5,000 AWESOME FACTS

(About Everything!)

NATIONAL GEOGRAPHIC

WASHINGTON, D.C.

CONtENTS

1 SPADEFOOT TOADS

SMELL LIKE PEANUT BUTTER.

(Follow the fact ticker at the bottom to see how many facts you've learned!)

15 PEANUT BUTTER

1 You need about **540** peanuts to make a **12-OUNCE** (340-g) jar of peanut butter.

2 One acre (0.4 ha) of peanuts could make **30,000** peanut butter SANDWICHES.

3 CARRAGEENAN, the ingredient that makes peanut butter so spreadable, comes from SEAWEED.

4 People living on the EAST COAST of the United States prefer CREAMY peanut butter; people living on the WEST COAST prefer CRUNCHY.

5 Americans have elected two PEANUT FARMERS to be President: Thomas Jefferson and Jimmy Carter.

6 ARACHIBUTYROPHOBIA is the fear of getting peanut butter stuck on the roof of your mouth.

7 The world's LARGEST peanut butter and jelly sandwich weighed **1,342** pounds (609 kg)—about as much as a POLAR BEAR!

FACTS THAT STICK

8 The world's **LARGEST** peanut butter factory produces 250,000 jars every day.

9 **ELVIS PRESLEY,** the King of Rock 'n' Roll, famously loved to eat **PEANUT BUTTER** and **BANANA** sandwiches.

10 The average American kid will eat about **1,500** peanut butter and jelly sandwiches before he or she graduates from **HIGH SCHOOL.**

11 Americans spend nearly $800 MILLION each year on peanut butter.

12 The U.S. Food and Drug Administration allows up to **29 INSECT FRAGMENTS** per 3.5 ounces (100 g) of peanut butter.

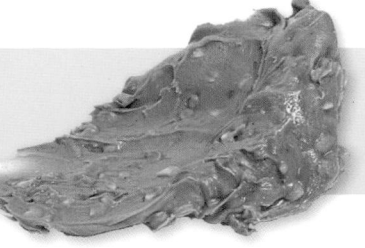

NET WT. 4 OZ. (113g) SALTED **BUTTER**

13 There's **NO BUTTER** in peanut butter.

14 A YouTube video of a banana **DANCING** to the song "It's Peanut Butter Jelly Time!!!" has been viewed more than **21 MILLION** times.

15 **ASTRONAUTS** in space eat peanut butter, but not on bread—bread is too crumbly—and **FLOATING** bits can get stuck in spacecraft filters or astronauts' eyes.

1 Castles are homes, fortresses, and symbols of power for monarchs and nobles.

2 About 1,000 years ago, castles became increasingly important in helping monarchs and nobles protect their land.

3 Castles could protect a 10-mile (16 km) radius. Monarchs and their lords had to construct many castles to watch over their realms.

4 Castles were homes not only to the kings and lords, but also to as many as 70 servants, craftspeople, and officials.

5 JOUSTING OFFERED ENTERTAINMENT FOR ROYALTY IN MEDIEVAL TIMES, AND A CHANCE FOR KNIGHTS TO SHOW OFF THEIR SKILLS AND EARN LARGE SUMS OF MONEY.

6 King Henry II of France died in 1559 while jousting after a lance pierced him in the face because the visor of his headpiece malfunctioned.

7 Caerphilly Castle, one of the largest castles in Wales, has a tower that leans ten feet (3 m).

8 The Tower of London has served as a prison, a treasury, and even a zoo!

9 Legend has it that a ghostly bear once appeared in the Tower of London, causing a guard to die of shock!

10 Two young 15th-century princes disappeared while staying in the Tower of London after their father's death. It is widely believed they were murdered by their uncle—Richard III—who saw them as a threat to the throne.

11 Krak des Chevaliers, a castle in Syria, had walls up to 80 feet (24.4 m) thick.

12 Himeji Castle in Japan is seven stories tall and built high on a hill. A maze-like entrance confused enemy attackers.

13 The ruins of 5,000 castles remain in France.

14 Some castles had water-filled moats up to 30 feet (9.1 m) deep to keep enemies from reaching the castle walls.

15 Some attackers would build a bridge to cross a moat—or fill the moat in with dirt.

16 Some moats were left dry and filled with sharpened sticks.

17 "Arrow loops" were vertical slits cut into castle walls through which defenders could fire arrows without getting hit themselves.

18 Arrows from long-range bows could fly about 1,000 feet (300 m).

19 A skilled archer could launch more than 10 arrows per minute.

20 Spiral staircases in castles generally spiraled clockwise (from the ascender's point of view), giving right-handed attackers a disadvantage.

21 In the Middle Ages, the knightly class was known as the chivalry. Knights were expected to be courteous and brave.

22 As many as 60 men worked on a trebuchet, a giant slingshot used in an attack.

23 Early cannons could be shot only ten times in an hour, partly because the metal became extremely hot and had to cool between shots.

24 A medieval cannon's range was about 50 yards (46 m).

25 Hay was used as toilet paper in castles.

26 MOATS WERE USED AS GARBAGE DUMPS AND A PLACE FOR EMPTYING TOILETS.

27 Defenders of castles dumped boiling water and hot sand on attackers from above.

28 No evidence has been found that crocodiles or alligators ever lived in castle moats in medieval Europe.

29 No one bothered to sweep castle floors. Instead, messes were covered with straw and flowers.

Caerphilly Castle, Wales

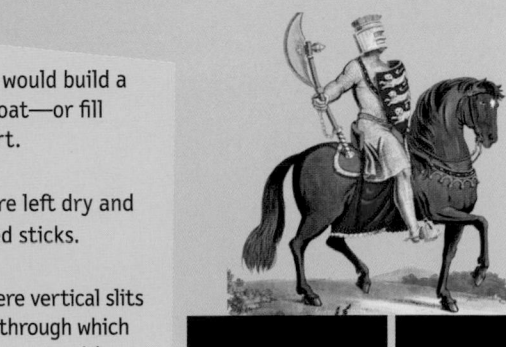

75 CASTLE FACTS FIT FOR A KING

30 A concentric castle had a court-yard ringed by several stone walls and a complex inside of towers, gatehouses, and buildings. It took thousands of workers years, even decades, to construct one.

31 King Edward I used concentric fortress designs discovered by Europeans during the Crusades to build his own castles in England.

32 Sleeping Beauty's Castle at Disneyland, modeled after Germany's Neuschwanstein Castle, was named after the princess in the Disney film, even though the park opened four years prior to the film's release.

33 Castles were built not just in northern Europe. The Moors built castles in northern Africa.

34 Castles were also built in medieval times in India, Japan, and Korea.

35 A CASTLE ON MONT ST. MICHEL, AN ISLAND IN FRANCE, CAN BE REACHED BY LAND ONLY DURING LOW TIDE.

36 In the 14th century, armies began using gunpowder and cannons and could easily knock down castle walls. Kings began moving into grand palaces and defended their realms with short, thick-walled fortresses.

37 By the 1600s, the use of castles for military reasons had ended.

38 Between 1347 and 1351, a plague called the Black Death swept Europe, killing about 25 million people. Castle dwellers were especially at risk because of the number of people living in close proximity.

39 Castles were often built near mountains or rivers as a natural defense against enemies.

40 Most castles were never finished. They kept growing and adapting to new threats and purposes.

41 If an English lord wanted to build a castle, he first had to get permission from the king, or his castle could be demolished.

42 Typically, a castle under construction grew 10 feet (3 m) in height per year.

43 Most castles had an underground well or rain-catching system so they could have a fresh supply of water, even if they were under attack.

44 The toilet in a medieval castle was called a garderobe.

45 A medieval pooper-scooper: The gong farmer was in charge of cleaning the pits beneath the garderobes.

46 Some squires followed the knights to war and fought in battle.

47 Centuries before television, medieval jesters were the ones who provided entertainment and told jokes at the castle and even made fun of visiting patrons.

48 ACCORDING TO LEGEND, A COUNTESS IN THE 11TH CENTURY HAD HER CASTLE'S ARCHITECT BEHEADED SO HE COULDN'T DESIGN CASTLES FOR HER RIVALS.

49 A 13th-century castle's gatehouse was designed as a dark tunnel so that emerging enemies couldn't see well for the attack.

50 Most knights started their training by the time they were about seven.

51 At around age 14, knights-in-training called squires became assistants to real knights.

52 A squire was ready by 21 to be dubbed a knight and given the title "sir" before his name.

53 When a knight went into battle, his armor weighed as much as 55 pounds (25 kg).

54 Switzerland's Chillon Castle sits on an island and can only be reached by drawbridge.

55 Japan's Matsumoto Castle is called the "Crow Castle" because of its black walls.

56 England's royalty uses Windsor Castle as a home. It's 200 times bigger than a typical house.

57 Cinderella's Castle at the Magic Kingdom looks larger than it really is thanks to a design trick called forced perspective: As the castle gets higher, the proportions get smaller.

58 The drawbridge on Disneyland's Sleeping Beauty's Castle really works, but it's only been used twice.

59 Tourists travel to Romania to see Bran Castle, also known as "Dracula's Castle" after the character in the book. The real person Dracula is based on may have only visited the castle and didn't live there.

60 In the Harry Potter books, Hogwarts is presumably located in Scotland. In the first film, Harry learned to fly his broomstick at England's Alnwick Castle.

61 Joan of Arc, a 15th-century French national heroine, was passionate about driving the English out of France and as a young woman was given armor and command of troops. She was eventually held by the English and burned at the stake.

62 King Arthur was a legendary character of medieval Britain. The real Arthur was probably a military leader, but the stories of his adventures have been spread by writers for almost 1,000 years.

63 The massive concentric castle Caernarfon in Wales cost about $22 million (in today's dollars) to construct in the 13th century.

64 Merlin was supposedly a magician and adviser to King Arthur. The story of Merlin may have originated in stories of a Celtic poet and prophet who lived 1,500 years ago.

65 King Arthur's table was round, legend says, to avoid fighting over who should occupy the seats of honor.

66 A wealthy man in California, U.S.A., began construction of Hearst Castle in 1919, but never finished. Now a state park, it has 56 bedrooms, 61 bathrooms, and a zoo.

67 The castle steward was a high-ranking servant who helped the lady manage the castle. He also collected rents from farmers who worked the fields around the castle.

68 A sapper had a risky castle job. He dug beneath an enemy castle's walls during sieges. Sappers were often squashed in cave-ins or cut down by castle defenders.

69 A serf was forced to farm the land that surrounded a castle and give a share of his crops to his lord, hoping he had enough left over to feed his own family.

70 THE GAME OF CHESS, WHOSE GAME PIECES DEPICT ROYALTY, KNIGHTS, AND SUCH, HAS BEEN PLAYED SINCE A.D. 600.

71 The castle barber did more than cut hair. He was often the dentist and surgeon.

72 A lady-in-waiting at a castle was a personal companion to the lord's wife who bathed and dressed the lady. She had to have a noble background and good connections.

73 At a holiday feast, castle cooks made exotic dishes, like peacock cooked in its feathers, roast porpoise, and fried stork.

74 Castle Island in South Boston, Massachusetts, U.S.A., is the home to star-shaped Fort Independence, an English fort originally established in 1634.

75 England's Donnington Castle suffered one of the longest known sieges—the siege lasted for two years in the mid-17th century.

1 Cats see SIX TIMES BETTER at night than humans.

2 During hotter months, ARMADILLOS FORAGE AT NIGHT to take advantage of COOLER TEMPERATURES.

3 SLOTHS SLEEP 15 HOURS A DAY and at night feed on leaves in the treetops.

4 PYGMY LORISES—tiny, tree-dwelling primates active after sunset—grip branches with their legs while using BOTH HANDS TO CATCH INSECTS.

5 HEDGEHOGS DON'T MAKE GREAT PETS: They are *very* active at night but sleep all day.

6 OWLS have the BEST NIGHT VISION of any animal.

7 FLYING SQUIRRELS GLIDE, not fly, between trees during the night using a FLAT TAIL AND SKIN that stretches from their forearms to their hind legs.

8 The HIGH-PITCHED, NIGHTTIME SCREECHES of feeding TASMANIAN DEVILS TERRIFIED early colonists on the island of Tasmania.

9 Burrowing WOMBATS DIG UP AS MUCH AS THREE FEET (0.9 M) of dirt during the night.

10 After dark, TREE KANGAROOS LEAVE RAIN-FOREST TREETOPS to search for grubs and plants on the ground.

11 The GREATER GLIDER, a tree-dwelling marsupial, can PARACHUTE MORE THAN 330 FEET (100 M) in the dark and land precisely on a tree trunk.

12 PORCUPINES make a GRUNTING SOUND WHILE FORAGING for bark, roots, and berries at night.

13 HIPPOS spend SIX HOURS a night eating an average of 88 POUNDS (40 KG) OF GRASS.

14 SCORPIONS GLOW if you shine a black light on them.

15 THE HISPANIOLA SOLENODON—a shrewlike nocturnal mammal—STUNS PREY such as lizards and insects with a POISONOUS BITE.

Vampire Bat

16 JAGUARS have SPECIALIZED EYES that are nearly TWICE AS POWERFUL at night as during the day to stalk and AMBUSH PREY in the dark.

17 TARANTULAS hunt at night. They use FLESH-DISSOLVING VENOM to capture insects, spiders, frogs, and snakes.

18 SPRING PEEPERS—a type of small frog—EMIT HIGH-PITCHED SOUNDS when they gather around bodies of water on spring nights.

19 A single BAT can eat HUNDREDS OF MOSQUITOES in one night.

20 Contrary to belief, BATS AREN'T BLIND; however, most species do see better at night than during the day.

21 The WHIP-POOR-WILL is named after the sound of its loud evening call.

22 Male Sydney FUNNEL WEB SPIDERS, whose VENOMOUS BITE CAN CAUSE DEATH, leave their homes and wander around outside after evening rainstorms.

23 The GREATER BULLDOG BAT uses LARGE, CLAWED FEET to catch an average of 30 TO 40 FISH a night.

24 To steer clear of PREDATORS, MOST SALAMANDERS are nocturnal and have TOXIC SKIN.

25 Asian VAMPIRE MOTHS use a TOUGH PROBOSCIS—a long feeding tube—TO PIERCE THE SKIN OF FRUITS AND ANIMALS during nighttime feedings.

35 FACTS ABOUT

26
THE FEATHERTAIL GLIDER, a rodentlike marsupial, uses a LONG, BRUSH-TIPPED TONGUE to gather nectar, pollen, and small insects from flowers at night.

27
North America's only marsupial, the nocturnal VIRGINIA OPOSSUM, PRETENDS TO BE DEAD— "PLAYING OPOSSUM"— for up to six hours when threatened.

28
RACCOONS use their HUMANLIKE FOREPAWS to pry open garbage cans and scrounge for food under the cover of night.

29
NORTHERN QUOLLS, catlike marsupials, RELEASE A SMELL that repels predators while they search for food at night.

30
LEADBEATER'S POSSUM—a tiny, nocturnal marsupial found only in SOUTHERN AUSTRALIA—was presumed EXTINCT for more than 50 YEARS until it was rediscovered in 1961.

31
MOONRATS spend their nights marking their territory with an ONIONLIKE SMELL and SWIMMING AFTER FISH.

32
A FLYING LEMUR GLIDES through the night using a FULL-BODY MEMBRANE that when fully extended makes the animals LOOK LIKE KITES.

33
VAMPIRE BATS use their teeth to CUT THE SKIN of unsuspecting sleeping animals, whose BLOOD THE BATS LAP UP WITH THEIR TONGUES.

34
Large FLYING FOXES, which are actually bats, get their name from their FIVE-FOOT (1.5 M) WINGSPAN and FOXLIKE FACE.

35
THE COMMON HOUSE GECKO'S silhouette can be seen at night inside LAMP-SHADES, where it feeds on INSECTS ATTRACTED TO THE LIGHT.

ANIMALS AFTER DARK

100 FLIGHT FACTS TO

1. Four hundred years before airplanes were invented, Leonardo da Vinci thought that people could learn to fly by watching birds. On his deathbed, he said he regretted that he never flew. **2.** The first airplanes used motorcycle or car tires for their landing wheels. **3.** In 1927, Charles Lindbergh became the first person to fly solo across the Atlantic Ocean. It took him 33½ hours to fly from New York to Paris. Today, it takes about 7½ hours. **4.** The U.S. military's Falcon HTV-2 can fly at speeds of 13,000 miles per hour (20,921 kph). Unfortunately, the super-fast bomber failed both of its test flights. **5.** The oldest kites were flown thousands of years ago in China. **6.** Before the Wright brothers built airplanes, they built bicycles. **7.** When astronauts landed on the moon in July 1969, they left their backpacks and an American flag behind. **8.** Early airplane flights across North America took 48 hours. Today they take about 6½ hours. **9.** The Antonov A-225, the largest plane ever made, has 32 landing wheels. **10.** Hot air balloons stay aloft because hot air (warmed by burners) is lighter than the cold air in the sky around the balloon. **11.** The world's biggest kite is almost as wide as a football field. **12.** In 2001, an American businessman became the first "space tourist." He paid $20 million to travel to the International Space Station. **13.** You can take a flight on a modified 727 airplane, where you experience weightlessness (or zero gravity), just like astronauts. **14.** The spacecraft that carried the first astronauts to land on the moon back to Earth reached speeds of 25,000 mph (40,200 kph). **15.** Some early inventors thought that one day people would fly on kites. **16.** The first airplane pilots were exposed to freezing temperatures and gusty winds because the cockpits were not enclosed. **17.** Only four years after the Wright brothers' historic flight, the first helicopter took flight. **18.** A duck, a sheep, and a rooster were passengers on the first balloon flight. **19.** Chimpanzees, dogs, monkeys, mice, and a guinea pig have all traveled into space. **20.** The flying monkeys in *The Wizard of Oz* were played by actors held in the air by piano wire. **21.** Early balloonists would throw bags of sand over the side of their balloons to keep them balanced in the air at a steady elevation. **22.** The first airplane flight lasted 12 seconds. **23.** The Apollo 8 spacecraft, the first manned craft to circle the moon, entered its orbit on Christmas Eve 1968. **24.** The youngest person to fly on a space shuttle was 28-year-old Sultan bin Salman bin Abdul-Aziz Al Saud. He flew on *Discovery* in 1985. **25.** In 1981, a solar-powered airplane flew from France to England. It took five hours and 23 minutes to fly 160 miles (258 km), a distance a jetliner can travel in 20 minutes. **26.** En route to the South Pole, Richard Byrd and his crew lightened their plane to get over the Queen Maud Mountains by throwing out their survival packs. **27.** There's a golf course nestled between two runways at an airport in Bangkok, Thailand. **28.** Bats are the only mammals that can fly (but others do glide, like "flying" squirrels). **29.** Some planes can be flown remotely using computers. **30.** The first hot air balloon flight happened in Paris in 1783. **31.** An airplane's "black box" records information on flights and is usually orange. **32.** The Concorde aircraft, in service from 1976 to 2003, flew at twice the speed of sound. **33.** The Airbus A380 is the world's largest passenger jet: It can seat 853 passengers. **34.** One of the earliest known birds, *Archaeopteryx*, lived 150 million years ago. **35.** In 1923, the U.S. Army refueled a plane in mid-air for the first time. **36.** Some 300 helium balloons were used to float a small house (with people inside) into the air—just like the Pixar movie *Up*. **37.** A 747-400 jet has six million parts. **38.** In 2000, the United States started developing an "exoskeleton" that would allow soldiers to wear a suit in which they could take off, fly, and land. **39.** Weather balloons are released twice a day from nearly 900 places worldwide to measure wind speed, humidity, and temperature. **40.** Early pilots had few instruments to tell them how far off the ground they were; they had to look out and down. **41.** In 1680, an Italian mathematician determined that the human body didn't have the muscles to be able to fly on its own. **42.** In July 1937, when Amelia Earhart and her co-pilot disappeared over the Pacific Ocean, the United States sent nine ships and 66 airplanes to search for them. **43.** The longest paper airplane flight ever lasted 27.6 seconds. **44.** NASA is developing a 300-pound (136-kg) personal "flying suit" nicknamed the Puffin. **45.** Before becoming a major star, the flying fairy Tinker Bell first appeared in the play *Peter Pan* in 1904. **46.** In 1979, the pilot of the human-powered *Gossamer Albatross* pedaled the

F-15 Strike Eagle
fighter jet

airplane across the English Channel. It weighed 70 pounds (32 kg). **47.** The Portuguese pilots who were the first to fly across the South Atlantic survived two plane crashes along the way. They finished in a third plane. **48.** The first man in space was the Soviet cosmonaut Yuri Gagarin. **49.** Daredevil David "The Bullet" Smith has been shot out of a cannon more than 5,000 times. **50.** An erupting volcano on Iceland caused thousands of flights to be canceled in April 2010 due to the thick ash in the air. **51.** In 1960, a U.S. Air Force pilot set the record for the highest-altitude jump when he flew a high-altitude balloon to 102,800 feet (31,333 m) before jumping out and free-falling back to Earth. He was protected by a pressure suit and carried parachutes to slow his descent. **52.** It's said that the rock band the B-52s named themselves after a beehive hairdo that resembles the nose of a Boeing bomber jet. **53.** More than 200 years ago, André Jacques Garnerin became the first person to parachute from a hot air balloon. **54.** In 1924, two airplanes each completed the first trip around the world. **55.** To fly "blind" means to pilot an aircraft using only navigational equipment and by not looking outside the cockpit. **56.** The first person to break the sound barrier in a plane was Chuck Yeager in 1947. He was going 700 mph (1,100 kph). **57.** NASA's five space shuttles flew 135 missions before the program ended in July 2011. **58.** Scientists think that theropod dinosaurs grew wings and feathers and evolved into modern-day birds. **59.** The X-15 rocket plane can fly at an altitude of 354,500 feet (108,052 m). **60.** A female pilot, Jacqueline Cochran, set more records than any other flier during her 30 years as a pilot. She broke the sound barrier six years after Chuck Yeager. **61.** Wandering albatrosses spend 70 percent of their lives flying over water. **62.** The multimillionaire inventor of the Learjet used by business executives and celebrities also invented the car radio. **63.** In 1931, the first hydrogen balloon reached the stratosphere—51,775 feet (15,781 m) in the air. **64.** The smallest airplane ever to fly, the *Bumblebee II*, was 8 feet 10 inches (2.7 m) in length. **65.** Aerophobia is the fear of flying. **66.** Seven-year-olds have piloted airplanes. **67.** The snipe (a small bird) can fly for 96 hours straight and cover more than 4,000 miles (6,437 km). **68.** U.S. Navy personnel wear different-colored jerseys for their jobs on the deck of aircraft carriers—crew in purple vests handle the fuel, whereas plane captains wear brown jerseys. **69.** A bird called the American woodcock flies at only five miles per hour (8 kph); you can bike faster than that! **70.** Birds can fly and humans can't, but both bird wings and human arms have the same bone structure. **71.** An airplane has an "elevator" on its back tail to allow the plane to move up or down. **72.** Airships filled with hydrogen used to travel between Europe and the United States, but after the *Hindenburg* exploded in 1937, people lost interest in this mode of air travel. **73.** Snoopy from the "Peanuts" comic strip would sit on his doghouse and pretend to be a pilot in a Sopwith Camel, a World War I fighter plane with only one seat. **74.** BASE jumping is the extreme sport of jumping off cliffs wearing a parachute to help coast to a landing. **75.** The McDonnell Douglas F-15, which began flying during the Vietnam War, has never been defeated in air-to-air combat. **76.** Some 4.5 billion birds (of 185 different species) migrate to Africa each winter. **77.** U2, the world-famous Irish rock band, is also the name of an American spy plane. **78.** You can buy a kit to build your own airplane (not a model one, either). **79.** Want to fly like a bird? Martin Aircraft sells a jetpack for $100,000 that you can wear on your back to take flight. **80.** The white-throated needle-tailed swift can fly 106 miles per hour (170 kph). **81.** Chefs on Gulf Air flights will prepare your meal for you, just as you like it. **82.** North American monarch butterflies migrate up to 3,000 miles (4,828 km) from the north to California and Mexico. **83.** The cabin air in the Airbus A-380 is always fresh since it is changed every three minutes. **84.** Helicopters can trace their history back more than 500 years to drawings by Leonardo da Vinci. **85.** Air moves faster over the top of the airplane wing and slower underneath; this is what creates lift. **86.** When a plane breaks the sound barrier it creates a loud "boom" called a sonic boom. **87.** Some skydivers use wingsuits—which make them look like flying squirrels—to slow their descent after they jump out of planes. **88.** Ultralight airplanes were first designed with engines similar to those in chainsaws. **89.** Planes that land on aircraft carriers have a runway of only 500 feet (150 m), so they have a hook on the tail of the plane that latches onto one of four sturdy cables. **90.** In 2005, Steve Fossett flew an airplane around the world without stopping—or refueling—and set a new record. His plane had 13 fuel tanks. **91.** In the late 1800s, Otto Lillienthal flew his own hang gliders some 2,000 times before he died from a fall during a flight. **92.** The largest pterosaurs, flying reptiles from the age of dinosaurs, had wingspans of about 40 feet (12 m)—as wide as an F-16 fighter jet. **93.** You can buy a ticket to space on Virgin Galactic, an airline that offers passengers 4 to 5 minutes of weightlessness in space. **94.** Three hundred and fifty-five people have flown on the space shuttle. **95.** *Air Force One*, the plane used by the President of the United States, includes medical facilities that can be used as an operating room. **96.** In 1984, Joe Kittinger became the first person to pilot a hot air balloon across the Atlantic; he traveled from Maine, U.S.A., to Italy in 83 hours and 40 minutes. **97.** You can rent your own private jet for $1,850 an hour. **98.** Bee wings and helicopter blades use the same principle to get the bee, or helicopter, into the air. **99.** The first nonstop hot air balloon flight around the world lasted 19 days, 21 hours, and 55 minutes. **100.** In the 1920s, an airplane ticket cost $5 (about $60 today).

MAKE YOUR MIND SOAR

50 Stupendous FACTS ABOUT SPIDERS

1
Web-making spiders have a **BRISTLED HOOK** on the end of their feet that allows them to grasp silk but not get stuck.

4
ARACHNOPHOBIA is the fear of spiders.

7
One type of spider in Nepal looks like **BIRD POOP**, for camouflage.

10
When the goliath bird-eating tarantula rubs its feet together it makes a **HISSING SOUND** that can be heard 15 feet (4.6 m) away.

13
North America's most venomous spider is the **BLACK WIDOW.**

14
The **BROWN RECLUSE** spider has a violin-shaped marking on its head.

15
As their name suggests, brown recluse spiders like to keep to themselves. When they do bite, their venom **KILLS THE VICTIM'S TISSUE** near the wound.

16
Spiders are popular in **FOLKLORE**. It is said that a spiderweb over your door means company is coming, and if a spider crawls into your pocket, you'll soon have money.

2
Scientists found a spiderweb that was spun **140 MILLION YEARS AGO**—when dinosaurs were on Earth—inside a piece of amber.

8
Spiders are capable of **REGENERATING LOST LEGS.**

17
Fishing spiders can **FLOAT ON WATER.**

3
Over 80 people spent four years collecting **SILK** from a million wild golden orb spiders in Madagascar and wove it into a large **CLOTH.**

5
A jumping spider can jump **40 TIMES** its body length.

9
Besides a venomous bite, a tarantula sometimes releases **BARBED HAIRS** at an attacker that act as an irritant.

11
The world's **MOST VENOMOUS SPIDER** is the Brazilian wandering spider—it's **15 TIMES** more venomous than a rattlesnake.

18
Engineers study spider webs to improve **BRIDGE DESIGNS.**

Weaver Spider

6
Most spiders only live one or two years, but **TARANTULAS CAN LIVE 20 YEARS.**

12
There is a town in South Carolina, U.S.A., named **SPIDERWEB.**

19
The largest spider in the world is wider than a **BASKETBALL.**

20
The smallest known spider is SMALLER than the period at the end of this sentence.

21
All spiders are meat-eaters.

22
E.B. White, the author of *Charlotte's Web*, got his **INSPIRATION** for the book when he walked into his barn and discovered a particularly beautiful **SPIDERWEB.**

23
Some spider species have evolved to look like ants—a disguise they use to prey on the ants.

24
A NEWLY DISCOVERED species of bark spider from Madagascar can cast a web across a stream or river more than 80 feet (25 m) long.

25
In 1973, Arabella and Anita were the first spiders to **TRAVEL TO SPACE.**

26
All spiders secrete silk from their abdomens, but tarantulas can also **SHOOT SILK FROM THEIR FEET.**

27
There are more than **38,000 SPECIES** of spiders in the world.

28
Some spiders **EAT THEIR OWN WEB** and recycle most of the protein into **FRESH SILK.**

29
Spiders are classified as **ARACHNIDS.** Other arachnids include scorpions, ticks, and mites.

30
Besides having eight legs, spiders have an extra pair of appendages called **PEDIPALPS**—they act like hands that help them feel their surroundings and hold on to prey.

31
Most spiders have **EIGHT EYES,** but the way they are arranged depends on the type of spider. A spider expert can often identify a spider by looking at its eyes.

32
Most spiders **DON'T HAVE PARTICULARLY GOOD VISION.** That's because seeing isn't that important for catching prey, when it just lands in your web.

33
A few species of spiders **STALK AND HUNT** their prey. These spiders have excellent vision.

34
Spiders taste and smell through special **SENSORY ORGANS ON THEIR LEGS.**

35
A spider **"HEARS"** by sensing vibrations through the hairs that cover much of its body.

36
Spiders are so **SENSITIVE TO VIBRATIONS** that they can tell the difference between a moth and a honeybee hitting a web.

37
Many orb weavers— spiders that spin flat, wheel-shaped webs—can spin their creations in **30 MINUTES.** Most build a new web every day.

38
Some spiders don't catch their prey in a web. They simply **HURL** a silken line and **REEL THEIR DINNER IN.**

39
Spiders can eat their weight in one meal.

40
Spiders often knock out their prey with a **PARALYZING VENOMOUS BITE.**

41
Spiders **SPIT A LIQUID** onto their food before they eat it that starts to break it down. Then they suck up their meal.

42
In 16th-century Italy it was believed that the only way to be cured from the bite of a wolf spider was to **DO A CERTAIN DANCE TO MUSIC.**

43
Many experts claim that the silk of an orb weaver spider is so strong that a strand as thick as a pencil **COULD STOP A JUMBO JET** in flight.

44
Baby spiders are called **SPIDERLINGS.**

45
After they hatch, spiderlings drift away on silk filament. This first flight is called **"BALLOONING."**

46
Some spiderlings balloon up **AS HIGH AS AIRPLANES!**

47
A European house spider can run **330 TIMES** its own body length in 10 seconds. That's like you running about the length of a soccer field six times in ten seconds!

48
In some parts of South America, people roast and eat **TARANTULAS.**

49
A person who studies spiders is called an **ARACHNOLOGIST.**

50
Scientists are studying spider silk to replicate it for human use, including making **BULLETPROOF VESTS.**

1 NEWBORN DOLPHINS HAVE A TINY **PATCH OF HAIR** ON THEIR CHINS.

24 DOLPHIN FACTS TO

2 IF A **DOLPHIN BECOMES SICK,** OTHER DOLPHINS WILL TAKE TURNS PUSHING IT TO THE SURFACE **SO IT CAN BREATHE.**

3 A PINK BOTTLENOSE DOLPHIN WAS DISCOVERED IN A LAKE IN LOUISIANA, U.S.A.

4 Every dolphin has a **SIGNATURE WHISTLE** it uses to identify itself.

5 Sometimes dolphins "surf" on boats' **BOW WAVES.** This gives them a boost of speed.

6 RISSO'S DOLPHINS CAN HOLD THEIR BREATH FOR **30 MINUTES.**

7 Dolphins have a special superpower that makes finding their way underwater easier. They use a type of sonar called echolocation to hunt and navigate.

8 SOME WILD DOLPHINS PLAY CATCH WITH **COCONUTS.**

9 DOLPHINS CAN SWIM UP TO **SEVEN TIMES** FASTER THAN THE FASTEST SWIMMING HUMAN AND DIVE UP TO **2,000 FEET** (610 M).

10 RIGHT WHALE DOLPHINS are the only members of the dolphin family that LACK DORSAL FINS.

SOCIAL SEAFARERS, they've been spotted in pods of nearly 3,000 individuals.

11 DOLPHINS HAVE BETWEEN 80 AND 100 TEETH.

12 **ORCAS** can bag some big prey. In the water, they'll take on **SEA LIONS, SHARKS,** and other whales. Orcas will even attack **DEER** or **MOOSE** that attempt to swim between islands in the Arctic Ocean!

13 A DOLPHIN BREATHES AIR THROUGH A **BLOWHOLE** LOCATED AT THE **TOP OF ITS HEAD.**

14 The freshwater-loving **AMAZON RIVER DOLPHIN** can be found in the Amazon and Orinoco Rivers in South America. Following a flood, they can swim through parts of forests.

15 FIFTY MILLION YEARS AGO, WHALE AND DOLPHIN ANCESTORS WALKED ON LAND! THEY ARE THE DISTANT RELATIVES OF HOOFED ANIMALS SUCH AS DEER, HIPPOS, AND BISON.

FLiP OVER

16 A dolphin "**SLEEPS**" for about eight hours a day, although it is never fully unconscious. Only half its brain is asleep at a time!

17 DON'T LET THE NICK-NAME FOOL YOU: "KILLER WHALES" ARE ACTUALLY DOLPHINS.

18 A DOLPHIN'S BEAK-LIKE SNOUT IS CALLED A ROSTRUM.

19 DOLPHINS HAVE **TWO STOMACHS.** ONE IS USED TO STORE FOOD, AND THE OTHER IS USED TO DIGEST IT.

20 The SMALLEST DOLPHIN, Hector's dolphin, is only four feet long (1.2 m). It's one of the rarest types, and it is shorter than an orca's dorsal fin.

21 THE iPAD is the latest high-tech tool researchers are using to help enhance communication between humans and dolphins.

22  Using **TEAMWORK**, long-beaked common dolphins herd sardines into a tight ball, making it a cinch to gobble them by the mouthful.

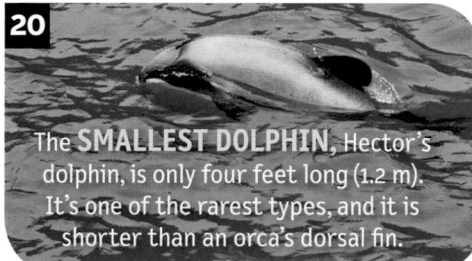

23 Some branches of the U.S. military use dolphins for jobs like **FINDING UNDERWATER EXPLOSIVES.**

24 A DOLPHIN'S EYEBALLS **MOVE INDEPENDENTLY** OF EACH OTHER. FOR EXAMPLE, ONE EYE CAN LOOK STRAIGHT AHEAD, WHILE THE OTHER LOOKS STRAIGHT UP.

15 SNEAKY FACTS

1 British author Ian Fleming, who created the character James Bond, was a **SPY** himself during World War II.

2 Aldrich Ames started working for the **U.S. Central Intelligence Agency** when he was in HIGH SCHOOL. Thirty years later, he was caught as a Soviet **DOUBLE AGENT.**

3 In the James Bond movies, "Q" makes **FUTURISTIC GADGETS** and weapons for 007's missions. The character is based on a real inventor who mastered disguising tools in ordinary objects—like a TINY METAL SAW sewn inside shoelaces.

4 "Bugs," which are small **MICROPHONES,** can be put **INSIDE** everyday objects like pens to pick up conversations without being obvious.

5 Why do U.S. Secret Service agents talk into their WATCHES? Because there's a **TINY MICROPHONE** inside used to talk to one another without drawing too much attention. Agents also wear an earpiece to **LISTEN** for instructions.

6 An **UMBRELLA** doesn't seem like much of a spy weapon—but in the 1970s a spy used one to shoot a **POISON-FILLED PELLET** at an unsuspecting man.

7 Some female spies during World War II **GATHERED INTELLIGENCE** by **POSING** as everyday housewives and using cameras disguised as purses.

8 **PERRY THE PLATYPUS,** the secret agent platypus on the Disney show *PHINEAS AND FERB,* has his own theme song.

ABOUT SPIES

9 The U.S. Central Intelligence Agency once strapped cameras on pigeons trained to fly over **ENEMY TARGETS.**

10 Josephine Baker, an American actress and dancer, VOLUNTEERED to be a spy for the Allies during World War II. She passed along information she heard from Italians and Germans at **PARTIES.**

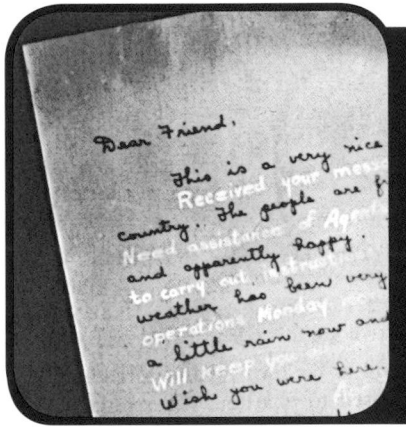

11 During the American Revolution, both sides used **INVISIBLE INK** when sending messages, in the hopes they wouldn't be detected. An invisible message was often written **BETWEEN THE LINES** of an ordinary letter. When the recipient of the letter heated or soaked the letter in chemicals, the message was revealed.

12 Special CAMERAS can take pictures of text or images and shrink them down to the size of the period at the end of this sentence. Called **MICRODOTS,** these easily hide information. In the movie *Mission Impossible III,* a microdot was placed on the back of a **STAMP,** but instead of text it held a tiny video.

13 To **CATCH A SPY,** invisible detection powder can be applied to important papers. The powder glows on the spy's hands under ultraviolet light—**PROOF** of snooping.

14 Spies are in **SPACE**—in the form of satellites. Special satellites can see a **GRAPEFRUIT** sitting on a picnic table from 250 miles (400 km) above Earth.

15 *Spy Kids: All the Time in the World* added an extra "D" to 3D. In addition to the 3D glasses, movie-goers got scratch-and-sniff cards so they could take in the smells of the film—from **BACON** to **CANDY** to **POOP!**

75 DiNO-MiTE DiNOSAUR FACTS

Tyrannosaurus rex

1 We have some idea of what dinosaur skin looked like, thanks to skin fossils—prints left in mud that later hardened.

2 Some dinosaurs had feathers.

3 *Ankylosaurus* had a large, fearsome club at the tip of its tail made from seven fused bones.

4 The smallest dinosaurs were tiny enough to hold in your hands.

5 Sauropods, a group of plant-eating dinosaurs, are the largest land animals that ever lived, weighing as much as 88 tons (80 MT).

6 ALL DINOSAURS WALKED ON THEIR TOES.

7 Almost all dinosaurs had curvy, S-shaped necks.

8 Some meat-eating dinosaurs had teeth that were serrated; that is they had sharp ridges like steak knives.

9 All dinosaurs laid eggs.

10 *Scansoriopteryx*'s long front limbs and very strong toe claws suggest that this meat-eating dinosaur climbed trees.

11 The tallest known dinosaur, *Sauroposeidon*, was taller than a five-story building.

12 The horned *Dracorex hogwartsia* was named after Hogwarts, Harry Potter's school.

13 The longest dinosaur name, *Micropachycephalosaurus*, belongs to one of the smallest dinosaurs, just shy of two feet (0.6 m) long.

14 The biggest dinosaur eggs could hold about as much fluid as 85 large chicken eggs.

15 Many dinosaurs had spikes on their back and tail, but *Tuojiangosaurus* had a spike sticking out from each shoulder.

16 *Carnotaurus*, a relative of *T. rex*, had a pair of stubby horns above its eyes.

17 *NIGERSAURUS* HAD ABOUT 500 SPARE TEETH IN ITS MOUTH.

18 *Deinocheirus*, which means "terrible hand," had eight-foot (2.4-m) -long arms with three 10-inch (25-cm) claws.

19 When *Parasaurolophus*, a duckbill dinosaur with a musical head, breathed through its nose, air passed through a tube inside the top of its head and created a trumpetlike sound.

20 *Epidendrosaurus* had an extra-long finger on each hand—its third finger was almost twice as long as the others.

21 During most of the time that dinosaurs roamed the Earth, there were only two continents: Gondwana, in the Southern Hemisphere, and Laurasia, in the Northern Hemisphere.

22 Dinosaurs first appeared about 230 million years ago and went extinct about 65 million years ago.

23 A sequence of preserved dinosaur footprints is called a trackway. Millions of trackways in Colorado, U.S.A., mark a route now known as the Dinosaur Trail.

24 Based on dinosaur tracks, the fastest dinos went about 26 miles per hour (42 kph).

25 Though mammals and dinosaurs lived at the same time, humans didn't appear until 62 million years after dinosaurs went extinct.

26 Dinosaurs were neither warm-blooded nor cold-blooded; they were dinosaur-blooded, meaning they combined conditions of both.

27 The word *dinosaur* is derived from Greek and means "fearfully great lizard." It first appeared in 1842.

28 Dinosaurs existed for a *long* time: The amount of time between *Tyrannosaurus* and *Apatosaurus*—65 million years—is more than the time between *Tyrannosaurus* and you.

29 Scientists have discovered the remains of nearly 1,000 different kinds of dinosaurs.

30 All dinosaurs fall into one of two groups: saurischians or ornithischians. Saurischians had one thumb that was significantly larger than the other; ornithischians had leaf-shaped teeth.

31 Fossils show that some dinosaurs laid their eggs in large nesting colonies with hundreds and perhaps even thousands of other dinosaurs.

32 Most dinosaurs could swim.

33 "Sue," on display at the Field Museum in Chicago, Illinois, U.S.A., is the largest (both in length and weight), most complete (90 percent of her bones) and best preserved *T. rex* skeleton ever found.

34 Dinosaur National Monument in Colorado and Utah, U.S.A., is famous for its abundance of dinosaur fossils, including a wall of 1,500 bones.

35 Dinosaurs usually are named after a characteristic body feature, where they were found, or a person involved in the discovery.

36 The shape of a dinosaur's eye sockets can tell scientists what time of day the animal was active.

37 *Sinornithosaurus*, a feathered, turkey-size dinosaur, had a poisonous bite.

38 *T. rex* had a mini-me in look-alike *Raptorex kriegsteini*, a human-size dino that weighed 90 times less than *T. rex*.

39 *T. REX*'S VISION WAS BETTER THAN THAT OF A HAWK.

40 Pterosaurs, the first backboned animals to fly, are closely related to, but not considered true, dinosaurs.

41 *Triceratops horridus* had a five-foot-wide (1.5 m) head.

42 The peculiar *Mononykus olecranus* had only one finger on each arm.

43 The bone at the top of *Pachycephalosaurus wyomingensis*'s skull could be up to nine inches (23 cm) thick.

44 *T. rex*'s jaw was four feet (1.2 m) long.

45 *T. rex* could eat up to 500 pounds (230 kg) of meat in one bite.

46 *Stegosaurus* was 30 feet (9 m) long but had a brain the size of a tangerine.

47 Many dinosaurs had hollow leg and arm bones, which helped them to be swift runners.

48 Eighty-nine kinds of dinosaurs have been found in the United States —more than in any other country.

49 *Fruitadens haagarorum* is the smallest known dinosaur in North America: It weighed about two pounds (0.9 kg) and was about two feet (0.6 m) long.

50 In 2007, explorers in India discovered a site that held more than 100 dinosaur eggs. Arranged in clusters of six to eight, some of the eggs were big enough that you would need two hands to hold them.

51 The 150-million-year-old *Turiasaurus riodevensis* weighed as much as seven adult male elephants.

52 SCIENTISTS HAVE NOT BEEN ABLE TO BRING DINOSAURS BACK TO LIFE LIKE IN *JURASSIC PARK*.

53 *Giganotosaurus* lives up to its name: It was five feet (1.5 m) longer and 5,952 pounds (2,700 kg) heavier than "Sue," the largest *T. rex*. It was discovered in the Argentine desert by a garage mechanic riding a dune buggy.

54 *Nothronychus* and its cousin *Therizinosaurus* had the biggest claws on their arms of any animal ever.

55 Big dinosaurs were probably too heavy to sit on their eggs so scientists think they piled plants on top of the eggs to keep them warm.

56 Dinosaur fossils have been found on every continent.

57 The world's largest dinosaur, the 100-ton (91-MT) *Argentinosaurus*, was found after a farmer turned up the dino's shinbone.

58 The backbone of *Argentinosaurus* is the world's biggest bone: It weighs two tons (1.8 MT), and it took weeks to dig up.

59 In 1825, Gideon Mantell, a British doctor, became the first scientist to identify a dinosaur—the 33-foot (10-m) -long *Iguanodon*.

60 *TSIN TAOSAURUS* HAD A LONG BONE SIMILAR TO A UNICORN'S HORN THAT SAT ATOP ITS SKULL.

61 Scientists think 42-foot (12.8-m) -long *Edmontosaurus* dinos migrated as far as 1,600 miles (2,575 km) a year.

62 *Apatosaurus* is the correct name for the dinosaur known as *Brontosaurus*.

63 *Diplodocus* had a 20-foot-long (6 m) tail that made a booming sound when the dinosaur snapped it.

64 *Mamenchisaurus* had the longest neck—more than 30 feet (9 m)—of any animal that ever lived.

65 More than 80 percent of all dinosaur fossils are discovered by accident.

66 Meat-eating dinosaurs laid eggs that were mostly long and thin, whereas plant-eating dinos laid eggs that were more rounded.

67 *T. rex* had the largest teeth of any dinosaur—they were the size of bananas and could dent metal.

68 Some meat-eating dinosaurs had retractable claws, like a cat.

69 Bones found in fossilized dinosaur stomachs reveal the diets of some meat-eating dinos.

70 *Cryolophosaurus* was found about 100 miles (161 km) from the South Pole and was the first dinosaur discovered in Antarctica.

71 When the bones of *Megalosaurus* were first discovered, people believed the fossils belonged to an ancient dragon.

72 *Lourinhanosaurus* swallowed stones to help grind up food in its gut, much like chickens swallow tiny pebbles and grains of sand to help with digestion.

73 The meat-eating *Baryonyx* had a foot-long (0.3 m) claw on each thumb.

74 *Spinosaurus* had tall, thin back spines measuring seven feet (2 m) high. Some scientists believe the spines created a sail-like structure that helped cool the dinosaur.

75 *T. rex*'s brain was twice the size of the brains of other giant meat-eaters.

35 HIGH-TECH

1 A modern cell phone has **MORE COMPUTING POWER** than **ALL OF NASA DID IN 1969** when the United States sent men to the moon.

2 **EMILY,** or the **EMERGENCY INTEGRATED LIFESAVING LANYARD,** is a robot that may one day save lives at beaches. She is **15 TIMES FASTER** than human lifeguards.

3 Some cars and trains use vegetable oil as an alternative fuel source, but the future may be in beef. A train running between Oklahoma and Texas, U.S.A., is using **BEEF FAT FOR FUEL!**

4 Using **RADAR SENSORS AND VIDEO CAMERAS,** Google and other companies are designing **CARS THAT DRIVE THEMSELVES.**

5 eLEGS allows some wheelchair-bound people to walk. The user's crutches send signals about where the person wants to go, and the **FITTED ROBOTIC LEGS** carry them there.

6 After the money-making success of *AVATAR,* **EVERYTHING WENT 3D**—including phones. One kind of cell phone lets you make videos in 3D.

7 **SEE YA, REMOTE!** Many toy cars, helicopters, and planes can now be **CONTROLLED WITH SMART PHONES.**

8 A special rubber wristband can track how many steps you take in a day and how many hours you sleep. If you haven't been active for a while, it **VIBRATES TO REMIND YOU TO GET MOVING!**

9 Within the **NEXT 30 YEARS,** people may be wearing contact lenses that allow them to **PULL UP INFORMATION** from the Internet when they **BLINK THEIR EYE.**

10 More than **FOUR MILLION APPLE iPHONE 4S** devices were sold the first weekend they were released in October 2011.

11 **FLYBOARD** is a **WATERPROOF JETPACK** that lets you dive in and out of the water like a dolphin. You can leap more than **30 FEET (9.1 M) ABOVE THE WATER.**

12 Companies are designing cars, refrigerators, and subway platform train schedules that use the same **INTERACTIVE TECHNOLOGY** as your smart phone touch screen.

13 One day, **LAPTOPS** will roll up like a **YOGA MAT.**

14 **GAMING DEVICES** will soon get even more interactive. You won't just tilt your game to make it move, **YOU'LL TWIST IT.** Upcoming models are **FLEXIBLE, LIKE RUBBER.**

15 Engineers are working on **SPECIAL EYEGLASSES** that will **INSTANTLY TRANSLATE FOREIGN LANGUAGES** and provide a transcript for the user to read.

16 Future cell phones will be as **THIN AS A CREDIT CARD AND BENDABLE.**

17 Upcoming **iPODS** will be worn on your wrist and **LOOK LIKE A BRACELET.**

18 **CELL PHONES** used to be the **SIZE OF A BRICK.**

19 Besides the **FIRST SUCCESSFUL PERSONAL COMPUTER, STEVE JOBS** was involved in the creation of the iPhone, the iPad, iTunes, and Pixar, the animators of *Toy Story.*

A green copper-vapor laser and an orange sodium-wavelength laser beamed by telescopes at the Starfire Optical Range in New Mexico

FACTS

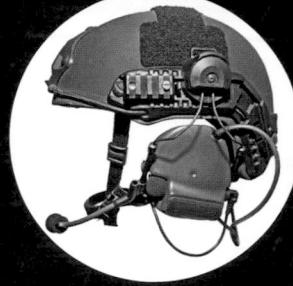

20 AIDA (Affective Intelligent Driving Assistant) is a dashboard computer that works like a GPS but also can scan your face to read emotion. Its comments try to suit your mood.

21 In the near future, **CARS MAY PARK THEMSELVES** and **COME PICK YOU UP** when you press a button on your phone.

22 Researchers are looking to **HARNESS ENERGY** created from the **OCEANS' WAVES AND TIDES TO POWER CITIES.**

23 People can now **USE THEIR PHONES** at the checkout **INSTEAD OF DEBIT CARDS OR CASH.**

24 Scientists **USE LASERS TO CALCULATE DISTANCES.** They even **BOUNCED A LASER BEAM OFF THE MOON** to measure the distance between it and Earth.

25 **KEVLAR**, a flexible fabric that is **FIVE TIMES STRONGER THAN STEEL**, is used for bulletproof vests, tennis rackets, helmets, and skateboards.

26 **SHARK SCALES** are designed for **FAST SWIMMING.** Scientists studied the fish to create swimsuit materials that can **INCREASE SWIMMERS' SPEEDS.**

27 **NINETY-SEVEN PERCENT** of people in **MOROCCO AND ICELAND** have Internet access—**MAKING** these countries the world's most **WIRED.**

28 More than **FIVE BILLION** of the world's **SEVEN BILLION** people have **CELL PHONES.**

29 In the United States, almost **197 BILLION TEXTS** are sent **EVERY MONTH.**

30 A dictionary definition of the verb "TWITTER" IS "TO TALK IN A CHATTERING FASHION."

31 Someday, **OUR SHOES MAY POWER OUR CELL PHONES.** An early version using rubber boots **CONVERTS THE WEARER'S HEAT** into current to charge a clipped-on phone.

32 The average user on **FACEBOOK** has **130 "FRIENDS."**

33 Surfers can now wear **WET SUITS** with a pull cord that inflates a suit to **BRING A SURFER TO THE SURFACE IN SECONDS.**

34 Some people who have had a brain trauma and can't speak have a brain chip that lets them move a computer's cursor **WITH THEIR THOUGHTS** to email or surf the Web.

35 In a Florida, U.S.A., school, kids don't pay cash for lunch. Each kid waves his hand over a sensor that detects a unique **VEIN PATTERN** and bills that kid's account.

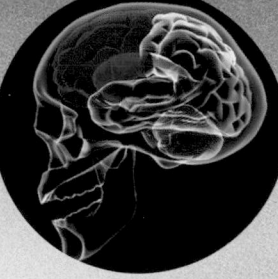

1

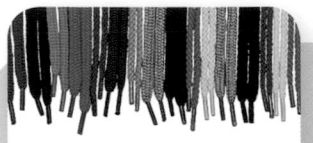

The covering at the end of a shoelace is called an **AGLET.**

5

A file cabinet labeled O–Z is rumored to have inspired L. Frank Baum to name his famous kingdom and wizard "Oz."

S

ANGRY AND HUNGRY are the only English words that end in —GRY.

12

The Pacific Ocean's name comes from the Latin *MARE PACIFICUM,* which means **"PEACEFUL SEA."**

A palindrome is a word that's spelled the same backward as forward, such as noon, kayak, and race car.

2

The word **"SYZYGY"** is used by astronomers to describe three objects in space that are positioned in a line.

6

The 267-page novel *Gadsby* by Ernest Vincent Wright has about 50,000 words, none of which contain the letter *e.*

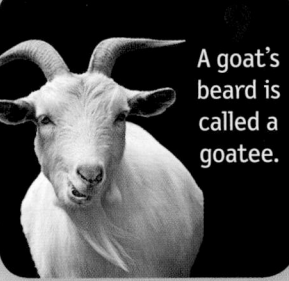

A goat's beard is called a goatee.

13

TRISKAIDEKAPHOBIA is the fear of the number **13.**

The 2,000-year-old Rosetta Stone, which helped scientists decode Egyptian hieroglyphs, is carved with Greek and two kinds of ancient Egyptian.

3

To **"86,"** or get rid of, something stems from a number code said to be used by restaurant workers to indicate they were out of a dish or wouldn't serve a customer.

7

It's impossible to know for certain, but English likely has more words—at least 250,000—than any other language.

10

Twenty-three of the world's languages have more than 50 million speakers each.

14

Cats communicate using at least 16 known "CAT WORDS."

In addition to hieroglyphs, ancient Egyptians had a more practical form of writing they called *sesh,* which means "writing for documents."

4

Describing a farewell as a "SWAN SONG" originated from the (false) belief that a swan was silent all its life but sang aloud right before it died.

11

India has 23 official languages.

18

The ancient Celtic culture existed for about 1,300 years but never had its own writing system. Instead, it borrowed from other cultures, such as Latin from the Romans.

50 WORD FACTS THAT WILL WOW YOU

19
Sign language is not a universal language—each country has its own sign language, and vocabulary and grammar vary by region.

26
ONOMATOPOEIA is the formation of a word based on the sound associated with it, such as cuckoo, hiccup, sizzle, and Ping-Pong.

32
Koko the gorilla understands 2,000 words of spoken English and can sign 1,000 words. Her statements usually contain three to six words.

39
A 2007 study found that women and men speak about the same number of words per day—16,000.

46
In 2011, the *Oxford English Dictionary* added the word LOL, which stands for Laughing Out Loud, in use since the 1980s.

20
The word "QUIZ" also means an "ODD PERSON."

27
Every **14 DAYS** a language dies out.

33
The ancient Romans called the Mediterranean Sea *Mare nostrum*, "Our sea."

40
The Hawaiian word "ALOHA" means both hello and goodbye.

46
The Swedish equivalent of LOL is ASG, short for *asgarv*, or intense laughter.

21
A sentence that uses all 26 letters of the English alphabet is called a **PANGRAM.** A famous pangram example is: The quick brown fox jumps over the lazy dog.

28
An **OOLOGIST** is a collector of bird eggs.

34
Pig latin is a play language formed by placing the first consonants of each word and "ay" at the end of the word; so shut becomes "utshay," door becomes "oorday."

41
A SNICKERSNEE is a large knife.

47
A HAIKU is an unrhymed three-lined verse, with five syllables in the first and third lines, and seven in the second.

22
The letter *e* is the most frequently used letter in the English alphabet.

29
There is a word that rhymes with orange: **SPORANGE,** a very rare, alternative form of the word "sporangium," a part of a fern.

35
Esperanto is a universal language—not tied to any one country or culture—invented in the late 1800s and spoken by an estimated two million people worldwide.

42
In Australian slang, **"BINGLE"** is a car accident, a **"CAPTAIN COOK"** is a look around, and a **"WHINGER"** is a complainer.

48
Sukanya Roy won the U.S. National Spelling Bee in 2011 by correctly spelling the word CYMOTRICHOUS, which means "having wavy hair."

23
A group of cats is called a CLOWDER.

30
In Wales, there's a community named LLANFAIRPWLLGWYNGYLLGOGERYCHWYRNDROBWLLLLANTYSILIOGOGOGOCH, commonly shortened to Llanfair PG.

36
The six official languages of the United Nations are Arabic, Chinese, English, Russian, French, and Spanish. Nearly three billion people worldwide speak these languages.

43
Nearly 80 percent of the world's population speaks only 1 percent of the planet's languages.

49
As of January 2011, no more than a dozen people speak fluent Huillichesungun, the language of Chile's Wequetrumao community.

24
A group of prisoners is called a PITY.

31
SCHADENFREUDE is a German word that means joy derived from the troubles of others.

37
The word MUGGLE—a nonwizard in the Harry Potter series—was included in the *Oxford English Dictionary* in 2003.

44
COULROPHOBIA is the fear of clowns.

50
The last two fluent speakers of Mexico's Ayapaneco language live less than a third of a mile (500 m) apart but won't speak to each other for reasons that remain unclear.

25
In Russian, the word for red also means "BEAUTIFUL."

38
The language of the Pirahã, a remote Amazonian tribe, has no words for "all," "each," "every," "most," or "few."

1. A frog in Brazil eats fruit. **2.** Waxy tree frogs create a waxlike cocoon around their bodies to survive dry spells. **3.** A group of frogs is called an army; a group of toads is called a knot. **4. Australian tree frogs create a range of smells, from rotting meat to roasted cashews to thyme leaves. 5.** The ornate horned frog can eat a mouse in one swallow. **6.** In dry, hot weather, the spatulate-nosed tree frog crawls into a hole and uses the tip of its alligator-shaped head to plug up the hiding spot. **7.** It's impossible for turtles to stick out their tongues. **8.** Frogs shed their skin about once a week and then eat it. **9. The goliath bullfrog can cover nearly ten feet (3 m) in one hop. 10.** You can't get warts from frogs or toads. **11.** Salamanders can't hear sounds, so they don't make any. **12.** Threatened ribbed newts can squeeze their muscles and force their sharp rib tips through their skin, piercing any unlucky predator. **13. Before a rainstorm, spadefoot toads come out by the hundreds and croak a call that sounds like "rain today." 14.** Horned toads aren't toads at all, they're lizards. **15.** More Americans die each year from bee stings than from snake bites. **16.** The tiny dwarf gecko is less than an inch (2.5 cm) long. **17. Snakes swallow prey headfirst. 18.** A snake stops eating about two weeks before it sheds its skin. **19.** Alligators have U-shaped snouts, crocodiles have V-shaped snouts. **20.** Sea turtles can sense Earth's magnetic field, and they use this sense in combination with others to orient themselves. **21. Dinosaurs were not reptiles but were related to them. 22.** Amphibians first appeared on Earth about 300 million years ago, about 70 million years before dinosaurs. **23.** A snake doesn't have taste buds on its tongue; instead, its taste receptors are in pits in the roof of its mouth. It flicks its tongue in and out to bring chemicals from the air back to the pit. **24.** The lizardlike tuatara may breathe as seldom as once per hour while resting during the day. **25. Tortoises are turtles that live on land. 26.** All turtles lack teeth and instead have a sharp beak. **27.** A turtle's ribs are fused to its shell. **28.** All turtles, even those that live in the sea, lay eggs on land. **29. The geometric plates on a turtle's shell are called scutes. 30.** The alligator snapping turtle, the world's largest freshwater turtle, weighs more than 220 pounds (100 kg) and has scissor-sharp jaws.

Loggerhead Sea Turtle

31. Loggerhead turtles are named for their large, powerful heads, which are equipped with jaws that can crush lobsters. **32.** Galápagos tortoises can weigh more than 550 pounds (249.5 kg) and live to be more than 100 years old. **33. The stinkpot turtle gets its name from a foul odor released as a defense. 34.** The four-eyed frog has only two eyes, but it appears to have four thanks to two black-and-white, eyelike spots on its rear. **35.** South American bullfrogs let out a loud shriek when grabbed by predators, which startles the predators into letting go of the frogs. **36.** The paradoxical frog is named for its odd trait: Tadpoles of the species grow to be about four times longer than adults. **37. When threatened, the European common toad stands on tiptoe to appear larger. 38.** The marine toad has poisonous glands covering its body that release a toxin that can kill predators in as little as 15 minutes. **39.** Most tree frogs have sticky pads on their toes that help them cling to surfaces. **40.** The world's largest frog, the goliath bullfrog, grows as long as 16 inches (40 cm) but can't make a sound—it lacks a vocal sac. **41. In most frog species, the females are larger than the males. 42.** The world's smallest lizard can fit on a dime. **43.** Abah River flying frogs don't have wings, but the webbing between their toes acts as a parachute that lets the frogs glide from tree to tree. **44.** Most burrowing frogs dig backward, using their hind feet.

100 COLD HARD FACTS ABOUT

45. African bullfrogs will stay underground for years at a time, waiting for heavy rains. **46.** Pit vipers and some boas and pythons use organs on their face called heat pits to detect small changes in air temperature produced by the presence of other animals. **47.** A snake's eyes are covered with a transparent scale that's replaced when the snake sheds its skin. **48.** A snake has up to 400 vertebrae along its back; a human has 26. **49.** A baby snake can be up to seven times longer than its egg when it hatches. **50.** Snakes keep their eggs warm by coiling on top of them and shivering to generate heat. **51.** Boas use their tails to hang from tree limbs while snatching lizards, birds, and mammals from lower branches. **52.** Both ends of a rubber boa look like a head, so when threatened, the snake coils into a ball and raises its tail to distract predators from its real head. **53.** The 550-pound (250 kg) anaconda is the world's heaviest snake; its body is strong enough to constrict an animal the size of a horse. **54.** The python is the world's longest snake, stretching 33 feet (10 m). **55.** The Arafura file snake, which looks like an elephant's trunk, has rough skin that helps the aquatic snake grip fish. **56.** The common egg-eating snake gobbles up whole eggs; spikes on the snake's backbone saw through the shell once it passes into the snake's throat. **57.** The Aesculapian snake is named after the Greek god of medicine and appears coiled around a staff on the medical profession symbol. **58.** The Mozambique spitting cobra sprays its victims with painful, blinding venom. **59.** All sea snakes are highly poisonous. **60.** The black mamba, which can grow to be 11 feet (3.5 m) long, can slither as fast as 12.5 miles per hour (20 kph). **61.** A threatened king cobra, the longest venomous snake, raises the front third of its body off the ground so that it stands up to five feet (1.5 m) tall. **62.** The adder lives in extremely cold climates, including the Arctic, where the snake hibernates for up to eight months of the year. **63.** A rattlesnake's rattle gains a segment each time the snake sheds its skin. **64.** The loose flap of skin under a lizard's head is called a dewlap. **65.** Chameleons change color mainly to adjust their temperature —darker skin absorbs more sun, warming the lizards—or to communicate with other members of their species. **66.** Flying lizards sail from tree to tree with the aid of "wings," which are really skin flaps stretched between long ribs. **67.** Marine iguanas are the only lizards that forage for food in the sea; they dive to depths of 39 feet (12 m) and can stay underwater for more than an hour. **68.** The plumed basilisk, a kind of lizard, can run upright on its hind legs across standing water. **69.** The Mexican beaded lizard and North America's Gila monster are the world's only poisonous lizards, but their bite is rarely fatal to humans. **70.** Komodo dragons can smell dead animals — a favorite food — up to three miles (5 km) away. **71.** Glass lizards and legless lizards, which look like snakes, lack legs but have very long tails. **72.** Geckos without eyelids use their tongues to lick their eyeballs clean. **73.** The three-foot-tall (0.9 m) sand monitor lizard uses its long, muscular tail to stand on its hind legs and have a look around. **74.** Chameleons' toes are fused into two opposite-facing groups that help the lizards grip slender branches. **75.** Amphisbaenians live underground and look like worms but are related to lizards. **76.** Nile crocodiles can kill prey as large as water buffalo and wildebeest. **77.** Crocodilians—crocodiles, alligators, caimans, and gharials—have a flap of skin at the back of their mouth that closes when the reptiles are underwater to keep water out of their lungs. **78.** All crocodilians have a powerful bite but can't chew — instead, they swallow whole chunks ripped from prey. **79.** The world's largest crocodilian is the saltwater croc, which can grow to 23 feet (7 m) and weigh more than 1 ton (0.9 MT). **80.** Crocs lie around with their mouths open to cool off. **81.** On the tip of a male gharial's long, slender snout is a bump the crocodilian uses to make sounds and bubbles. **82.** Some land-dwelling salamanders lack lungs and instead breathe through their skin, mouth, and throat. **83.** Sirens, a kind of eel-like amphibian, breathe through lungs and external gills on the sides of the neck that resemble a feather boa. **84.** The 4.5-foot (1.4-m) Japanese giant salamander can live for more than 50 years. **85.** Female great crested newts lay dozens or hundreds of eggs and wrap them—individually, or in groups of two or three—in leaves for protection. **86.** The sticky slime from a slimy salamander takes several days to wash off. **87.** Caecilians, limbless, wormlike amphibians are rarely seen because they live either underground or underwater. **88.** Unlike frogs and toads, newts and salamanders keep their tails as adults. **89.** Frogs and toads have four digits on their forelegs, five on their hind legs. **90.** When swallowing food, frogs and toads shut their eyes, which rolls the eyeballs downward and creates more pressure in the mouth, meaning fewer swallows to finish a meal. **91.** Frogs live on every continent except Antarctica. **92.** The quarter-sized coqui frog makes a sound like its name: "CO-KEE!" **93.** A kind of frog that lives near noisy waterfalls dances instead of croaks. **94.** If your tongue were as long as a frog's, it would reach your bellybutton. **95.** The smallest known frog is the size of a person's fingernail. **96.** Tadpoles are baby frogs adapted for life in the water: They use gills to breathe and tails to swim. **97.** In the Florida Everglades, pet Burmese pythons released into the wild constrict and eat alligators. **98.** A crocodile can't move its tongue — it's attached to the bottom of the croc's mouth. **99.** A type of thread snake found on the Caribbean island of Barbados is the smallest known serpent in the world—it's as thin as a spaghetti noodle and about as long as a computer mouse. **100.** Komodo dragons, which weigh on average about 155 pounds (70 kg), can eat up to half their weight in a single meal.

Gila Monster

REPTILES & AMPHIBIANS

1

FIRE ANTS—

red, stinging ants native to South America— were accidentally brought to the United States on ships in the 1900s.

2

THE HOTTEST **TEMPERATURE EVER RECORDED ON EARTH WAS** 136°F (58°C) **IN LIBYA IN 1922.**

3

CAMELS HAVE ADAPTED TO LIVE IN HOT, DRY DESERT CLIMATES.

The thick fur on the top of their bodies provides shade, while the thin fur everywhere else helps heat escape their bodies.

4

USING REFLECTIVE MATERIALS TO HARNESS THE SUN'S ENERGY, PEOPLE MAKE SOLAR OVENS TO COOK FOOD.

5

MAGNIFYING GLASSES

can concentrate the sun's rays into a **FIRE-STARTING BEAM.**
Some campers use a magnifying glass to start a fire instead of matches.

25 RED HOT

6

Energy from lightning heats the air up to **60,000°F** (33,316°C). That's six times hotter than the surface of the sun!

9

The surface temperature on **VENUS,** the hottest planet in our solar system, is **854°F** (457°C).

11

MOST LOBSTERS ARE GREENISH BROWN, BUT TURN BRIGHT RED WHEN PUT IN A POT OF BOILING WATER.

7

THE RING OF FIRE IS A ZONE IN THE PACIFIC BASIN WHERE THREE-QUARTERS OF EARTH'S ACTIVE VOLCANOES LIE.

10

One-third of all the lava that has erupted from Earth in the past 500 years has flowed out of **ICELAND.**

8

ORIENTAL FIRE-BELLIED TOADS

SHOW THEIR TRUE COLORS WHEN THEY FEEL UNDER THREAT.

Green on top with black spots, they reveal their bright red belly by arching their back or even flipping over as a warning to predators that they are toxic.

12

TALK ABOUT HOT AIR: A MAN ONCE EXTINGUISHED 39 FIRE-LIT TORCHES IN 30 SECONDS BY PUTTING THEM IN HIS MOUTH.

13

Rarely seen FIRE TORNADOES occur when intense heat and turbulent winds spur whirling currents of air, called eddies. The eddies form a tornado-like structure that sucks in burning debris.

14

AMELIA EARHART
OFTEN DRANK
HOT CHOCOLATE
ON HER FAMOUS FLIGHTS.

15

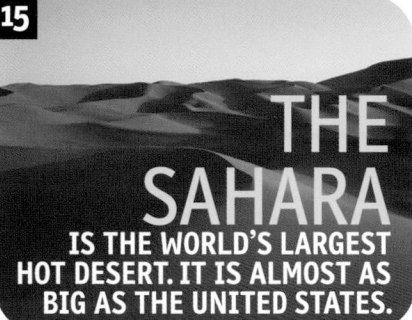

THE SAHARA IS THE WORLD'S LARGEST HOT DESERT. IT IS ALMOST AS BIG AS THE UNITED STATES.

16

Every year, there is a "solar egg frying contest" in Arizona, U.S.A. Contestants try to fry an egg on a sidewalk—often using mirrors, magnifying glasses, and other contraptions to help the egg cook faster.

FACTS

17

THE RITUAL OF WALKING ON HOT COALS has been around for thousands of years. While coals reach temperatures of around

1,000°F (537°C),

most people aren't badly injured because only a small amount of heat transfers to their feet.

18

THE INFINITY CHILI, THE WORLD'S HOTTEST PEPPER, IS **200** times hotter than a jalapeño. It often brings to tears people who taste just a sliver.

19

A FIREFIGHTER'S GEAR— including the helmet, pants, jacket, boots, belt, gloves, and breathing apparatus—weighs about 60 POUNDS (27 kg)—about the same as three car tires!

20

THE LONGEST HOT DOG EVER MADE WAS 668 FEET (204 M)— THAT'S THE LENGTH OF TWO FOOTBALL FIELDS!

21

THE HOTTEST SEA IN THE WORLD IS THE RED SEA. AT ITS WARMEST SPOT IT'S 87°F (31° C).

22

IN THE HOT AUSTRALIAN DESERT, KANGAROOS LICK THEIR ARMS TO STAY COOL.

23

In some countries, VOLCANIC STEAM AND HOT WATER are used to generate electricity.

24

EATING A HOT PEPPER CAN MAKE YOUR MOUTH FEEL ON FIRE, but drinking water won't help. Water doesn't easily wash away the oil in the pepper that causes the burn. Eating bread or rice, which will soak up the oil, is a quicker fix.

25

Over 200 years ago, two men invented the first practical hot air balloon when they were inspired by a piece of paper floating in the updraft of a fire.

35 AWESOME

1 ASIA is the LARGEST CONTINENT— even the surface of the moon is smaller.

2 Asia and Europe have the same number of countries—46.

3 The MANGO is the national fruit of INDIA, and the capital of Thailand, Bangkok, is known as the BIG MANGO.

4 The 50 TALLEST MOUNTAINS in the world are in Asia.

5 Asia is home to the world's most populous countries, China and India. Each one has more than ONE BILLION INHABITANTS.

6 More than 10,000 people formed a HUMAN DOMINO CHAIN in Inner Mongolia, China, in 2010.

7 The world's LOWEST AND HIGHEST POINTS are in Asia. The lowest, in the Dead Sea, is 1,385 feet (422 m) below sea level. The highest, Mt. Everest, is more than 5 miles (8 km) above sea level.

8 Professional video game players in South Korea are TREATED LIKE ROCK STARS. Some practice for 16 hours a day and can't go out without people asking for autographs.

9 Forty jumbo jets would fit inside the Sarawak Chamber in Malaysia's GOOD LUCK CAVE. It's the LARGEST UNDERGROUND CHAMBER ever found.

10 RICE BALLS WRAPPED in seaweed are popular in Japan. They are called *onigiri*.

11 A dam in NUREK, TAJIKISTAN, rises nearly 100 STORIES (984 ft or 300 m) above the Vakhsh River.

12 A zoo in SINGAPORE is ONLY OPEN AT NIGHT. It features NOCTURNAL ANIMALS, like the leopard, tapir, Malayan tiger, and the slow loris.

13 People have been living in SANA'A, the capital of Yemen, for more than 2,500 years. More than 40 walled "secret" gardens can be found within the walls of the city.

14 The FORBIDDEN CITY, in the middle of BEIJING, CHINA, was built with 3.1 MILLION BRICKS.

15 In KAZAKHSTAN a traditional sport, called *kokpar*, requires two teams on horseback to try and move a GOAT'S CARCASS to a goal in the center of the field.

16 In Vietnam you can stay in a HOTEL CARVED OUT OF A TREE. Some people call it the "CRAZY HOUSE."

17 The CHINESE INVENTED FIREWORKS. Blue-violet fireworks are the hardest to create because the concentrations of chemicals are so UNSTABLE AND DANGEROUS.

Forbidden City, Beijing, China

18 HAMSTERS were first found in SYRIA. These cuddly pets like to hoard any extra food they find.

19 In MALAYSIA, BATS OUTNUMBER any other mammal, including humans.

20 There are NO MOVIE THEATERS in Saudi Arabia.

21 The KOREAN form of SUMO WRESTLING requires the winner to throw his opponent to the ground. In JAPAN, the winner must push his opponent out of the ring.

22 Every day, people in the Philippines send an average of 400 MILLION TEXT MESSAGES.

FACTS ABOUT ASIA

23 Some kids in **AFGHANISTAN** participate in **KITE FIGHTING.** Players try to cut each other's strings by gluing glass to their strings.

24 Some **70 PERCENT** of the drinking water in Saudi Arabia is actually **PURIFIED SALT WATER.**

25 Japan gets hit by more than **1,000 EARTHQUAKES EVERY YEAR,** and has one of the world's most effective earthquake warning systems.

26 In Mongolia, people like to drink **AIRAG—FERMENTED HORSE MILK—**during the summer.

27 The **ASIAN LONG-HORNED BEETLE** likely arrived in the U.S. in **WOOD PALLETS** from China in the 1980s. The beetle is a serious pest to some North American hardwood trees.

28 When the Philippines is at war, its **FLAG IS FLOWN UPSIDE DOWN.**

29 The **HANGING GARDENS OF BABYLON** were one of the **SEVEN WONDERS OF THE ANCIENT WORLD.** Their exact location remains a mystery.

30 A small species of deer, the **LEAF DEER,** lives in **MYANMAR.** It's less than two feet tall (0.6 m), and males have tiny 1-inch (3.2 cm) antlers.

31 The **LARGEST EMPIRE** ever to exist was founded in Asia by **GENGHIS KHAN.** At its height, it stretched from Asia into eastern Europe.

32 **ISTANBUL,** the largest city in Turkey, is located in **BOTH EUROPE AND ASIA.**

33 **TURKEY** has a national holiday for kids every April during which the children get **NEW CLOTHES.**

34 The **TORAJA** in Indonesia build their houses **WITHOUT NAILS.** They use just wood and bamboo.

35 **KOMODO DRAGONS** live on the islands of Indonesia. They are the **LARGEST LIVING LIZARDS** in the world and can reach **TEN FEET** (3 m) in length.

15 FACTS THAT ARE

1 The **LARGEST S'MORE EVER** made used **40,000** marshmallows, **8,000** chocolate bars, and **55,000** graham crackers.

2 A Swiss man has collected nearly **9,000** "DO NOT DISTURB" SIGNS from different hotels.

3 A driver on Long Island, New York, U.S.A., has **DRIVEN HIS VOLVO NEARLY THREE MILLION MILES (4.8 MILLION KM).**

4 In **LOS ANGELES, CALIFORNIA, U.S.A.,** you can buy a hot dog wrapped in bacon and then fried and topped with mayo.

5 **THE BIG SHOT RIDE** in Las Vegas, Nevada, U.S.A., sits ON TOP OF A SKYSCRAPER, and shoots riders 160 feet (49 m) into the air.

6 A Canadian **ICE-BREAKING SHIP WEIGHS 33 MILLION POUNDS** (15,000 MT) and can break through thick ice sheets that are **62 FEET (19 M) THICK.**

7 There's a **CHILI PEPPER SO HOT** that two out of every three people who eat it THROW UP.

WONDERFULLY WEIRD

8 **THE GREAT WALL OF CHINA** spans an estimated **5,500 MILES** (8,850 km)—that's longer than the continent of Africa.

9 A church in Barcelona, Spain—THE SAGRADA FAMÍLIA—has been UNDER CONSTRUCTION FOR MORE THAN 100 YEARS. It's one of Barcelona's most popular tourist attractions.

10 IN 2011, SAMIT IJON achieved a new world record by walking a **49-FOOT** (15-m) **HIGH WIRE** suspended between TWO HOT AIR BALLOONS ABOUT 100 FEET (30 M) IN THE AIR.

11 In 2009, more than **2,500 PEOPLE DRESSED UP AS SMURFS** and hung out in a town square in Great Britain.

12 In 1960, an Air Force pilot SKYDIVED OUT OF A BALLOON 102,800 FEET (31,333 m) above Earth.

13 THE ROYAL GORGE BRIDGE in Colorado, U.S.A., stretches more than **956 FEET** (291 m) above the Arkansas River. The ROYAL RUSH SKYCOASTER takes riders at **50 MILES AN HOUR** (80 kph) to hang over the river **A THOUSAND FEET (305 M) BELOW.**

14 In 2010, TWO MEN JUMPED FROM THE TALLEST BUILDING ON EARTH, the Burj Kalifa in Dubai, using parachutes to slow their fall. The building is 2,717 FEET (828 M) TALL.

15 Some people have a **FEAR OF SLIME, OR MYXOPHOBIA.**

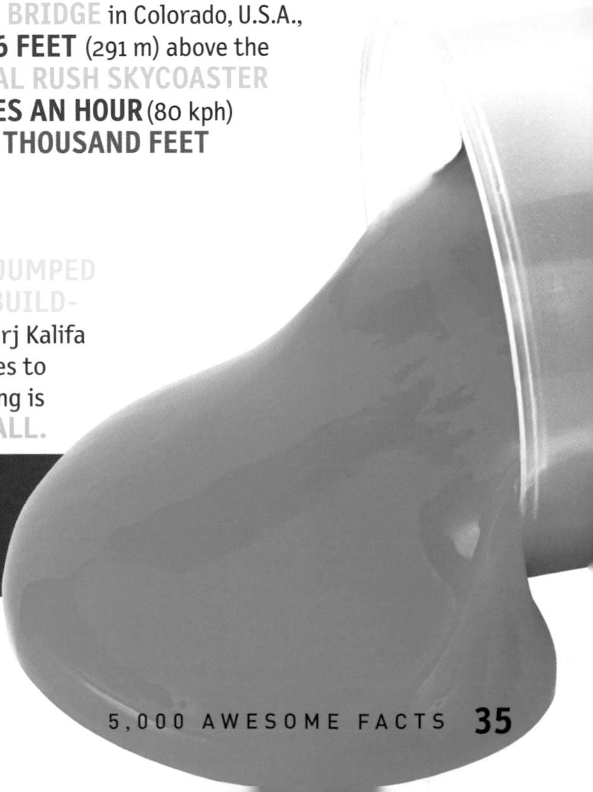

1 Feathers are made from keratin—the same material in mammal hair and reptile scales.

2 Almost all birds shed and replace their feathers at least once a year.

3 The oldest bird fossil is 150 million years old and has wings and feathers like a bird, but a snout like a reptile.

4 Most bird bones are hollow—lighter bones make flying easier.

5 BIRDS HAVE NO TEETH.

6 Most birds are born blind and without feathers.

7 Ostriches are the largest birds, weighing as much as 350 pounds (160 kg) and standing more than nine feet (2.8 m) tall.

8 Only ostriches have two toes on each foot; all other birds have three or four toes on each foot.

9 Ostriches can't fly, but they can run 45 miles per hour (70 kph) for up to 30 minutes.

10 The wandering albatross has the longest wingspan of any bird—up to 11 feet (3.5 m). That's about a foot (0.3 m) shorter than a Mini Cooper.

11 Flamingoes get their pink color from the algae and shrimp they eat.

12 Flamingoes stand on one leg to keep warm.

13 Hummingbirds are the only birds that can fly backward and upside down.

14 The bee hummingbird is the smallest known bird. It is just over two inches (or 6 cm) long and weighs less than a penny.

15 The smallest bird egg is about the size of a pea.

16 Owls swallow their prey whole and later cough up pellets that contain fur, feathers, bones, and other indigestible parts.

17 Hummingbirds don't use their feet to hop or walk, only for perching and scratching.

18 Some birds use silk from spider webs to hold their nests together.

19 Male bowerbirds build elaborate structures made of twigs, bugs, flowers, and even found objects such as toys, mirrors, and CDs to woo females.

20 The longest tail of any bird belongs to the ribbon-tailed astrapia: At three feet (0.9 m) long, its tail feathers are three times the length of its body.

21 BIRDS ARE MODERN-DAY DINOSAURS.

22 The superb lyrebird can expertly mimic many sounds, including those of a chainsaw and a car alarm.

23 A YouTube video of a dancing cockatoo revealed that some birds have rhythm; prior to this, scientists believed only humans were capable of keeping a beat.

24 New Caledonian crows are able to make and use their own tools—despite having no hands.

25 Each year 100,000,000 to 1 billion birds are killed from flying into glass windows.

26 *Sesame Street*'s Big Bird is 8 feet, 2 inches (2.5 m) tall—about a foot (0.3 m) shorter than a real-life ostrich.

27 Einstein, an African grey parrot, had a vocabulary of more than 200 words and sounds.

28 "BIRD" IS BRITISH SLANG FOR GIRL.

29 A peacock's tail is more than half its total body length.

30 A female peacock is called a peahen.

31 Contrary to popular belief, ostriches do not bury their heads in the sand.

32 The Arctic tern travels nearly 25,000 miles (40,230 km) a year during its migration between the Arctic and Antarctica. That's like traveling around the Earth at the equator one full time every year!

33 Brown-headed cowbirds sneak their eggs into the nests of other birds, which raise the cowbird young as their own.

34 THERE ARE ABOUT 10,000 KNOWN BIRD SPECIES IN THE WORLD.

35 Each March, half a million sandhill cranes come together for a month along Nebraska's Platte River to rest and eat during their migration.

36 In the United States, there is a ban on importing live birds from Afghanistan, Albania, Azerbaijan, Bangladesh, Benin, Burkina Faso, Cameroon, Cambodia, Djibouti, Egypt, Ghana, Hong Kong, India, Indonesia, Iran, Iraq, Israel, Ivory Coast (Côte d'Ivoire), Japan, Jordan, Kazakhstan, Kuwait, Laos, Malaysia, Myanmar, Nepal, Niger, Nigeria, Pakistan, Palestinian Autonomous Territories, People's Republic of China, Romania, Russia, Saudi Arabia, South Africa, South Korea, South Sudan, Sudan, Thailand, Togo, Turkey, Ukraine, and Vietnam.

37 The heavy, flightless dodo bird went extinct less than 80 years after it was discovered.

38 Clark's nutcrackers store between 20,000 and 30,000 nuts each year in as many as 1,000 different hiding spots. Studies show the birds remember 75 percent of these hiding spots.

75 AMAZING

39 American crows sometimes form flocks in the millions.

40 BIRDS ARE FEATURED ON THE FLAGS OF 15 COUNTRIES.

41 The hooded pitohui of New Guinea is the first bird ever found by scientists to be toxic—its feathers and skin are poisonous.

42 The tundra swan has more feathers—roughly 25,000—than any other bird.

43 Peregrine falcons can achieve flight speeds of up to 117 miles per hour (188 kph). That's faster than a major league baseball pitch.

44 Pelicans have a pouch just beneath their bills that can store more food than their stomachs.

45 The laughing kookaburra's call has appeared in many movies; it's used as a substitute for the sound of a group of monkeys.

46 Common kingfishers can dive through a layer of thin ice in pursuit of fish below.

47 THE OLDEST RECORD OF A PET PARROT DATES TO 400 B.C.

48 The hammerkop stork builds a nest that can measure six feet (2 m) around and can weigh more than 100 pounds (45 kg).

49 The kiwi—a chicken-size, flightless bird—is the national symbol of New Zealand, and people from New Zealand are often referred to as "Kiwis."

50 Kiwis have existed for more than 30 million years, making them the most ancient living bird.

51 More than 100 families of sociable weavers will occupy an apartment complex–like nest that measures 20 feet (6 m) wide and 10 feet (3 m) high.

52 Hindus consider peafowl sacred because the spots on a peacock's tail are said to resemble the eyes of the gods.

53 A cassowary's booming call is the lowest sound of any bird.

54 Emus—large, flightless Australian birds—can't back up.

55 Hunters in Kazakhstan use trained golden eagles—very fast, powerful raptors—to catch antelope and deer.

56 Ancient Egyptians considered ibis to be sacred and mummified more than one million of them.

57 A flock of crows is called a murder.

58 A flock of chickens is called a peep.

59 Whip-poor-will hatchlings emerge ten days before a full moon.

60 Osprey carry fish headfirst back to the nest; holding the prey this way makes for more aerodynamic flight.

61 SONGBIRDS SING LOUDER AROUND CITY TRAFFIC NOISE.

62 Female barn swallows are attracted to males that have the longest and most symmetrical tails.

63 Ravens attract wolves' and coyotes' attention to prey by calling loudly, and they feast on what the larger predators leave behind.

64 Beijing's Olympic stadium—built for the 2008 Games—was designed to look like a bird's nest.

65 In 2010, India reported an increase in pet owls, caused in part by the popularity of Hedwig, Harry Potter's pet snowy owl.

66 Wild turkeys can run up to 25 miles per hour (40 kph).

67 Some ducks close one eye while sleeping, which lets one half of the brain rest while the other stays alert.

68 PENGUINS ARE THE ONLY BIRDS UNABLE TO FOLD THEIR WINGS.

69 Hummingbirds can eat as much as their body weight in one day.

70 Birds play; common ravens like to slide down snowbanks on their tails and roll down hillsides for fun.

71 Turkey vultures rely on their sense of smell to find dead prey.

72 Birds can see a greater variety of colors than humans.

73 Brown thrashers can sing as many as 2,000 different songs.

74 To find food, hairy woodpeckers tap trees and listen for the sound of insects moving inside.

75 Pelicans stand on their eggs to keep them warm.

Ostrich

AVIAN FACTS

1 DRINKING SALT WATER IS WORSE than not drinking any water at all. Salt water actually DEHYDRATES YOU.

2 The INTERNATIONAL SIGN OF DISTRESS when using fire is to BUILD THREE FIRES IN A TRIANGLE.

3 Since 1937, the Hershey Company has issued MILITARY GRADE CHOCOLATE to service men and women. It is designed to be a high-fat ENERGY BOOSTER.

4 THIRTY-THREE MEN IN CHILE were STUCK IN A MINE FOR 69 DAYS—the longest anyone has ever been trapped underground. THEY ALL SURVIVED.

5 In Missouri , U.S.A., a high school boy was PICKED UP BY A TORNADO AND TOSSED 1,307 FEET (398 m). He had a cut on his head, but no other injuries.

6 The best way to escape QUICKSAND is to calmly lean back as if doing a backfloat. Slowly move your feet in small circles until you free yourself and can paddle to safe land.

7 Some LIZARDS' TAILS are constructed to BREAK OFF EASILY so they can ESCAPE IN AN ATTACK. A new tail is REGENERATED, usually within a few months.

8 MOVING YOUR ARMS LIKE YOU'RE SWIMMING and KEEPING YOUR MOUTH SHUT so snow doesn't pack into your throat can help you SURVIVE AN AVALANCHE.

9 COMPACTED SNOW is like a recording studio: SOUNDPROOF. When buried in snow, IT'S A WASTE OF OXYGEN TO SHOUT for help unless someone is very close by.

10 You are more LIKELY TO SURVIVE A SHARK CIRCLING YOUR SURF-BOARD if you stay calm. THRASHING AROUND makes you look like its FAVORITE FOOD— A SEAL.

11 People have been POISONED BY SNAKE VENOM even AFTER THE SNAKE IS DEAD.

12 It takes TEN MINUTES TO LOSE FEELING IN YOUR ARMS AND LEGS after falling through ice into water.

13 SHIMMYING UP LIKE A WALRUS and kicking your feet LIKE A DOLPHIN is the safest way to GET OUT OF A FROZEN POND and back onto the ice.

14 THREE FISHERMEN SURVIVED NINE MONTHS AND NINE DAYS adrift in the Pacific Ocean after RUNNING OUT OF FUEL. They survived on RAW FISH AND SEA-BIRDS.

15 You lose 10 PERCENT of your BODY HEAT through your HEAD.

16 To SIGNAL DISTRESS WITH SOUND, like with a whistle, REPEAT THE SOUND QUICKLY THREE TIMES.

17 The signal for S.O.S., which can be used as a VISUAL OR AUDIO, IS THREE SHORT, THREE LONG, AND THEN THREE SHORT SIGNALS.

18 WIRELESS OPERATORS aboard the *TITANIC* called for help USING S.O.S. IN 1912.

19 People often resort to EATING INSECTS TO SURVIVE because they are a GOOD SOURCE OF PROTEIN AND FAT.

20 A New York, U.S.A., man was STUCK IN AN ELEVATOR FOR 41 HOURS.

21 If you're in a PLUM-METING ELEVATOR, you cannot save yourself by jumping up just before it crashes. Humans can't jump up fast enough to counter the elevator's speed.

22 Juana Maria, who inspired the book *Island of the Blue Dolphins*, survived 18 YEARS ALONE on San Nicolas Island after her tribe was attacked by Russian hunters in 1835.

23 The first episode of *GILLIGAN'S ISLAND* was filmed on the Hawaiian ISLAND OF KAUAI. The rest were FILMED ON A STUDIO LOT.

24 CONTESTANTS ON *SURVIVOR* are NOT GIVEN BUG REPELLENT, but they do get sunscreen.

35 LIFESAVING

25

The best way to SURVIVE A TORNADO if you're outside and nowhere near shelter is to FLATTEN YOURSELF ON THE GROUND LIKE A PANCAKE.

26

Some backpackers now bring along a device that can pinpoint the EXACT LOCATION OF A STRANDED HIKER via satellite and send a message to alert a search-and-rescue-team.

27

ERNEST SHACKLETON and his crew set out in 1914 to CROSS ANTARCTICA, but instead became trapped in sea ice and didn't return home for TWO YEARS. Miraculously, no one died.

28

A BEAR CUB that survived a NEW MEXICO, U.S.A., FOREST FIRE IN 1950 was nursed back to health and taken to the National Zoo. He became known as SMOKEY BEAR.

Personal locator beacon

29

PUNCHING OR KICKING A SHARK in its most sensitive areas—NOSE, EYES, AND GILLS—can send it swimming the other direction in the middle of an attack.

30

SHARKS HAVE ATTACKED PEOPLE because they were ATTRACTED TO THEIR BLING, such as earrings and watches, which look like fish scales to a hungry shark.

31

SHARKS are attracted to STRONG SMELLS, INCLUDING URINE.

32

You can START A FIRE with the BATTERY OF A CELL PHONE, STEEL WOOL, AND DRY STICKS.

33

They now make SOLAR-POWERED CELL PHONES for hikers and campers. You put the phone on a rock in the sun for an hour and you get 25 minutes of chat time.

34

During WWII, JOHN F. KENNEDY'S U.S. Navy boat was hit by a Japanese destroyer. He and other surviving crew swam to a small island. They were rescued several days later.

35

Some people say TWINKIES are the best food for a survival kit because they NEVER SEEM TO SPOIL, but their SHELF LIFE IS ONLY 25 DAYS.

TerraFix™ 406
GPS Interface/Onboard PLB

GPS I/O

OK TEST

Push & Together x 1 Sec.

ON

OFF

DO NOT COVER GPS ANTENNA

ACR

FACTS ABOUT SURVIVAL

100 SHARK FACTS YOU CAN

1. The great white shark is the largest carnivorous fish in the sea. **2.** There are about 350 species of sharks. **3.** Sharks live in all of Earth's oceans. **4.** Sharks lived on earth 170 million years before dinosaurs. **5.** Sharks are fish, but they don't have bony skeletons. They are made from a flexible, rubbery material called cartilage. **6.** The tip of your nose and your earlobe are made of cartilage. Cartilage helps sharks twist and turn. **7.** At 65 feet (20 m), the whale shark is the world's largest shark, but it's a harmless giant. It feeds mostly on floating plankton. **8.** Whale sharks weigh up to 74,970 pounds (34,000 kg)—about as much as 12 large white rhinos. **9.** A newborn whale shark is only 25 inches (64 cm) long. **10.** A whale shark has 3,000 tiny teeth that are 1/12 of an inch (3 mm) long. **11.** A whale shark's mouth opens to about 4.6 feet (1.4 m), almost as wide as a car. **12.** The five-foot-long (1.5 m) leopard shark is spotted like its namesake. **13.** Pilot fish hover around nurse sharks and eat parasites off their skin. **14.** More than half of a shark's weight is muscle. **15.** All that bulk makes them heavier than seawater, so they must swim constantly to avoid sinking to the ocean floor. **16.** Most sharks also swim to keep water flowing through their gills so they can breathe. **17.** Bottom-dwelling sharks are often seen resting on the ocean floor. They find spots with a slow-flowing current or oxygen-rich water. **18.** A shark's skin is as tough as sandpaper and is covered in pointed scales. **19.** Sharks have six or more rows of teeth. Only the outer one or two are functional. **20.** A shark's rows of teeth act as replacements that move forward as older teeth wear out or are lost. **21.** On average, a shark loses about one tooth a week. **22.** Sunlight penetrates the ocean to a depth of only about 400 feet (122 m). Below that it is pitch-black. Some sharks have a mirrorlike layer at the back of their eyeballs to increase brightness. **23.** Sharks have a very good sense of smell. Some can smell one drop of blood in 25 million drops of ocean. **24.** Sharks use their ears for a sense of balance just like we do. **25.** Every shark has a lateral line—a canal filled with fluid—running down the inside of its body. This allows it to feel pressure waves (produced by movement or underwater sound) in the water around it. **26.** Sharks have tiny sensory pits across their snouts that can detect electric currents produced by other animals, which helps them find food. **27.** A few sharks—like dogfish—hunt in groups when attacking a larger prey, but most sharks eat alone. **28.** Hammerheads use their head to pound their prey—like stingrays—against the ocean floor. **29.** Great whites hunt by surprising their prey from below and disabling them with one massive bite. If they like how it tastes, they finish it off. **30.** Great whites are colored dark on the back and shade to light on the belly. This makes them hard to see from above (in contrast to the dark sea) and from below (in contrast to the water surface or sky). **31.** Fast sharks tend to hold their bodies stiff while their tails give quick, powerful thrusts. Slower sharks' bodies flex as they move. **32.** The upper lobe on a thresh shark's tail is about as long as the rest of its body! It uses its tail to splash the water while rounding up prey. **33.** Port Jackson sharks use their flattened teeth to feed on shellfish and sea urchins. **34.** Whale sharks, basking sharks, and megamouth sharks are all filter feeders. They open their mouths wide to suck in gallons of water, then strain the water out through their gills to trap the plankton inside. **35.** Basking sharks get their name because they lie with their back at the water's surface like a sunbather. **36.** Sharks are light eaters relative to their body weight. They don't need to use food as energy to keep their body warm because they are cold-blooded. **37.** Worldwide, there are 50–80 unprovoked shark attacks each year. On average, only a dozen people die. **38.** The most common places for shark attacks to occur are Florida, U.S.A.; California, U.S.A.; South Africa; and Australia. **39.** Far more people are killed each year by dogs, elephants, and bees than by sharks! **40.** Great white, tiger, and bull sharks are considered the most dangerous to people. Often their attacks are because of mistaken identity: These sharks normally eat prey similar in size to humans. **41.** Some shark species are known to live 100 years or longer. **42.** One of the

Great White Shark

fiercest sharks is the 20-inch (51-cm) cookie-cutter shark. It will bite chunks from whales more than 20 times its body length! **43.** Shark babies are called pups. Some pups grow inside their mothers. Others hatch from eggs. **44. Shark skin is used to make purses and shoes. Shark teeth are used for jewelry. 45.** Swell shark pups hatch from eggs. The mother sharks lay the eggs in hard cases. People call these cases mermaid's purses. **46.** Swell shark mothers lay up to five egg cases at a time. In nine months, the swell shark pups hatch. **47.** In the light, our vision is about the same as a shark's. In the dark, a shark's eyes are ten times more sensitive to light. **48. A shark uses up more than 10,000 teeth in its lifetime. 49.** Prehistoric sharks had teeth up to six inches (15 cm) long! **50. The prehistoric shark** *Carcharocles megalodon* **is estimated to have been 60 feet (16.2 m) long and weighed 55,125 pounds (25,000 kg). That's the size and weight of a fully loaded semi. 51.** The spiny pygmy shark is about eight inches (20 cm) long. It has a glow-in-the-dark belly. **52. When a great white bites its prey, its eyes roll back into its head. This protects its eyes in case the prey fights back. 53.** Mako sharks leap clear out of the water to catch prey. **54. The tiny lantern shark is covered with glow-in-the-dark slime. 55.** The lantern shark is a deep-sea shark. Scientists think glowing might help predators attract prey. **56. Wobbegong sharks are colored like the seafloor. Their mouths have parts that look like seaweed. 57.** A surfer named Bethany Hamilton was attacked by a tiger shark in Hawaii, U.S.A., when she was 13. It took a big bite out of her surfboard, and it took her left arm. Bethany continues to surf. The movie *Soul Surfer* was made about her. **58. The great white shark has the largest teeth of any living shark. They are two inches long (5 cm). 59.** Sharks are close cousins to rays. **60. A shark has five to seven gill openings on each side of its head. A bony fish has just one. 61.** Scientists use bone, teeth, or scales to determine the age of a bony fish. But since sharks don't have bones, permanent teeth, or scales, it is hard to determine the age and life span of a shark. **62. Red tail sharks, popular in home aquariums, are bony fish, not sharks. 63.** The dwarf lantern shark is only the size of a pencil. **64. When threatened, a swell shark doubles in size by gulping water. Once safe, it makes a doglike bark and burps out water. 65.** Mako sharks are faster than bottlenose dolphins and killer whales. They can swim up to 31 miles per hour (50 kph). **66. During the day, as many as 36 nurse sharks pile on top of each other as they rest in caves and crevices. 67.** A shark cage is the only safe way to observe and photograph larger, and more aggressive, sharks. **68. A shark's taste buds line its whole mouth, not just its tongue. 69.** The prickly dogfish gets its name from its super-rough scales. The best way to see this shark is from a deep-sea submersible off the coasts of New Zealand and Australia. **70. Greenland sharks live in the North Atlantic and Arctic. They eat seabirds and dead whales. Indigenous people use their hides for boots and teeth for knives. 71.** The nurse shark is active at night in the mangrove reefs and rocky shores of the eastern and western Atlantic, the Gulf of Mexico, and the eastern Pacific from Mexico to Peru. **72. Spinner sharks hunt schools of fish while jumping and spinning out of the water. 73.** Blacktip reef sharks are common in the reefs of the Mediterranean Sea and the Pacific and Indian Oceans. **74. Six rare shark species call the freshwater rivers of Borneo, Australia, and India home. 75.** The heart of a whale shark weighs more than 40 pounds (18 kg). That's 80 times bigger than your heart! **76. Researchers and fishermen have found everything from license plates to boat cushions in the bellies of sharks. 77.** Great white sharks travel 6,897 miles (11,100 km) in 99 days to migrate from South Africa to Australia. That's like swimming the distance of the U.S. from coast to coast—twice! **78. Waders, surfers, and divers in Florida are usually unaware that swimming nearby are sand devils, bonnet-head, blacktip, sandbar, spinner, and scalloped hammerhead sharks. 79.** As much as two-thirds of a shark's brain is devoted to its sense of smell. **80. A shark's fat-filled liver provides buoyancy and stores energy. A basking shark's liver is 25 percent of its body weight. 81.** Some sharks, like carpet sharks, can change their skin color to blend into their surroundings. **82. Tiger sharks aren't picky about what they eat. They gobble up fish, other sharks, seabirds, iguanas, sea snakes, sea turtles, and sea scraps such as garbage and carrion. 83.** Great white sharks grow to an average of 15 feet (4.6 m) in length, though some larger ones have been recorded at more than 20 feet (6 m) and weighed up to 5,000 pounds (2,268 kg). **84. If the current and light are just right, a shark: hears prey 820 feet (250 m) away; smells blood one-half mile (1 km) away; sees movement up to 50 feet (15 m) away; and feels the flutter of moving animals one to two body lengths away. 85.** A shark's sense of smell is 10,000 times better than ours! **86. Great white and oceanic whitetip sharks poke their heads out of the water to pick up airborne scents. 87.** A major predator of sharks is another shark. **88. Unlike mammals, a shark's upper jaw is not fused to its skull. When biting, the upper and lower jaws drop and move forward, rotating the teeth outward. This gives a shark a larger bite or better suction to capture prey. 89.** A large adult great white shark is three times longer than a person. **90. The oldest known intact shark skeleton (a** *Doliodus problematicus***) was found in Canada. It lived 409 million years ago. 91.** Frilled sharks have changed very little since prehistoric times. These squid-eating, deep-sea sharks can grow as long as a Jeep. **92. Angel sharks hide beneath the sand and wait perfectly still for their prey. 93.** The Greenland shark has poisonous flesh. It has been known to snatch caribou straight from the water's edge. **94. If you ate like a shark, you'd only eat one small meal, like a piece of pizza, every few days. And you'd have to swallow it whole! 95.** A great white shark's first dorsal fin is about 3.2 feet (1 m) tall—larger than a four-year-old kid! **96. How far can you swim in five seconds? A shortfin mako can zip 239 feet (73 m)—the length of a soccer field. A great white can make it 183 feet (56 m)—first to third base. Megamouth is a bit of a slowpoke. It can only travel 4.5 feet (1.3 m)—that's like moving over two seats in a baseball stadium. 97.** An ichthyologist is a person who studies marine fish, including sharks. **98. People are a bigger danger to sharks than sharks are to people. Millions of sharks die in nets set to catch other fish. Others are killed on purpose. 99.** 900,000 tons (816,466 MT) of shark have been caught every year for the last 20 years. **100. Some sharks are caught for shark fin soup, a Chinese delicacy.**

SiNK YOUR TEETH INTO!

50 Furious Facts ABOUT EXTREME EARTH

1 The **BASE** of most volcanoes usually begins **60 MILES** (96 km) or more **BELOW THE SURFACE OF THE EARTH.**

2 When **VOLCANOES** erupt, they throw out all kinds of debris besides lava, including **VOLCANIC BOMBS**—huge rocks that can be as large **AS AN ELEPHANT.**

3 **MAUNA LOA,** the world's largest active volcano, rises 30,000 feet (9,144 m) from ocean floor to summit. That's bigger than **MOUNT EVEREST!**

4 There are about **1,900 ACTIVE VOLCANOES** on Earth.

5 All of the **HAWAIIAN ISLANDS** were formed by **VOLCANISM,** but only the Big Island's Mauna Loa and Kilauea are currently active.

6 Each year, **400,000** people make a pilgrimage to **MOUNT FUJI IN JAPAN** and scramble to its 12,388-foot (3,776-m) summit.

7 U.S.A.'s Yellowstone National Park sits atop a **MASSIVE SUPER VOLCANO.** Super volcanoes can erupt with greater intensity than any eruption in human history.

8 On average, **A VOLCANO ERUPTS** somewhere in the world each week.

9 **KILAUEA VOLCANO** in Hawaii, U.S.A., has **ERUPTED CONTINUOUSLY SINCE 1983.** The material it's spewed has made Hawaii's south shore 500 acres (202 ha) bigger.

10 When **MOUNT ST. HELENS ERUPTED** in Washington, U.S.A., in 1980, four billion board feet (9.4 million m³) of timber were lost from trees downed by the powerful blast.

11 In some cultures, volcanoes are thought to **HOLD A BEAST INSIDE**—or they are an entrance into a **HORRIBLE PLACE.**

12 The word "volcano" comes from the name of the **ROMAN GOD OF FIRE, VULCAN.**

13 There are volcanoes **INSIDE GLACIERS IN ICELAND.**

14 Nevados Ojos del Salado on the Chile/Argentina border is the world's **HIGHEST VOLCANO** above sea level at **22,595 FEET (6,887 M).**

15 **EARTHQUAKES AND TREMORS** almost always occur before **VOLCANIC ERUPTIONS.**

16 California, U.S.A.'s **SAN ANDREAS FAULT,** a crack in the Earth's crust, moves at the same rate as **HUMAN FINGERNAILS GROW**—about two inches (5 cm) a year.

17 Alaska has **MORE EARTHQUAKES THAN ANY OTHER STATE** in the United States.

18 **MOONQUAKES** are earthquakes on the moon.

19 During an earthquake, the **WATER IN SWIMMING POOLS MAY SLOSH AROUND.** A pool in Arizona, U.S.A., once lost water from an earthquake 1,240 miles (2,000 km) away.

20 The interior of **ANTARCTICA HAS ICEQUAKES.** Icequakes are like earthquakes, but they occur within the ice sheet instead of the land underneath the ice.

21 On average, **HALF A MILLION EARTHQUAKES** are detected around the world every year, but only **100,000** can be **SENSED BY HUMANS.**

22 The **HIGHEST MAGNITUDE EARTHQUAKE** ever recorded, a **9.5,** was centered off the **COAST OF CHILE IN 1960.**

23
The **TALLEST TSUNAMI WAVE** ever known to make landfall was **SEVEN STORIES HIGH.** The wave hit Alaska in 1958.

24
The amount of energy in a stroke of **LIGHTNING COULD POWER AN AVERAGE-SIZE CAR** for as many as **910 MILES** (1,465 km).

25
LIGHTNING can jump from **ONE PERSON TO ANOTHER.**

26
If you count the seconds between the **LIGHTNING FLASH AND THE THUNDER** and then divide by five, that's how many miles away the lightning is.

27
LIGHTNING can travel through **PHONE LINES.**

28
In 1885, **FIVE LIGHTNING BOLTS STRUCK THE WASHINGTON MONUMENT,** yet no thunder was heard.

29
On average, **EVERY U.S. COMMERCIAL AIRPLANE** is struck by lightning **MORE THAN ONCE EACH YEAR.**

30
A **FOREST FIRE** can travel more than **SIX MILES PER HOUR** (9.7 kph).

31
Forest fires **TRAVEL FASTER UPHILL** than downhill.

32
The **LOMA PRIETA EARTHQUAKE** in 1989 **DELAYED THE WORLD SERIES** between the San Francisco Giants and the Oakland Athletics **TEN DAYS.**

33
For centuries, scientists have been baffled by reports of "**BALL LIGHTNING**"—glowing spheres of electricity ranging in size from a tennis ball to a beach ball.

34
ANGEL FALLS IN VENEZUELA is Earth's **LARGEST WATERFALL.** It drops **3,212 FEET** (979 m) and barely makes contact with the sheer face of rock it falls past.

35
The **DEAD SEA** is Earth's **LOWEST ELEVATION** at **1,365 FT** (416 m) below sea level.

36
The **DEEP OCEAN** is under as much **PRESSURE** as 9,000 pounds per square inch (62,053 kPa). That's **300 TIMES** the air pressure of a **CAR TIRE!**

37
GLACIAL ICE isn't the same color as ordinary ice— **IT APPEARS TO BE BLUE!**

38
EARTH MOVES around the sun at a rate of **19 MILES PER SECOND** (30 km/s).

39
There are **MORE GEYSERS** in U.S.A.'s Yellowstone National Park than anywhere else on Earth.

40
The **WORST FOREST FIRE** in American history **BURNED THREE MILLION ACRES** (more than 1.2 million hectares) of timberland in Idaho and Montana in 1910.

41
SHIFTING TECTONIC plates in East Africa will someday cause the **HORN OF AFRICA TO SPLIT** from the rest of the continent.

42
37,000–78,000 TONS (33,600–70,800 MT) of **SPACE MATERIAL** falls on Earth each year— most of which is dust-size particles.

43
SANDSTORMS occur all over Earth, but are strongest in the Middle East and China. There is evidence there are even **SANDSTORMS ON MARS!**

44
The **KUTIAH GLACIER** in Pakistan has the record for the **FASTEST GLACIAL SURGE.** In 1953, it moved more than seven miles (12 km) in three months.

45
THE OLDEST VOLCANIC ROCKS on Earth are in Canada. They have been dated at **3.8 BILLION YEARS OLD.**

46
The **OLDEST PERSON** to climb the **HIGHEST MOUNTAIN** on Earth was **76 YEARS OLD.**

47
The **PACIFIC** is the **OLDEST** of all the current oceans on Earth. Because of plate tectonics, the **PACIFIC SHRINKS** a little bit every year while the **ATLANTIC GROWS.**

48
RUSSIA'S LAKE BAIKAL is the world's **OLDEST LAKE.** It holds more water than all of the Great Lakes combined.

49
The **COLDEST PLACE** on Earth with permanent residents is the **SIBERIAN VILLAGE OF OYMYAKON.** The temperature there once reached **-90°F** (-68°C).

50
The **GOBI IS THE COLDEST HOT DESERT.** Temperatures there can drop below **-4°F** (-20°C).

1 Demand to vacation on Croatia's uninhabited, HEART-SHAPED GALEŠNJAK ISLAND increased after satellite images revealed its

SWEET SHAPE.

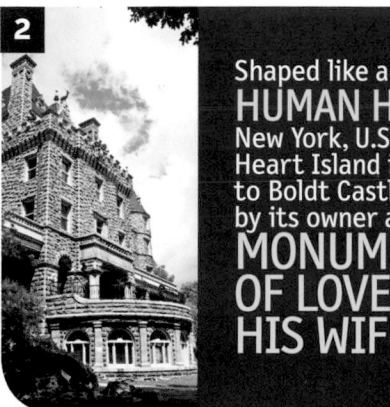

2 Shaped like a **HUMAN HEART**, New York, U.S.A.'s Heart Island is home to Boldt Castle, built by its owner as a **MONUMENT OF LOVE TO HIS WIFE.**

3 Check in to Memphis, Tennessee, U.S.A.'s Heartbreak Hotel, and you can swim in its **HEART-SHAPED SWIMMING POOL.**

4 An elephant's heart weighs as much as **46** pounds (21 kg), about as much as a four-year-old kid.

5 A SEARCH FOR "HEART" ON *BILLBOARD'S* WEBSITE **TURNS UP MORE THAN**

50,000

SONGS THAT CONTAIN THE WORD.

25 HEART-

6 The human heart weighs just over **HALF A POUND** (283.5 g) and is shaped like a fist.

8 The human heart beats 100,000 times a day, or **40 MILLION TIMES A YEAR.**

11 A giraffe's heart is **2** FEET (.6 M) **LONG** and weighs **25** POUNDS (11 KG).

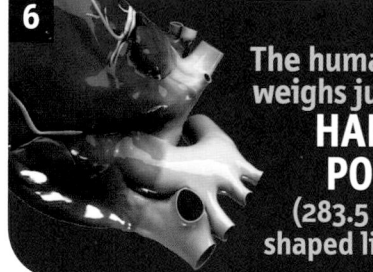

7 More than **8 BILLION SWEETHEARTS CONVERSATIONS HEARTS CANDIES** are manufactured **EACH YEAR.**

9 A HUMAN HEART **CIRCULATES** NEARLY SIX QUARTS (5.6 L) OF BLOOD THROUGH THE BODY.

10 A DEVELOPING HUMAN HEART FIRST RESEMBLES A **FISH HEART,** THEN A **FROG'S**, THEN A **SNAKE'S**, AND FINALLY A **HUMAN'S.**

12 THERE'S A **HEART-SHAPED CORAL REEF IN AUSTRALIA.**

13 SEA STARS—COMMONLY CALLED STARFISH—HAVE **NO HEARTBEAT,** BECAUSE THEY HAVE **NO HEART.**

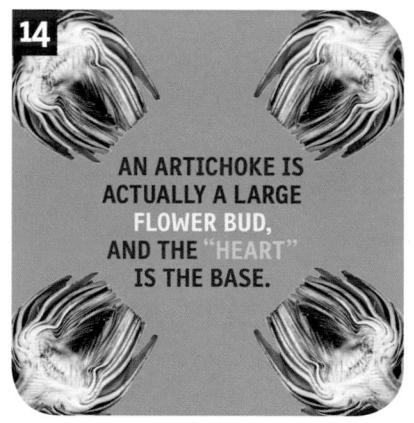

14 AN ARTICHOKE IS ACTUALLY A LARGE FLOWER BUD, AND THE "HEART" IS THE BASE.

15 **EARTHWORMS** HAVE FIVE HEARTS.

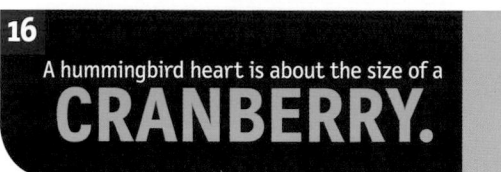 

16 A hummingbird heart is about the size of a **CRANBERRY.**

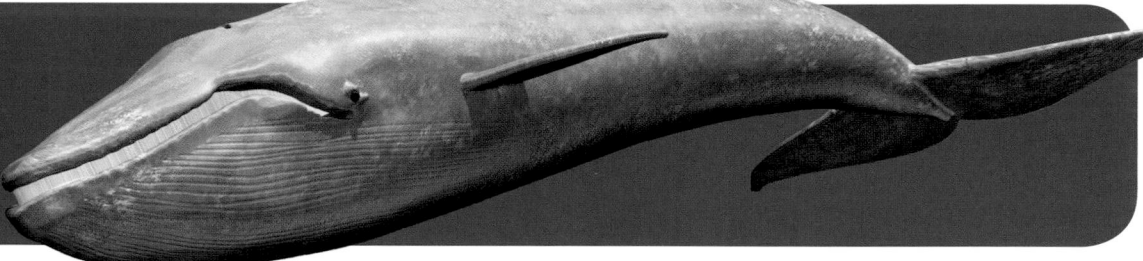

17 A BLUE WHALE'S HEART IS AS LARGE AS A **SMALL CAR.**

PUMPiNG FACTS

18 The human heart pumps blood through a network of blood vessels **60,000 MILES (96,500 KM) LONG.**

19 **EACH HUMAN HEARTBEAT** fills a four-chambered heart with fresh blood.

20
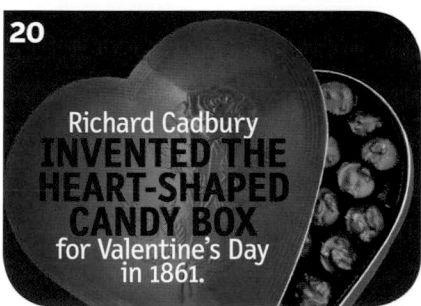
Richard Cadbury **INVENTED THE HEART-SHAPED CANDY BOX** for Valentine's Day in 1861.

21 The heart symbol is meant to represent love. The feeling of love actually has **NOTHING TO DO WITH YOUR HEART**—it comes from neurological responses that **PRODUCE CHEMICALS IN YOUR BRAIN.**

22
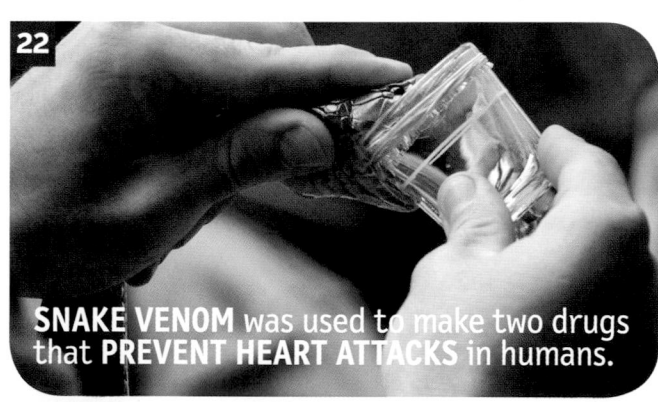
SNAKE VENOM was used to make two drugs that **PREVENT HEART ATTACKS** in humans.

23 The world's largest heart-shaped pink emerald weighs **169** CARATS AND IS VALUED AT **2.5 MILLION DOLLARS.**

24 At some restaurants in Vietnam, you can order up a **STILL-BEATING SNAKE'S HEART**

25 An adult human heart averages **72 BEATS PER MINUTE;** a beluga whale's heart averages **100 BEATS PER MINUTE,** though it slows to 12 to 20 beats per minute while diving.

1 **ONE IN FOUR AMERICANS** believes Earth has already been visited by EXTRATERRESTRIALS.

2 Scientists have started looking for **LIGHT AND AIR POLLUTION** on other planets—these would be SIGNS OF TECHNOLOGY GENERATED BY INTELLIGENT LIFE.

3 For the movie *AVATAR*, a linguist was hired to construct the ALIEN LANGUAGE NA'VI. Designed to be a language the actors could pronounce, it doesn't resemble any language here on Earth.

4 A group of scientists have created A WEBSITE ASKING ALIENS TO SEND THEM AN EMAIL. So far, they've only received **HOAX MESSAGES.**

5 Ancient Greeks considered the idea that THERE ARE OTHER PEOPLE IN THE UNIVERSE BESIDES US.

6 In their search for possible life, **SCIENTISTS LOOK FOR STARS WITH HEAVY METALS.** Stars without these metals can't form terrestrial planets or life. They also SCAN FOR LASER LIGHT—the kind that can only be made from an intelligent source.

7 Thirty-five years ago, an engineer working at a telescope detected a **MYSTERIOUS 72-SECOND PULSE** that originated a long way from Earth. Some say it could have been a black hole event. The long pulse has never been repeated.

8 People once believed that **MARTIANS BUILT CANALS** on the **RED PLANET.**

9 Scientists have only looked closely at a few thousand stars within 100 light years or so of Earth for intelligent life. With **400 BILLION STARS SPREAD OVER 100,000 LIGHT YEARS OF SPACE,** they have a lot more searching to do —**AND THAT'S JUST OUR GALAXY.**

FACTS ABOUT ALIENS

10 UFO sightings have long been linked to **"AREA 51,"** part of an Air Force airfield in **NEVADA, U.S.A.,** that was once used for testing experimental aircraft.

11 IN 1947, there was a crash near **ROSWELL, NEW MEXICO, U.S.A.,** which the Air Force says was an experimental surveillance balloon. Others say it was an ALIEN CRAFT, and the creatures inside were **SECRETLY CAPTURED AND STUDIED.**

12 The SETI INSTITUTE is a group of scientists trying to detect intelligent life outside Earth. They get data from radio telescopes, including the world's largest at **PUERTO RICO'S ARECIBO OBSERVATORY.** That radio telescope, which is 1,000 feet (305 m) in diameter, was featured in THE MOVIE CONTACT.

13 Roughly 98 PERCENT of all stars in the universe could host planets with life.

14 IN 1977, **TWO SPACECRAFT WERE LAUNCHED** that carried sounds and images representing life on Earth. It will be 40,000 YEARS before these spacecraft are close to any other planetary system.

15 IN 1938, a radio broadcast reported that a huge meteorite had smashed into a New Jersey farm and New York was **UNDER ATTACK BY TENTACLED MARTIANS.** It was actually a dramatization of **THE WAR OF THE WORLDS**, but thousands of people **BELIEVED IT WAS TRUE AND PANICKED.**

75 PLANT FACTS TO

11 Morning glory flowers typically open in the morning, triggered by the sun's light and warmth, but close in the evening when temperatures cool and light fades.

12 Mandrake roots, famous for their eerie screaming in the Harry Potter series, were once used to relieve pain and cause "deliriousness" during operations.

13 A potion in *Harry Potter*, wolfsbane was used centuries ago to poison wolves in Europe.

14 In the Middle Ages, the poisonous deadly nightshade was believed to help witches fly.

15 The ancient Greeks believed holly could protect from lightning, poison, and witchcraft.

16 The wand of *Harry Potter*'s Voldemort was made of yew; in real life the tree contains a chemical used to treat several kinds of cancer.

17 HINDUS BELIEVE COCONUTS ARE SACRED, AND THEY ARE OFTEN GIVEN AS AN OFFERING TO THE GODS.

18 Olive trees are a symbol of peace in many cultures.

19 Bamboo is the largest grass in the world.

20 In 2004, scientists discovered a Norway spruce—which are often used as Christmas trees—with roots that had been growing underground for 9,550 years.

21 Bristlecone pines are among the longest-living trees in the world. One in California, U.S.A.—nicknamed the Methuselah Tree—has been growing for more than 4,700 years.

22 A sunflower is not one flower; the black center of the flower is actually 1,000 to 2,000 tiny flowers that grow in two opposite spirals.

1 The Queen of the Andes plant blooms only once every 80 or more years.

2 Some spiders and small bats sleep in between the folds of tree bark.

3 Hairs around the flowers of the woolly lousewort trap the sun's heat and raise the temperature around the plant's bloom by as much as 34°F (20°C).

4 THE GIANT CORPSE FLOWER IS NAMED AFTER ITS FOUL STENCH—LIKE ROTTING MEAT—THAT ATTRACTS FLIES AND OTHER INSECTS THAT POLLINATE THE PLANT.

5 Animals couldn't exist without plants, which convert the sun's energy into food and "exhale" oxygen into the atmosphere.

6 The ancient Greeks, Romans, and Egyptians made funeral arrangements out of celery.

7 More than one million trees were planted in Nebraska, U.S.A., in 1876 to celebrate the first Arbor Day.

8 Strings of dried apples were found in the 4,500-year-old royal tomb of a queen who ruled the ancient city-state of Ur, in present-day Iraq.

9 In 1623, a European colonist arrived in New England with the first apple seeds to be planted in the Americas.

10 THE THOUSANDS OF CHERRY TREES RINGING WASHINGTON, D.C.'S TIDAL BASIN WERE A GIFT TO THE UNITED STATES FROM TOKYO, JAPAN'S MAYOR IN 1912. IN RETURN, THE U.S. SENT FLOWERING DOGWOOD TREES TO JAPAN.

Morning glories

GROW YOUR MIND!

23 Eating any part of the monkshood plant can be fatal.

24 Giant hogweed sap can cause painful blisters, but only if the sticky stuff is exposed to sunlight.

25 Cherry trees are toxic to horses.

26 FORTUNATELY FOR SQUIRRELS, ACORNS ARE POISONOUS TO HUMANS.

27 Smoke from burning poison ivy is toxic.

28 There are about 400,000 known plant species in the world—less than half the number of insect species.

29 Contrary to popular belief, poinsettias *aren't* poisonous to humans.

30 A massive underground vault on a Norwegian island holds hundreds of millions—and one day will hold billions—of seeds for safekeeping.

31 Dutchman's breeches plants are named after their flowers, which look like a pair of pants hanging upside down.

32 In 1981, a scientist spotted the first plant—a purple prairie lupine—growing on the dry, empty blast zone created by Mount St. Helens's May 1980 eruption in Washington, U.S.A.

33 The White House Christmas tree can be any of several species of evergreen, but it must be about 18.5 feet (5.6 m) tall to reach the ceiling.

34 Sundew plants use sticky globs that resemble dewdrops to lure and trap insects, which the carnivorous plants then eat.

35 Pitcher plants' sweet smell attracts bugs and slugs to a slippery-sided chamber filled with chemicals that digest trapped prey.

36 A Venus flytrap snaps shut after a bug brushes tiny hairs in the plant's mouth twice.

37 There are *lots* of orchids: One-fourth of the world's flowering plants are orchids, and there are four times as many orchid species as mammal species, and twice as many orchids as birds.

38 If the history of Earth were squeezed into one hour, flowering plants would exist for only the last 90 seconds.

39 The world's largest tree by volume is a sequoia nicknamed General Sherman that's more than 52,500 cubic feet (1,487 cubic m).

40 Sugar pine cones can grow to be nearly two feet (61 cm) long.

41 The active substance in aspirin originally came from willow trees.

42 Mosses, ferns, and many kinds of algae produce spores instead of flowers and seeds.

43 The delicate yellow flowers of *Azara microphylla* smell like chocolate and vanilla.

44 The leaves of the sensitive plant, also called the shame plant, fold up and droop when touched.

45 LIVING ROCKS ARE ACTUALLY SMALL, FLAT DESERT PLANTS THAT RESEMBLE STONES.

46 Without water, the desert resurrection plant will shrivel into a dried ball and appear dead for years. When it finally rains, the plant will unfurl and grow green again.

47 A California, U.S.A., redwood named Hyperion is the world's tallest living tree—at 379.1 feet (115.3 m), it's more than 70 feet (21 m) taller than the Statue of Liberty.

48 Maple syrup, made from the sap of the sugar maple, can be collected only when days are sunny and cold—but not freezing—and nights are frosty.

49 In 2010, the names Lily and Jasmine—both fragrant flowers—were among the top 100 most popular U.S. baby names for girls.

50 Amber is fossilized tree resin, a fluid plant material different from sap.

51 KOPI LUWAK COFFEE IS MADE FROM COFFEE BEANS THAT HAVE BEEN EATEN AND POOPED OUT BY A CATLIKE MAMMAL IN INDONESIA.

52 Licorice flavor comes from licorice root, but also from the herbs anise and fennel.

53 Balsa trees bloom only at night, and their inch-deep (2.5 cm) pool of nectar attracts birds, bats, kinkajous, opossums, and monkeys.

54 The stem of a sugar cane can grow to be more than 17 feet (5 m) tall.

55 Most coal is formed from ancient plant remains.

56 Corn is the most planted field crop in the United States.

57 Aladdin, Dreaming Maid, Ice Cream, Kung Fu, and Mrs. John T. Scheepers are types of tulips.

58 The flowers of the evening primrose, moonflower, and night phlox open from dusk until dark.

59 Coco-de-mer, a kind of palm tree, produces the biggest seeds in the plant kingdom—each weighs up to 66 pounds (30 kg).

60 You would have to line up end-to-end 300 of the world's smallest seeds—produced by a kind of orchid—to make an inch (2.5 cm).

61 Monarch caterpillars eat milkweed, which makes the insects' skin poisonous and foul tasting to predators.

62 Cinnamon spice is the ground-up, dried bark of the cinnamon tree.

63 All of the plants at Disney's Tomorrowland in Anaheim, California, U.S.A., are edible.

64 The tree tumbo has only two leaves, but they can grow up to 29.5 feet (9 m) long and live for 1,500 years.

65 The world's biggest flower, found in the Indonesian rain forest, can grow wider than a car tire.

66 Johnny Appleseed's real name was John Chapman; he was a New Englander who headed across the American West about 200 years ago, planting apple trees as he traveled.

67 The "seeds" of a fig are actually more than 1,000 tiny fruits.

68 The Jerusalem artichoke is not an artichoke.

69 Rocket is another name for arugula, a peppery, leafy green used in salads.

70 The ancient Greeks planted parsley on graves.

71 THE SEEDS OF THE STAR ANISE TREE ARE IN STAR-SHAPED PODS.

72 Vanilla comes from a kind of orchid.

73 Ginger has been used for medicinal purposes longer than it has been used for food.

74 Kudzu, a climbing vine from Asia, is a major invasive species in North America thanks to the plant's ability to grow as much as one foot (30.4 cm) a day.

75 A saguaro cactus can reach a height of 50 feet (15.2 m), but in the first eight years of its life it grows only 1 to 1.5 inches (2.5–3.8 cm).

1 Australia and New Zealand are known as the **"LAND DOWN UNDER"** because of their location in the Southern Hemisphere.

2 Australia is part of a region known as **OCEANIA**, which contains islands in the Pacific and New Zealand. Australia and New Zealand are as far apart as Miami and New York, U.S.A.

3 You can walk on the **GRASS-COVERED ROOF** of the Parliament House in Canberra.

4 **KOALAS**, native to Australia, rarely drink water. They get most of the water they need from the leaves they eat.

5 While Australia is the smallest of all the continents, it is **THREE TIMES LARGER** than the largest island in the world—Greenland.

6 There are 40 **SPECIES**—some poisonous—of funnel web spiders in eastern Australia.

7 The famous **OUTBACK**, or dry, middle region of Australia, contains the country's largest deserts with scorching hot temperatures and little water.

8 The largest **VOLCANIC ERUPTION** in history happened in Taupo, New Zealand, some 26,500 years ago. The eruption reached 30 miles (50 km) into the sky.

9 Before 1995, the **INTERNATIONAL DATE LINE** divided the island nation of **KIRIBATI**, so in the western part of the nation it was Monday and in the eastern part it would be Tuesday.

10 Many of the first settlers in Australia were **CRIMINALS**—sent by the British to live there as punishment.

11 The world's ten most **VENOMOUS SNAKES** call Australia home. Sea snakes can have venom **TEN TIMES** more potent than that of a **COBRA**.

12 Rains during the **RAINY SEASON** bring more water to northern Australia in two months than London sees in a year.

13 People in **PAPUA NEW GUINEA** speak more than **700 LANGUAGES**—the most of any country.

14 **SALTWATER CROCODILES**, native to Australia, are considered among the deadliest animals in the world.

15 In Australia people play **NETBALL**, which is similar to basketball except there is no dribbling.

16 The **POPULATION** of Australia nearly **DOUBLED** in less than eight years after gold was found in 1851.

35 AWESOME AUSTRALiA

17 DINGOS, wild Australian dogs, first arrived 3,500 YEARS AGO aboard ships from Asia.

18 Ski resorts in south-east Australia are popular. An international ski event called the KANGAROO HOPPET takes place every August, with the longest race covering 26 miles (42 km).

19 The first English settlers arrived in Australia in 1788, but Aboriginal Australians had lived on the continent for 60,000 YEARS.

20 Thousands of years ago, the island of TASMANIA was connected to Australia by a land bridge.

21 In Papua New Guinea, SUNKEN SHIPS from World War II are a popular attraction for scuba divers.

22 Australia has more than 9,300 protected areas that help to conserve its UNIQUE PLANTS and animals.

23 New Zealand has about 10 SHEEP for every PERSON in the country.

24 Nearly a quarter of the people who live in Australia were born in ANOTHER COUNTRY.

25 The FLIGHTLESS EMU, Australia's largest bird, can run as fast as 40 miles per hour (64 kph).

26 The tough bark of the EUCALYPTUS TREE protects it from dangerous fires, which happen naturally in Australia and occur in dry areas.

27 More KANGAROOS live in Australia than people.

28 WALLAROOS are marsupials smaller than a kangaroo. They swim by moving each rear leg separately, which is something they don't do on land.

29 About 90 PERCENT of the plants in New Zealand are found NOWHERE ELSE in the world.

30 Festivities in PAPUA NEW GUINEA include sing-sings, where people PAINT THEIR BODIES and faces and perform traditional songs and dances.

31 Samoans drink KAVA at important functions. The beverage, made from the root of the kava plant, is said to have relaxing properties.

32 The EMU can reach 6.5 feet (2 m) in height. Since they can't fly, if they are attacked by birds of prey they run in a zigzag pattern.

33 At the 2000 Summer Olympic Games in Sydney, Australia won 58 MEDALS—the most ever for the country.

34 The world's largest rock, ULURU, located in the middle of Australia, is taller than a 114-story building.

35 A public park in Rotorua, New Zealand, has bubbling and hissing GEO-THERMAL POOLS. In 2001, rocks and globs of mud the size of footballs were launched 33 feet (10 m) into the air.

FACTS ABOUT OCEANiA

1. A special airline allows only pets as passengers. **2.** A cheetah can accelerate faster than a race car. **3.** A sailboat made of 12,500 soda bottles sailed from San Francisco, California, U.S.A., to Australia. **4.** Cars didn't come with ignition keys until 1949. **5.** Two pilots set a world record by flying around the world in a helicopter in 11 days, 7 hours. **6.** In 1930, two men drove a car from New York City to Los Angeles and back using only the reverse gear. It took them 42 days. **7.** A Minnesota, U.S.A., motorcyclist got a speeding ticket for going 205 miles per hour, (330 kph), which police believe is a state record for breaking the speed limit. **8.** The first steam-run vehicle was a tractor, built in 1769. It could go 2.5 miles per hour (4 kph). **9.** Horsepower is a unit of measurement for how much power an engine has. One horse can do 33,000 foot-pounds of work every minute, and has 1 horsepower. A Honda Civic has 140 horsepower. **10.** The first true automobile had just three wheels. **11.** Aircraft are able to write in the sky by adding a special oil to a plane's exhaust. A company in New York, U.S.A., writes more than 50 marriage proposals in the sky every year. **12.** Japan holds the current title for fastest passenger train, which has reached speeds of 361 miles per hour (581 kph). **13.** U.S. Route 66 was nicknamed the Main Street of America. In 1926 it was designated as a public thoroughfare to link the Midwest, Southwest, and southern California. **14.** Peach Springs, Arizona, U.S.A., was the inspiration for Radiator Springs, the town in the Disney Pixar movie *Cars*. Like the fictional town, it was once a Route 66 gem, but turned into a ghost town after it was bypassed by an interstate. **15.** The first car wheels were bicycle wheels. **16.** The first gas-engine car had the power of three horses and could travel at 20 miles per hour (30 kph). **17.** Early cars had additional passenger seats in front of the driver seat, not behind it. The driver had to peer around heads to see the road! **18.** Starting in 1901, most countries began using numbered license plates, but drivers had to make their own—and they often used cardboard! **19.** The "Clarion Bell" was an early version of today's car horn and was rung to tell pedestrians to get out of the way. Drivers operated the bell with their foot so their hands could stay on the steering wheel. **20.** Before there were turn signals and taillights on cars, drivers used hand signals to tell other cars which direction they were headed or if they were slowing down. **21.** Costing around $500, Henry Ford's Model T Ford was the first affordable car; 250,000 Model T's were sold in five years. **22.** Model T Fords only came in one color—black. It kept painting prices down to just use one color. **23.** Before headlights came along in the 1920s, cars were equipped with candle lamps. **24.** Racing cars use smooth tires called "slicks." The rubber heats up and gets sticky during a race to provide grip on the track. **25.** Most American car horns honk in the musical key of F. **26.** The first American to get a speeding ticket was a New York City taxi driver. He was going 12 miles per hour (19 kph). **27.** The world's first traffic signal was installed in London in 1868 before cars were invented. It directed horse-drawn carriages. **28.** In 1920, Detroit, Michigan, U.S.A., was the world's first city to use red, green, and yellow lights to control traffic. Traffic officers had to push a button or flip a switch to change the signal. **29.** Oklahoma City, Oklahoma, U.S.A., put up the first parking meters in 1935. It cost a nickel per hour to park. **30.** The first McDonald's drive-thru opened in 1975 near an Arizona, U.S.A., military base. Soldiers couldn't get out of their cars in uniform so the drive-thru solved the problem. **31.** A man once set a world record by riding a bumper car for 24 hours. **32.** The Smart For Two city car is the shortest two-seater production car. It is 8 feet (2.5 m) long. A Toyota Camry is almost twice as long. **33.** The Toyota Corolla is the world's best-selling automobile. More than 32 million have been built. **34.** The first motorcycles had small steam engines. **35.** Pistons in motorcycle engines can go up and down 100 times in a second. **36.** Motorcycles don't have a reverse gear. **37.** Theodore Roosevelt was the first U.S. President to own a car. **38.** The first cable car debuted in 1873 after the inventor saw horses struggling to pull horse cars up San Francisco's steep cobblestone streets. The cars latch on to an underground moving cable that propels them forward. **39.** The world's largest ferry can hold 230 cars and 300 freight vehicles. It travels from Holland to Britain in six and a half hours. **40.** The world's fastest car, called the Bloodhound, is set to release in 2013. It is expected to reach a maximum speed of 1,000 miles per hour (1,609 kph). **41.** The U.S. Marines have full-size helicopters that operate by remote control and can deliver goods to isolated bases. **42.** A new airplane equipped with anti-turbulence technology adjusts for bumps to keep you from getting motion sickness. **43.** A Frenchman has designed a futuristic luxury yacht that can transform into an airplane. Its four sails fold into wings and its bullet shape allows it to glide through the air and sea. **44.** Swiss engineers designed an airplane with enough solar cells to power the electric motors on board for 24 hours of continuous flight. **45.** Steam locomotives get their power from steam generated from fuel burned in boilers. It takes three hours to make enough steam to move a steam locomotive. **46.** The east to west U.S. railroad was completed in 1869. The final railroad spike driven into the rail was made of gold. **47.** A car was invented to run on wood chips. **48.** The Sydney Harbor Bridge in Australia is the world's largest steel arch bridge—its arch stretches 440 feet (134 m) above the sea below. **49.** Actor Tom Hanks played six roles in the movie *The Polar Express*. **50.** The Qinghai-Tibet Railway is the world's highest railway, traveling up to 15,220 feet (5,072 m). Passengers are provided oxygen to combat altitude sickness. **51.** The "Chunnel"—an underground tunnel in the English Channel—links England with Belgium and France. The train traveling through it reaches speeds of more than 200 miles per hour (322 kph). **52.** Japan introduced the first modern high-speed train in 1964, which was coined the "Bullet Train." **53.** There are 31,180 turnstiles in the New York City subway system. The busiest station is Times Square. **54.** People take 3.2 billion rides on Tokyo subways every year. **55.** About two billion vehicles have crossed over the Golden Gate Bridge since it opened in 1937. **56.** The 26.4-mile (42.5-km) Jiaozhou Bay Bridge in China is the world's longest bridge over open water. If you run from end to end, you will have run a marathon! **57.** The Silk Road wasn't an actual road—it was an ancient 4,000-mile (6,400-km) trade route that carried goods between Rome and China. **58.** Abbey Road is a street in London the Beatles were famously photographed crossing. The photo appears on their album with the same name. **59.** When the 35-mile (57-km) Gotthard Rail Tunnel in the Swiss Alps opens, it will reduce hours of travel time between the north and south ends of Europe—and it will become the world's longest tunnel. **60.** San Francisco's Lombard Street is considered the most crooked street in the world. There's a one-block section with eight turns. **61.** The Trans-Siberian Railroad is the longest train route in the world. It extends 5,771 miles (9,288 km) and passes through seven time zones! **62.** A hovercraft is not a boat but rather an air-cushioned vehicle that floats above the water. **63.** The difference between rafts and boats is that you usually sit in a boat and on a raft. **64.** More than 500 cars were destroyed during the making of *Transformers: Dark of the Moon*. **65.** Ancient Greeks and Romans made warships that were rowed by as many as 1,800 people! **66.** The world's largest riverboat is the *Mississippi Queen*. It can hold 422 passengers. **67.** The world record for fastest boat—a jet-powered hydroplane—is 318 miles per hour (511 kph). **68.** A dinghy is a small boat attached to or towed behind a larger ship as a lifeboat. **69.** Dragon boats, traditionally from China, are human-powered with an ornamental dragon head at the bow. The longest recorded trip made by a dragon boat was about 294 nautical miles (545 km) down the Missouri River in the U.S.A. **70.** The flag that flew on explorer Ernest Shackleton's ship *Endurance*, which was trapped in ice for 11 months en route to Antarctica in 1915, sold for $180,600. It was the most expensive flag ever sold. **71.** The world's largest passenger ship is 1,187 feet (362 m) long. That's more than 300 feet (91 m) longer than the *Titanic*. **72.** Scientists are working on powering cars using coffee grounds and used diapers! **73.** A man once spun 24 circles in one minute on a motorcycle. **74.** Drivers in Washington, D.C., and Chicago, Illinois, U.S.A., spend more than 70 hours a year stuck in traffic. **75.** The airbag was patented in 1953, but it didn't show up in cars for several decades because it was hard to make one that inflated fast enough. Today's airbags take 1/25th of a second to inflate. **76.** In NASCAR races, four tires are changed and the car is fueled in 15 seconds or less. **77.** The first fire trucks were water pumps on wheels pulled by horses. **78.** The tires on a mining dump truck are as tall as two adult men! **79.** White-colored cars get in fewer accidents than cars of other colors. **80.** There are 756 cars for every 1,000 people in the U.S., a higher ratio than any other country. **81.** A fan boat has an airplane-like propeller on the back to move it through shallow water. It is commonly used to get around the U.S.A.'s Florida Everglades. **82.** In Venice, Italy, gondolas are used to travel the city's waterways; all are painted black. **83.** Taxicabs get their name from the taximeter, an instrument used to measure the distance traveled and time spent by a car. **84.** There are about 13,000 licensed taxis in New York City. **85.** Sled dogs have been used as transportation for hundreds of years. In Alaska, U.S.A., the Iditarod is a 1,150-mile (1,851-km) sled-dog race that runs from Anchorage to Nome. **86.** In India's Kaziranga National Park, guards ride elephants to make their patrols. **87.** Virgin Galactic is a private company that plans to take passengers on a flight 360,000 feet (109,728 m) above Earth, where they will experience zero gravity. The cost: $200,000. **88.** A Habel-Habel is a motorcycle used in the Philippines with an extra-long seat that can carry four to five people. **89.** In Thailand, taxis come in the form of tuk-tuks, three-wheeled cars with open sides and a covered top. **90.** Road construction in Beijing once caused a ten-day traffic jam. **91.** A Toyota Prius is 85 percent recyclable. **92.** The first use of a rearview mirror in a car was during the first Indianapolis 500 race in 1911. **93.** Because camels can go up to eight days without drinking and can carry heavy cargo, they have been a common form of transportation in African and Middle Eastern deserts for thousands of years. **94.** The Couchbike is exactly what it sounds like—a couch with bike wheels on the sides that can be pedaled around town. **95.** Rearview cameras and sensors have been used in construction trucks since the 1970s, but the technology just caught on with passenger cars. **96.** Disneyland's Monorail was the first daily operating monorail in the Western Hemisphere when it opened in 1959. **97.** London's subway system is called the Underground and also the Tube. **98.** Oftentimes, "ambulance" is spelled backward on the hood of the vehicle so that when it is approaching drivers from behind the word will be shown correctly in the rearview mirror. **99.** At $1.7 million, the Bugatti Veyron is the most expensive street-legal car sold. Its top speed is 253 miles per hour (407 kph). **100.** China is considering "straddling buses" to solve traffic jams. The buses take up two lanes and carry up to 1,200 people seven feet (2.1 m) above the road, allowing cars to pass underneath.

100 MOVING FACTS ABOUT THINGS THAT GO!

45 ADORABLE FACTS ABOUT BABY ANIMALS

(AND 5 NOT SO CUTE ONES...)

1 Baby **SEAHORSES** are birthed by their **DADS, NOT THEIR MOMS!**

2 A **BABY GIANT ANTEATER** spends its first year of life **RIDING PIGGYBACK** on its mother.

3 **BABY GOATS** are called **KIDS.**

4 Baby **ARMADILLOS** have **SOFT SHELLS** that harden within a few days after birth.

5 Baby **BAT-EARED FOXES** look like **CHIHUA-HUAS.**

6 **CHEETAH CUBS** have a mane on their neck and shoulders that looks like a **MINI-MOHAWK!**

7 Some kinds of baby **CAECILIANS**, wormlike amphibians, use **SPECIALIZED TEETH** to eat a layer of skin off their **MOTHER'S BACK** shortly after hatching.

8 Baby **TASMANIAN DEVILS** have a lot of growing to do. They start life the size of a **GRAIN OF RICE** and grow to be as big as **18 POUNDS (8 KG).**

9 When a baby **GIRAFFE** is born, it **DROPS HEADFIRST SIX FEET (1.8 M)** to the ground.

10 **BABY ROCK HYRAXES EAT POOP** to get bacteria they need to digest plants.

11 Most piglets are born **STRIPED.**

12 **FLAMINGO CHICKS** drink crop milk, a substance that forms in the upper digestive track, from both their moms and dads.

13 Porcupine babies are called **PORCUPETTES.**

14 The Australian gastric-brooding frog has a weird way of entering the world: **TADPOLES HATCH IN THEIR MOTHER'S STOMACH** and then she **VOMITS THEM OUT.**

15 **SLOTH BABIES** hang onto their **MOTHER'S HAIR** from the moment they're born.

16 Chimps **CAN'T COMPLETELY WALK** on their own until they're about **FOUR YEARS OLD.**

17 **OKAPIS**, the only living relatives of giraffes, **DON'T POOP** for the first time until they're **A MONTH OLD.**

Cheetah Cub

✳ YOU HAVE LEARNED **1,210** FACTS

18
The babies of **HONEY BADGERS**, relatives of skunks, get their characteristic **WHITE STRIPE THREE WEEKS AFTER BIRTH.**

19
Baby **HIPPOS** can be born underwater or on land.

20
A **BABY SEA LION** can **FIND ITS MOM** in a crowd by **RECOGNIZING THE SOUND** she makes.

21
ZEBRAS are **DARK BROWN** and **WHITE** at birth.

22
A **BABY PANDA** is as big as a **STICK OF BUTTER.**

23
A **BABY ECHIDNA**, a spiny marsupial, is called a puggle, and even though it is a mammal, it hatches from an egg!

24
Zookeepers working with **BABY KOALAS** wrap them in a blanket to make them **FEEL LIKE** they're in a **MOTHER'S POUCH.**

25
OTTERS CAN'T SWIM until they are **TWO MONTHS OLD.**

26
A **TWO-DAY-OLD PRONGHORN ANTELOPE** can run faster than a **FULL-GROWN HORSE.**

27
Practice makes perfect: **BABY ELEPHANTS ARE CLUMSY** with their trunks at first.

28
Baby **HEDGEHOGS** have quills at birth, but they are **SOFT AND FLEXIBLE.**

29
CASSOWARIES—large, flightless birds—are raised **ONLY BY THEIR FATHERS.**

30
A **ONE-DAY-OLD** reindeer can **OUTRUN** you.

31
HUMMINGBIRD BABIES have **BUMPS FOR BILLS.**

32
MOST HUMMINGBIRD hatchlings are 1 inch (2.5 cm) long **WHEN THEY ARE BORN.**

33
OSTRICH NURSERIES have as many as 300 CHICKS.

34
Baby **SCORPIONS CAN'T STING.**

35
The **TADPOLES** of Panamanian golden frogs use their **TEETH TO CLING TO ROCKS** when a stream flows faster after a storm.

36
POISON FROG TADPOLES hatch on land and then **WRIGGLE ONTO THE BACK OF A PARENT** to hitch a ride to water.

37
A **BABY WOMBAT**, called a **JOEY**, waits **SIX MONTHS** to peek out of its mother's pouch.

38
Many **BABY REPTILES** use a **TOOTH** on the front of their snout to **BREAK OUT OF THEIR EGG.**

39
Baby crocodiles and alligators sometimes **SWIM INTO THEIR MOTHER'S MOUTH** for safety.

40
The day it hatches, a **BABY COBRA** can spread its **HOOD AND STRIKE.**

41
After **HATCHING UNDERGROUND**, baby tortoises can take as long as a month to **DIG THEIR WAY TO THE SURFACE.**

42
After a week or two, a **BABY RATTLESNAKE FORMS THE FIRST SEGMENT OF ITS RATTLE.**

43
BABY CAMELS are born **WITHOUT A HUMP.**

44
BROWN BEAR CUBS spend at least the first month of their lives with **A SLEEPING MOTHER**—she's even **ASLEEP WHEN SHE GIVES BIRTH!**

45
BABY RHINOS can weigh as much as an **ADULT HUMAN.**

46
A **PYGMY MARMOSET NEWBORN** is about the **SIZE OF YOUR THUMB.**

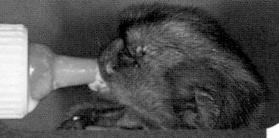

47
Most **BABY BIRDS** eat **REGURGITATED**, or partly eaten, food **RIGHT OUT OF THEIR MOTHER'S MOUTH.**

48
A **PARSON'S CHAMELEON** can take **TWO YEARS TO HATCH.**

49
A **BABY BLUE WHALE** gains about 200 **POUNDS (90.7 KG) EVERY DAY.**

50
Newborn **KANGAROOS** are about **AS LONG AS A PAPER CLIP.**

1 More than **200 PEOPLE** could fit inside the world's **BIGGEST IGLOO.**

2 **DURING THE LAST ICE AGE 11,500 YEARS AGO,** one-third of Earth's surface was covered in ice. Today, ice only covers one-tenth.

3 **90% OF ALL RECOVERED METEORITES** come from Antarctica because weather conditions preserve them—and because they're easy to spot on the ice.

4 **WHEN LIGHTNING OCCURS WITH A SNOWSTORM IT'S CALLED THUNDERSNOW.**

5

IT'S POSSIBLE TO SNOW SKI IN HAWAII, U.S.A.

25 COOL FACTS TO MAKE YOU

6 An **ICE PALACE** built in St. Petersburg, Russia, was an exact replica of one Empress Anna Ivanovna had built 200 years ago.

7 **SNOW CONES** sold during the Great Depression were called "hard times sundaes" because they were cheap to make.

8 **DON'T TRY THIS AT HOME:** If you touch your tongue to a metal pole on a below freezing day, **IT COULD GET STUCK THERE.**

9 Early hockey pucks were **FROZEN COW DUNG** (poop).

10 **WATER BOILS AT TEN DEGREES ABOVE FREEZING ON MARS.**

11 **WOOD FROGS** have special antifreeze-like chemicals in and around their cells that allow them to **NEARLY FREEZE SOLID,** then hop back to life after they thaw.

12 A **BRAIN FREEZE** **ACTUALLY HAS NOTHING TO DO WITH YOUR BRAIN. IT OCCURS WHEN THE BLOOD VESSELS IN YOUR HEAD SWELL.**

13 A hotel in Sweden is made from a mixture of snow and ice and rebuilt each year. **EVEN THE CHAIRS, TABLES, AND BEDS ARE MADE OF ICE!**

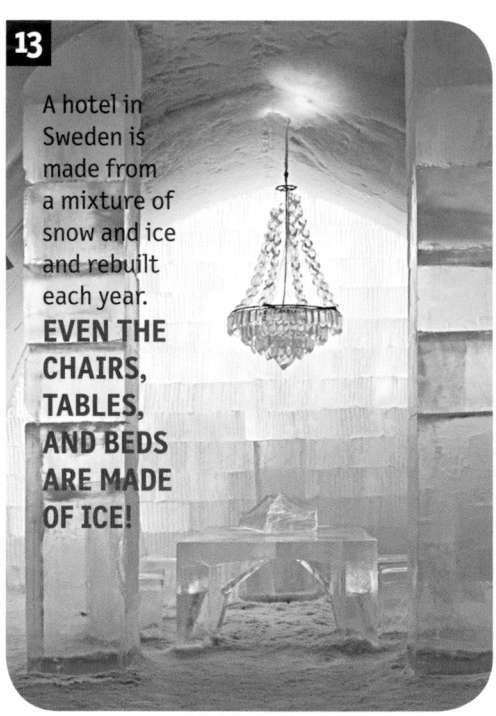

14 YOU COULD FILL 12 OLYMPIC-SIZE POOLS **WITH THE NUMBER OF** SLURPEE DRINKS **SOLD EVERY YEAR.**

15 A WOMAN SET A WORLD RECORD BY STACKING 73 FROZEN WAFFLES IN HER HANDS.

16 Kids get an average of **8** COLDS per year.

CHiLLOUT

17 A Dutch artist is making an ice sculpture called **SUNGLACIER IN THE MIDDLE OF THE DESERT** to get people to think about **CLIMATE CHANGE.**

18 An **"ICEBERG"** is a chunk of ice larger than 16 feet (5 m) across. **"BERGY BITS"** are chunks less than 16 feet (5 m). **"GROWLERS"** are chunks less than 6.6 feet (2 m) across.

19 IN SOME PARTS OF ANTARCTICA, THE ICE IS **3 MILES (5 KM) THICK!**

25

Over 100 years ago, an 11-year-old boy named **FRANK EPPERSON** left a soda-filled cup with a stick in it on his porch on a cold night. He called it an Epsicle. When he had kids, they called it a **POPSICLE,** and Frank patented the name.

20 IN THE ANTARCTIC, THERE IS A **30-30-30 RULE:** When the temperature is **30 below (-34.4°C),** and the wind is **30 miles per hour (48.3 kph),** human skin freezes in **30 seconds.**

22 Earth's two ice sheets cover most of **GREENLAND AND ANTARCTICA** and make up more than **99 percent** of the world's glacial ice.

23 ICEBERG LETTUCE IS ALSO CALLED **"CRISPHEAD."**

21 The lowest temperature ever recorded on Earth was **-128.6°F (-89.2°C)** IN ANTARCTICA.

24 Icebergs are formed from glaciers on land and drift out to sea. **THEY ARE MOSTLY MADE FROM FRESH— NOT SALT—WATER.**

15 LITTLE FACTS

1 Around the **WORLD,** people believe **LADYBUGS** are a sign of **GOOD LUCK.**

2 For more than **2,600** years, people in Western Europe have considered the feet of **RABBITS** to be lucky.

3 Many people believe **CROSSING THEIR FINGERS** brings good luck.

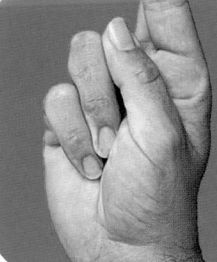

4 Wearing **YELLOW** underwear on New Year's Day in Peru is considered lucky.

5 In Germany, it's good luck to **TOUCH** a chimney sweep's brush.

6 **EIGHT** is a lucky number in China: More than 300,000 **COUPLES** in the country got married on **8/08/08.**

7 Four-leaf clovers are considered **LUCKY,** but perhaps the most lucky clover is the **WORLD RECORD–HOLDER** for most leaves, **56.**

ABOUT LUCK

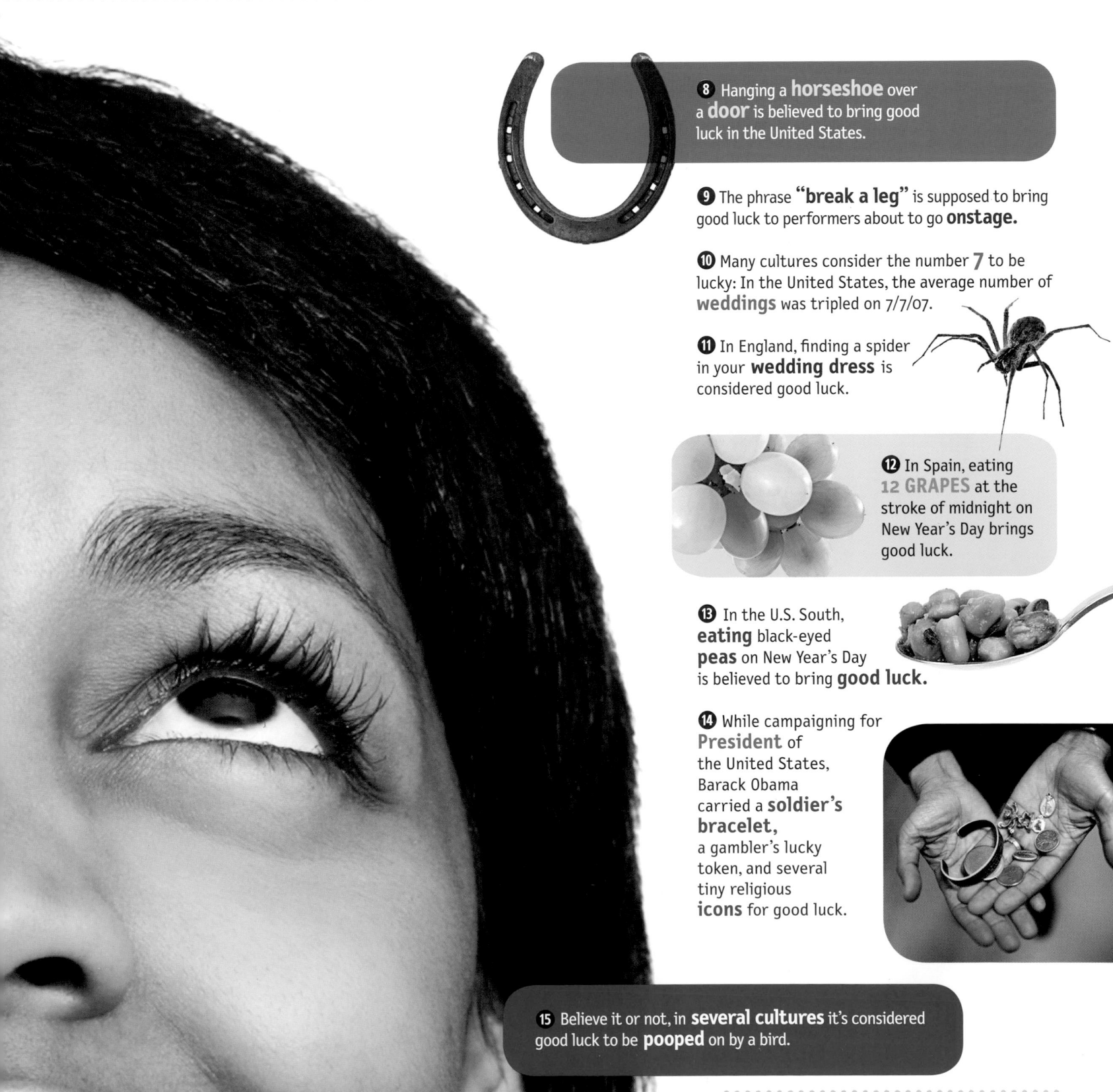

8 Hanging a **horseshoe** over a **door** is believed to bring good luck in the United States.

9 The phrase **"break a leg"** is supposed to bring good luck to performers about to go **onstage.**

10 Many cultures consider the number **7** to be lucky: In the United States, the average number of **weddings** was tripled on 7/7/07.

11 In England, finding a spider in your **wedding dress** is considered good luck.

12 In Spain, eating **12 GRAPES** at the stroke of midnight on New Year's Day brings good luck.

13 In the U.S. South, **eating** black-eyed **peas** on New Year's Day is believed to bring **good luck.**

14 While campaigning for **President** of the United States, Barack Obama carried a **soldier's bracelet,** a gambler's lucky token, and several tiny religious **icons** for good luck.

15 Believe it or not, in **several cultures** it's considered good luck to be **pooped** on by a bird.

Mandrill Monkey

75 FACTS TO MONKEY AROUND WITH

1 Monkeys are not apes. Apes include gorillas, chimpanzees, bonobos, orangutans, and humans.

2 MONKEYS HAVE TAILS, APES DON'T.

3 Some monkeys in Thailand teach their children how to floss their teeth.

4 Unlike many monkey fathers, male siamangs help take care of their children.

5 There are 12 monkeys in the Barrel of Monkeys game—which was created in 1965.

6 Saki monkeys have shaggy fur. If they get wet, they'll sometimes suck water off it.

7 To "stop monkeying around" means to stop acting mischievously.

8 There's a town in western Kentucky, U.S.A., called Monkeys Eyebrow.

9 Apes and monkeys groom each other by picking through their neighbor's fur to pull out bugs and dirt.

10 A gorilla named Koko was taught to use sign language to communicate.

11 Howler monkeys are named for their strong cries of warning that can travel almost two miles (3 km) through forest trees.

12 When Jane Goodall first began studying chimpanzees in Tanzania in 1960, the authorities made her bring her mother with her.

13 Wild lemur monkeys only live on the island of Madagascar.

14 When one baboon shows the bottom of his foot to another, it means he is accepting the other as the alpha male, or boss.

15 Superman's pet monkey is named Beppo. He first appeared in the comic strip in 1959.

16 One in three orangutans has fallen out of a tree and broken a bone.

60 5,000 AWESOME FACTS

17 Macaques are quick learners. Once a macaque named Imo learned how to wash sand off her sweet potato snack, and soon her whole troop was imitating her.

18 People in Thailand attend a monkey festival where sweets, vegetables, and fruits are given to the monkeys which can eat as much as they like.

19 Male and female gibbon couples sing songs together.

20 Mike, a chimpanzee Jane Goodall studied, beat on a gasoline can to intimidate his rivals.

21 DOUC MONKEYS CAN LEAP 20 FEET (6 M) BETWEEN TREES.

22 An orangutan named Fu Manchu used to escape from his Omaha zoo enclosure by keeping a wire to pick the lock hidden in his mouth.

23 Speeding along the ground, the patas monkey can reach speeds of 35 mph (56 kph).

24 Just like humans, monkeys can go bald in old age.

25 Most apes have longer arms than legs. Orangutans have arms that are almost twice as long as their legs.

26 Spider monkeys got their name from their resemblance to spiders when they move their long arms and tails.

27 A group of gorillas is called a band.

28 Colobus monkeys burp to be friendly to other monkeys.

29 Adult male mandrill monkeys have red-and-blue noses. The color becomes brighter when they are excited or upset.

30 Chimpanzees fish for termites by poking long sticks into termite mounds.

31 The emperor tamarin uses its mustache to make itself appear larger.

32 Active at night, small owl monkeys in the Amazon are prey to the great horned owl.

33 Old windup toys featuring a monkey drumming or hitting cymbals can fetch hundreds of dollars on eBay.

34 In 1996, a gorilla named Binti Jua rescued a three-year-old boy who had fallen into her enclosure at a Brookfield, Illinois, U.S.A., zoo.

35 Siamangs are a type of gibbon. They sing to communicate their location to other siamangs.

36 Japanese macaque monkeys have snowball fights.

37 Monkeys have the same number of teeth as an adult human—32.

38 Most monkeys and apes like to build a cozy nest out of branches to go to sleep.

39 Dian Fossey studied gorillas in Rwanda, Africa. The first gorilla to reach out and touch her hand was named Peanuts.

40 Chimpanzees use leaves as umbrellas to protect themselves from the rain.

41 HUMANS ARE THE ONLY APES THAT CAN SPEAK IN WORDS.

42 Langur monkeys are sacred to Hindus, who even let them take food straight from their gardens.

43 Chimpanzees can build a nest in ten minutes.

44 Just like humans might nap during the day, nocturnal owl monkeys take naps in the middle of the night.

45 In 1966, a gorilla with white fur, "Snowflake," was found in West Africa. He made his home in a zoo in Barcelona, Spain, where he had 30 babies!

46 Gibbons are so fast they can catch birds mid-flight by leaping out of trees.

47 MONKEYS AND APES CAN CATCH DISEASES FROM HUMANS.

48 Allen's swamp monkeys have a unique way of fishing. They place leaves on the water and then grab the fish that come to hide underneath.

49 Monkeys peel their bananas and toss away the skins.

50 Chimpanzees hug each other.

51 Marmoset monkeys eat tree sap.

52 Monkeys make faces when they play together.

53 The first monkeys to survive a trip into space spent 15 minutes there in 1959.

54 In Malaysia, pig-tailed macaques climb trees and pick coconuts. They are paid for their work in bananas.

55 The Phoenix Suns basketball team's mascot is a gorilla, who performs slam dunks during breaks in the game.

56 Some 500 long-tailed macaques make their home on Bali in the Sacred Monkey Forest. They are believed to guard the forest's temples.

57 Gorillas cry when upset.

58 Michael Jackson had a pet monkey named Bubbles. They sometimes wore matching outfits.

59 Chimpanzees take leaves and use them to soak up water. Then they have a "sponge" they can drink water from.

60 Grape Ape, the purple gorilla that starred in Hanna-Barbera cartoons in the '70s was said to be 40 feet (12.2 m) tall. Real gorillas are only four to six feet (1–2 m) tall.

61 Four paintings made by a chimpanzee were exhibited at an art show and praised by critics, who thought a human had painted them.

62 The actress who played Jane in the Tarzan movies complained that Tarzan's chimp sidekick, Cheetah, bit her "at every opportunity."

63 Siamangs and gibbons don't like water and will not try to cross streams or ponds.

64 Langur monkeys were used in Delhi, India, to keep smaller macaques from bothering people.

65 In 1981, Universal Studios sued Nintendo for violating their trademark of King Kong, saying that Donkey Kong was too similar. The studio did not win.

66 Macaques' cheek pouches can hold as much food as their stomachs.

67 CHIMPANZEES HUNT ANIMALS FOR FOOD. THEY EVEN USE SPEARS.

68 Scientists used to think that bonobos were just another kind of chimpanzee, but they are their own species.

69 Monkeys' fingerprints are as distinctive as those of humans.

70 Underneath the fur of different apes is different color skin. Orangutan skin can have a blue tinge.

71 Howler monkeys might pee on humans walking beneath them.

72 Gibbons live together in family groups, with a mom and dad and their offspring.

73 Monkey wrenches are adjustable wrenches used for heavy tasks.

74 Japanese macaques soak in hot springs to keep warm.

75 Vervet monkeys in the Caribbean often steal beverages from sunbathers lying on the beach.

1 An 11-year-old girl wrote a letter to presidential candidate **ABRAHAM LINCOLN** suggesting he grow a beard; he did.

2 The comic book superheroine **WONDER WOMAN**—who fights villains with her Lasso of Truth—first appeared in 1941 and graced the cover of the first issue of *Ms.* magazine in 1972.

3 The famous **BRONTË SISTERS**—Charlotte, Emily, and Anne—published their novels under **FAKE MEN'S NAMES**—Currer Bell, Ellis Bell, and Acton Bell.

4 **QUEEN VICTORIA** ruled from 1837 to 1901, the longest reign in British history and one of the longest in the world.

5 **MARY WALKER**, a surgeon for the Union Army in the American Civil War, was awarded the U.S. Medal of Honor in 1866, the first and **ONLY WOMAN** ever to receive the recognition.

6 **JULIA WARD HOWE**, a women's rights activist and the author of the famous song "**BATTLE HYMN OF THE REPUBLIC**," first suggested Mother's Day as a day dedicated to peace.

7 In 2006, archaeologists unearthed a 1,600-year-old **MUMMY** of a king who turned out to be a woman, casting doubts on the idea that the ancient Peruvians were ruled only by men.

8 In 1903, **MARIE CURIE** became the first woman to win a **NOBEL PRIZE**, in physics. She won another in 1911, in chemistry, and her daughter went on to win one in 1935.

9 **NOBEL PEACE PRIZE** winner and environmental activist **WANGARI MAATHAI** inspired her fellow Kenyans to plant more than 45 million trees in their country since 1977.

10 **ELIZABETH I**, who ruled England from 1558 to 1603, was **25 YEARS OLD** when she became queen.

11 The ancient **SUMERIAN QUEEN PUABI** was found buried with heaps of gold jewelry, a board game, a lyre, and ten hand-maidens and five soldiers sacrificed upon her death.

12 Runner **WILMA RUDOLPH** overcame childhood polio to win **THREE GOLD MEDALS** at the 1960 Olympics, the first American woman ever to reach three golds in one race.

Queen Victoria

35 FACTS ABOUT WOMEN WHO MADE HISTORY

13
Nearly 2,000 years ago, sisters **TRUNG TRAC** and **TRUNG NHI** led Vietnamese forces in a rebellion against Chinese rulers, capturing dozens of forts over several years.

14
CLARA BARTON founded the **AMERICAN RED CROSS** in 1881 at age 60 after risking her life to give clothing, food, supplies, and support to American Civil War soldiers in the field.

15
In the spring of 1943, 60 American women were selected from tryouts at Chicago's Wrigley Field to play in the first ever **WOMEN'S PROFESSIONAL BASEBALL** league.

16
ELLEN SIRLEAF JOHNSON, the president of Liberia since 2006, is Africa's first female elected head of state.

17
In 1805, American Indian **SACAGAWEA**, who appears on the dollar coin, explored the American West as a translator for Lewis and Clark—all while carrying her infant son on her back.

18
Before she became a famous chef, **JULIA CHILD** worked for the U.S. government during World War II, helping to develop shark repellent and conducting top-secret work in Asia.

19
African-American **ROSA PARKS** sparked peaceful protests against discrimination in 1955 when she refused to give up her seat on an Alabama bus to a white person.

20
In 1893, **NEW ZEALAND** became the first nation where women could **VOTE**. In 2011, 118 years later, Saudi Arabian women were given the right.

21
Harry Potter author **J.K. ROWLING** has sold more than 450 million books in 70 languages and is the best-selling author of the first decade of the 21st century.

22
In 1901, **ANNA EDSON TAYLOR** became the first person to successfully go over **NIAGARA FALLS** in a barrel.

23
In 2011, **GERMAN CHANCELLOR ANGELA MERKEL** ranked #4—the only woman in the top 10— in a list of the 100 most powerful people in the world.

24
MARY ANDERSON invented windshield wipers in 1903 after watching New York City drivers crane their necks out their windows to see in the rain.

25
In 1926, **GERTRUDE EDERLE** became the first woman to swim the **ENGLISH CHANNEL,** covering 35 miles (56 km) of frigid water in 14 hours and 39 minutes.

26
HELEN KELLER became blind and deaf before age two but still learned to **READ, WRITE, AND SPEAK,** and graduated from college with honors.

27
In 2007, India elected its **FIRST FEMALE PRESIDENT:** 72-year-old **PRATIBHA PATIL.**

28
BENAZIR BHUTTO, who served two terms as prime minister of Pakistan in the 1980s and 1990s, was the first woman leader of an Islamic country.

29
VALENTINA V. TERESHKOVA became the first woman in **SPACE** when she orbited Earth 48 times in 70.8 hours in 1963.

30
At the 2008 Beijing Summer Olympics, sisters **VENUS** and **SERENA WILLIAMS** took home gold medals for women's doubles tennis.

31
Japan's **JUNKO TABEI** became the first woman to summit **MOUNT EVEREST** on May 16, 1975.

32
On July 17, 1984, **SVETLANA SAVITSKAYA** became the first woman to spacewalk— float in space outside a spacecraft.

33
At least 35 women have run for **PRESIDENT OF THE UNITED STATES.**

34
German-born international movie star **MARLENE DIETRICH** worked as a **SPY** for the United States during World War II.

35
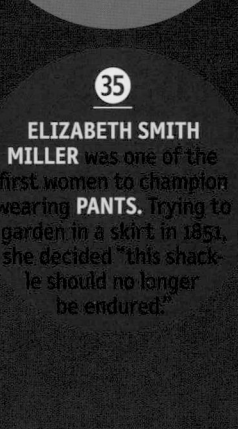
ELIZABETH SMITH MILLER was one of the first women to champion wearing **PANTS**. Trying to garden in a skirt in 1851, she decided "this shackle should no longer be endured."

1. Trees in a rain forest canopy can be as tall as a 20-story building. **2.** Rain forests are made up of different "layers." Animals that live at the bottom layer are completely different from animals that live at the top. **3.** Trees from an area the size of a football field are cut down every second in a rain forest somewhere in the world. **4. There are 700 species of fish in the Congolese rain forests. 5.** Due to the dense plant life on the rain forest floor, animals that live on the ground must rely on their voices to communicate. **6.** Canoes are a common way to get around a rain forest. **7.** The higher elevations of El Yunque National Forest in Puerto Rico can get 200 inches (508 cm) of rain a year. The forest is the only tropical rain forest protected by the U.S. National Forest system. **8. Half of the Earth's plants and animals live in rain forests. 9.** Male rhinoceros hornbill birds seal their babies and mates in hollow trees to keep them safe. They feed them through a hole just big enough for their beaks. **10.** Sloths spend 15–18 hours a day sleeping to conserve energy. **11.** Fewer than one out of every 100 rain forest plants has been studied by scientists to see if it can be used in medicine. **12. In the rain forest, camouflage is king! Some flowers are shaped like insects, and some insects are shaped like leaves. 13.** You can go to school to learn how to survive in a rain forest. **14.** The top of the rain forest canopy acts as an umbrella, keeping much of the wind, water, and light from reaching the plants and animals below. **15.** Tropical rain forests began to grow over 100 million years ago. **16. When a tree falls, it can become a "nurse" log that other plants soon overtake by growing on it and getting nourishment from it. 17.** Twenty percent of all the fresh water on Earth can be found in the Amazon basin. **18.** Violet plants in the rain forest can grow as big as apple trees. **19.** Rain forests usually receive at least 80 inches (203 cm) of rain a year—if all of the rain pooled on the ground at once, it would be deeper than a grown man is tall. **20. Rain forests once blanketed the Earth; today, they cover only 2 percent of Earth's surface. 21.** The trees are so thick in a rain forest that no more than two percent of the sun's light penetrates to the forest floor. **22.** A single rain forest tree can be more than a thousand years old. **23.** Antarctica is the only continent without a rain forest. **24. Rubber is made from sap from the rubber tree, which grows in the Amazon. 25.** One type of rain forest tree flowers once, releases its seeds, and then dies. **26.** Even though they are blind, millions of army ants will advance through the rain forest in a column that eats everything in its path. **27.** We can thank the rain forest for pineapple, cinnamon, chocolate, vanilla, and other foods we eat every day. **28. The rain forest isn't home just to animals—more than 30 million people live there too. 29.** A medicine to treat malaria, a killer disease spread by mosquitoes, comes from rain forests. **30.** The Brazilian nut tree produces flowers that only last for one day. **31.** A quarter of the world's known butterfly species live in South American rain forests. **32. More than 4,000 miles (6,437 km) of rivers can be found in the Amazon rain forest.**

African Grey Parrot

100 FACTS ABOUT

33. Sloths are the slowest mammals on Earth: They move about six to eight feet (1.8 to 2.4 m) per minute. **34.** Scientists think that more than 2,000 rain forest plants might be used to fight cancer. **35.** The durian fruit, which tastes great but smells like dirty socks, grows in the forests of Southeast Asia, and is a favorite food of orangutans. **36. Cayenne red pepper, black pepper, and chili pepper all come from rain forests. 37.** The bright colors of some butterflies signal that they are poisonous. **38.** More than half the trees cut down in the Amazon are removed to make room for cattle ranches. **39.** It takes sloths up to one month to process their food. **40. The flooded forests of the Amazon are the only places on Earth where fish feed on fruits and seeds. 41.** The rain forest is home to brightly colored snakes, including purple eyelash pit vipers. **42.** Some scientists estimate that 30 million different species of insects live in rain forests. **43.** The largest butterfly in the world, the Queen Alexandra's birdwing, can have a wingspan up to one foot across (30.5 cm). **44. Ancient Central Americans used the jaguar as a symbol of royalty and believed that jaguars protected them from evil. 45.** During the annual rains in the Amazon, an area the size of England is inundated with water. **46.** The Roosevelt elk, the largest elk in North America, lives in a temperate rain forest. Males can be five feet (1.5 m) at their shoulders. **47.** There is a rain forest in Alaska. **48.** It can take ten minutes for rain falling on a rain forest to reach the ground. **49. Tree kangaroos live in Australia's rain forests. While they are clumsy on the ground, they are swift and fast once in the trees. 50.** Some piranhas in the Amazon will remove nuts from their shells and eat them. **51.** Manatees in the Amazon can weigh as much as 1,000 pounds (454 kg). **52.** The goliath beetle can weigh as much as 3.5 ounces (100 g)—or the same as a medium-sized apple. **53. You might cross an acre (0.4 ha) of rain forest and never see the same kind of tree more than once—now try that in your backyard! 54.** Howler monkeys howl to let other monkeys know the territory is occupied. **55.** The people of the Amazon eat a fish called the tambaqui, and no wonder: It can weigh as much as a cheetah! **56.** The Amazon rain forest is twice the size of India. **57. Strangler figs got their name because they take the place of a tree they have grown on and killed. 58.** Some plants create "cups" with their leaves that can hold gallons of water. **59.** After feasting on rotting leaves, a bird called the hoatzin smells like cow manure. **60.** Armadillos live in rain forests, and they can hold their breath for six minutes to cross a body of water. Sometimes they do it by walking along the river bottom. **61. Organisms living in a sloth's fur will tint it green; the sloth then becomes even harder to spot in the trees. 62.** When a leaf falls in a rain forest it decomposes in about six weeks, but when a leaf falls in a northern pine forest, it can take seven years for it to decompose. **63.** Capuchin monkeys, which live in the Amazon rain forest, are very clever. It's recently been discovered that they can be trained to help people with disabilities. **64.** Rain forests are rich with beetles; scientists found nearly 1,000 species of beetles on one tree in Panama. **65. Red-eyed tree frogs use a sticky mucus on their toes to help them grip wet, slippery surfaces. 66.** Notorious for their carnivorous appetites, some piranhas are actually vegetarian. **67.** To get around in the forest canopy, some tree snakes glide from limb to limb, avoiding the ground altogether. **68.** The colorful Morpho butterflies of rain forests can be so vivid that they can be seen from low-flying airplanes. **69. Dolphins in the Amazon River are different shades of pink. 70.** Brazil is home to 30 percent of the world's tropical rain forests; in second place: the Democratic Republic of Congo. **71.** Tropical rain forests don't have cold winters—the average temperature is a warm 75°F (24°C). **72.** Some orchids grow underground. **73. The Maya and the Inca built great civilizations in their rain forest homes. 74.** You can buy chocolate bars that are made using rain forest-friendly cocoa. **75.** In one year, a canopy tree in a tropical forest can release about 200 gallons (760 L) of water through its leaves. **76. A tropical downpour can rain two inches (5 cm) in one hour. 77.** Some animals never travel from the forest canopy to the ground. **78.** Grasshoppers in Peruvian rain forests can be rainbow-colored. **79.** Fruit bats eat fruit; after the seeds pass through their digestive systems, they poop them out as they fly overhead. **80. Rain forests at higher elevations are called "cloud forests" because of the presence of fog and clouds. 81.** Brightly colored scarlet macaws are sometimes illegally caught in forests and then sold as exotic pets. **82.** Researchers use hot air balloons to float over rain forests in order to study them. **83.** If logging continues in the Amazon at its present rate, more than half of its forests could disappear by 2030. **84. Vines in the rain forest can grow to be as thick as your leg. 85.** Red-eyed tree frogs are colored bright neon on their bellies. When attacked they flip over to startle the predator and make a quick getaway. **86.** Chewing gum originally came from rain forest trees; now it can be made artificially. **87.** As many as 100 African grey parrots will perch in one single tree. **88. Rain forests act to absorb carbon dioxide, which is one of the gases that cause global warming. 89.** In Australia, you can stay in an eco-friendly tree house and watch the wildlife. **90.** Carnivorous piranhas will chomp down on goats that have fallen into the water. **91.** Some tarantulas will flick hairs from their bodies at animals that might try to attack them. **92. Rubber trees produce a sticky latex so that when an animal tries to eat the tree, its mouth sticks together instead. 93.** Some bamboo plants can grow as much as one foot (0.3 m) a day. **94.** Rain forests are most "alive" at night—80 percent of all the animal activity takes place in the darkness. **95.** A baby orangutan will cling to its mother's belly as she searches for fruit to eat. When the baby gets older, it will go for piggyback rides! **96. Leaf cutter ants eat more than 15 percent of all the leaves grown in some forests. 97.** In the Amazon, after a canoe is made, it is burned to make it waterproof. **98.** Perfectly at home in the forest, some Amazonian peoples have never seen a cell phone or car. **99.** Baby Brazilian tapirs have stripes and spots, but adults are all brown. **100. The large eyes of the nocturnal bush baby let in as much nighttime light as possible.**

1 Many **BROWN BEARS** that live in North America are also called grizzly bears.

2 Polar bears have rough pads on their paws that prevent them from slipping on ice.

3 When a polar bear and a grizzly bear have a baby, it's called a **"GROLAR BEAR"** or a **"PIZZLE."**

4 **SUN BEARS** usually have **ONE CUB** at a time. Other bears have two to three cubs in a litter.

5 The **SAMI**, an indigenous people of Scandinavia, refer to bears as "step-wideners" or "winter-sleepers."

6 A **BROWN BEAR** can **LOSE HUNDREDS OF POUNDS** (kilograms) when it hibernates— that's like losing the weight of a washing machine.

7 Giant anteaters are also known as **"ANT BEARS."**

8 **POLAR BEARS** have been known to swim up to 100 miles (161 km) in one stretch!

9 Sloth bears have a gap in their front teeth that they use to suck up termites.

10 The Asiatic black bear, also called a **MOON BEAR,** has a white stripe on its chest that looks like the crescent moon.

11 **SPECTACLED** bears might climb a cactus to eat the fruit at the top.

12 You can ski downhill at **BEAR MOUNTAIN** in Southern California, U.S.A., and cross-country at Bear Mountain in upstate New York, U.S.A.

13 When bears hibernate, they usually don't wake up for anything—they **MAY NOT EVEN GO TO THE BATHROOM FOR MONTHS.**

14 Outside of zoos, **PANDAS** only live in the remote mountains of central China.

15 Though very rare, black bears can be all white. These are often referred to as **"SPIRIT BEARS."**

16 Spectacled bears are the only bears that live in **SOUTH AMERICA.**

17 Sun bears, contrary to their name, are mostly active at night.

18 The **ANCIENT GREEKS** believed that men could turn into bears.

50 FURRY FACTS ABOUT BEARS

19
Polar bears **DO NOT HIBERNATE** if conditions are right for them to hunt year round.

20
Baloo from *The Jungle Book* is a **SLOTH BEAR.**

21
U.S. President Thomas Jefferson **KEPT TWO GRIZZLY BEARS AS PETS** in a cage at the White House.

22
Polar bears actually have **BLACK SKIN.**

23
YOGI BEAR was named after baseball legend Yogi Berra.

24
Researchers tracked a polar bear that **SWAM FOR NINE DAYS** without stopping—the same as swimming from Washington, D.C., to Boston, Massachusetts, U.S.A.

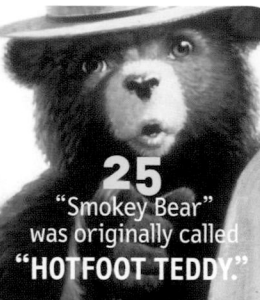

25
"Smokey Bear" was originally called **"HOTFOOT TEDDY."**

26
Brown bears used to live in **MEXICO** but are now **EXTINCT** in that region.

27
When a brown bear **STANDS** on its hind legs, it's not always trying to be threatening. It's often just getting a **BETTER LOOK** at its surroundings.

28
Polar bears have **TRANSPARENT HAIR** with a hollow core that reflects sunlight, making them appear to be white.

29
Pandas spend **10 TO 16 HOURS** of every day eating up to 40 pounds (18 kg) of bamboo.

30
Sun bears are the **SMALLEST OF ALL BEARS** and can weigh as little as 60 pounds (26 kg)—that's about the size of a golden retriever.

31
A "bear claw" is the name of a tasty pastry filled with almond paste.

32
A **NEWBORN PANDA CUB** is the same size and weight as an **ICE-CREAM SANDWICH!**

33
Sloth bear cubs are the **ONLY CUBS** that will **HITCH A RIDE** on their mom's back.

34
Although the **KOALA** is actually a marsupial, early English-speaking settlers called it **"KOALA BEAR"** due to its similarity in appearance to bears.

35
Polar bears have no natural enemies.

36
MALE BLACK BEARS can have a home range as large as 80 square miles (207 square kilometers).

37
SUN BEARS are also called "honey bears" because they eat honey using their long tongues.

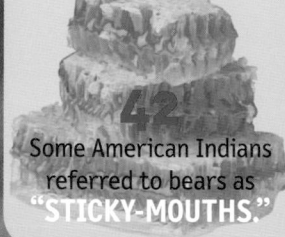

38
A group of bears is called a **"SLOTH,"** but you won't often see a sloth of bears, since the animals generally hang out alone.

39
To fatten up in the fall before it hibernates, a brown bear may eat as much as **90 POUNDS** (40 kilograms) **OF FOOD** a day. That's like eating **340 BANANAS!**

40
Most of the world's **BEAR SPECIES** are in danger of becoming **EXTINCT.**

41
GRIZZLIES are speedy. They can run up to 30 miles an hour (48 kph)— **FASTER THAN A HORSE.**

42
Some American Indians referred to bears as **"STICKY-MOUTHS."**

43
SPECTACLED BEARS will sit in a tree for days waiting for their **FRUIT TO RIPEN!**

44
In England, gummi bears are called **JELLY BABIES.**

45
Bears even **APPEAR IN THE SKY**—as the constellations the Big Bear and the Little Bear (Ursa Major and Ursa Minor).

46
Rather than building a den, a sun bear mother **BUILDS A NEST** on the ground to have her babies.

47
It's a myth that black bears "hoot." They do grunt and bellow.

48
Pixar made a fake commercial for **LOTS-O'-HUGGIN' BEAR** in *Toy Story 3*.

49
WINNIE THE POOH started out named **"EDWARD BEAR."**

50
Teddy bears were named after **PRESIDENT THEODORE ROOSEVELT.** The first ones were called **"TEDDY'S"** bears.

1
POISONOUS ANIMALS
HAVE POISON IN THEIR BODIES, BUT THEY MUST BE EATEN TO AFFECT ANOTHER ANIMAL.

3
Some **FESTIVE HOLIDAY PLANTS** can make cats sick. The sap from **POINSETTIAS**, for instance, can cause **VOMITING** but is not thought to cause death.

5
STEVE IRWIN, "THE CROCODILE HUNTER," died from a strike by the poisonous barb of a stingray to the heart, A VERY RARE OCCURRENCE.

2
BROWN RECLUSE SPIDERS
live in **DARK PLACES** but only have **THREE PAIRS OF EYES. MOST OTHER SPIDERS HAVE FOUR SETS.**

4

VENOMOUS ANIMALS
HAVE POISON IN THEIR BODIES THAT THEY CAN INJECT INTO OTHER ANIMALS.

6
THERE ARE CERTAIN KINDS OF **BACTERIA** THAT ARE HARMFUL TO HUMANS, BUT NOT TO ANIMALS, AND VICE VERSA.

25 Poisonous

7
A small amount of
NUTMEG
can safely add flavor to desserts, but large amounts can cause people to become **VERY SICK TO THEIR STOMACHS.**

8
When it eats certain
BEETLES
the flesh of the African spur-winged goose can be TOXIC TO EAT.

9
BLACK WIDOW SPIDERS DON'T HAVE TEETH. Instead they inject poison from needle-like "chelicerae" that turns the insides of their prey into **GOO THAT THEY CAN DRINK.**

10
A FORMER PRESIDENT OF UKRAINE WAS
POISONED
IN 2004 AND LIVED.

11
President Abraham Lincoln's mother died from "milk sickness." She drank milk after the cows who made it had grazed on a poisonous plant, **WHITE SNAKEROOT.**

12
THE LONGEST VENOMOUS SNAKE IN THE WORLD, THE
KING COBRA,
CAN BE AS LONG AS A CAR.

13
EXPOSURE TO
POISON IVY
CAN CAUSE EXTREME ITCHING AND RASHES. REMEMBER THE RHYME, "LEAVES OF THREE, LET IT BE."

14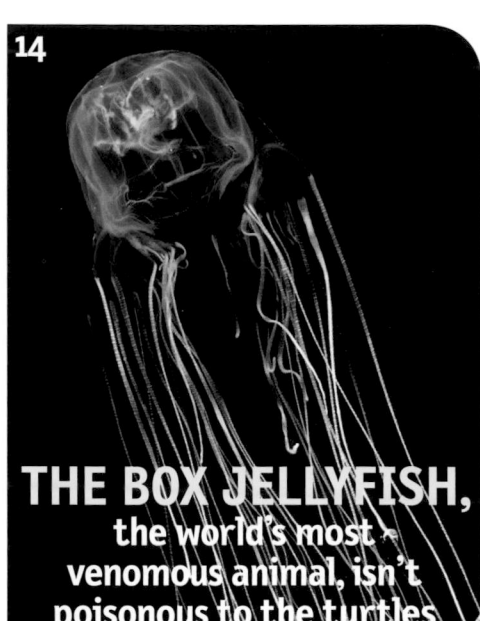

THE BOX JELLYFISH, the world's most venomous animal, isn't poisonous to the turtles that eat them.

15 WATCH OUT FOR THE

SLOW LORIS.

THEY LICK VENOM FROM THEIR INNER ELBOW AND MIX IT WITH THEIR SALIVA AND THEN BITE THEIR PREY.

16 THE ONLY POISONOUS LIZARD IN THE UNITED STATES, **THE GILA MONSTER,** CAN INJECT POISON WHEN IT BITES ITS **PREY.**

17 THE UNRIPE BERRIES OF THE

BLACK NIGHTSHADE

PLANT ARE MORE TOXIC THAN THE RIPE ONES.

FACTS to Die For

18

19 PUSS MOTH CATERPILLARS are even dangerous when dead. Their venom can still be injected from hairs on its body.

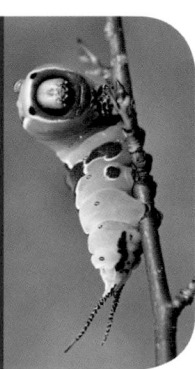

20

FISH,

such as sea bass and grouper, can carry a poison. If you eat an infected fish, it can cause you to feel SEARING HOT PAIN WHEN TOUCHED BY AN ICE CUBE.

The poisonous western

DIAMONDBACK RATTLESNAKE

has diamond-shaped markings on its skin.

21 THE

MISTLETOE

PLANT

can cause a slow heartbeat and an upset stomach if eaten.

23

Early settlers in North America developed an easy rhyme to tell the difference between the poisonous coral snake and other, nonpoisonous snakes with the same coloration: "Red touches black, friend of Jack. Red touches yellow will kill a fellow." THIS DOESN'T WORK IN OTHER PARTS OF THE WORLD!

24  RAW BEAN SPROUTS can carry deadly bacteria and the only way to kill the bacteria is to steam them; just washing them won't kill them.

22  Many MUSHROOMS are safe to eat, but a few wild varieties can cause death. Some of them are known as "destroying angels" or "death caps."

25 DRINKING TOO MUCH

WATER

AT ONCE CAN CHANGE THE SALT CONTENT IN YOUR BLOOD AND

KILL YOU.

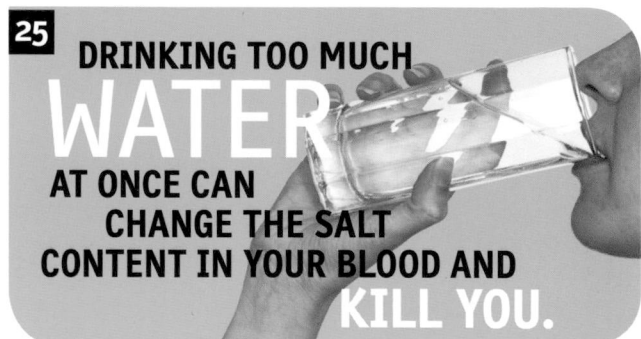

15 ROLLER COASTER

1 The **EARLIEST ROLLER COASTERS** were likely **ICE SLIDES**—wood covered in several inches of ice—that first appeared in **17TH-CENTURY RUSSIA.**

2 The **KINGDA KA** roller coaster in Jackson, New Jersey, U.S.A., climbs as high as **456 FEET** (139 m) and drops **418 FEET** (127.4 m) in a single dip.

3 Japan's **STEEL DRAGON 2000** roller coaster has just over **8,133 FEET** (2,479 m) of track—**691 MORE FEET** (210.6 m) than the next-longest roller coaster.

4 A roller coaster scheduled to open in China in 2012 will turn riders **UPSIDE DOWN 11 TIMES, A WORLD RECORD.**

5 On **FOURTH-DIMENSION** roller coasters, people sit in individual pods that **FLIP 360 DEGREES** during the ride.

6 **RIDDLER'S REVENGE** in California, U.S.A., **HOLDS EVERY RECORD**—fastest, longest, highest, farthest drop, most inversions—for roller coasters on which people **RIDE STANDING UP.**

FACTS TO GET YOUR HEART RACING

7 Riders on California, U.S.A.'s **SUPERMAN: ESCAPE FROM KRYPTON** roller coaster experience **WEIGHTLESSNESS FOR 6.5 SECONDS**, more than one-quarter the total ride time.

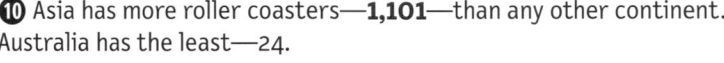

8 The **FASTEST ROLLER COASTER** in the world, in Abu Dhabi, reaches 149.1 miles per hour (240 kph) — in **FOUR SECONDS** — and requires riders to wear **SAFETY GOGGLES**.

9 The **LONGEST** roller coaster marathon ride lasted **405 HOURS AND 40 MINUTES** and took place over several weeks in 2007.

10 Asia has more roller coasters—**1,101**—than any other continent. Australia has the least—24.

11 Riders have climbed aboard Pennsylvania, U.S.A.'s wooden **LEAP-THE-DIPS**, the **OLDEST OPERATING** roller coaster, since 1902.

12 The first roller coaster to reach **100 MILES PER HOUR** (160.9 kph) was Australia's **TOWER OF TERROR**, opened in 1997.

13 In **ONE HOUR**, as many as **1,920 PEOPLE** ride Florida, U.S.A.'s **INCREDIBLE HULK** roller coaster.

14 At the top of **DISNEYLAND'S MATTERHORN BOBSLEDS** roller coaster, there is a **BASKETBALL HOOP** for employees to use while on break.

15 On August 8, 2010, **102 NAKED PEOPLE** rode the **GREEN SCREAM** roller coaster in England, setting a world record for **MOST NUDE PEOPLE** on a theme park ride.

75 FACTS THAT WILL TOTALLY CREEP YOU OUT

1 *The Book of the Dead*, written by ancient Egyptians, is a collection of spells believed to help the dead safely navigate the dangerous journey to the afterlife.

2 The Winchester Mystery House in California is said to be one of the world's most haunted places. Some report the smell of chicken soup coming from kitchens that haven't been used in decades.

3 A MAN SCULPTED A STATUE OF HIMSELF, USING HIS OWN TEETH, HAIR, AND NAILS.

4 Cave paintings in Europe show animals that existed at the time, such as woolly mammoths, and also shapes that look like flying saucers.

5 Tiny leeches can live in your nose. The first case was discovered in 2007 in Peru.

6 Beef tapeworms can grow to be as long as 25 feet (7.6 m) inside a person's intestine. Eating undercooked beef that has the worm cysts is a way to get them. You also can get them by eating undercooked meat that is infested with worms.

7 Elements of a book published in 1898 have uncanny similarities to the sinking of the *Titanic* in 1912. In the book, a huge ocean liner called the *Titan* strikes an iceberg on its first voyage in the month of April.

8 A medieval artist painted a devil face in the clouds of a painting featured in the Basilica of St. Francis in Assisi, Italy.

9 You can damage your hearing by holding in a sneeze.

10 In Asia, male vampire moths can suck human blood for 20 minutes before they're full.

11 THE FEAR OF REPTILES, OR OTHER CREEPY CRAWLY THINGS, IS HERPETOPHOBIA.

12 Some brands of gelatin are made from the hides and bones of animals, including cows and pigs.

13 An apparition is the appearance of a ghost. An apparition of a bride and a young girl are said to appear at Major Graham Mansion in Virginia, U.S.A.

14 Several people have reported hearing a screaming woman in Fort Mifflin in Philadelphia, Pennsylvania, U.S.A.—a fort used during the Revolutionary War. The screams are reportedly so loud that people nearby have called the police to investigate.

15 A theme park in the Ukraine closed right after it opened because of a nuclear disaster at a nearby plant, which made the area radioactive.

16 In 1932, Harry Price, a ghost hunter, tried to turn a German goat into a boy.

17 Christopher Columbus recorded three mermaid sightings in his journal.

18 A sea-dwelling parasite called the isopod eats the tongue of a fish, and then takes the tongue's place and lives in the fish's mouth.

19 A HUNDRED GRAMS OF CHOCOLATE CAN HAVE 60 INSECT FRAGMENTS AND STILL BE SOLD IN STORES.

20 The idea of vampires has been around for a long time—a 2,300-year-old Babylonian piece of art shows a vampire being chased by a vampire hunter.

21 "Ring Around the Rosy" is a nursery rhyme about the plague.

22 MIKE THE CHICKEN LIVED FOR 18 MONTHS WITHOUT HIS HEAD.

23 A paint color called bone black is made from cow bones.

24 There's about a soup can full of bacteria in your stomach at any time.

25 Stories of the Kraken, a terrifying sea monster that destroys ships, might be based on real sightings of a giant squid. It wasn't until 2004 that scientists got a good look at this sea creature.

26 The International UFO Museum and Research Center in Roswell, New Mexico, U.S.A., showcases the alleged UFO visit to the area. After you visit, you can eat at a UFO-themed restaurant.

27 A crater in Turkmenistan has been on fire for more than 38 years. A drilling rig accidentally punctured a hole in a big pocket of natural gas. To burn off the dangerous fumes, the gas was set on fire.

28 Elephantiasis causes swelling of the arms and legs. The disease is transmitted by mosquitoes found in some tropical areas.

29 A man in South Korea collapsed after he played an online video game for 50 hours. He later died.

30 A CHURCH IN THE CZECH REPUBLIC HAS A CHANDELIER MADE OUT OF HUMAN BONES.

31 A man received 3,900 body piercings in 7 hours and 46 minutes.

32 Some intestinal diseases are treated by swallowing live worm eggs.

33 A Romanian noble, Vlad Dracul, inspired the fictional character Dracula. Vlad Dracul lived more than 500 years ago in Transylvania and was known for his cruelty and for impaling his victims. He is said to have killed tens of thousands of people.

34 Some people believe that planes and ships "disappear" in an area of the Atlantic Ocean called the Bermuda Triangle. In reality, the area has no more wreckages than any other part of the ocean, but a strong Gulf Stream current can erase evidence of disasters.

35 The crew of the *Flying Dutchman*, a ship that sank off the coast of South Africa in 1641, is rumored to have to find souls to take their places before they can rest.

36 Turkey vultures, known to feast on the carcasses of dead animals, can't actually tear into meat. Instead, they have to wait for the animal to start decomposing before having a meal.

37 The Maya used some cenotes, or deep holes, in Central America to sacrifice people as offerings to their gods.

38 In Europe during the Middle Ages, millions of black cats were killed because people believed they had magical powers.

39 The Sanzhi U.F.O. houses were luxury "pods" built in Taiwan in the 1980s for wealthy vacationers. The project was abandoned midway through, after a series of mysterious accidents caused people to think the houses were haunted. The pod ghost town stood for 30 years until it was torn down in 2010.

40 People with lycanthropy believe they are wolves.

41 A hungry python decided to snack on an alligator in the Florida Everglades. The alligator was so big that scientists think the python burst.

42 COCKROACHES CAN LIVE FOR A FEW WEEKS WITHOUT THEIR HEADS.

43 In ancient Russia, people believed they could recite a chant to turn into a werewolf. Some believed that if you were scratched by a werewolf you became one.

44 A giant blue earthworm can grow to be 6.5 feet (2 m) long. That's longer than you are tall!

45 The ancient megalodon shark had a mouth full of teeth about the size of your hand (7 inches or 18 cm).

46 People who have the eating disorder pica want to eat things that aren't food—like burnt matches, stones, sand, and hair.

47 Five nuclear submarines have sunk to the bottom of the Atlantic Ocean with their radioactive cargo on board.

48 Spiders have clear blood.

49 In the 1940s, a grandmother had a hobby of creating miniature crime scenes inside nutshells. Local police used them as teaching tools.

50 The tadpoles of flying vampire frogs have two fangs that stick out from their mouths.

51 A feature in Death Valley National Park is known as the Devil's Golf Course because of its spiky salt formations as tall as two feet (0.6 m).

52 A BLOOD-RED WATERFALL FLOWS SLOWLY OUT OF A GLACIER IN ANTARCTICA. THE COLOR COMES FROM THE WATER'S HIGH IRON CONTENT.

53 Astrologer John Hazelrigg made a prediction that the men elected president of the U.S. in the 1920, 1940, and 1960 elections would die during their terms. They all did.

54 Some pet owners pay to have plastic surgery performed on their pets.

55 The goliath bird-eating spider is as big as a dinner plate. It's found in South America.

56 "Zombie walks" are events in which people dress in their scariest costume for a parade. Seven hundred zombies walked in the 2011 Detroit, Michigan, U.S.A., walk.

57 Dogs can get heartworms by being bit by a mosquito carrying the larvae. The larvae grow into heartworms that can be found in the dog's heart and lungs.

58 Dust mites eat your dead skin. Without them, you would be up to your eyeballs in dead skin cells.

59 A myth holds that if you hear the sorrowful wailing of an old hag in the wind, the death of a loved one is soon to follow.

60 Worms don't have arms or legs, or even eyes. One million worms can live on one acre (0.4 ha) of land.

61 The Museum of the Weird in Austin, Texas, U.S.A., showcases shrunken heads and tarantulas.

62 The goliath tigerfish lives in Africa's Congo River. It has razor-sharp teeth, weighs more than the average ten-year-old, and grows to be five feet (1.5 m) long.

63 People play a musical instrument called a theremin without touching it. The musician's hands move near its two antennas to produce a creepy sound.

64 Caecilians are legless amphibians that look like large earthworms or small snakes. They live underground in tunnels and use their razor-sharp teeth to swallow prey whole.

65 In 1692, 19 women and men were hanged in the town of Salem, Massachusetts, U.S.A., accused of being witches.

66 Jellyfish can sting you even when they are dead.

67 Dead blackbirds fell from the sky on New Year's Eve in Arkansas, U.S.A. Scientists think that poor nighttime vision might be to blame.

68 "Sleep tight—don't let the bed bugs bite" is based on a real insect. Bed bugs come out at night and feed on human blood.

69 The Hachioji Castle in Tokyo, Japan, is supposedly haunted by women who jumped to their deaths from the castle's walls when it was under attack.

70 There was once a paint made from ground-up Egyptian mummies. It was just called "mummy."

71 A river once ran red in Canada. Heavy rains had washed sediment into the river.

72 IN 1942, A LAKE FULL OF SKELETONS WAS FOUND IN A VALLEY IN INDIA. SCIENTISTS THINK THAT SOME 200 PEOPLE DIED AROUND A.D. 850 FROM A FREAK HAILSTORM.

73 Only 23 people live on the Skull Valley Reservation in Utah, U.S.A.

74 People report hearing the ghost of King Edward II of England screaming every year on the anniversary of his death in 1327.

75 The African crested rat chews on a toxic tree and then smears the mixture on its fur. Any predator that tries to eat the rat gets sick and dies.

35 NUMBER

1 Alex, an African grey parrot, could count up to SIX.

2 If you COUNTED ONE NUMBER A SECOND without stopping until you reached a BILLION, it would take 31 years, 259 days, 1 hour, 46 minutes, and 40 seconds.

3 In British English, a billion is equivalent to a MILLION MILLION, whereas in American English, it means a THOUSAND MILLION.

4 A pool with a million gallons of water would be 267 FEET (81 M) long, 50 FEET (15 M) wide, and 10 FEET (3 M) deep.

5 ONE MILLION DAYS is about 2,700 years; 1 million hours is just over 114 years; 1 million minutes is nearly two years.

6 In the early 1900s, a HORSE named CLEVER HANS solved simple math problems by stomping the ground. It turns out the trainer was giving clues with his body language.

7 A PRIME NUMBER can only be divided evenly by one and itself.

8 When asked to choose a NUMBER BETWEEN 1 AND 20, the most common number people choose is 17.

9 There are about 1,000 grains in a PINCH OF SALT. There are 100,000 in a TABLESPOON — and to fill up a bathtub with salt, it would take 1 billion grains.

10 A bowl large enough to hold a billion goldfish would be the size of a FOOTBALL STADIUM.

11 There are more than ONE BILLION CARS in the world.

12 Depending on your stride, there are between 2,000 AND 2,500 STEPS in one mile (1.6 km).

13 Seven is the MOST COMMON ROLL with two six-sided dice.

14 Disney's The Twilight Zone Tower of Terror DROPS RIDERS 13 STORIES in a runaway service elevator.

15 There are 64 SQUARES on a checkerboard.

16 All apples have FIVE SEED POCKETS, but the number of seeds in each apple depends on the health of the tree.

17 A GOOGOL is the number 1 with 100 ZEROES after it.

FACTS YOU CAN COUNT ON

18 A palindromic number is the same whether it is read frontward or backward, like this: 523,325.

19 When **BABE RUTH** hit his 60th home run in 1927, he didn't have a number on his back. Jersey numbers weren't common until 1929.

20 A **TRIDECAGON** is a **13-SIDED** polygon.

21 The **NUMBER 4** is considered **UNLUCKY** in some Asian cultures. There **ISN'T A MARKED FOURTH FLOOR** in some buildings.

22 You can't really catch the **HOGWARTS EXPRESS** at London's King's Cross Station, but there is a 9¾ sign on a blank brick wall near Platform 9.

PLATFORM 9¾

23 A **CENTENARIAN** is someone who is 100 years of age or older.

24 A man once jumped **238 TIMES IN ONE MINUTE** on a pogo stick.

25 An octagon has **8 SIDES.** An octacontagon has 80.

26 The largest **MILLIPEDES** have **750 LEGS,** not 1,000 as their name suggests.

27 The word "centipede" means 100 LEGS, but the insects actually have anywhere from **30 TO 300 OR MORE.**

28 A solar year is **365.2422 DAYS LONG.**

29 The **EMERGENCY NUMBER** in the **UNITED STATES** is 911. In the United Kingdom, Saudi Arabia, and Hong Kong it's 999.

30 A man once scored **365 POINTS** for the word "QUIXOTRY" in a game of Scrabble.

31 **NUMEROLOGY** is the study of the mysterious significance of numbers.

32 Tweets are limited to **140 CHARACTERS** because most text messages are limited to a similar character length.

33 The **SYMBOL FOR *PI*** is the 16th letter in the **GREEK ALPHABET.** In the English alphabet, *p* is the 16th letter.

34 A **DOZEN** is 12. A **BAKER'S DOZEN** is 13.

35 Basketball player **SHAQUILLE O'NEAL** wears a **SIZE 23 SHOE.**

100 FAR-OUT FACTS ABOUT THE UNIVERSE

1. In four days, the Deep Space 1 spacecraft traveled 621,400 miles (1,000,000 km). To cover that distance in a jet, you would have to fly nonstop for six weeks. **2.** NASA's space shuttle program shut down on July 21, 2011, after more than 30 years of missions. **3.** At liftoff, a NASA space shuttle weighed about 4.5 million pounds (2,041 mt). **4.** NASA's space shuttles were the world's first reusable spacecraft. **5.** Snoopy, the dog from the Peanuts comic strip, is the safety mascot of NASA astronauts. **6.** The International Space Station weighs 861,804 pounds (390,908 kg) and has been continuously occupied by astronauts since November 2, 2000. **7.** Space doesn't have a temperature, only things in space have a temperature. **8.** An astronomical unit, or AU, is a measurement used to calculate distances in our solar system. One AU is about the distance from the sun to Earth: 92,960,000 miles (149,597,890 km). **9.** Earth is the only planet in our solar system with liquid water. **10.** Venus is covered in thick clouds that reflect a lot of sunlight, making it the brightest planet in the night sky. **11.** The Big Bang, which formed the universe 13.7 billion years ago, wasn't an explosion but rather an event similar to an enormous balloon inflating. **12.** The Barringer Crater in southern Arizona, U.S.A., is a depression three-quarters of a mile (1.2 km) across and nearly 600 feet (183 m) deep created by a meteorite that crash-landed to Earth 50,000 years ago. **13.** The universe is filled with visible light and radiation—a kind of light invisible to the naked eye that includes x-rays and radio waves. **14.** In our solar system—formed about 4.5 billion years ago—13 planets orbit our home star, the sun. Scientists have identified about 300 different stars with orbiting planets. **15.** The universe is so vast that scientists measure cosmic distances using light-years. A light-year is the distance that light travels in one year—about 5.88 trillion miles (9.46 trillion km). **16.** Venus has the densest atmosphere of any planet in the solar system; it's so dense that if you tried to walk on the planet's surface, you would be crushed instantly like a soda can. **17.** Viewed from Earth, the three brightest objects in the sky are the sun, the moon, and Venus. **18.** It never rains on Venus and the temperature never changes—it's always a blistering 864°F (462°C) on the planet. **19.** One day on Mercury is equal to 176 days on Earth. **20.** Mercury is home to one of the largest craters in the solar system: The Caloris Basin is about 800 miles (1,287 km) across and was formed when a giant asteroid hit the planet. **21.** In star years, the sun, more than four billion years old—is middle-aged. **22.** One million Earths could fit inside the sun—but the star is considered average-size. **23.** The sun, like all stars, is primarily an enormous ball of hydrogen gas. It has no solid surface. **24.** While the planets in our solar system orbit the sun, the sun itself moves around our home galaxy, the Milky Way. **25.** All the elements in your body are recycled from two previous star explosions. **26.** The sun appears white to an astronaut in space. **27.** The sun's corona—the halo-like outer layer that can be millions of times hotter than the star's surface—is visible from Earth only during a solar eclipse. **28.** The sun's surface has sunspots—slightly cooler areas that appear as dark blotches—and the largest ones are nearly twice the size of Earth. **29.** When people say they were "born under the sign of…" they mean that on their birthday, the sun was directly between Earth and their constellation. **30.** Martian volcanoes can grow to be about 100 times larger than those on Earth. **31.** You can't walk on Jupiter, Saturn, Uranus, or Neptune because they have no solid surface. **32.** Astronaut Alan Shepard hit three golf balls on the moon while exploring its surface in 1971. **33.** A storm nearly three times the size of Earth has been raging on Jupiter for centuries. **34.** Earth has one moon; Jupiter has 50, maybe more; Mercury has none. **35.** Saturn, Jupiter, Neptune, and Uranus all have rings, but only Saturn's are visible with a telescope from Earth. **36.** Scientists haven't found life beyond Earth yet, but in 2010, a Vatican astronomer announced that the Catholic Church would welcome alien life forms. **37.** Uranus tilts 98° on its axis, so it appears to be lying on its side. **38.** Most of Uranus's moons are named for characters in William Shakespeare's writings. **39.** On Neptune, winds blow more than 1,200 miles per hour (2,000 kph). **40.** Neptune's core is hotter than the surface of the sun, but the clouds surrounding the planet are -350°F (-212°C). **41.** Stars die when they run out of fuel, and the heavier the star, the shorter its life span: Massive stars live for only a few million years, but lighter stars can live for trillions of years. **42.** All stars come from cosmic nurseries called nebulas—giant hydrogen gas clouds. **43.** Heavy stars are blue; lighter stars are red. **44.** A supernova is the explosive death of a very large star. Black holes, which have the strongest gravitational pull in the universe, can form from supernova leftovers. **45.** Astronomers have found hundreds of planets orbiting distant stars. Some circle two stars, which means the planets have double sunsets and sunrises. **46.** Our home galaxy, the Milky Way, is spiral-shaped and contains billions of stars (the sun is merely one of these). **47.** Our closest galactic neighbor is Andromeda, about twice the size of the Milky Way. The two galaxies are moving toward each other at about 300,000 miles per hour (483,000 kph) and will collide in a few billion years. **48.** Astronauts grew potatoes on the space shuttle. **49.** The universe is expanding—literally creating more space—at an ever-increasing speed. **50.** Some scientists believe that there are other universes, but even if these exist, we can't communicate with or travel to them. **51.** On several missions, NASA has launched into space LEGO figurines resembling the astronomer Galileo Galilei and the Roman god Jupiter and his wife Juno. **52.** Comets are leftovers from the creation of our solar system about 4.5 billion years ago, and they consist of sand, ice, and carbon dioxide. **53.** A comet's tail, which always points away from the sun, can be hundreds of millions of miles long. **54.** The brightest explosions in the universe are called gamma ray bursts; these occur when a black hole is born. **55.** The sunset on Mars appears blue. **56.** In 1969, U.S. astronaut Neil Armstrong became the first person to walk on the moon. **57.** The Kuiper Belt is a region beyond Neptune that's home to comets, icy objects, and the dwarf planets Pluto, Haumea, Makemake, and, sometimes Eris. **58.** In 2006, Pluto—smaller than Earth's moon—was demoted to a dwarf planet. **59.** The coldest, farthest object found in our solar system is the dwarf planet Eris. It orbits the sun once every 557 years. **60.** Because of its tilt, each side of Uranus has 42 years of sunshine followed by 42 years of darkness. **61.** The Sun burns an estimated 661 million tons (600 million MT) of hydrogen every second. **62.** A supermassive black hole is millions or even billions of times as massive as the sun. **63.** Scientists crashed a rocket into the moon in October 2009 to study its surface. The impact kicked up water vapor and ice, proving the moon is at least partly made of water (not cheese). **64.** Since 1991, astronomers have discovered more than 550 exoplanets—worlds outside our solar system. **65.** More than half a million kids and adults have attended Space Camp in Huntsville, Alabama, U.S.A., since the program began in 1982. **66.** Most galaxies are spiral-shaped, like the Milky Way. But galaxies can take other forms, including the shape of an egg, toothpick, or ring. **67.** Mars has two moons, Phobos and Deimos, and both are shaped like a potato. **68.** Mars was named by the Romans after their god of war. The Egyptians called the planet "Her Desher," which means "the red one." **69.** On April 5, 2010, four female astronauts—three American, one Japanese—gathered aboard the International Space Station and set the record for most women in orbit at once. **70.** Uranus shares its name with the Greek god of the sky, though the astronomer who discovered the planet in 1781 wanted to name it after King George III. **71.** A car-size asteroid enters Earth's atmosphere roughly once a year, but it burns up before it can make impact. **72.** NASA monitors more than 1,200 Potentially Hazardous Asteroids, or PHAs, which are rocky bodies orbiting Earth closely enough to pose a threat of impact. **73.** The Asteroid Belt, which lies between Mars and Jupiter, is home to most of the solar system's asteroids. **74.** In 2005, a Japanese spacecraft landed on an asteroid. **75.** Asteroids tend to have unusual names: Mr. Spock, Donald Duck, Santa, and Yes, to name a few. **76.** Asteroids range in size from 592 miles (952 km) to 0.6 miles (1 km) across. **77.** About 150 of the roughly 550,000 known asteroids have moons orbiting them. **78.** According to the International Astronomical Union, the definition of a planet is an object that orbits the sun, is nearly round, is not a moon, and steers clear of other nearby planets. **79.** If you weigh 100 pounds (45 kg) on Earth, you'd weigh a fraction of a pound—0.01 pounds (0.005 kg)—on a comet, and 38 pounds (17 kg) on Mercury. **80.** On Venus, the sun rises in the west and sets in the east—the opposite as on Earth. **81.** Shooting stars are really meteors, space material that heats up and burns bright once it enters Earth's atmosphere, and several can be seen every hour on any given night. **82.** Meteorites are meteors that don't burn up completely in Earth's atmosphere and make impact with the planet's surface. The largest meteorite ever found on Earth landed in southwest Africa and weighed 119,000 pounds (54,000 kg). **83.** In 1954, an eight-pound (3.6 kg) meteorite crashed through the roof of an Alabama woman's house. **84.** About 1,000 to 10,000 tons (907 to 9,072 MT) of meteoric material falls on Earth every day, but most is in the form of tiny particles, or space dust. **85.** On the asteroid Vesta, there is a mountain three times as tall as Mt. Everest. **86.** Saturn's moon Enceladus is covered in 330 feet (100 m) of snow. **87.** Jupiter's moon Europa has a surface layer of ice that scientists believe covers a giant ocean that could harbor alien life. **88.** Hubble, a space telescope the length of a school bus and the weight of two elephants, has been orbiting Earth at 17,500 miles per hour (28,160 kph) since 1990. It has taken hundreds of thousands of images of distant planets, stars, and galaxies. **89.** Astronauts eat tortillas in space because they don't crumble, so nothing can get stuck in the equipment. **90.** Astronauts don't bring dirty laundry home with them; they place the clothes in a bag that burns up in Earth's atmosphere during re-entry. **91.** Astronauts working aboard the International Space Station get weekends off. Popular pastimes include racing through the station, doing somersaults and backflips, and simply staring out the windows at space. **92.** Mayan astronomers made detailed observations of Venus more than 1,300 years ago. **93.** The word "planet" comes from the Greek word "planetes," which means wanderer. **94.** The Cassini spacecraft took less than seven years to travel nearly two billion miles (3.2 billion km) to Saturn. To cover this distance by car, you would have to drive 62 miles per hour (100 kph) for 3,653 years. **95.** There are six American flags planted on the moon. **96.** A 1967 international law prohibits any one country from owning planets, stars, or any other natural objects in space. **97.** If you could fly a plane to Pluto, the trip would take more than 800 years. **98.** Neptune has storm clouds the size of Earth. **99.** The ancient Greeks called the sun "Helios" and the ancient Romans called it "Sol." **100.** Neptune was discovered in 1846 and didn't complete an orbit of the sun until 2011.

1

There are **12 PIECES** of candy in a regular-size roll of **PEZ**.

2

The founder of **HERSHEY'S** started his candy-making business when **HE WAS JUST 18.**

3

HERSHEY'S KISSES didn't have their **PAPER "FLAG"** for the first **14 YEARS** they were made.

4

CHARLES SCHULZ, the creator of the "**PEA-NUTS**" comic strip, said he was inspired to name **PEPPERMINT PATTY** when he saw a dish of candy sitting on a table.

5

The **BLUE JELLY BELLY** was invented for U.S. President Reagan's inaugural festivities. Over three tons (2.7 MT) of red, white, and blue beans were ordered for the occasion.

6

ROCK CANDY is one of the oldest candies. It was first available in the U.S. **FROM PHARMACISTS AND WAS USED AS MEDICINE.**

7

Alexander the Great **ATE LICORICE.**

8

Ancient Greeks believed that **MINT CURED HICCUPS.**

9

Sugar isn't what **ROTS YOUR TEETH.** The strep-tococcus **BACTERIA IN YOUR MOUTH LIKE TO EAT SUGAR** on your teeth and excrete acids that can give you a cavity.

10

There is salt and water in **SALTWATER TAFFY,** but it's **NOT MADE FROM SEAWATER.**

11

Sales of **REESE'S PIECES** went up at least 65 percent when the movie *E.T.* skyrocketed them to fame. (**THE M&M FOLKS TURNED DOWN THE ROLE.**)

12

MOLASSES TAFFY was among the first kinds of candy made in the United States.

13

The world's **LARGEST LOLLIPOP** weighed **6,514 POUNDS** (2,955 kg) and was **25 FEET** (7.50 m) high. It took a crane to stand it up.

14

WINTERGREEN LIFESAVERS make a **SPARK IN YOUR MOUTH** when you crunch them.

15

Ancient Egyptians made **MARSHMALLOWS.**

16

In many Asian countries, **PICKLED AND PRESERVED FRUITS** covered in a **SWEET AND SOUR POWDER** are a popular dessert treat.

17

The **FRENCH WORD "BONBON"** —a candy with a chewy center— means "**GOOD-GOOD.**"

50 SWEET FACTS ABOUT CANDY

✳ YOU HAVE LEARNED **1,810** FACTS

18
In Central and South America, COCOA BEANS WERE ONCE USED AS CURRENCY.

19
TIC TACS—introduced in 1969—first featured flavors such as grape and cinnamon. New favorites include STRAWBERRY FIELDS and FRUIT ADVENTURE.

20
A survey of parents showed that 90 PERCENT SNEAK some of their KIDS' HALLOWEEN CANDY.

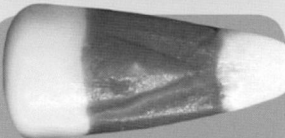

21
October 30th is NATIONAL CANDY CORN DAY in the U.S.

22
CONVERSATION HEART CANDIES were once shaped like HORSESHOES AND BASEBALLS.

23
Enough CANDY CANES are made every year to stretch from SANTA CLAUS, INDIANA, U.S.A., to NORTH POLE, ALASKA, U.S.A., and back again 32 TIMES.

24
54 PERCENT OF KIDS eat their candy cane by sucking on it. Boys are almost TWICE AS LIKELY to crunch their candy canes as girls.

25
Two different universities created LICKING MACHINES to see how many licks it took to get to the center of a Tootsie Roll Pop. One got 411 LICKS, the other got 364.

26
It is a MYTH THAT SWALLOWED GUM takes SEVEN YEARS to pass through the digestive system.

27
SUGAR DOESN'T STRETCH, to blow BIGGER GUM BUBBLES, chew until the sugar dissolves.

28
COTTON CANDY was originally called FAIRY FLOSS.

29
ICE CUBES help UNSTICK GUM from clothing.

30
THE BIGGEST-SELLING candy holiday is HALLOWEEN.

31
M&MS were on all SPACE SHUTTLE MISSIONS after 1981. Astronauts gobbled them up like PAC-MAN as they floated in the craft.

32
GUMMI BEARS were originally called "DANCING BEARS."

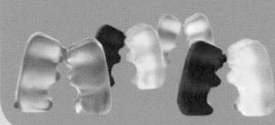

33
Enough JELLYBEANS are made in the U.S. each year to FILL AN EASTER EGG 89 FEET (27 m) HIGH and 60 FEET WIDE (18 m).

34
200 MILLION INDIVIDUAL SKITTLES candy pieces are made every day.

35
Early lollipop machines made 40 LOLLIPOPS IN ONE MINUTE. Today's machines make 5,900 LOLLIPOPS in the same amount of time.

36
In the summer, more than HALF OF ALL MARSHMALLOWS sold are TOASTED OVER A FIRE.

37
Some candy—LIKE TOOTSIE ROLLS—were once marketed as HEALTH FOODS.

38
76 PERCENT of people eat the EARS OFF THEIR CHOCOLATE BUNNY FIRST.

39
The world's largest chocolate EASTER EGG was made in Italy. It was THREE STORIES TALL and WEIGHED AS MUCH AS AN ELEPHANT.

40
In 1953, it took 27 HOURS to create a MARSHMALLOW PEEP. Today, it takes SIX MINUTES.

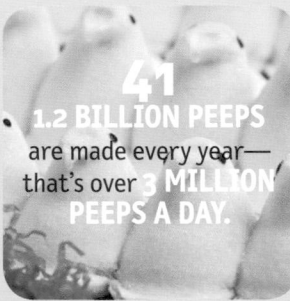

41
1.2 BILLION PEEPS are made every year—that's over 3 MILLION PEEPS A DAY.

42
THE EYES ON THE FIRST PEEPS WERE PAINTED ON BY HAND. Now, machines create 3,500 PEEPS' eyes per minute.

43
Chocolate, marmalade, spinach, earwax, and vomit are a few of Bertie Bott's EVERY FLAVOR BEANS in *Harry Potter*. The beans are now available in the Muggle world.

44
THE CHOCOLATE RIVER in the original *Willy Wonka & the Chocolate Factory* movie WASN'T MADE OF CHOCOLATE. It was colored water.

45
More than 60 years ago, the FIRST "M" STAMPED ON M&M'S WAS IN BLACK, NOT WHITE.

46
There are about 700 DIFFERENT BAZOOKA JOE COMICS.

47
Red-colored RED VINES DON'T HAVE LICORICE IN THEM. Only the black vines do.

48
M IS THE FIRST LETTER OF THE LAST NAME of both of the founders of the M&M candy company.

49
POP ROCKS are mixed with CARBON DIOXIDE GAS under high pressure, which causes TINY BUBBLES of carbon dioxide gas to form in the candy.

50
POP ROCKS DON'T JUST POP IN YOUR MOUTH. If you crush them in a bowl, you can hear them pop too.

1 **NANOROBOTS** ARE ATOM-SIZED AND CAN CRAWL, BUT THEY AREN'T MADE OF METAL; THEY'RE MADE OF **HUMAN DNA**.

2 THE FIRST INTERNATIONAL **ROBOT OLYMPICS** WAS HELD IN 1990 IN SCOTLAND AND INCLUDED SUCH EVENTS AS **WALL CLIMBING, SPEAKING, AND COLLISION AVOIDANCE.**

3 THE SMALLEST HUMANLIKE ROBOT IS **6 INCHES** (15.3 CM) TALL AND CAN WALK, KICK, AND DO PUSH-UPS.

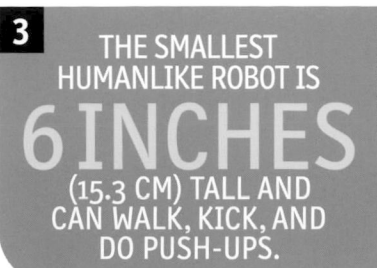

4 Scientists studied **CHIMPANZEE** behavior to develop Nao, a humanlike robot that can mimic the emotions of a one-year-old.

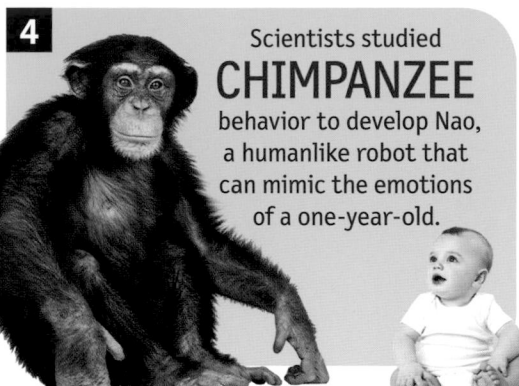

5

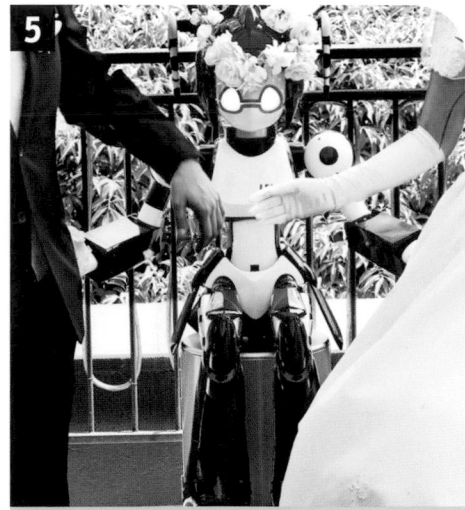

On May 16, 2010, **TOMOHIRO SHIBATA** and **SATOKO INOUE** were married by **I-FAIRY**, the first robot to perform a wedding ceremony.

25 FAR-OUT

6 THE WORD "ROBOT" IS LESS THAN 100 YEARS OLD—IT FIRST APPEARED IN A 1920 CZECH PLAY.

7 **LINGODROIDS** use a combination of **BEEPS** to create their own **SPOKEN LANGUAGE** and **COMMUNICATE WITH ONE ANOTHER.**

8

9 **PAPERO THE CHILDCARE ROBOT** is a mechanical babysitter that uses a 3,000-word vocabulary, two "eyes," and eight "ears" to interact with kids.

IN FEBRUARY 2011, NASA LAUNCHED THE FIRST **HUMANLIKE ROBOT** INTO SPACE: **ROBONAUT 2** WILL HELP ASTRONAUTS PERFORM EVERYDAY TASKS ABOARD THE INTERNATIONAL SPACE STATION.

10

Every year, **TEAMS FROM ALL OVER THE WORLD** gather for **ROBOCUP, A SOCCER GAME WITH ROBOTS** as players instead of people.

11 The woman who lent her voice to **ROSIE THE ROBOT** on *The Jetsons* also voiced **WILMA FLINTSTONE.**

12 THE SMALL, MOBILE **SNACKBOT** DEMONSTRATES HOW ROBOTS INTERACT WITH PEOPLE— AND DELIVERS SNACKS TO THEM.

13 A team of Swiss researchers built a **ROBOT SMALL ENOUGH TO SWIM THROUGH HUMAN ARTERIES.**

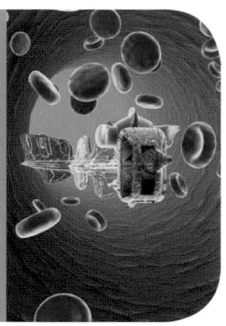

15 **CORNELL UNIVERSITY RESEARCHERS BUILT A FOUR-LEGGED ROBOT** that can teach itself to walk and then, when damaged, **TEACH ITSELF TO LIMP.**

17 **STAR WARS' C-3PO** stands 5 feet 7 inches (1.7 m) tall;

R2-D2 is 3 feet 2 inches (.97 m) tall.

14 Scientists at the University of California, San Diego built an **ALBERT EINSTEIN** –lookalike robot that can teach itself to smile, frown, and make other facial expressions.

16  **ROBOTICIST HIROSHI ISHIGURO BUILT A ROBOT WITH A FACE JUST LIKE HIS TO STUDY HOW PEOPLE REACT TO LIFELIKE MACHINES.**

ROBOT FACTS

18 **THE FIRST ROBOT DEBUTED IN 1961 AND WORKED IN A GENERAL MOTORS AUTOMOBILE FACTORY.**

21 *WALL·E,* a movie about a trash-collecting robot, won the 2009 Oscar for Best Animated Feature Film.

23 **AT HONG KONG'S ROBOT KITCHEN,** ROBOTS GREET, SEAT, AND SERVE CUSTOMERS.

19 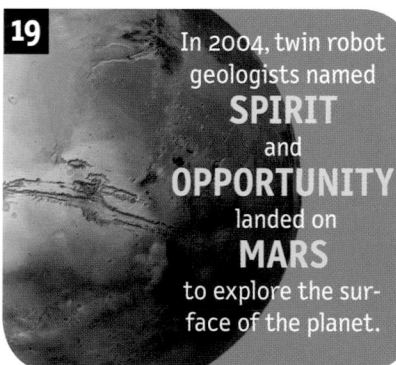 In 2004, twin robot geologists named **SPIRIT** and **OPPORTUNITY** landed on **MARS** to explore the surface of the planet.

24 **SCIENCE FICTION AUTHOR ISAAC ASIMOV WROTE THE THREE LAWS OF ROBOTICS:**

1) **A ROBOT** may not injure a human being, or, through inaction, allow a human being to come to harm.

2) **A ROBOT** must obey the orders given it by human beings, except where such orders would conflict with the First Law.

3) **A ROBOT** must protect its own existence as long as such protection does not conflict with the First or Second Law.

20 THE CUBE STORMER II ROBOT SOLVED A RUBIK'S CUBE IN **5.7** SECONDS IN 2011—THE FASTEST TIME YET.

22 SEASWARM—a fleet of oil-absorbing robots—could be used to clean up future oil spills: Each 'bot can absorb up to 20 times its own weight in oil.

25 On September 19, 2010, **525 Illinois high school students SET THE RECORD** for the largest group of people performing **"THE ROBOT"** dance move.

① The perfectly **CUBE-SHAPED BOXFISH** found in the waters around Indonesia was the inspiration for a fuel-efficient **MERCEDES-BENZ CAR.**

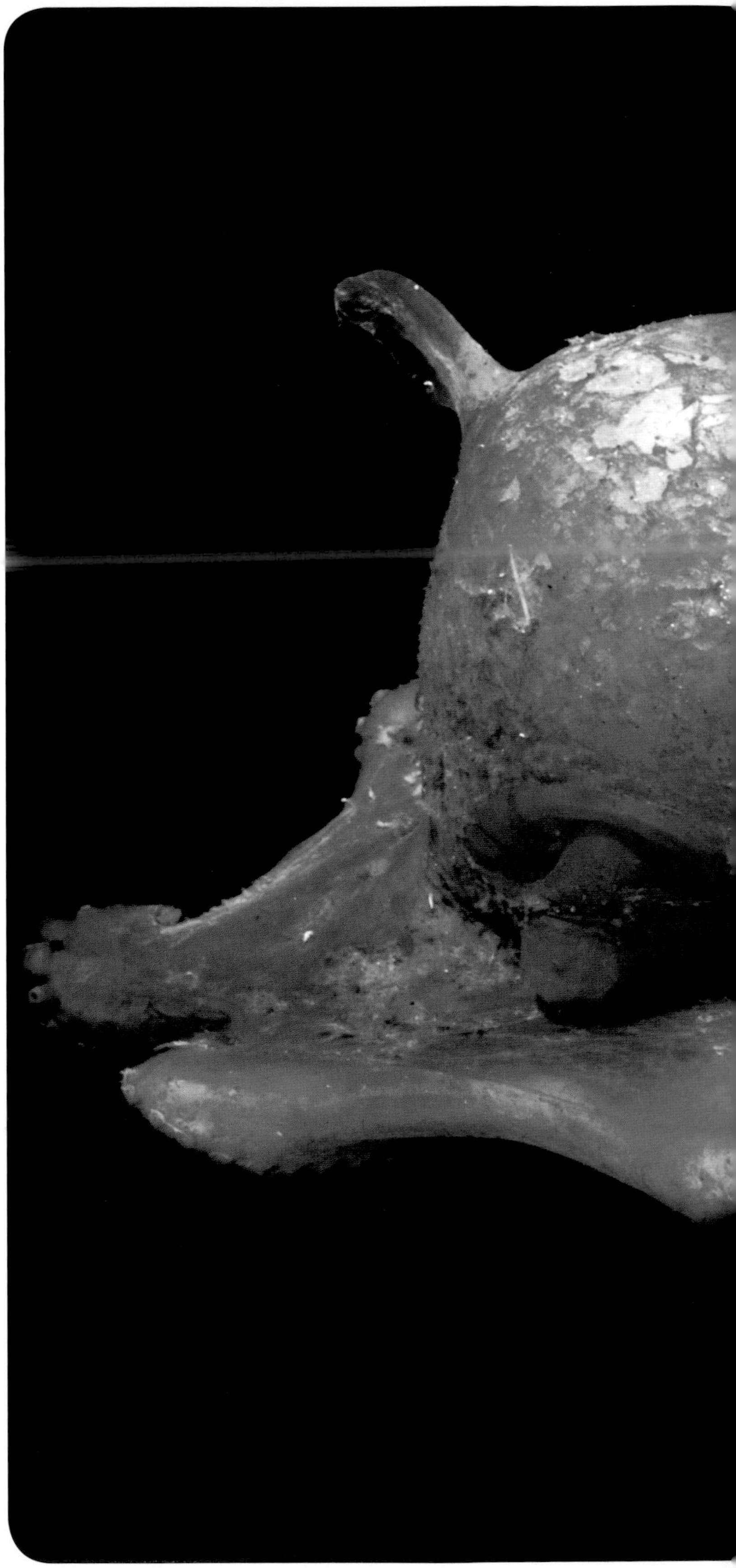

② The six-inch (15-cm)-long **VAMPIRE SQUID** lives in the dark depths of the ocean and avoids attack by pulling its arms around the rest of its body, making it look **INSIDE OUT.**

③ The **BLOB FISH** lives up to its name. Pasty white with floppy skin, this ocean dweller looks like a frowning old man with a **VERY LARGE NOSE!**

④ The spines on a **REEF STONEFISH'S** dorsal fins contain some of the **MOST TOXIC FISH VENOM** in the world.

⑤ The **CHRISTMAS TREE WORM** found on the Great Barrier Reef looks like a **COLORFUL, SEASONAL DECORATION** but when a predator comes near, it retreats into the tunnel it carves in live coral.

⑥ The **VENUS FLYTRAP ANEMONE,** which lives in the Gulf of Mexico, looks remarkably like the bug-catching rain forest plant. Instead of snatching insects, however, this anemone **STINGS PREY** with its tentacles.

⑦ Silky white **YETI CRABS** have furry claws that give them the look of an under-the-sea **ABOMINABLE SNOWMAN.**

SEA CREATURES

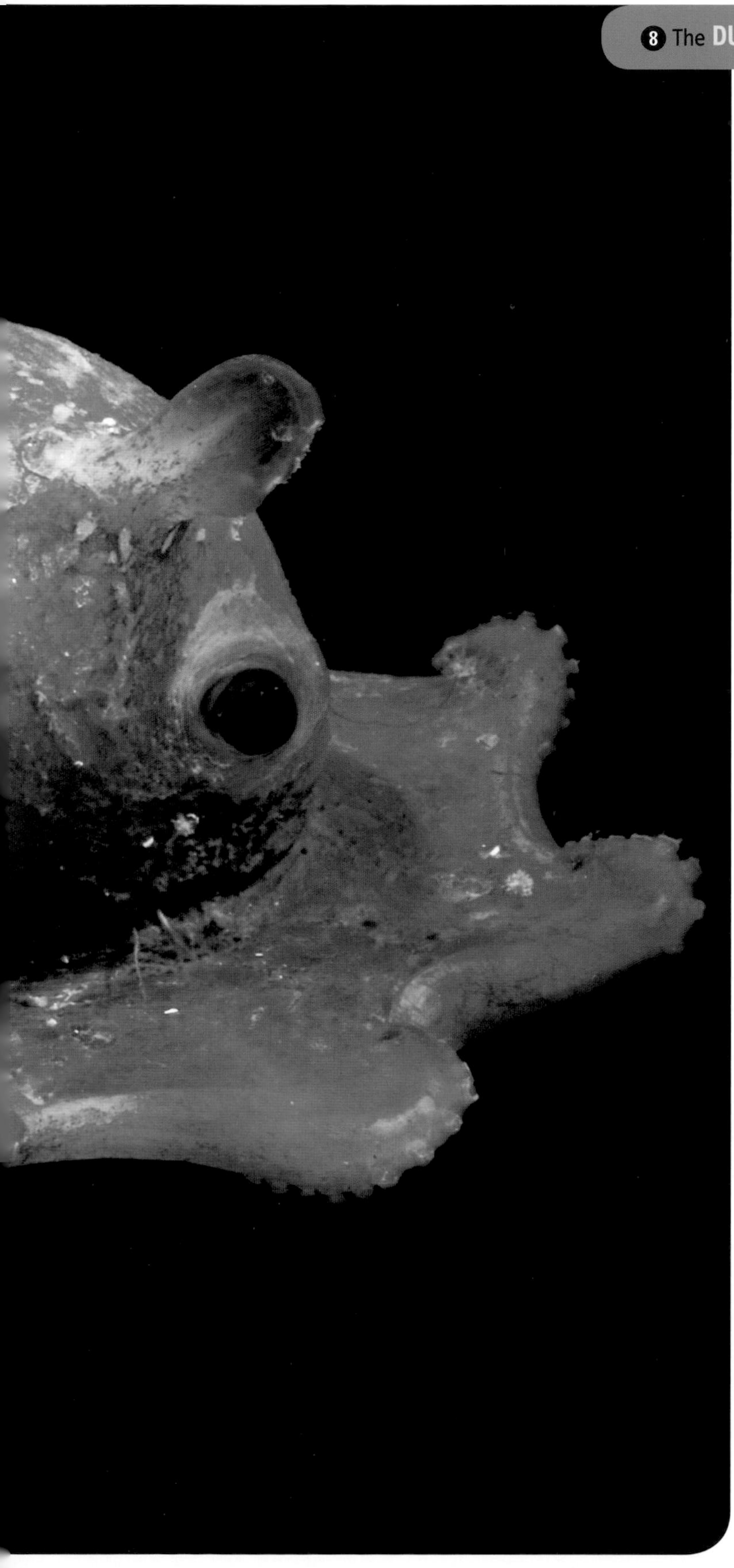

8 The **DUMBO OCTOPUS** flaps its earlike fins to swim in deep ocean waters.

9 The four-inch (10-cm)-long **PINK HANDFISH** doesn't swim—it uses its fins to WALK on the ocean floor near Tasmania.

10 A **SEA PEN** looks more like **HARRY POTTER'S QUILL** stuck into the ocean floor than a sea creature. Each "pen" is a community of many polyps—anemone-like individuals that work together for the survival of their colony.

11 The **LEAFY SEA DRAGON**—a close relative of the seahorse—is perfectly camouflaged to look like **SEAWEED**.

12 The DEEP-SEA DANA OCTOPUS SQUID captures prey after stunning it with blinding, bright flashes that come from its arms.

13 **GIANT SEA SPIDERS** the size of dinner plates crawl in the icy waters off Antarctica.

14 One of the world's smallest seahorses, **DENISE'S PYGMY SEAHORSE,** is about the SIZE OF A PAPERCLIP.

15 A jellyfish found in waters near Tasmania looks like a LITE BRITE! Its rainbow glow is made by light reflecting off the **TINY PROJECTIONS** it uses to swim.

75 BRIGHT-iDEA

7 An iPad-like tablet computer was invented in 1968 for kids, but the Apple version—along with Angry Birds—didn't show up until 40 years later.

8 Scientists invented an armband that sends electricity through your joints and muscles to control your fingers' movements. You can slip it on, grab a guitar and play a song without even thinking about it!

9 A NEWLY INVENTED LIGHTBULB ONLY HAS TO BE CHANGED ONCE EVERY 20 YEARS!

1 A high school student invented a glove that translates sign language into words that appear on a screen.

2 An aerodynamic umbrella was recently designed to withstand winds of up to 70 miles per hour (113 kph).

3 TV remotes were invented in the 1950s, but early versions emitted a sound that annoyed dogs' keen hearing.

4 One company invented a line of everyday items with a bacon twist: Bacon dental floss, bacon air fresheners, bacon candy canes, and bacon soap!

5 THE OWNER OF NIKE INVENTED THE WAFFLE SOLE RUNNING SHOE IN 1971 BY POURING HOT RUBBER INTO HIS WIFE'S WAFFLE IRON.

6 The first smart phone, invented in 1992, was named Simon and weighed five times as much as an iPhone.

10 The Inkling pen remembers everything you draw. When you plug it in to the computer, your sketch appears on screen.

11 Fashion designers invented cat ears that clip on your head and respond to your moods. If you're curious, they prick up. If you're relaxed, they droop.

12 The computer company IBM created "Watson," a computing system designed to find the correct answers on the quiz show *Jeopardy!* In 2011 Watson beat the 74-time reigning *Jeopardy!* champion.

13 Humans' first invention? Tools. By chipping away at the edges of stones they made axes, arrowheads, and hammers.

14 The wheel was invented about 5,000 years ago in what is now the Middle East.

15 The Nyfork is a fork that has a pizza wheel attached to the side of it so you can slice your food and gobble it up using one utensil—and one hand!

16 Before the Wright brothers took flight in the first controllable, self-propelled, heavier-than-air machine in 1903, they spent years researching and making test models.

17 John Deere, known for his shiny green tractors, invented the cast steel plow in 1846. By 1855, he was selling 13,000 plows a year. Today Deere & Co. is worth more than $31 billion.

18 Thomas Edison didn't invent the first incandescent light bulb, but he invented the first one that worked well. His first successful bulb burned for 13½ hours straight.

19 In 1455, Johannes Gutenberg invented the printing press, which allowed printers to make thousands of copies of a book page. Before that, it took months or years to copy a book by hand.

20 When Alexander Graham Bell invented his telephone, the first words he spoke into it were, "Mr. Watson—come here—I want to see you."

21 The first TV broadcast in color was on January 1, 1954, but only 200 of the newly invented color TVs had been sold to see the show.

22 Samuel Morse was an artist before he invented the electric telegraph used to transmit Morse code—a series of dots and dashes that translate into letters and numbers—in 1838.

23 Thomas Edison began to lose his hearing when he was a child, but he said it made him a better inventor, since he could work with fewer distractions, and he slept more deeply.

24 THOMAS EDISON'S LABORATORY IN NEW JERSEY WAS NICKNAMED "THE INVENTION FACTORY."

25 In 2009, a 19-year-old college student invented an environmentally-friendly one-wheeled electric motorcycle.

26 As a boy, Benjamin Franklin invented paddles that slipped over his hands to help him swim faster.

27 Benjamin Franklin invented a stove, bifocal glasses, and a "long arm" used to take books down from high shelves.

28 The lightning rod, invented by Benjamin Franklin in 1752, provides a safe path to the ground for lightning. It is still used on houses and buildings to prevent fires today.

29 Benjamin Franklin proved that lightning is electricity by reportedly flying a kite in a thunderstorm. Lightning struck the kite, which sent sparks flying from a key attached to the kite string.

30 Instant ramen noodles were invented by a Japanese man who became known as "Mr. Noodle." When first introduced, they were an expensive luxury item.

31 Early cars didn't have windshield wipers—people simply pulled over and wiped the window down when it got so bad they couldn't see. That all changed in 1905, when Mary Anderson got a patent for her device that swung an arm with a rubber blade on the end.

32 PLASTIC WAS INVENTED IN 1907. EARLY USES WERE BUTTONS, BILLIARD BALLS, AND TOILET SEATS!

33 The first functional submarine was called the "Turtle." It was made of wood and used in the American Revolution to plant bombs on enemy ships.

34 Gatorade was invented in 1965 by a Florida, U.S.A., doctor who wanted to give athletes something to drink that would boost their energy. He named it after the University of Florida's football team, the "Gators."

35 The man who created Velcro in 1955 came up with the idea after examining burrs stuck to his dog's fur under a microscope!

FACTS ABOUT INVENTIONS

36 Band-Aids were invented in 1917 but weren't popular until seven years later, when the company gave free ones to Boy Scouts across the country. Since then over 100 billion have been made!

37 Scotch tape was invented in 1930. At first, it only had adhesive along the edges and not in the middle.

38 George Ferris unveiled his 264-foot (80-m)-high Ferris wheel in 1893. The tallest Ferris wheel today is in Singapore; it soars 42 stories, or 542 feet (165 m), high.

39 The Slinky was invented by accident. In the 1940s, an inventor was trying to make a spring that would keep instruments stable on ships, but when one got away and "walked" down a pile of books, he realized it could be a fun toy.

40 THE SUPERSOAKER WAS INVENTED IN 1989 BY A NUCLEAR ENGINEER.

41 The zipper, invented in 1893, was originally called the "clasp locker."

42 Will Kellogg invented corn flakes in 1894 by accident from a dough recipe gone wrong. But Kellogg quickly realized it could be a new product. Within a few years, Kellogg's Corn Flakes were a household name.

43 In the 1970s a man invented the "Pet Rock." The small stone sold in a doggy carrying case with breathing holes for $4. He became an instant millionaire.

44 The inventor of the trampoline named it after the Spanish word for diving board: *el trampolin*.

45 The inventor of Coca-Cola was a pharmacist, doctor, and surgeon. It was first sold as a medicine claiming to get rid of fatigue and headaches.

46 A Canadian filmmaker who lost his vision in one eye as a boy developed a replacement eye that is also a battery-powered wireless video camera. He can make a digital video of everything he sees.

47 Platform shoes were invented in Venice, Italy, in the 16th century to keep feet dry in the flooded streets.

48 In 1877, an 18-year-old from Maine, U.S.A., got a patent for the "Ear Protector"—the world's first earmuffs. He had the idea when he was 15 and wanted to play outside but couldn't keep his ears warm.

49 The telescope was invented in 1608, and within a year Galileo constructed his own to observe the moon.

50 Duct tape was invented during World War II because soldiers needed waterproof tape that they could easily tear off to fix things. Now it's used for everything—including the world's largest duct tape wallet, which is 106.5 inches (2.7 m) long.

51 Dreaming of the day when cars will fly? It might not be too far off. NASA has already invented a flying car called "Highway in the Sky."

52 The man who invented the flushable toilet in 1596 took his commode straight to England's Queen Elizabeth I, who promptly had it installed in one of her palaces.

53 The Sonic Bomb alarm clock was invented for heavy sleepers. It has a 113-decibel ringer that's as loud as thunder.

54 SCIENTISTS HAVE INVENTED A CLOCK THAT IS POWERED BY DEAD FLIES.

55 Before the inflatable rubber tire was invented in 1888, wheels were made of wood, sometimes with steel rims.

56 The Pool PC is a waterproof computer than can attach to an inner tube so you can surf the Internet in the pool while you splash around.

57 The first email was sent in the U.S.A. in 1969 between the University of California, Los Angeles, and Stanford University. The sender was trying to type "login" but the system crashed at the "G," so the message just read "Lo."

58 When Harry Wesley Cooper was experimenting with super sticky adhesive for the military in the 1940s and 50s, he ruined a lot of plastic parts for guns. He turned his mistake into profit by marketing it as "Super Glue."

59 THE THREE-POINT SEAT BELTS USED IN CARS TODAY WERE INVENTED IN 1959. THEY SAVE ROUGHLY 400,000 LIVES A YEAR.

60 Post-It notes were invented in 1980 when an adhesive was discovered that was sticky but not permanent like glue. Now the notes are one of the top five office products sold.

61 Before a way to manufacture aluminum cheaply was found, the stuff of soda cans was once considered a precious metal and used for fine jewelry.

62 No more getting to school late because of ice on the windshield: A newly invented special box connects to the car's battery and heats up washer fluid before it hits the frosty glass, instantly melting snow and ice.

63 While wearing a cap with sensors that monitor brain activity, a man was able to send a computer a 23-character tweet just by thinking.

64 One of the first escalators was used as a ride at Coney Island in New York, U.S.A., in 1896. It took riders up seven feet (2.1 m) and about 75,000 people rode it!

65 The inventor of the first portable electric vacuum was a janitor. He made the vacuum from a fan motor, a soap box, and a broomstick handle.

66 The revolving door was invented for skyscrapers. The tall buildings created a pressure difference between the column of warm air on the inside and the cold air outside, making conventional doors hard to open.

67 To get an ice arena's surface smooth, it used to take a team of sweepers an hour and a half. The first Zamboni, unveiled at the 1960 Winter Olympics, took just 15 minutes.

68 Before 1855, locks were easily picked. Then came the "Yale Magic Infallible Bank Lock"—a design still used in banks—which allowed owners to change the combination.

69 AstroTurf, invented in 1967 and used in indoor sports stadiums, was first named Chemgrass.

70 The man who invented the Dyson vacuum recently invented a bladeless fan. A stream of uninterrupted cool air runs through a circle and blasts into the room.

71 When a plumber visited a school in 1906, he noticed kids shared a cup to drink water, which he knew spread germs. Within five years he patented the first water fountain.

72 Levi Strauss opened his San Francisco, California, U.S.A., shop in 1853 selling goods to gold miners. He and his partner took denim and added rivets to make the jeans sturdy. Levi's are still among the most popular jean brands today.

73 Gelatin was discovered in the 17th century by boiling animal bones, but it wasn't considered the fun treat that we call Jell-O until 1902. Today's gelatin—which is still processed the same way—is Utah, U.S.A.'s official state snack.

74 Lipstick has been worn for thousands of years, but it wasn't until 1915 that it came in a tube.

75 SKATEBOARDS WERE INVENTED BY SURFERS IN THE 1950S AS A WAY TO PRACTICE ON LAND IN BAD WEATHER OR WHEN WAVES WERE ROUGH. SURFERS NAILED ROLLER-SKATE WHEELS TO PIECES OF WOOD.

1 Preserved by chemicals or their natural environment, the bodies of **MUMMIES DON'T DECAY.**

2 So-called **BOG MUMMIES** are preserved in cold peat bogs in northern Europe. They look exactly like they did when they died—they even have hair.

3 A mummy from A.D. 450 that was discovered in a **PERU PYRAMID** had images of spiders and snakes and imaginary creatures **TATTOOED** on her body.

4 **HUNGRY?** Albert's, a novelty candy company, makes **GUMMY MUMMY** candy coffins.

5 In 1800s London, people attended shows during which performers **UNWRAPPED REAL EGYPTIAN MUMMIES** on stage.

7 Just as doctors can use machines to **LOOK INSIDE YOUR BODY,** they also use them to peer inside mummies.

8 A **TWO-YEAR-OLD GIRL** who died in 1920 is so perfectly preserved scientists have dubbed her **"SLEEPING BEAUTY."**

9 The 2,500-year-old **SIBERIAN ICE MAIDEN** mummy was found frozen in ice; her eyeballs had been replaced by tufts of fur.

10 **TUTANKHAMEN,** or "King Tut," died when he was only **19 YEARS OLD,** but he had already been pharaoh for ten years.

11 The 2,400-year-old **"TOLLAND MAN"** found in Denmark was thought to be a criminal who was hanged and then thrown into a peat bog.

12 A mummy known as the **"BEAUTY OF KRORÄN"** found in China's Tarim Basin had a **FOOT OF HAIR** rolled up in an elaborate headdress.

13 Egyptians mummified **HIPPOPOTAMUSES,** apes, dogs, and cats.

14 The mummy of **EUNG TAE,** who died from an illness in 1586, was found in 1998 by construction workers on the job in South Korea.

15 The word "mummy" comes from the Arabic word for a **BLACK, GOOEY SUBSTANCE** that people believed was used to prepare Egyptian mummies.

17 More than one hundred **CHILDREN** of the Chinchorro people of northern Chile died from accidental **ARSENIC POISONING** and were then mummified.

18 Mummies found above the Arctic Circle were **FROZEN IN TIME** by an ice slide.

19 King Tut's tomb was discovered by Howard Carter in 1922, but there is evidence that **ROBBERS** had gotten there first.

20 Puruchuco, a site near Lima, Peru, contained more than **2,200 MUMMIES.**

35 FACTS ABOUT

22 Egyptian mummies are often found with a **RISING SUN AMULET,** which symbolized **ETERNAL LIFE.**

23 An Egyptian mummy was buried in a **SARCOPHAGUS,** or stone coffin, that sometimes was shaped like a human body and decorated to look like the dead person.

24 In Papua New Guinea, the Anga tribe mummified their **VILLAGE CHIEF** when he died in 1950; he was then **SUSPENDED FROM A CLIFF WALL** for decades.

25 Mummies aren't just from long ago; the Soviet leader **VLADIMIR LENIN** was mummified in 1924.

26 Scientists can tell that the **ICEMAN MUMMY** died when someone shot him from behind with an **ARROW.**

29 Ancient Egyptians buried their **PHARAOHS** with many of their belongings to ensure a **HAPPY AFTERLIFE.**

30 Some people believe that King Tut cursed the members of the excavation team that unearthed him, but no evidence exists of the so-called **CURSE OF THE MUMMY.**

31 One Egyptian mummy was found with his **TONGUE STICKING OUT.**

32 Mummies have been found on every continent **EXCEPT ANTARCTICA.**

33 Archaeologists think that the **INCA ICE MAIDEN** was sacrificed high up in the Andes Mountains some 500 years ago as a gift to the gods her people believed in.

6

In 2007, a reindeer herder found a **BABY WOOLY MAMMOTH MUMMY** in the Russian Arctic. Some 40,000 years old, she was preserved by the mud that suffocated her.

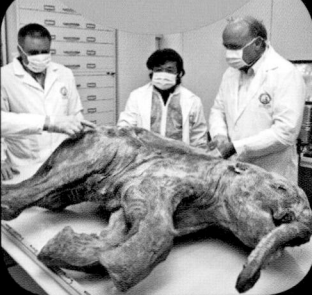

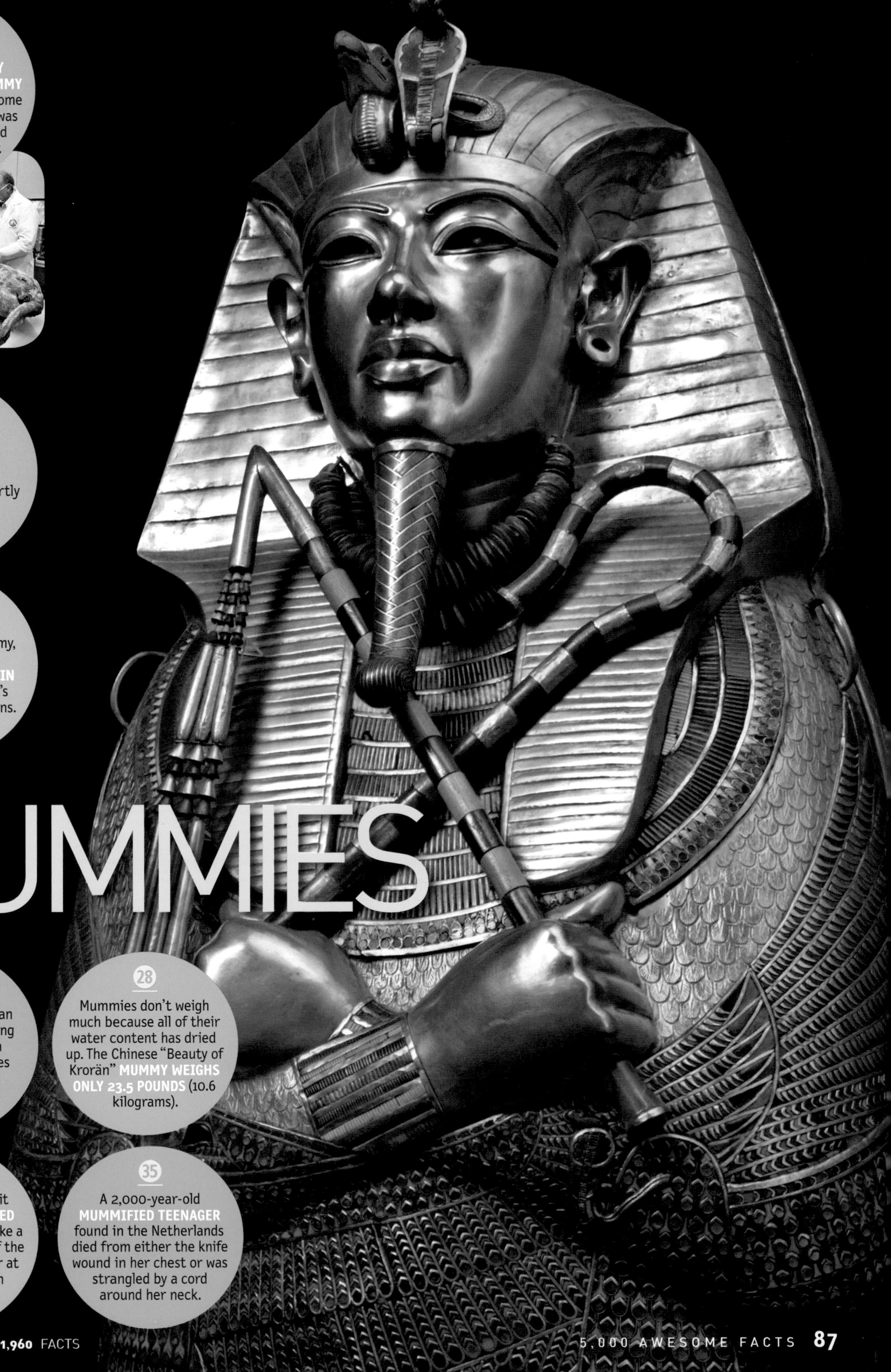

16

The 5,300-year-old **ICEMAN MUMMY** ate a hearty meal shortly before he died.

21

When making a mummy, ancient Egyptians **THREW OUT THE BRAIN** but kept the person's heart and other organs.

MUMMIES

27

GLOBAL WARMING can lead to mummies being **DISCOVERED,** when they defrost in places such as the Andes or Siberia.

28

Mummies don't weigh much because all of their water content has dried up. The Chinese "Beauty of Krorän" **MUMMY WEIGHS ONLY 23.5 POUNDS** (10.6 kilograms).

34

Want to know what it feels like to be **CHASED BY MUMMIES?** Just take a ride on the Revenge of the Mummy roller coaster at Universal Studios in Florida, U.S.A., to find out!

35

A 2,000-year-old **MUMMIFIED TEENAGER** found in the Netherlands died from either the knife wound in her chest or was strangled by a cord around her neck.

YOU HAVE LEARNED **1,960** FACTS

1. Skin cells live 14 to 28 days; red blood cells live 120 days. **2.** Humans share 99.9 percent of their genes with each other. **3.** Humans and chimps share 98.8 percent of their genes; humans and fruit flies share only 60 percent of their genes. **4.** Your body releases about two cups (400–500 mL) of sweat a day. **5.** Identical twins are always the same gender. **6.** Every minute, your body sheds 30,000 to 40,000 dead skin cells. **7.** Skin is the thinnest on your eyelids, the thickest on your palms and heels. **8.** Eighty-five percent of kids have acne. **9.** When exposed to direct sunlight, the body makes vitamin D, which boosts bone health and the immune system. **10.** Your sweat contains many of the same substances as your pee. **11.** Fingerprints never change and no two are alike. **12.** Five million hairs grow on the body, but the scalp contains only about 100,000. **13.** The hair on your head grows about 0.01 inches (0.35 mm) a day. **14.** Hair on the top of your head grows faster than hair sprouting from the side of your head. **15.** It takes 6 months to grow a fingernail, 18 months to grow a toenail. **16.** Children's nails grow fastest during the summer. **17.** More than 400 joints connect the 206 bones in a human skeleton. **18.** The average adult skeleton weighs 20 pounds (9 kg). **19.** The thighbone is the longest bone in the body, measuring about 18 inches (46 cm) in an adult. **20.** The shortest bone in the body is in the ear and is only 0.1 inches (2.6 mm) long. **21.** Every day, your body produces more than 100 billion new blood cells. **22.** There are 14 bones in the face. **23.** Teeth are not made of bone, but rather of hard substances called enamel, dentin, and cementum, and a soft tissue called pulp. **24.** Each hand has 27 bones; each foot has 26. **25.** Babies have more bones than adults; as people grow, some of their smaller bones fuse together. **26.** Almost everyone is born with flat feet (having no arches in their feet). **27.** The word "muscle" comes from the Latin word "musculus," which means "little mouse." The Romans thought a flexing muscle looked like a rodent moving beneath the skin. **28.** Of

100BODYFACTS

the body's 650 muscles, the gluteus maximus (or butt muscle) is the largest. **29.** The body uses 12 leg muscles to walk. **30.** It takes 12 muscles to smile, 11 to frown. **31.** All of an adult's blood vessels laid end-to-end could circle Earth two and a half times. **32.** Blood travels 12,000 miles (19,000 km) in one day. **33.** The heart pumps blood through its largest artery at about one mile per hour (1.6 kph). In tiny vessels, blood moves only 43 inches an hour (109 cm per hour). **34.** A soft tissue called marrow inside bones produces most new blood cells. **35.** Blood itself is about 100.4°F (38°C)—a little hotter than the average body temperature. **36.** Blood is always red, but its shade varies by location in the body. **37.** Being afraid and angry increases your heart rate by 30 to 40 beats per minute. **38.** Squeezing a tennis ball with your hand gives you a good idea of how hard the heart works to pump blood. **39.** The human heart weighs half a pound (0.2 kg) in women, slightly more in men. **40.** The smallest blood vessels in the body are much tinier than a human hair, and just big enough that red blood cells can pass through single file. **41.** A Brazilian man set a world record by holding his breath underwater for 20 minutes and 21 seconds. **42.** The amount of air that passes through the lungs each day could fit into 2,600 gallon (10,000 L) milk jugs. **43.** The word "lung" comes from a Germanic word meaning "light"; together your two lungs weigh only 2.5 pounds (1.1 kg). **44.** Myth Busted! Your heart does not stop when you sneeze. **45.** It's very difficult to keep your eyes open during a sneeze. **46.** Ten to 15 minutes of laughing burns about 50 calories. **47.** Americans eat about 100,000 pounds (45,359 kg) of food in a lifetime. **48.** Each day, your mouth makes about 1 to 1.5 quarts (0.9 to 1.4 L) of saliva. **49.** A stomach can expand from two ounces (59 mL) to one gallon (3.8 L). **50. It takes food about three to five hours to make its way through the ten-foot (3-m)-long small intestine. 51.** The liver weighs about three pounds (1.3 kg) and is the largest gland in the body. **52.** The average adult produces 48 gallons (181.7 L) of gas in a year. **53. Goose bumps are caused by the contraction of muscles at the base of body hairs. 54.** Your stomach growls both when it's hungry and when it's digesting food. **55.** About 50 to 100 hairs fall out of your head every day. **56. When walking, a person's foot hits the ground with a force about three times their body weight. 57.** The lower jawbone is the skull's only movable bone. **58.** Another name for the thumb is the pollux. **59. A cough can expel material at speeds of up to 100 miles per hour (161 kph). 60.** The left lung is about 10 percent smaller than the right because it has a notch where it curves around the heart. **61.** Lungs are pale pink at birth but over time darken to gray or black as they collect carbon. **62. It is physically impossible to hold your breath until you die; your brain forces your body to take a breath. 63.** Scientists working on the Bellybutton Biodiversity Project have found more than 1,400 different types of bacteria living in people's belly buttons. **64.** The human body requires two to three quarts (1.9–2.8 L) of water a day. **65. Stomach acid is strong enough to dissolve metal nails. 66.** Red blood cells are flattened in the center because they lack a nucleus, which all other cells have. **67.** Stretched flat, the lungs' alveoli—tiny air sacs—would cover 861 square feet (80 sq m). **68. The human body loses about 11 ounces (0.3 L) of water every day through breathing. 69.** Breathing in lasts about two seconds; breathing out about three. **70.** The human heart at rest beats about 70 to 80 times a minute; a blue whale's only beats 6 times per minute. **71. Adults usually have 32 teeth, although the record is 35. 72.** An adult body has 50–100 trillion cells. **73.** The nerve cells that run from the spine to the toe are more than three feet (0.9 m) long. **74.** Every minute of every day, the kidneys purify about one quart (0.9 l) of blood. **75. It takes a meal 15 hours to 2 days to completely pass through you. 76.** Tiny, fingerlike folds called villi on the small intestine increase its size more than eight times. **77.** Heterochromia, or having different-colored eyes, is rare in humans but common in dogs. **78. The human brain can detect more than 10,000 different smells. 79.** Your brain is only 2 percent of your total body weight, but it uses 20–25 percent of your body's energy. **80.** The spinal cord is only about 1.4 feet (44 cm) long, but it contains 1 billion nerve cells. **81. The human tongue**

THAT WILL RATTLE YOUR BONES

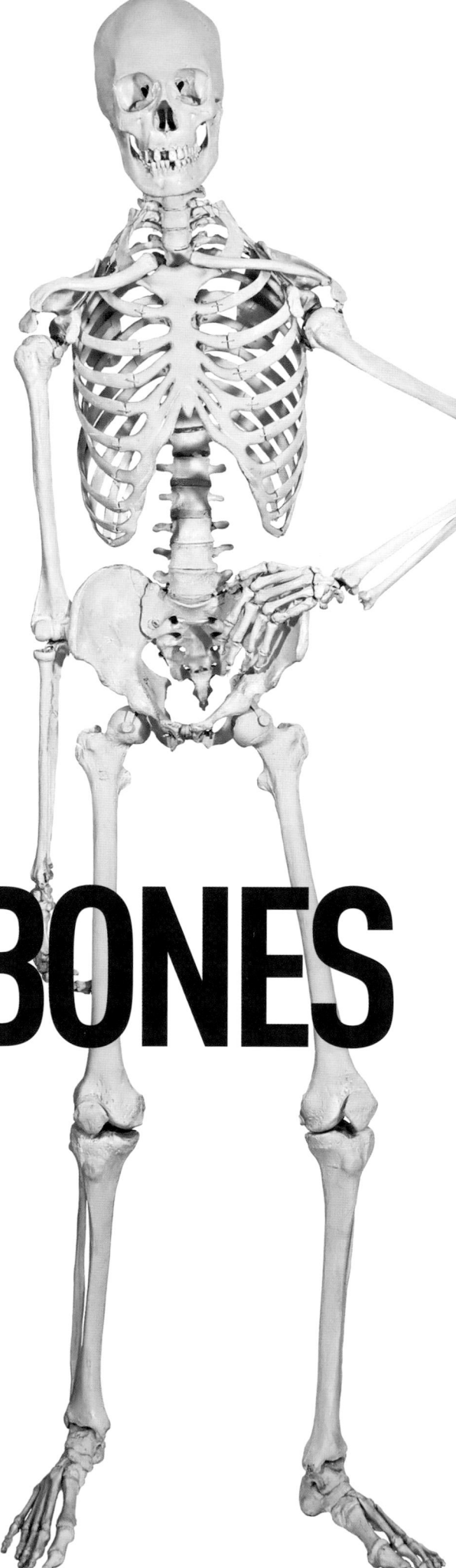

has about 9,000 taste buds. **82** The ancient Greek physician Hippocrates recommended that people use a ball of wool moistened with honey to brush their teeth. **83.** Food must be dissolved in water to have taste; this is one of the reasons why your mouth produces spit. **84. There are ten times more bacteria cells in your body than human cells. 85.** If you were to hold a nickel and a penny in your hand, together they would weigh about the same as your eyeball, 7.5 grams. **86.** The average time between blinks is 2.8 seconds. **87. Human skin weighs nine pounds (4.1 kg). 88.** If you could take off all your skin and spread it out on the floor, it would cover 20.8 square feet (1.9 sq m). **89.** In shorter, heavier people, the stomach tends to lie horizontally; in taller, thinner people, the stomach more often lies vertically. **90. Alien hand syndrome is a condition that causes a person to lose control of their hands' movements. 91.** The world's longest fingernails are a total of 19 feet, 9 inches (6 m)—about as long as a killer whale. **92.** The longest tongue ever measured sticks out 3.86 inches (9.8 cm) from the record-holder's mouth. **93. The longest nose on a living person is 3.46 inches (8.8 cm) from bridge to tip. 94.** The proud owner of the world's longest ear hair has hair more than half a foot long sprouting from the middle of his ear. **95.** The world's strongest tongue can lift a 27-pound (12.5 kg) weight. **96. The woman with the world's longest hair—18.5 feet (5.6 m)—hasn't had a haircut since 1973. 97.** It's impossible to tickle yourself. **98.** Hair and nails do not continue to grow after death; that's just a creepy myth. **99. Eating too many carrots will turn your skin orange. 100.** Just like fingerprints, no two tongue prints are alike.

1
MEERKATS, which live in dry places, get moisture from the roots and fruits they eat.

2
WARTHOGS dash from their burrows at top speed to escape any PREDATORS waiting outside.

3
KOALAS are excellent climbers, thanks to TWO THUMBS ON EACH FRONT PAW.

4
KINGFISHER NESTS, dug into the sides of hills and cliffs, OFTEN SLOPE UPWARD to avoid flooding.

5
WOMBAT POUCHES open toward the MARSUPIAL'S REAR instead of toward its head to keep dirt out while digging.

6
The BELLY FUR ON A SLOTH—an animal which spends most of its life up-side down—parts toward the back so water runs off and away from the head during a rainstorm.

7
SPINY HEDGEHOGS roll into a ball to protect their SOFT BELLIES from predators.

8
TRAP-JAW ANTS can fling themselves into the air and away from preda-tors by snapping their jaws shut at 145 MILES PER HOUR (233 kph).

9
Camels' two rows of EXTRA-LONG EYE-LASHES help keep sand out of their eyes.

10
The VEILED CHAMELEON looks like it's wearing a birthday hat, but the structure actually collects and channels water into the lizard's open mouth.

11
OWLS' FRINGED FEATHERS allow the birds to fly—and at-tack—QUIETLY.

12
CAMELS can drink up to 32 GALLONS (145 L) of water at a time.

13
A Saudi Arabian sand gazelle can SHRINK ITS LIVER to a third its usual size to CONSERVE WATER.

14
SAND GROUSES soak their chest feathers in water to bring back to babies in the nest. Chicks suck the water up from the feathers LIKE A SPONGE.

15
Some birds fish from the backs of FLOATING HIPPOS.

16
OWLS have an excellent range of motion for their heads because their EYES ARE TOO BIG to move from side to side or up and down.

17
THOMSON'S GAZELLES follow WILDEBEEST AND ZEBRAS, since the larger animals eat tougher grasses but leave behind the tender grasses that gazelles like.

50 AMAZING ANIMAL ADAPTATIONS

18
NAKED MOLE RATS have no hair: They don't need it to keep warm or as protection from the sun because they spend their lives underground in warm deserts.

19
Most vultures have FEATHERLESS HEADS so that eating dead animals is LESS MESSY.

20
A SCORPION CAN'T STING ITSELF: It's immune to its own venom.

21
The honey-loving HONEY BADGER HAS A STENCH that causes bees to flee their hive and thick skin that withstands their stings.

22
ZEBRA'S STRIPES make it difficult for predators to PICK OUT ONE animal from the herd to attack.

23
To avoid getting sunburned, RHINOS WALLOW IN THE MUD.

24
GIANT ANTEATERS use their long snouts as SNORKELS WHILE SWIMMING.

25
Having its eyes, ears, and nostrils along the TOP OF ITS HEAD allows the HIPPO to stay mostly underwater, where it's cooler, for long periods of time.

26
CHEETAHS' LARGE NOSES let in more air after a sprint.

27
A lion's THICK MANE PROTECTS ITS NECK during fights with other cats.

28
A TOUCAN'S LARGE BILL lets it grab food at the end of branches too tiny to support the bird's weight.

29
ARCTIC MUSK OXEN'S short legs and tail MINIMIZE HEAT LOSS.

30
Downy feathers on a PTARMIGAN'S FEET keep the BIRD'S TOES TOASTY in chilly temperatures.

31
Arctic birds keep warm by STANDING ON ONE LEG and TUCKING THEIR HEAD UNDER A WING.

32
FLAPS BETWEEN THE TOES OF DESERT GECKOES keep the animals from sinking into the sand.

33
AGOUTIS, rain forest rodents, FOLLOW MONKEYS AND PARROTS moving through the treetops to score food accidentally dropped to the ground.

34
South American thorn bugs' spiky shape both DISGUISES THEM and makes them HARD TO SWALLOW.

35
When PEANUT BUGS feel threatened, they spread wings with GIANT, EYE-LIKE SPOTS to make themselves look bigger.

36
ROCK-HOPPING HYRAXES, which resemble short-eared rabbits, have small feet with SOLES LIKE SUCTION CUPS.

37
LEMMINGS' FRONT CLAWS GROW LARGER in the winter to help them tunnel through snow.

38
The JACANA CAN STAND AND WALK ON FLOATING LEAVES thanks to the bird's long, widely spaced toes.

39
HIPPOS DON'T SWEAT but instead SECRETE A RED FLUID from their skin that keeps the animals moist and shields them from the sun's rays.

40
Water spiders USE SILK TO MAKE A BUBBLE that serves as a dry underwater nursery.

41
Many deep-sea fish CREATE THEIR OWN LIGHT to attract prey.

42
Some deep-sea creatures have CLEAR BODIES that make them nearly INVISIBLE TO PREDATORS.

43
The LUMPFISH uses a SUCKER ON ITS BELLY to stick to sea rocks in strong currents.

44
The sensitive WHISKERS around a sea otter's mouth help it TO DETECT FISH.

45
In the mountains, MANY INSECTS ARE WINGLESS to avoid being blown away by strong winds.

46
A TIGER'S STRIPES CAMOUFLAGE IT in the tall grass it hunts in.

47
A WOODPECKER'S SKULL IS EXTRA THICK to absorb the shock from all that banging.

48
MANATEES ARE VERY GASSY, which makes the mammals float, but heavy bones help them stay underwater.

49
ZEBRAS' LONG, TWISTY EARS let the animals detect where a sound is coming from without looking around.

50
WHEN THREATENED, TAMANDUAS, anteater relatives, free their front claws for fighting by PROPPING THEMSELVES UP ON THEIR TAIL.

1 Each year Americans buy **48 MILLION** pounds (21.8 million kg) of chocolate for **VALENTINE'S DAY.** That's the same weight as **128 BLUE WHALES!**

2 **WHITE CHOCOLATE IS TECHNICALLY NOT CHOCOLATE.** THE PALER TREAT IS MADE WITH ONLY COCOA BUTTER— NOT COCOA POWDER, AS REAL CHOCOLATE BARS ARE.

3 HERSHEY, PENNSYLVANIA, U.S.A., smells like chocolate. Why? The Hershey's chocolate factory there produces (among other things) more than 20 MILLION HERSHEY'S KISSES A DAY.

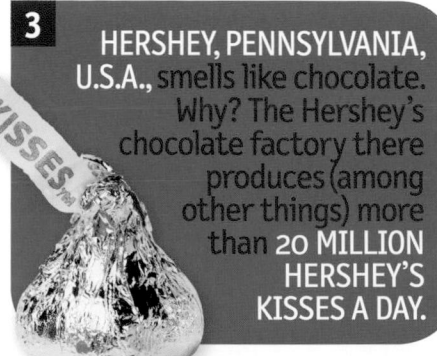

4 CHOCOLATE-COVERED **BACON** IS A POPULAR TREAT AT MANY U.S. STATE FAIRS.

5 CHOCOLATE IS MADE FROM THE SEEDS OF THE CACAO PLANT, WHICH GROWS ONLY IN AREAS NEAR THE EQUATOR.

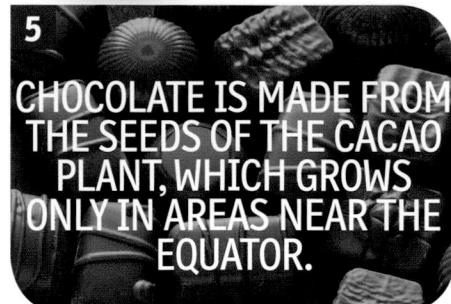

25 COOL THINGS ABOUT

6 U.S. SOLDIERS SERVING IN WORLD WAR II (1941–45) WERE THE FIRST TO EAT M&M'S. THE CANDY COATING ALLOWED TROOPS TO CARRY THE HIGH-ENERGY TREAT WITHOUT IT MELTING.

7 Ever feel like you'd RATHER EAT CHOCOLATE THAN DINNER? You're not alone: An early advertisement for the candy claimed it was more filling than meat.

8 A MINIATURE STATUE OF LIBERTY WAS BUILT OUT OF **229** POUNDS (104 KG) OF CHOCOLATE.

9 THE SCIENTIFIC NAME FOR CHOCOLATE, *THEOBROMA CACAO,* MEANS "FOOD OF THE GODS."

10 THERE ARE 30 TO 50 SEEDS IN EACH FOOTBALL-SHAPED CACAO POD—THAT'S ENOUGH TO MAKE SEVEN BARS OF MILK CHOCOLATE.

MMM... CHOCOLATY HISTORY

21  AS EARLY AS 1000 B.C. The ancient Olmec (famous for their gigantic head statues, left) of what is now Mexico and Central America are believed to be the first people to use the cacao plant.

22  1300 The Aztec mixed cacao seeds with chilies to make a frothy, spicy drink.

11 THE AVERAGE AMERICAN EATS ABOUT **12 POUNDS** (5.4 KG) OF CHOCOLATE A YEAR.

12 A SWISS COMPANY INVENTED A CHOCOLATE THAT WON'T MELT UNTIL TEMPERATURES REACH 131°F (55°C).

13 The ancient Aztec of what is now Mexico and Central America believed chocolate had magical properties; royalty drank a spicy, bitter mixture from golden goblets.

14 THE NEXT TIME YOU HAVE A COLD, ask for a piece of chocolate. A natural chemical in the treat helps suppress coughs.

CHOCOLATE

15 People in the United Kingdom eat 1,000 chocolate bars for every one bar eaten in China.

16 RUMOR HAS IT THAT AZTEC EMPEROR MOCTEZUMA II DRANK MORE THAN A GALLON (3.8 L) OF CHOCOLATE A DAY.

17 CHOCOLATE-COVERED **ANTS** ARE A TREAT IN **MEXICO.**

18 JUST ONE WHIFF OF CHOCOLATE CAN MAKE PEOPLE FEEL HAPPY. A CHEMICAL IN CACAO RELEASES FEEL-GOOD VIBES IN THE BRAIN.

19 Maria Theresa, Queen of France from 1660 to 1683, appointed a royal hot chocolate maker to her court.

20 IT WOULD TAKE 15,133,852,800 HERSHEY BAR SQUARES LAID END-TO-END TO REACH THE MOON.

23 1528 Explorer Hernán Cortés brought the Aztec drink back to Spain.

24 MID-1500s French and Spanish nobles sweetened the bitter beverage with cinnamon and cane sugar.

25 1847 Joseph Fry & Sons of England cooked up the first chocolate bar.

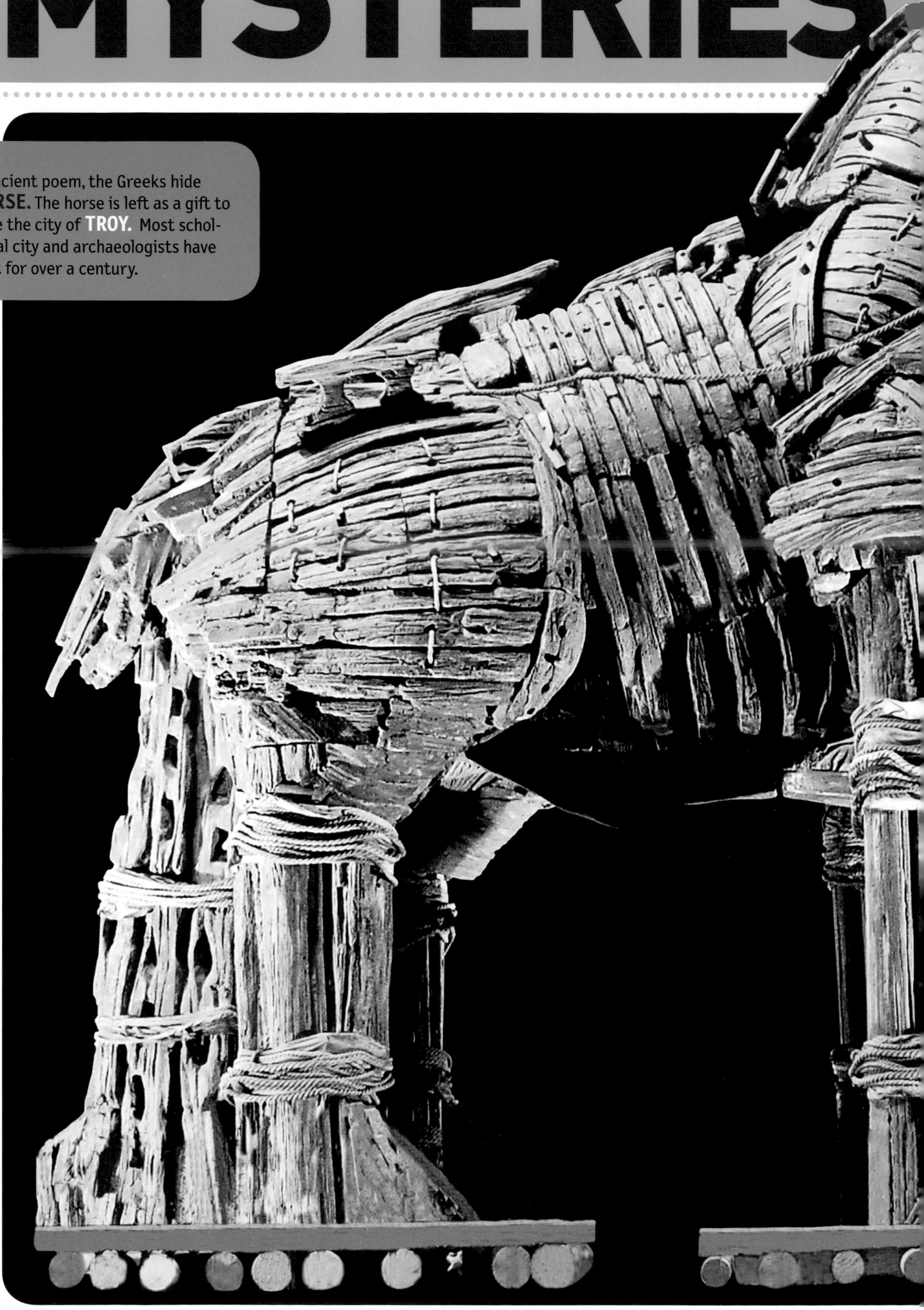

❶ In *The Iliad*, an ancient poem, the Greeks hide inside a **GIANT HORSE.** The horse is left as a gift to get the Greeks inside the city of **TROY.** Most scholars agree it was a real city and archaeologists have been searching for it for over a century.

❷ The **RONGORONGO HIEROGLYPHS** were found on pieces of wood on Easter Island, but no one has been able to read them. Every other line is inscribed upside down.

❸ In 1937, **AMELIA EARHART** attempted to be the first woman to fly around the world. After radioing that she was running low on fuel in the South Pacific, she, her navigator, and her plane were never heard from again.

❹ Evidence found on a small island in the South Pacific indicates Amelia Earhart was possibly a **CASTAWAY** after her plane crashed.

OF HISTORY

5 When supply ships arrived at the first **ENGLISH COLONY** in North America on Roanoke Island, the colonists had vanished. All the crew found was the word **"CROATAN"** carved on a tree.

9 Ancient people etched giant shapes and animals in the Peruvian desert. Called **NASCA LINES,** researchers think they could have been **OFFERINGS TO GODS** to bring rain.

10 Some people think Peru's Nasca Lines were designed to be seen from primitive hot air balloons. Another theory: They were landing strips for **ALIEN SPACECRAFT.**

6 Around 360 B.C., Greek philosopher **PLATO** wrote about the **LOST CITY OF ATLANTIS**—a civilization made of half-god, half-human peoples that existed thousands of years before him. While people have searched for the metropolis, most scientists don't think it was real.

11 The largest stones at England's **STONEHENGE**—each weighing as much as a small pickup truck—were transported 250 miles (400 km) to the site. No one is sure how its builders managed to move them there.

7 No one knows what happened to the **EASTER ISLANDERS** who built the famous 13-foot (4-m) -tall stone statues called **MOAI.** Changes in their environment— or being overrun with rodents— may have caused them to leave.

12 Experts debate why **STONEHENGE** was built. Leading theories: **AN ASTRONOMICAL CALENDAR;** a place of sun worship; a place for healing; or a combination of uses.

13 As tall as a six-story building, the human-headed lion **SPHINX** in Egypt is one of the **LARGEST STATUES** in the world, but what does it mean? New findings show that the Sphinx and the pyramids align with the sun at key times throughout the day.

14 Some experts say the huge limestone blocks that make up the **EGYPTIAN PYRAMIDS** were likely floated down the Nile on **RAFTS** from quarries and **PUSHED** up ramps and into position.

8 In 1911, an American explorer in Peru was guided to **MACHU PICCHU**—a "lost" city on a high mountain ridge. The Inca had abandoned the city centuries before. No one is sure why.

15 The Egyptian pyramids' positioning is so **PRECISE** that some people have wondered if, rather than tombs, the pyramids were built as **GIANT ASTRONOMICAL OBSERVATORIES.**

1 Established in 1872, Yellowstone was the world's first national park.

2 Yellowstone National Park is in three U.S. states—96 percent in Wyoming, 3 percent in Montana, and 1 percent in Idaho.

3 Death Valley National Park, in California and Nevada, is the hottest place in the U.S. Temperatures have soared to 134°F (56.7°C).

4 The tallest tree on Earth, the coast redwood, only grows in Oregon and California, U.S.A., including in Redwood National Park. The tallest coast redwood is 379 feet (115 m).

5 The deepest lake in the U.S. fills the crater of a volcano at Crater Lake National Park in Oregon. It's 1,943 feet (593 m) deep.

6 The tallest dunes in North America—found at Great Sand Dunes National Park in Colorado, U.S.A.—are 75 stories tall.

7 A BRISTLECONE PINE TREE IN GREAT BASIN NATIONAL PARK IN NEVADA, U.S.A., LIVED NEARLY 5,000 YEARS BEFORE IT WAS CUT DOWN.

8 After being nearly extinct in the lower 48 states, wolves were reintroduced to Yellowstone National Park in 1995 by biologists. Now almost 100 live there.

9 Galápagos National Park, 600 miles (965 km) off the coast of Ecuador, protects the native species—like tortoises, iguanas, and sea lions—but it's also where Charles Darwin studied how species evolve.

10 Sagarmatha National Park in Nepal protects Mount Everest. At 29,035 feet (8,850 m), Everest is the tallest mountain in the world.

11 Rocks mysteriously move on their own, probably from slick silt underneath them and wind, at a place called the Racetrack in Death Valley National Park.

12 More than three million people visit Great Smoky Mountains National Park in Tennessee and North Carolina every year—more than any other U.S. national park.

13 You can take an elevator down 750 feet (229 m) into a cave at Carlsbad Caverns National Park in New Mexico, U.S.A.

14 Yellowstone is home to 67 species of mammals—including grizzly bears, moose, mountain lions, bighorn sheep, and buffalo.

15 Bryce Canyon National Park in Utah, U.S.A., is filled with hoodoos—limestone spires created by weather and erosion.

16 Death Valley's Badwater Basin is 282 feet (86 m) below sea level—the lowest point in the U.S. It is only 90 miles (145 km) from Mount Whitney, the tallest peak in the lower 48 states.

17 Alaska's Wrangall-St. Elias is the largest national park in the U.S. and is known for its 150 glaciers. It is twice as big as Yellowstone, Grand Canyon, and Death Valley combined.

18 63 million people visit the U.S.'s 58 national parks every year.

19 Mammoth Cave National Park in Kentucky, U.S.A., is home to the largest cave system in the world. More than 390 miles (563 km) of cave passages have been mapped.

20 Dinosaurs once roamed in what is today Badlands National Park in South Dakota, U.S.A. Paleontologists have found 75-million-year-old fossils.

21 Wolves migrated to Michigan, U.S.A.'s Isle Royale National Park by walking 14 miles (22 km) across frozen Lake Superior.

22 There are over 500 islands in Minnesota, U.S.A.'s Voyageurs National Park.

23 THE GRAND CANYON IS 18 MILES (29 KM) WIDE AND A MILE (1.6 KM) DEEP.

24 Yosemite National Park in California, U.S.A., is as big as Rhode Island, U.S.A.

25 About 600 humpback whales visit the areas around Glacier Bay National Park in Alaska, U.S.A., every year.

26 The road to the summit of the volcano in Hawaii, U.S.A.'s Haleakala National Park is 38 miles (61 km) long and travels from the seafloor to 10,000 feet (3,048 m). It is one of the world's steepest roads.

27 More than 2,000 Alaskan brown bears live in Katmai National Park in Alaska and can be spotted fishing for salmon in the park's rivers.

28 A safari in South Africa's Kruger National Park takes you to see the park's "big five"— buffalo, lion, elephant, rhino, and leopard.

29 A 23-YEAR-OLD MAN CLIMBED THE 2,130-FOOT (649-M) GRANITE FACE OF HALF DOME IN YOSEMITE NATIONAL PARK WITHOUT ROPES OR ANY OTHER SAFETY GEAR. IT TOOK HIM 2 HOURS AND 45 MINUTES.

30 Yellowstone's Old Faithful Inn is one of the oldest log hotels in the world.

31 Yosemite Falls, which is 2,425 feet (739 m) high, is the highest waterfall in North America. It is fed by snow melt.

32 Before he was a U.S. President, Gerald Ford worked as a park ranger in Yellowstone National Park.

33 Mount McKinley, in Alaska's Denali National Park, has some of the coldest temperatures in the U.S. The windchill can reach -118°F (-83°C).

34 113,000 National Parks and similarly protected areas cover approximately 6 percent of the land surface of Earth.

35 Established in 1885, Banff National Park was Canada's first national park and the third established in the world. It is home to over 1,000 glaciers.

36 The General Sherman Tree in California's Sequoia National Park is the largest living thing on Earth. It weighs approximately 2.7 million pounds (1.2 million kg) and is 2,100 years old—and it's still growing!

37 The 287.4-foot (87.6-m) -long Kolob Arch in Zion National Park in Utah, U.S.A., is one of the world's largest freestanding natural arches.

38 There are more than 2,000 arches in Utah, U.S.A.'s Arches National Park. To make the list, an arch must measure at least three feet (.9 m) across. The largest, Landscape Arch, is longer than a soccer field.

39 U.S.A.'s Everglades National Park is the only place in the world where alligators and crocodiles coexist.

40 Water that originates in Montana, U.S.A.'s Glacier National Park eventually winds up in the Pacific Ocean, the Gulf of Mexico, and the Hudson Bay.

41 Grand Canyon National Park has some of the cleanest air in the U.S. You can see 90 to 110 miles (145 to 177 km) in any direction.

42 The world's largest national park is North and East Greenland National Park at 603, 973 square miles (972,000 sq km).

43 Yosemite's El Capitan, the largest exposed granite rock in the world, is 350 stories high.

44 Letterboxing began in England's Dartmoor National Park in 1854. Map readers use clues to find treasure boxes hidden across the countryside. Inside is a notebook to sign and a stamp to say you've been there.

45 The Petit Train d'Artouste, the little railway in France's Pyrénées National Park, takes tourists up 6,562 feet (2,000 m) for mountain views. It is Europe's steepest railway.

46 Free rock climbing (without the aid of any equipment) is said to have started in Saxon Switzerland National Park in the 19th century.

47 Greece's Olympus National Park is named after the country's highest mountain and legendary home of the gods.

48 Ireland's Killarney National Park is home to the country's tallest mountain range, the MacGillycuddy's Reeks. Their highest point is 3,414 feet (1,041 m).

49 ITALY'S ETNA NATIONAL PARK HOLDS ONE OF THE MOST ACTIVE VOLCANOES ON EARTH. MOUNT ETNA HAS BEEN IN A STATE OF NEAR-CONTINUOUS ERUPTION FOR HALF A MILLION YEARS!

50 Hundreds of animal species— including elephants, gazelles, rhinos, lions, cheetahs, leopards, wildebeest, and zebras—migrate to Kenya's Masai Mara National Reserve to feast in the summer months.

51 You can take a *Lord of the Rings* tour in New Zealand's Fiordland National Park, where the trilogy was filmed.

52 In the Star Wars movie *Return of the Jedi,* some scenes featuring ewoks on planet Endor were filmed in Redwood National Park.

53 Kilimanjaro National Park in Tanzania protects the highest point in Africa, Mount Kilimanjaro, which stands 19,341 feet (5,895 m).

54 BANDHAVGARH NATIONAL PARK IN INDIA IS HOME TO ABOUT 50 WILD TIGERS.

55 India's Kaziranga National Park is home to 2,000 one-horned rhinos that can run 25 miles per hour (40 kph).

56 SKAFTAFELL NATIONAL PARK'S SVARTIFOSS (BLACK FALLS) ARE SURROUNDED BY HEXAGONAL COLUMNS MADE FROM LAVA FLOWS.

57 Most of South Africa's wild lion population lives in and around Kruger National Park.

58 Ruins from Mayan settlements more than 1,000 years old are found at Tikal National Park in Guatemala.

59 Kaieteur Falls in Kaieteur National Park in Guyana are five times higher than Niagara Falls.

60 More than 200 different types of birds fly through Zion National Park in Utah, U.S.A., every year.

61 Bighorn sheep are found in Rocky Mountain National Park in Colorado, U.S.A. You can tell a male from a female by their horns. An adult male's curl whereas an adult female's grow to a straight sharp point.

62 RESEARCHERS FOUND THAT MOOSE IN ROCKY MOUNTAIN NATIONAL PARK ARE PREDICTABLE EATERS. THE SAME MOOSE WILL RETURN TO THE SAME CLUMP OF WILLOWS ON ALMOST THE SAME DAY EVERY WINTER.

63 Serengeti National Park in Tanzania sees the annual migration of hundreds of thousands of wildebeest, zebra, and gazelle. It is considered to have one of the oldest ecosystems.

64 Swiss National Park in Switzerland protects the edelweiss, a flower that grows thousands of feet above sea level and is the subject of a song in *The Sound of Music.*

65 The area in and around Lake District National Park in England was said to have inspired Beatrix Potter, author of *Peter Rabbit.*

66 Manuel Antonio National Park in Costa Rica contains such rain forest animals as sloths, iguanas, and squirrel monkeys.

67 Kakadu National Park in Australia has been inhabited by Aboriginals for more than 50,000 years.

68 Joshua Tree National Park in California, U.S.A., is home to tarantulas with 2–3 inch (5–7.5 cm) -long bodies and four-inch (10-cm) legs.

69 Petrified wood made from fossilized trees at Petrified Forest National Park in Arizona, U.S.A., is almost solid quartz. You can only cut it with a diamond-tipped saw!

70 California, U.S.A.'s Lassen Volcanic National Park has all of the four types of volcanoes found in the entire world—shield, plug dome, cinder cone, and composite.

71 Saguaro National Park in Arizona, U.S.A., has 25 species of cactus, including the pinkflower hedgehog cactus and teddybear cholla cactus.

72 The West Indian manatee in Everglades National Park spends up to eight hours each day grazing on seagrasses.

73 Iguanas in Virgin Islands National Park can fall 40–50 feet (12–15 m) onto a hard surface without injuring themselves.

74 In winter, many roads in Yellowstone National Park are only open to snow coaches and snowmobiles. Snow coaches are vans with tracks instead of wheels.

75 MORE THAN 5,000 BATS PER MINUTE POUR OUT OF CARLSBAD CAVERN AT PEAK HOURS IN THE EVENING.

Arches National Park, Utah, U.S.A.

75 SPECTACULAR FACTS ABOUT NATIONAL PARKS

1 One of the first PEZ CANDY dispensers was shaped like a space gun.

2 The BAZOOKA was named after the MUSICAL INSTRUMENT of the same name.

3 "SMART BOMBS" don't just go until they run into something and explode. They are fitted with special guided equipment that takes aim at a specific target.

4 One fan spent $240,000 on the original LIGHT SABER used in the first two *Star Wars* movies.

5 FLAMETHROWERS launch burning fuel, and have been weapons in war for thousands of years.

6 A BAYONET is a dagger at the end of a rifle or musket and is used for close-combat fighting, especially when the gun is not reloaded.

7 People began using SLINGSHOTS shortly after the invention of rubber in 1839, and they are firmly embedded in the gaming world, where colorful (and angry) birds are flung from them.

8 Aboriginal Australians used BOOMERANGS to hunt small animals like birds and rabbits.

9 In the time it took an early U.S. settler to load a MUSKET, a Native American was capable of firing at least a dozen ARROWS.

10 The VICTORINOX SWISSCHAMP has 33 tools packaged into one pocket knife—including a magnifying lens, toothpick, fish scaler, and wood saw.

11 Japanese SAMURAI fought on horseback with bows and arrows. They only used their SWORDS in hand-to-hand combat when they had used all their arrows.

12 When archaeologists found what is believed to be Blackbeard's *Queen Anne's Revenge*, the cannons were still loaded with bolts, nails, and spikes intended to shred the sails of other ships.

13 Notorious bank robber John Dillinger escaped from a county jail using a FAKE GUN whittled out of WOOD.

14 The RED RYDER BB gun, like the one featured in the movie *A Christmas Story*, is named after a comic strip cowboy.

35 SURE-FIRE FACTS ABOUT WEAPONS

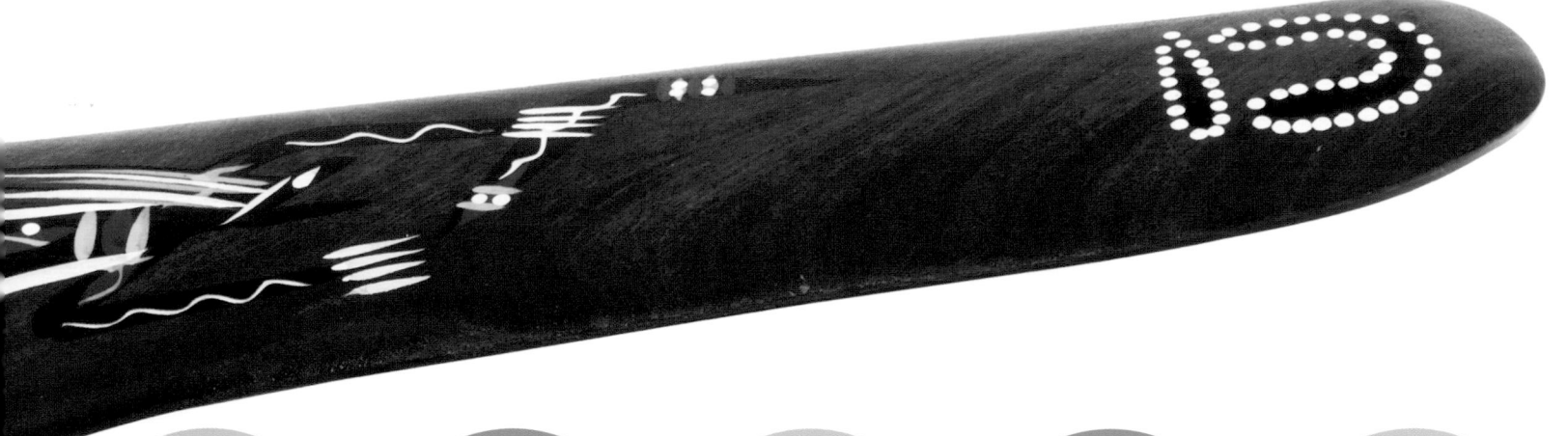

15
A pump-action **MARSHMALLOW SHOOTER** launches mini marshmallows the length of two minivans.

16
ALFRED NOBEL developed **DYNAMITE** with the intention that it be used for construction only. He left his fortune to **REWARD SCIENTISTS** who work for the benefit of humanity.

17
In the Olympic sport of the **BIATHLON,** an athlete with a rifle slung over one shoulder skis and then stops at certain points to shoot at targets.

18
Legends say that **JAPANESE NINJAS,** working as spies or warriors, wore a katana sword on their back and threw stars and darts.

19
FENCERS in tournaments use electric foils that have a button on the end that keeps track of points.

DYNAMITE

20
A 13th-century Scottish warrior once used a **FIVE-AND-A-HALF-FOOT** (1.7 m) **SWORD** to fight the English.

21
A **SPUD GUN** packs a punch. It works under air pressure and can launch a potato at speeds of more than 300 miles per hour (483 kph).

22
TOXIC SECRETIONS from poison dart frogs are put on the tips of **BLOWGUN DARTS** and used to hunt in Central and South America.

23
The U.S. Navy created a "SUPERGUN" that's the size of a bus and shoots bullets that travel at 5,637 miles per hour (9,072 kph)—more than seven times the speed of sound.

24
Gladiators used **SWORDS, SPEARS, DAGGERS, SLINGS,** and **TRIDENTS** when they battled in an arena.

25
A new kind of **TANK** acts like a **CHAMELEON.** It has special panels on it that make it look like a cow or car when viewed through heat-sensitive scopes.

26
GUNPOWDER was first used as fireworks and signals before being used in weapons for war.

27
The **FIRST GUN** was made about 1,000 years ago. It was a piece of bamboo, and gunpowder was used to fire a small spear.

28
Every time a gun is fired it leaves a mark on the bullet. Police try to **MATCH BULLETS WITH WEAPONS** as evidence to who committed a crime.

29
In the 15th century, **GRENADES** were made by pouring gunpowder into a pot and lighting it.

30
The word "DYNAMITE" comes from a Greek word that means "POWER."

31
People long before Robin Hood used **BOWS AND ARROWS.** They've been around for **40,000 YEARS.**

32
In recent wars in Iraq and Afghanistan, **GUN-CARRYING ROBOTS** were used in battle.

33
You can see the pistol **JOHN WILKES BOOTH** used to kill U.S. President Abraham Lincoln at Ford's Theatre in Washington, D.C.

34
A **TORPEDO** with explosive TNT inside could put a hole in a ship the size of a barn door.

35
50 years ago, the U.S. blew up a **HYDROGEN BOMB** in outer space as a weapons test. The sky flashed red and green, and colors could be seen from Hawaii, U.S.A., to New Zealand.

1. Houseflies use their feet to taste things. **2.** Ticks grow from the size of a grain of rice to the size of a marble. **3.** It takes 2,000 silkworm cocoons to produce 1 pound (0.45 kg) of silk. **4.** A bee searching for food may fly up to 60 miles (97 km) in one day. **5.** Ants can lift and carry more than 50 times their own weight. **6.** Mexican jumping beans "jump" because of a caterpillar that lives inside. **7.** One hundred monarch butterflies weigh one ounce (30 g). **8.** Dung beetles were imported to Australia to combat an excess of poop from millions of cattle. **9.** The queen of a certain kind of termite can lay 40,000 eggs a day. **10.** Insects have been around for about 350 million years. **11.** About one third of all insects are carnivorous, and most hunt for their food rather than eating decaying meat or dung (poop). **12.** When alarmed, some hawk moth caterpillars from Brazil can inflate their bodies to look like the head of a snake. **13.** There are 1.5 million named insects in the world. **14.** Only female mosquitoes bite humans; male mosquitoes live off juices from plants and decaying material. **15.** In the winter, many insects replace the water in their bodies with a chemical that acts as antifreeze against cold temperatures. **16.** There are more kinds of beetles than plants. **17.** For two weeks each June in Tennessee, U.S.A.'s Great Smoky Mountains National Park, thousands of fireflies gather at night and flash in unison. **18.** Dung beetles eat poop and roll it away and bury it underground to feed to their young. **19.** The postman butterfly caterpillar looks just like bird poop, a disguise that helps hide the insect from predators. **20.** Insects have three pairs of legs. **21.** Insect hearts are tube-shaped. **22.** Insects were the first flying animals. **23.** Most insects have two pairs of wings, but true flies have only one pair of wings, and sometimes none at all. **24.** Flies can fly backward, sideways, and upside down. **25.** Prior to takeoff in cold weather, many insects warm up their flight muscles by vibrating them. **26.** A midge can beat its wings 62,760 times a minute—more than 10 times faster than a hummingbird can. **27.** The flower mantid has an ear between one pair of legs. **28.** Mantids are the only insects able to turn their head around and look behind them. **29.** Wooly bear moths can produce ultrasonic sounds to warn off predators and confuse bats looking for a tasty treat. **30.** Predacious diving beetles carry air bubbles beneath their wings to use for breathing while diving. **31.** One in three insects is a beetle. **32.** Female sheep nose bot flies deposit their young in the nostrils of sheep. After a year of living in the sheep's head, the young flies are sneezed out. **33.** Hawk moths can fly as fast as 30 miles per hour (50 kph). **34.** The "fur" on bees keeps them warm while flying in cold temperatures. **35.** Ant colonies can live as deep as 20 feet (6 m) underground. **36.** After living underground for 17 years, millions of periodical cicadas will suddenly emerge within a few hours to live aboveground for about a month. **37.** The Jivaro Indians of Ecuador wear brightly colored beetle wing covers as earrings. **38.** Museums use carpet beetles—which will eat almost anything—to clean the skeletons of mammals. **39.** In ancient Egypt, the dung beetle represented the morning sun god, Khepri. **40.** In 1889, an enormous swarm of locusts crossed the Red Sea—the swarm was estimated to contain 250 billion locusts, cover an area of 2,000 square miles (5,180 sq km) and weigh 500,000 tons (453,600 MT). **41.** There are more than ten quadrillion ants in the world (that's 10,000,000,000,000,000!). **42.** A trap-jaw ant can close its jaws at a speed of 145 miles per hour (233 kph)—the fastest in the animal world.

100 INCREDIBLE INSECT

Above: Leaf Beetle
Left: Giant Grasshopper
(*Tropidacris collaris*)
Right: Ladybug

43. Queens of a kind of African driver ant lay about 50 million eggs a year. **44.** A group of 200,000 army ants on the move is 45 feet (13.7 m) across. **45.** Four out of five animals on Earth are insects. **46.** A cockroach can live for weeks without a head. **47.** Cockroaches can survive underwater for as long as 15 minutes. **48.** Insects breathe air through holes on the sides of their bodies. **49.** Monarch butterflies have been seen flying as high as 3,937 feet (1,200 m) in the air. **50.** Non-biting midges live 4,462 feet (1,360 m) below the surface of Russia's Lake Baikal. **51.** The most heat-tolerant insects are desert-dwelling ants that forage at temperatures above 140°F (60°C). **52.** The longest insect, a kind of beetle, is about half a foot (16.7 cm)—longer than some small Chihuahas. **53.** The fastest insect—an Australian tiger beetle—can run 5.6 miles per hour (or 2.5 meters per second). **54.** Carpenter bees produce the largest insect eggs—three millimeters in diameter (one-sixth the width of a dime). **55.** Fleas can jump incredibly far—some fleas that are only a few millimeters across can jump more than 10 centimeters, or 50 times their body length. If you're five feet (1.5 m) tall, that's like jumping 250 feet (76 m)! **56.** The oldest found fossil of an insect is of a 400 million year old springtail, which looks like a flea. **57.** A 50-million-year-old ant fossil reveals a queen that was two inches long (5.08 cm)—as large as a hummingbird without its beak. **58.** In a flood, fire ants float by clinging together to make a waterproof raft. **59.** Body lice—which live in the folds of clothing—have been around for 190,000 years, about as long as people have been wearing clothes. **60.** To escape predators, some caterpillars quickly curl into a ball and roll away at speeds of up to 8 inches (20 cm) per second. **61.** Bug Appétit at the Audubon Insectarium in New Orleans, Louisiana, U.S.A., serves "chocolate chirp cookies": chocolate chip cookies, but with toasted grasshoppers. **62.** Many cultures consider insects, from ants to scorpions, to be a delicious snack. **63.** In Mexico, 1,700 different kinds of insects are eaten. **64.** Love-struck mosquitoes harmonize their buzzing. **65.** Crickets create a chirping sound by rubbing their front wings together. **66.** Female praying mantids often eat male praying mantids. **67.** Silkworms—farmed for their silk—no longer exist in the wild. **68.** Tiger beetles have ears under their wings and can hear only while flying.

Blue Dragonfly

69. When threatened, ladybugs play dead and release a foul-tasting fluid from their leg joints. **70.** Flies don't have eyelids, so they rub their eyes clean with their feet. **71.** Ants give directions: They're able to communicate to each other where food is. **72.** Kissing bugs suck blood from around the mouths of sleeping people. **73.** Millipedes have two pairs of legs on each body segment; centipedes, which aren't actually insects, have one pair of legs on each body segment. **74.** Stink bugs emit a pungent odor when disturbed. **75.** Madagascar hissing cockroaches make their namesake noise while fighting; winning roaches hiss more than losing roaches. **76.** Walking sticks look exactly like twigs and can grow as long as 13 inches (33 cm). **77.** Velvet ants are actually wingless female wasps. **78.**

FACTS

African termite mounds can grow to be 42 feet (13 m) tall. **79.** Leaf cutter ants trim off sections of leaves and carry them underground to add to fungi gardens used to feed baby ants. **80.** Forty-one of the 50 U.S. states have an official state insect. **81.** Water scorpions have breathing tubes on their butts, which enables them to breathe air while the majority of their body is underwater. **82.** In general, butterflies fly during the day, and moths fly at night. **83.** The white witch moth has a wingspan of 11 inches (28 cm). **84.** In Japan, insects are commonly kept as pets: Crickets in bamboo cages are sold at the market. **85.** In the Democratic Republic of the Congo, lightly fried termites are sold as a snack. **86.** When army ants encounter holes along their path, they will position themselves over the hole and let other ants walk over them. **87.** Four ladybugs and a jar of aphids were carried on a space shuttle flight to study how they moved in zero gravity. Scientists found ladybugs were able to capture prey without an assist from gravity. **88.** Dragonflies and damselflies are older than dinosaurs. **89.** Dragonflies have two pairs of wings that they can beat in unison or separately; this flexibility allows the insects to act like a helicopter, hovering and flying backward. **90.** Dragonflies rest with their wings spread; they are unable to fold them. **91.** Beetles use their legs to clean their antennae. **92.** The American walking stick can release a defensive chemical that temporarily blinds predators, including mice and birds. **93.** Insects don't have bones; instead, they have a tough exterior called an exoskeleton. **94.** Instead of blood, insect bodies are filled with a fluid called haemolymph. **95.** Insect wings are made of cuticle, the same material at the base of your fingernails. **96.** Mayflies live for two to three years but often spend only one day as an adult. **97.** When walking sticks are attacked, they can lose a leg and later grow it back. **98.** Most insects lay eggs, but some cockroaches give birth to live young. **99.** Cicadas make sounds that can be heard up to one mile (1.6 km) away. **100.** A swarm of 50 billion grasshoppers can eat up to 100,000 tons (90,718 MT) in a single day.

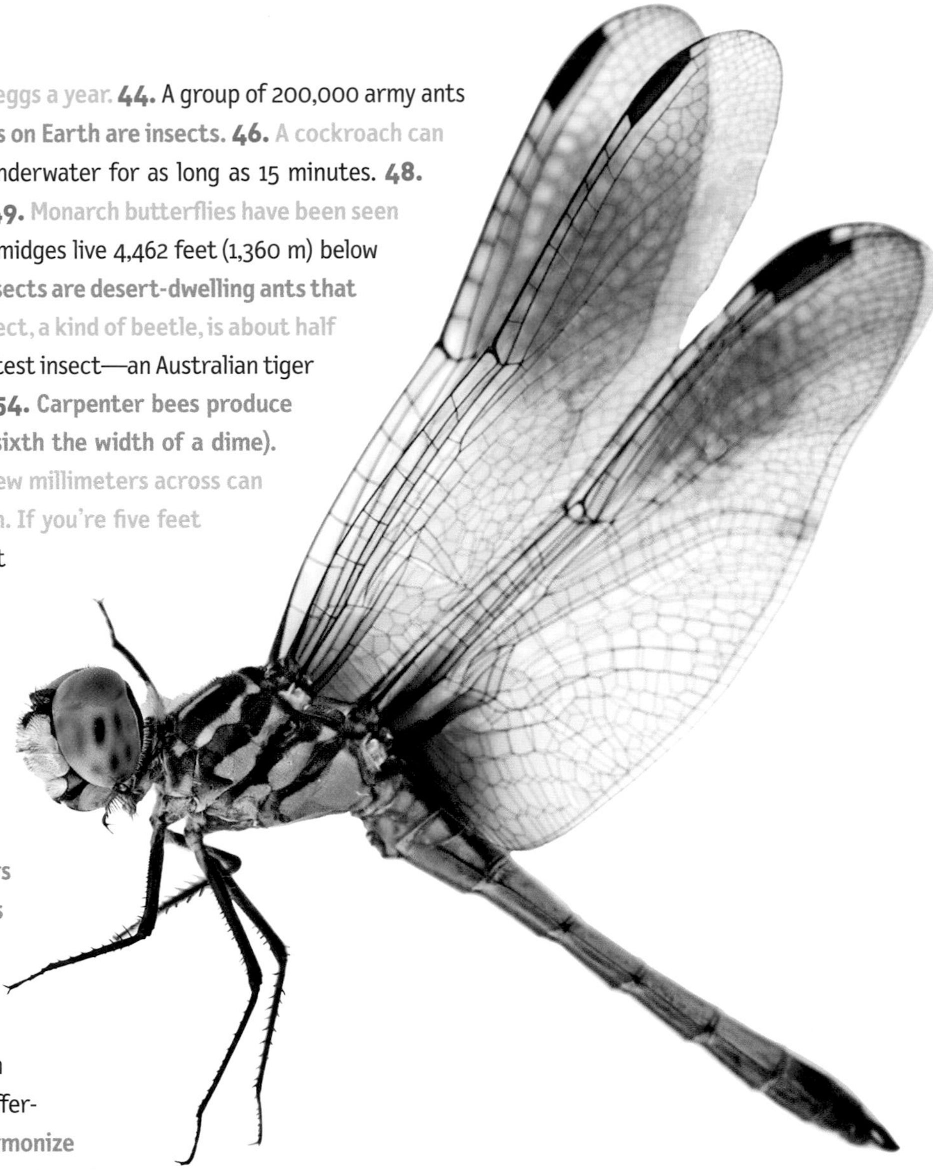

✳ YOU HAVE LEARNED **2,360** FACTS

1
Scientists measure penguins to tell if they are getting **ENOUGH TO EAT.** From height, they can determine if there are enough fish in the ocean.

2
Some penguins can dive 1,000 feet (305 m)— that's about **150 TIMES DEEPER** than an Olympic swimming pool.

3
Penguins have flat corneas in their eyeballs that give them **CLEAR UNDERWATER VISION.**

4
Penguins **CAN'T FLY.** They use their wings (called flippers) to push their bodies forward while underwater.

5
Birds that fly have light, hollow bones. Penguins have solid, **HEAVY BONES** that help them dive for food.

6
There's a **TOWN NAMED PENGUIN** on the coast of Tasmania. It was named after the fairy penguin.

7
Penguins are found almost exclusively in the **SOUTHERN** Hemisphere.

8
Penguins catch their food **IN THE WATER,** but raise their **CHICKS ON LAND.**

9
At 16 inches (.41 m) tall, the **FAIRY PENGUIN** is the smallest of the penguins—smaller than most newborn humans.

10
At 3.7 feet (1.1 m) tall, the **EMPEROR PENGUIN** is the tallest of the penguins—about the size of a **FOUR-YEAR-OLD KID.**

11
If a penguin makes it past the chick stage, it can live for **15 TO 20 YEARS.**

12
MANNERS MATTER! When two penguins make a nest together, they announce the union by bowing to one another.

13
Penguins can spend up to **75 PERCENT** of their lives in the water.

14
King and emperor penguins lay one egg at a time. All other species of penguin lay **TWO EGGS** at a time.

15
African penguins have spots on their chest that are just like human **FINGERPRINTS:** No two spot patterns are the same.

16
The **CHINSTRAP** penguin has a thin line that wraps from behind one eye under the chin to behind the other eye, like a bike helmet strap.

17
A group of penguins is called a **COLONY.**

18
Emperor penguins establish their colonies about 62 miles (100 km) from the ocean, but must **WADDLE** back to sea to gather food.

19
Penguins' tuxedo-like appearance is called **COUNTERSHADING;** it helps keep them camouflaged in the water.

20
Some penguins do not make nests. The egg rests on top of their feet, and it is kept warm with a flap of feathered skin called a brood pouch.

21
Male emperor penguins stand with their egg for **65 DAYS** in icy temperatures and harsh winds without eating while females get food.

22
An emperor penguin egg weighs about **16 OUNCES** (450 grams)—that's about the same as **EIGHT** chicken eggs.

23
ADÉLIE penguins build nests by scooping out a spot in the ground and lining it with small stones, which help their eggs stay dry and warm.

24
Some penguins slide on their **BELLIES,** using their feet to push them forward.

25
In the movie *Mr. Popper's Penguins*, the gentoo penguins were real (but computer-enhanced). The movie had to be filmed on a **REFRIGERATED SET.**

26
Penguins **DON'T SLEEP LYING DOWN.** They stand and usually tuck their beak under their wings.

27
An adult **GENTOO** penguin makes as many as **450 DIVES** a day looking for food.

28
Most penguins waddle, but **ROCKHOPPER** penguins live up to their name—they hop around shorelines.

29
Rockhopper penguins have a crest of spiky yellow and black feathers on top of their head, **BLOOD-RED EYES,** a red-orange beak, and pink, webbed feet.

30
Rockhopper penguins often burst from the water near shore and land on rocks with a **BELLY FLOP.**

31
ADÉLIE penguins know there's safety in numbers. Making their home in Antarctica, these birds nest in colonies of 400,000.

32
A scientist found a **36-MILLION-YEAR-OLD** fossil of a penguin that would have stood shoulder-height to a man.

33
A king penguin parent spends four hours and **2,000 PECKS** a day fighting off birds trying to attack its chick or egg.

40 ELEPHANT SEALS snack on penguins in the water, but on land, penguins can wander around elephant seals and rarely be bothered.

43
Penguin feet don't get **FROSTBITE**, thanks to a special circulation system that keeps them warm in freezing temperatures.

48
ORCAS purposely beach themselves on the shore of a penguin colony, grab a penguin in their teeth, and return to sea.

34
Every penguin has its own **UNIQUE VOICE**, which helps find its mate or chick in a crowd.

46 EARLY PENGUINS lived in Earth's oceans before **WHALES AND SEALS** arrived.

49 MAGELLANIC penguins are named after the explorer Ferdinand Magellan, who saw the birds in **1520** at the tip of South America.

41 LEOPARD SEALS eat as many as 15 penguins a day.

44
The emperor penguin can eat up to **31 POUNDS** (14 kg) of food at a time. That's like eating **900 CHICKEN NUGGETS!**

47
Not all penguins live in chilly climates. The **GALÁPAGOS** penguin swims in warm waters at the Equator.

35
Penguin parents **THROW UP** partly digested food from their bellies to feed their chicks.

50 MACARONI penguins have yellow tufts above each eye.

45
On land, Galápagos penguins **PANT LIKE A DOG** to lose heat on the warm islands.

42
Unlike humans, penguins can **DRINK SEAWATER.** They have a special gland that takes the salt out of the water.

36
Chicks tell their parents they want food by **TAPPING** on the side of their parents' beak.

37
Penguins' top layer of feathers is **OILY AND WATERPROOF.**

50 EYE-POPPING PENGUIN FACTS

38
Some penguins leap out of water for a breath of air like a **DOLPHIN.**

39
Penguin **POOP** changes color depending on what they're eating. White poop means they're eating a lot of fish. If it's green, it means they can't find food and they're hungry.

Macaroni Penguin

✳ YOU HAVE LEARNED **2,410** FACTS

1 BUZZARDS CAN SEE RODENTS FROM **15,000 FEET** (4,572 M) IN THE AIR.

2 ANIMALS ARE ABLE TO SENSE NATURAL DISASTERS BEFORE HUMANS.

3 A species of bug uses **INFRARED LIGHT** (heat-based light invisible to humans) to find pinecone seeds, which are about 27 °F (15°C) **WARMER** than their surroundings.

4 HUMAN TONGUES have five kinds of taste cells— **SALTY, SWEET, SOUR, BITTER, AND SAVORY** —and bitter cells are also found in the GUT, NOSE, AND LUNGS!

5 FLIES CAN HEAR EACH OTHER LAND ON A BLADE OF GRASS.

25 SENSE-

6 A DRAGONFLY EYE HAS **30,000** lenses; a human eye has only one.

7 PENGUINS ARE ATTRACTED TO THE SMELL OF ROTTING EGGS.

8 CATFISH HAVE **10** TIMES AS MANY TASTE BUDS AS HUMANS.

9 The same cells that detect SOURNESS ALSO DETECT FIZZINESS.

10 HOUSEFLIES taste with their feet, which are **10,000,000** TIMES MORE SENSITIVE THAN HUMAN TONGUES.

11 BATS HAVE THE BEST HEARING OF ALL LAND MAMMALS.

12 MANY ANIMALS USE CHEMICAL SIGNALS CALLED PHEROMONES TO COMMUNICATE WITH EACH OTHER.

13 A BOX JELLYFISH HAS 24 EYES;

A SCALLOP HAS ABOUT 100.

14 SEA STARS DON'T HAVE EYES; INSTEAD THEIR ARMS SENSE LIGHT.

15 MOST PEOPLE WHO ARE COLOR BLIND CAN'T TELL THE DIFFERENCE BETWEEN GREEN AND RED.

16 Chameleon eyes and seahorse eyes MOVE INDEPENDENTLY; they can see in two DIFFERENT DIRECTIONS at the same time.

ATIONAL FACTS

17 PEOPLE WITH MOTION BLINDNESS CAN'T SEE MOTION— for example, water flowing out of the tap or a car driving away.

18 THE SNOUT OF A STAR-NOSED MOLE IS SIX TIMES MORE SENSITIVE THAN A HUMAN HAND.

19 FISH CAN TASTE THINGS NOT ONLY IN THEIR MOUTHS, BUT ALL OVER THEIR BODIES.

20 AN OWL CAN HEAR A MOUSE STEP ON A TWIG 75 FEET (23 M) AWAY.

21 PEOPLE WITH PROSOPAGNOSIA have difficulty recognizing faces, EVEN THEIR OWN.

22 A COYOTE can hear a mouse moving under ONE FOOT (30 CM) OF SNOW.

23 YOUR EYES CAN SEE ABOUT 10 MILLION DIFFERENT COLORS.

24 PEOPLE WITH SYNESTHESIA HAVE BLENDED SENSES: For example, they see pizza when they hear the sound of drums, or smell smoke when someone touches their right arm.

25 Many animals, such as the TEXAS BLIND SALAMANDER, HAVE LOST THE ABILITY TO SEE because they live in TOTAL DARKNESS.

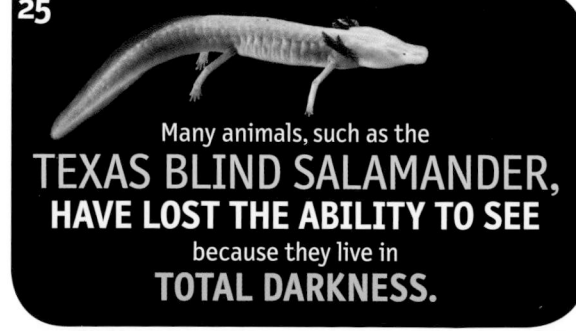

35 FASCINATING

1
South American rain forests are home to **ONE-QUARTER OF ALL BUTTERFLY SPECIES** on Earth.

2
ONLY A FOOT TALL (30 cm) at its shoulder, a **SMALL DEER CALLED THE PUDU** lives in South America. It sometimes has to stand on its hind legs to reach food.

3
You can ski at the **WORLD'S HIGHEST SKI RESORT IN BOLIVIA.** It takes about **30 MINUTES** to hike up to the only ski run.

4
A smaller version of the **STATUE OF LIBERTY** can be found in Buenos Aires, Argentina.

5
VENEZUELANS BURN LIFE-SIZE DOLLS representing their problems each New Year's Eve to mark the beginning of a new year.

6
VENEZUELA'S ANGEL FALLS—the world's highest at **3,212 FEET** (979 m)—is named for an American aviator who first flew over the falls.

7
Isolated some 620 miles (1,000 km) from the mainland, the 19 islands of the Galápagos are home to the **FOUR-FOOT** (1.4-m) **-LONG IGUANA** and many other unique animals.

8
Peru has more than 3,000 different kinds of **POTATOES.**

9
ROBINSON CRUSOE—a book about a castaway stranded on a tropical island—was **INSPIRED BY A REAL MAN** who was shipwrecked on an island off the coast of Chile.

10
ARICA, CHILE, is the world's **DRIEST PLACE**—it hardly ever rains there.

11
You can find yellow, green, and red **MINIATURE BANANAS** in Ecuador.

12
In the 19th century, Peruvians made **MONEY BY SELLING BIRD DROPPINGS,** which were used as a fertilizer.

13
COLOMBIA is named after **CHRISTOPHER COLUMBUS.**

14
BRAZIL SHARES A BORDER with all the countries in South America except Ecuador and Chile.

15
A kind of dance called the *gallopa* in **PARAGUAY** includes women **BALANCING BOTTLES** on their heads.

16
BUENOS AIRES, ARGENTINA, is home to one of the world's **WIDEST STREETS**: It's nine lanes wide.

17
More than **700,000** different kinds of insects live in **BRAZIL.**

18
COLOMBIA is the only country in South America where can you **SWIM IN BOTH THE PACIFIC AND ATLANTIC OCEANS,** since it has a coastline on each.

19
South America's rain forests are home to the world's **SMALLEST MONKEY** (PYGMY MARMOSET) and the **LOUDEST (THE HOWLER MONKEY).**

FACTS ABOUT SOUTH AMERICA

20 INCA RULERS wore clothes made from the wool of the *vicuña*, a LLAMA-LIKE ANIMAL prized for its SOFTNESS.

21 PATAGONIA in southern Chile has a shoreline divided by fjords, islands, and inlets that stretches over 50,000 MILES (90,000 km). That's about twice around the globe.

22 URUGUAYAN COWBOYS, called GAUCHOS, wear black hats.

23 The MAJORITY OF THE WORLD'S EMERALDS come from Colombia.

24 The ANDES is the world's LARGEST ABOVE-WATER MOUNTAIN RANGE. If laid in a straight line, the mountains would stretch from Chicago, U.S.A., to Berlin, Germany.

25 Argentina's president works in a building known as "THE PINK HOUSE" (La Casa Rosada).

26 CHILI PEPPERS were used to flavor foods and traded across South and Central America some 6,000 years ago. Today, chilies can be so "hot" they can burn through latex gloves.

27 LLAMAS are related to CAMELS, but don't have a hump. South Americans use llamas as PACK ANIMALS, but if too much weight is added most llamas will refuse to move.

28 PEOPLE LIVE ON FLOATING ISLANDS made out of woven reeds in LAKE TITICACA, on the border between Peru and Bolivia. The largest islands can house up to ten families.

29 CHILE IS A SKINNY COUNTRY—its average width is only about 109 miles (175 km)—but the country stretches some 4,000 miles (6,440 km) down along the Pacific Ocean.

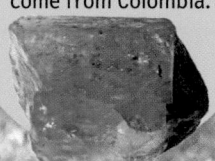

30 SOCCER is a big deal in BRAZIL. Its national team has WON FIVE WORLD CUPS—more than any other country.

31 A FAVORITE FOOD IN COLOMBIA is *hormiga culona*, or ROASTED ANTS.

32 PERU'S MANÚ NATIONAL PARK has six species of colorful macaws and more than 100 SPECIES OF BATS. Jaguars also roam the park.

33 A tower made out of a HALF-MILLION LEGOS and standing taller than 102 FEET (31 m) was built in São Paulo, Brazil, in April 2011. That's about the size of a ten-story building.

34 Since the EQUATOR runs through ECUADOR, you can stand in both the Northern and the Southern Hemispheres at once. "ECUADOR" MEANS EQUATOR IN SPANISH.

35 There's a SILVER MINE in BOLIVIA that's so dangerous it is known as the "MOUNTAIN THAT EATS MEN."

(15) WILD CAT FACTS

1 There are **MORE TIGERS IN CAPTIVITY** in the United States alone than in the **WILD THROUGHOUT THE WORLD.**

2 **THREE** of the ORIGINAL EIGHT SUBSPECIES of tiger are extinct.

3 Most **BIG CATS ROAR;** most **SMALL CATS PURR.**

4 The **BENGAL TIGER** is **INDIA'S NATIONAL ANIMAL.**

5 A **LION PRIDE** can be as few as **3 ANIMALS** or as many as **30.**

6 Cats **CANNOT TASTE SWEET**—they LACK the TASTE RECEPTORS.

7 **SNOW LEOPARDS** can **TAKE DOWN PREY THREE TIMES THEIR WEIGHT.**

Bengal Tiger

THAT WILL MAKE YOU PURR

8 A **CHEETAH** can **ACCELERATE FASTER** than a **RACE CAR.**

9 There are 35 **SPECIES OF WILD CATS** in the world.

10 **TIGERS CAN EAT** more than 80 **POUNDS (36 KG) OF MEAT** in one meal—that's like eating 70 **T-BONE STEAKS!**

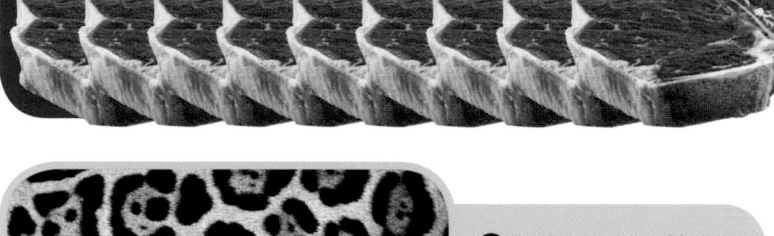

11 Each species of big cat has **A UNIQUE COAT FOR CAMOUFLAGE.**

12 A **PUMA** is also called a **MOUNTAIN LION, A PANTHER, AND A COUGAR.**

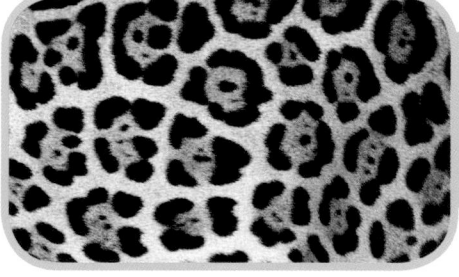

13 A **SERVAL'S BIG EARS** help it **HEAR THE SOFT SOUNDS** of scurrying prey.

14 A **LEOPARD** can drag a small antelope **UP A 50-FOOT (15-M) TREE.**

15 A **LION'S TOP RUNNING SPEED** is **36 MILES PER HOUR (58 KPH).**

50 FACTS that will be MUSIC to your EARS

1
If the vibration from an object is not in a regular pattern it's considered noise. If it has a **STEADY BEAT**, it's considered musical.

2
A musician hit **669 PIANO KEYS** in one minute at a 2011 concert to raise money to end curable blindness in India.

3
In an orchestra, instruments that produce **SOFT SOUNDS** are located up front. **LOUDER INSTRUMENTS** such as drums are located in the back.

4
Archaeologists can still **PLAY ANCIENT FLUTES** made from animal bones that are between **7,000** and **9,000** years old.

5
The newest building on the UNESCO World Heritage List is the **SYDNEY OPERA HOUSE.** It was completed in 1973.

6
Thomas Edison recorded the lines of **"MARY HAD A LITTLE LAMB"** on a tinfoil phonograph to test his invention. The phonograph was an early way to record music.

7
MOZART is said to have composed the last movement of his "Piano Concerto in G Major" to sound like the **CALLS FROM HIS PET BIRD.**

8
Three artists created a song called **"THE MOST UNWANTED MUSIC,"** after surveying music people didn't like. The song includes holiday tunes and cowboy music.

9
DAVID BYRNE from the Talking Heads turned empty buildings into music by wiring an antique organ into the buildings' pipes, pillars, and beams.

10
Famous composer **BEETHOVEN** went completely **DEAF** at the height of his career.

11
Composer **JEM FINER** created a computer-generated song called "Longplayer" that will last for **1,000 YEARS.**

12
Some high-frequency cell phone ring tones **CAN'T BE HEARD BY ADULTS,** because as you get older your ears can't detect certain frequencies that you hear when you're younger.

13
A **SHOFAR** is a musical instrument made from the horn of a ram that was used by the ancient Hebrews. It is still used today during Jewish religious ceremonies.

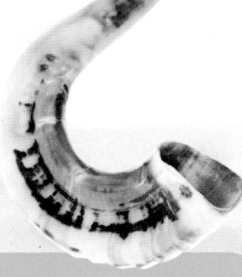

14
A musician created an album of harp music to **SOOTHE WOUNDED ANIMALS.** Dogs responded with a lowered heart rate and respiration and less anxiety.

15
Mozart was only **SIX YEARS OLD** when he first performed in front of Bavarian royalty.

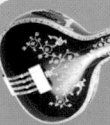

16
A musician must sit to play the **INDIAN SITAR,** a large guitarlike instrument.

17
Strings for Spanish acoustic guitars used to be made from **SHEEP INTESTINES.**

18
HIP-HOP began in the **MID-1970S** when deejays used two turntables to make music for **DANCING CROWDS.**

19
The saxophone was named after its inventor, **ADOLPHE SAX.**

20
"THE STAR-SPANGLED BANNER," the U.S. national anthem, is based on a poem and set to the tune of an old English song.

21
A musician in Iceland created a **16-FOOT, 5-INCH-LONG (5 M) RECORDER.** Each hole is almost 4 inches (8.5 cm) wide.

22
The **GRAMMY AWARD** was named after the **GRAMOPHONE,** an early device used to play music.

23
Some **AMERICAN INDIANS** of the Great Plains kept their drums in special buildings called **"DRUM HOUSES."**

24
A HYMN found on a stone tablet in **SYRIA** from **1400** B.C. is the oldest known written song.

25
The Swiss **ALPENHORN** can be heard for very long distances and was traditionally used to call herdsmen in the Alps Mountains.

26
There are more than **200,000 ELVIS PRESLEY IMPERSONATORS** worldwide, including "The Flying Elvi," a group of skydivers who parachute from planes.

27
Composer **JOHN WILLIAMS** used the London Symphony to create the music for the **STAR WARS** movies.

28
The company that holds the copyright to **"HAPPY BIRTHDAY TO YOU"** makes some **$2 MILLION** a year on the song.

29
A **JUG BAND** uses such household items as **WASHBOARDS, SPOONS, AND EMPTY BOTTLES** as musical instruments.

30
Left-handed guitar legend **JIMI HENDRIX** played a right-handed guitar that he restrung **UPSIDE DOWN.**

31
While a piece called "Music for Fireworks" played at a royal show in London in the 18th century, **A BUILDING CAUGHT ON FIRE FROM THE FIREWORKS.**

32
Composer **JOHN CAGE'S** song *4'33"* is four minutes and thirty-three seconds of **SILENCE.**

33
Macaque monkeys and chimpanzees will sometimes **DRUM ON DEAD TREES.**

34
JUSTIN BIEBER taught himself to play guitar by the time he was **SIX.**

35
The first time **MICHAEL JACKSON MOONWALKED** in front of an audience was during the Motown's 25th anniversary special televised broadcast in **1983.**

36
Beijing Opera performances include music and **MARTIAL ARTS.**

37
According to tradition, **ONLY MEN** are allowed to play the **DIDGERIDOO**— an ancient instrument used by the Aborigines of Australia.

38
Greece has one of the longest national anthems in the world, with a total of **158 VERSES.**

39
Critics didn't like the *NUTCRACKER* **BALLET** when it was first performed in 1892. Today, it has become a tradition during the Christmas season.

40
HEITOR VILLA-LOBOS, a Brazilian composer, appears on the Brazilian **$500 BILL.**

41
The ancient Greeks invented the **MUSIC NOTATION** system many musicians still use today.

42
The **FIRST CD** manufactured in the United States was Bruce Springsteen's album *BORN IN THE USA* in 1984.

43
One of **JOHN LENNON'S TEETH** sold at auction for around $31,000.

44
Traditionally, West Indians reused **OIL DRUMS** as **STEEL DRUMS.**

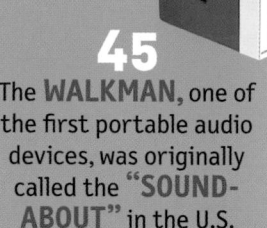

45
The **WALKMAN,** one of the first portable audio devices, was originally called the **"SOUND-ABOUT"** in the U.S.

46
In 1979, the Sugarhill Gang's song **"RAPPER'S DELIGHT"** became so popular that **"RAP"** became the name for this new type of music.

47
Before he was 16, **PRINCE** could **PLAY A DOZEN INSTRUMENTS.**

48
U.S. PRESIDENT **BARACK OBAMA** awarded cellist **YO-YO MA THE PRESIDENTIAL MEDAL OF FREEDOM** in November 2010.

49
NEIL ARMSTRONG took a recording of **DVORAK'S FAMOUS SYMPHONY "FROM THE NEW WORLD"** with him to discover a new world— **THE MOON.**

50
It took more than **1,000 CAT SOUNDS** for a producer to create 20 songs by the **JINGLE CATS,** cats who "sing" holiday songs like "Jingle Bells" and "Silent Night."

35 EYE-OPENING

1 People can nap with their **EYES OPEN.**

2 On average, we spend a third of each day sleeping—that's about four months a year! If you live to be 70, you'll spend **23 YEARS OF YOUR LIFE SLEEPING.**

3 **YAWNING CAN BE CONTAGIOUS!** When someone near you yawns, you are likely to yawn yourself, especially if you know the person.

4 **MYTH BUSTED!** The chemical tryptophan, found in turkey, **DOES NOT** actually **MAKE YOU SLEEPY.**

5 In the 1700s, scientist Carolus Linneaus designed a **"FLOWER CLOCK"** that could tell the time by which flowers were opened or closed during the day. He never built it.

6 In 2005 a teenage girl in London **SLEEPWALKED OUT OF HER HOUSE,** climbed to the top of a 130-foot (40 m) crane and then walked out onto the beam and fell asleep.

7 To protect itself while it sleeps, a **PARROTFISH OOZES MUCUS** that surrounds its entire body like a cocoon, disguising its scent from any lurking predators.

8 The Singapore Changi airport has won the **"GOLDEN PILLOW AWARD"** for 15 years in a row for being the most comfortable airport in the world to sleep in.

9 **PILLOWS** have been found in **ANCIENT EGYPTIAN TOMBS.**

10 People who take a short nap during the day, **A SIESTA,** may be more productive than those who don't.

11 Giraffes sleep for a little **LESS THAN TWO HOURS** a day.

FACTS ABOUT SLEEP

12 When you dream, it can **FEEL LIKE HOURS HAVE PASSED,** but in reality, it's only been **MINUTES.**

13 In 1965, high school student Randy Gardner intentionally **STAYED AWAKE 264 HOURS (11 DAYS)** for a science project.

14 Astronauts on the space shuttle slept in **SLEEPING BAGS THAT HUNG FROM THE WALL.**

15 Birds can sleep for **30-SECOND INTERVALS**—this might be how they fly without resting during long migrations.

16 Elephants sleep **BOTH STANDING UP AND LYING DOWN.** They lie down for REM sleep, which is the stage of sleep when most dreams happen.

17 During **REM SLEEP** (the dreaming stage), a person's body actually becomes **PARALYZED** so you don't act out your dreams. This is called sleep paralysis, or atonia.

18 **DOLPHINS** that are closely bonded might **SWIM IN SYNCHRONY.**

19 **HARRIET TUBMAN** often fell asleep when she was helping people in the **UNDERGROUND RAILROAD.** Most likely she suffered from narcolepsy, a disease of excessive sleepiness.

20 To stay warm, **GARTER SNAKES HIBERNATE TOGETHER** by lying on top of each other in big heaps, usually in rocky crevices.

21 In the 1960s, **DION MCGREGOR TALKED SO CLEARLY IN HIS SLEEP** that his roommate recorded it and called it "The Dream World of Dion McGregor: He Talks in His Sleep."

22 Medical experts have seen a rise in what is called **SLEEP TEXTING,** in which people wake up and are shocked to find messages they **TEXTED IN THEIR SLEEP.**

23 The **POSITION** you sleep in may provide **CLUES TO YOUR PERSONALITY.** If you sleep curled up, you are most likely shy.

24 The **BRITISH MILITARY** was the first to develop a way for soldiers to stay **AWAKE.** When they would get sleepy, they put on a special pair of visors that mimic a sunrise.

25 **KOALAS** sleep for as many as **22 HOURS A DAY.** Their **DIET OF EUCALYPTUS** leaves is low in nutrition so they sleep to conserve energy.

26 Sometimes your **BRAIN IS MORE ACTIVE WHILE YOU ARE SLEEPING** than when you are awake.

27 The **OJIBWE** of the northern United States traditionally hang a **DREAM CATCHER** over a baby's cradle to capture bad dreams.

28 **STEPHENIE MEYER,** the author of the **TWILIGHT SERIES,** got the idea for the story and started writing it after she had a very **VIVID DREAM** about the two main characters.

29 It takes the average **TEN-YEAR-OLD KID** about **TWENTY MINUTES** to fall asleep.

30 To stay awake on his flight over the Atlantic Ocean, Charles Lindbergh **HELD HIS EYES OPEN WITH HIS FINGERS.** He almost crashed his plane when he dozed off for a few minutes.

31 Bee-eater birds sleep by lining up side-by-side on a wire. The two birds on the ends stay awake and **WATCH FOR DANGER** while the birds in the middle sleep. After a while they change places.

32 You can only **SNORE** if you are not in **REM SLEEP.**

33 **HOT NIGHTS** can cause sleep problems because we need to be able to **COOL OFF TO FALL ASLEEP.**

34 The loudest human snores are **LOUDER THAN A JACKHAMMER.**

35 **NIGHT TERRORS,** which are **DIFFERENT THAN NIGHTMARES,** occur in kids in the first few hours of sleep, during deep sleep, which is why they don't remember them.

1. Gravity is the force that pulls objects (like a basketball) to the ground, and it causes each thing on Earth to have a specific weight. 2. **Atoms are microscopic, but the nuclei, or the center of atoms, are *really* small. If an atom was the size of a baseball stadium, its nucleus would be the size of a fly sitting in the center of the field.** 3. There is a neutron star that moves roughly 3 million miles per hour (4.8 million kph). It is the fastest object in space. 4. The flavors in soda come partly from phosphoric acid, which gives bubbly water a fruity, acidic taste. 5. **Water molecules in foods in your freezer can escape to a colder place in your freezer—causing "freezer burn," or dry spots and frost on your food.** 6. Objects appear 30 percent larger underwater. 7. Movies are just a series of still pictures, and most are filmed at 24 frames every second. 8. **The world's largest human-made hole is the Bingham copper mine in Utah, U.S.A. It covers an area the size of nearly 25,000 basketball courts.** 9. The ancient Greeks thought there were four kinds of matter, or elements: earth, water, fire, and air. Today, we count more than 100 elements. 10. Scientists use Petri dishes to grow bacteria, cells, and algae. Some Petri dishes today even transmit data to a computer. 11. **The whereabouts of Albert Einstein's brain remained a mystery for 20 years after his death, until a New Jersey reporter located it, sitting on the shelf of the doctor who removed it (it was preserved in a jar).** 12. Scientists use tools called pipets to measure the exact volume of different liquids. 13. Albert Einstein started studying calculus when he was 12. 14. **Since cold salt water is denser than warm fresh water, it sinks below fresher water and keeps the ocean currents moving.** 15. Ultrasound machines used to see a baby inside a mother's womb use sonar technology adapted from submarines. 16. **Tiny particles in the air all around you have weight and press down on you all the time. This is called air pressure.** 17. Phycologists study algae. They even use satellites to analyze algae blooms in lakes and oceans. 18. Scientists have created a battery about the size of your fridge that can power your home. When it's time to recharge, just plug it into your solar panels or windmills. 19. **Thousands of years ago, our ancestors could use only the iron they found in meteorites. Today, we produce iron by heating iron ore in a blast furnace.** 20. Gamma rays, which can come from nuclear explosions, travel through most objects. Only thick lead or steel can stop them. 21. Antoni van Leeuwenhoek discovered bacteria and blood cells using lenses he had made that magnified things up to ten times better than in the past. 22. **When a skater does a kick flip, the skateboard spins around its center of gravity, which is the average location of the skateboard's weight.** 23. Socrates, the Greek philosopher, figured out some 2,400 years ago that by building your house to face the sun in the winter, it could be warmed

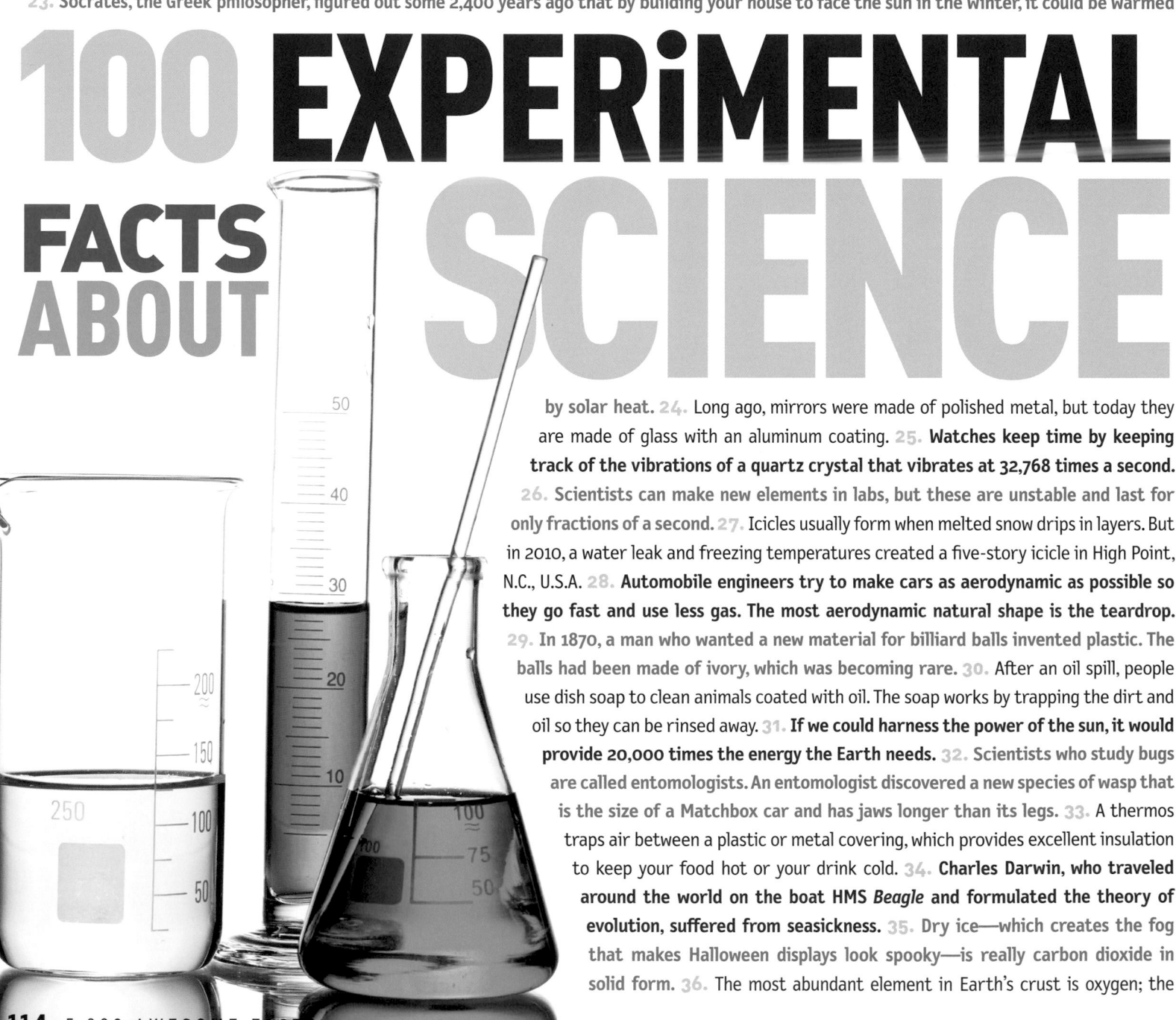

100 EXPERiMENTAL FACTS ABOUT SCIENCE

by solar heat. 24. Long ago, mirrors were made of polished metal, but today they are made of glass with an aluminum coating. 25. **Watches keep time by keeping track of the vibrations of a quartz crystal that vibrates at 32,768 times a second.** 26. **Scientists can make new elements in labs, but these are unstable and last for only fractions of a second.** 27. Icicles usually form when melted snow drips in layers. But in 2010, a water leak and freezing temperatures created a five-story icicle in High Point, N.C., U.S.A. 28. **Automobile engineers try to make cars as aerodynamic as possible so they go fast and use less gas. The most aerodynamic natural shape is the teardrop.** 29. **In 1870, a man who wanted a new material for billiard balls invented plastic. The balls had been made of ivory, which was becoming rare.** 30. After an oil spill, people use dish soap to clean animals coated with oil. The soap works by trapping the dirt and oil so they can be rinsed away. 31. **If we could harness the power of the sun, it would provide 20,000 times the energy the Earth needs.** 32. Scientists who study bugs are called entomologists. An entomologist discovered a new species of wasp that is the size of a Matchbox car and has jaws longer than its legs. 33. A thermos traps air between a plastic or metal covering, which provides excellent insulation to keep your food hot or your drink cold. 34. **Charles Darwin, who traveled around the world on the boat HMS *Beagle* and formulated the theory of evolution, suffered from seasickness.** 35. Dry ice—which creates the fog that makes Halloween displays look spooky—is really carbon dioxide in solid form. 36. The most abundant element in Earth's crust is oxygen; the universe's is hydrogen. **37. Forensic scientists study how human bodies decompose on a "body farm" outside of Knoxville, Tenn., U.S.A. 38.** Using x-rays, art researchers discovered a hidden picture under a painting by the Spanish artist Goya. **39.** Sound travels faster in water than in air. **40. All matter is made up of atoms. The Greek thinker Leucippus first developed this idea more than 2,400 years ago. 41.** Surfers ride a wave by staying in front of the wave and moving along with it. Surfers can even surf the fast current in some rivers. **42.** In the future, electric wands may be used to put out fires. The wands would use an electric field to separate burning fuel from fuel that's not. **43. Galileo used a telescope to become the first person to observe Jupiter's moons. 44.** When skydivers jump out of airplanes, they fall at a constant speed of around 124 miles per hour (200 kph). **45.** Scientists send bottles thousands of feet down using a wire to collect water samples from deep in the ocean. The largest bottles hold 66 gallons (250 L). **46. Salt is used to produce chemicals that make soap and glass. 47.** Scientists have found evidence that there was once a lake the size of England in the Sahara. **48.** Bungee-jumping ropes are made out of rubber because it's stretchy and good for absorbing shocks. **49. Green lasers look brighter than red lasers of the same wattage because our eyes are more sensitive to green light than to red light. 50. The largest radio telescope is located in Puerto Rico. It's wider than the length of 12 tennis courts (1,000 feet, or 310 m). 51.** Only two elements are liquid at room temperature (70°F or 25°C)—bromine and mercury. **52. A spinning top slows down because of friction, the force that exists whenever objects come in contact with each other. Without friction the top could spin pretty much forever. 53.** A ball sitting on the seat of a car will appear to move forward and fall off the seat if the driver stops suddenly. In truth, the ball just kept moving forward when the car slowed. **54.** The Earth travels more than 5,000 miles (8,047 km) in 5 minutes. **55. Pure water freezes at 32°F (0°C). If you add salt to the water it lowers the freezing point, so the water will freeze at temperatures below zero. 56.** Many plastic water bottles have a curve at the center, which helps make the bottles stable and lets the manufacturer use thinner plastic. **57.** In 1996, Dolly the sheep became the first cloned mammal. **58. Anything that gives off heat also gives off infrared waves; these waves are what night-vision goggles pick up and make visible. 59.** Rotten eggs float in water because they are lighter than fresh eggs. **60.** The pistol shrimp makes a "clicking" sound that is louder than a blue whale's call. **61. If you weigh 100 pounds (45 kg) on Earth, you'd weigh 236 pounds (107 kg) on Jupiter. 62.** Hot water will turn into a frozen mist almost instantaneously when thrown into supercold air at -30°F (-34°C) or below. **63.** The energy we get from food is measured in calories. **64. The element helium was named after the Greek word for the sun. 65.** The sun is always behind you when you see a rainbow. **66.** Sticky substances called epoxy resins have been used to stick cars to billboards. **67. The word "engineer" comes from the Latin word for cleverness. 68. Windmill power can be used to grind grain or produce electricity. 69.** The only diamond mine in the United States is in Murfreesboro, Arkansas. It is owned by the U.S. government. **70. Fiber optic cables transmit information using light. They even stretch under the sea to connect continents. 71.** Artists create sculptures in bronze because it doesn't rust. "The Thinker," a sculpture by Rodin that was featured in the movie *Night at the Museum,* was made out of bronze and marble. **72.** Inventor Thomas Edison liked to take catnaps during the day—including on his lab table. **73. Botanists, scientists who study plants, have collected seeds and stored them in the Svalbard Global Seed Vault on a remote island in the Arctic. The collection can store 2.25 billion seeds. 74. Water under high pressure can cut through metal. 75.** All animals—that includes you—get energy from eating plants or by eating animals that have eaten plants. **76. Scientists who study birds are called ornithologists. 77.** It takes the same amount of gas to fill a car's gas tank as it does to make chemicals to produce three plastic trash cans or ten polyester shirts. **78.** Power stations don't always produce the same amount of power. Engineers can vary the amount depending on how much energy is needed. **79. Iron melts at a temperature that is 15 times hotter than boiling water: 2,795°F (1,535°C). 80. A man in New Hampshire, U.S.A., made an alarm clock in 1787, but it only rang at one time: 4 a.m., when he wanted to wake up. 81.** When you rub a balloon against your body, you can then stick it to the wall using electrostatic force, or slow-moving electrical charges. **82. Only three countries in the world don't use the metric system of measurement: the United States, Liberia, and Myanmar (Burma). 83. The first scientific journal was published more than 340 years ago, in 1665. 84.** Scientists created an airbag that could be used by skiers during an avalanche to help keep them near the top of the racing snow. **85. When famous physicist Stephen Hawking was nine, he was one of the worst students in his class. 86. Miners work nearly 2.4 miles (3.9 km) underground in the TauTona mine in South Africa digging for gold. 87.** The grandfather clock got its name from a song title, "My Grandfather's Clock." **88. Gum can be removed from your hair by using peanut butter. The oils in the peanut butter get in between the gum and hair and work to make the gum less sticky. 89. If you sprinkle pepper in a dish of water and put your finger in the water, the pepper will gather around your finger. If you put dish soap on your finger and do the same thing, the pepper scatters. That's because the dish soap changes the surface tension of the water. 90.** Pickles are cucumbers soaked in salt water, which lets bacteria eat the cucumbers' sugars. This makes the pickles taste tart. **91. You get shocked when an electric charge has built up on the surface of something, like a light switch or a pet rubbing itself on a carpet, and you touch it. 92. The Chinese invented the first compass more than 2,000 years ago by magnetizing iron needles. These needles always pointed north when floated in water. 93.** Glowsticks work because a chemical reaction creates light when you break the tubes inside the stick. **94. Driving fast on the interstate may get you to your destination faster, but it burns more gas. 95. In the 16th century, people mailed descriptions of the animals they observed to the Swiss naturalist Konrad von Gesner. He published them in a book, and some oddities were included, like a giant sea serpent. 96.** It can be hard to make a soapy lather if you are using "hard" water. That's water with dissolved chemicals from rocks it came in contact with. **97. The sound a whip makes when it "cracks" comes from the tip when it's moving faster than the speed of sound. 98. The big spinning globe outside of Universal Studios in Orlando, Florida, U.S.A., spins in the wrong direction. 99.** Stunt glass invented for movie props is mostly made of plastic so that it breaks easily but looks realistic. **100. A TV remote control uses infrared light to change channels and adjust the volume.**

1
"THE HEART OF THE OCEAN" is the name of the heart-shaped blue stone worn by Rose in *Titanic*. In the film, she throws it into the ocean, but fans can buy replicas of their own.

2
DANIEL RADCLIFFE, the actor who played Harry Potter in the films, was allergic to his first pair of glasses on set.

3
One pair of RUBY SLIPPERS that the actress Judy Garland wore in the dance scenes of *The Wizard of Oz* are on display at the National Museum of American History.

4
MOTION-CAPTURE ANIMATION is when actors perform their character's movements while wearing hundreds of sensors, which transfer the movement to animation.

5
During the filming of *Pirates of the Caribbean: On Stranger Tides*, 773 COCONUT TREES were harvested to prevent the fruit from dropping on the cast and crew.

6
FOURTEEN REAL CARS WERE WRECKED to film the Whomping Willow scene in *Harry Potter and the Chamber of Secrets*.

7
The makers of *THE MUPPETS* movie didn't want to "erase" puppeteers out of the film. Instead, they created sets that hid them—including hollowed-out furniture that puppeteers scrunched into.

8
Avatar has made more money at the box office than any other movie—$2.8 BILLION WORLDWIDE!

9
Titanic, *The Lord of the Rings: The Return of the King*, and *Ben-Hur* each won 11 OSCARS, more than any other movie.

10
JULIE ANDREWS played a nanny in three movies: *Mary Poppins*, *The Sound of Music*, and *Eloise at the Plaza*.

11
Before *THE WIZARD OF OZ* became a movie, it was a book, a comic, a stage musical, and a silent movie!

12
In the Pixar movie *Cars*, LIGHTNING MCQUEEN'S racing number is 95, a reference to the year *Toy Story* was released—1995.

13
JIM HENSON, the creator of the Muppets, was the original voice of Kermit the Frog, Rowlf the Dog, Dr. Teeth, and the Swedish Chef (even though he didn't know Swedish!).

14
R2-D2 of *Star Wars* fame was sometimes operated by remote control and other times by an actor who crouched inside and moved the DROID.

15
Star Wars' C-3PO was said to be fluent in over six million languages. There are just over 7,000 languages spoken on Earth.

16
The first sound cartoon was *Steamboat Willie*, released in 1928. This early version of MICKEY MOUSE was voiced by Mickey's creator, Walt Disney.

17
Pixar brought BUZZ LIGHTYEAR and WOODY to life in *Toy Story*, the first computer-animated feature-length film.

18
When the classic book *Where the Wild Things Are* was turned into film, the Wild Things were a mix of computer animation and people in GIANT MONSTER SUITS.

19
Scenes from *INDIANA JONES AND THE LAST CRUSADE* of a temple carved out of a sandstone rock face were filmed at a real building called the "Treasury" in Petra, Jordan.

20
THE WHITE HOUSE has its own movie theater. It seats 42 people.

21
The actor who was the voice of YODA also gave a voice to MISS PIGGY.

22
Americans reach for popcorn as their go-to snack at the movies. In Japan a popular treat is BAKED FISH SKELETONS coated with soy and sugar. In Korea, it's roasted chestnuts.

23
The world's biggest IMAX theater screen is in Sydney, Australia. It is 96 feet (29 m) high by 117 feet (36 m) wide—OVER HALF THE SIZE OF AN OLYMPIC-SIZE POOL—and seats 540 people.

24
The BATMOBILE used in the movie *Batman Forever* sold at auction for $335,000.

25
A man in India set a world record for the longest marathon of film-watching. He watched movies for 120 HOURS, 23 MINUTES STRAIGHT.

26
JOHNNY DEPP cannot see his own movies in 3-D. He is one of a small percentage of the population with "stereo blindness," which means his eyes don't align to see 3-D properly.

27
It took TWO AND A HALF HOURS to apply makeup to JIM CARREY for *How the Grinch Stole Christmas*. The film took 92 days of shooting. That's 230 HOURS OF SITTING STILL!

28
Oftentimes in animated movies, the actors NEVER EVEN MEET EACH OTHER. They record their parts separately, and these are put together to make the dialogue.

29
SHREK means "MONSTER" in Yiddish.

30
When a new DVD of *E.T. the Extra-Terrestrial* was re-released, guns held by police officers in the original film were digitally erased and replaced with WALKIE-TALKIES.

31
After *Night at the Museum* was released, attendance at the American Museum of Natural History in New York, U.S.A., increased **20 PERCENT.**

32
Classic movies are shown on summer evenings in the middle of a **LOS ANGELES CEMETERY!**

33
The letters in the Hollywood sign are **FOUR-AND-A-HALF STORIES TALL.**

34
The actor **JOHN RATZENBERGER** has lent his voice to every full-length Pixar movie, including as a school of fish in *Finding Nemo* and Mack, the semi-truck in *Cars.*

35
Snow White and the Seven Dwarfs was the first full-length animated film **IN COLOR AND WITH SOUND.**

36
Shaving cream was used for the goo of the **STAY-PUFT MARSHMALLOW MAN** after he exploded at the end of *Ghostbusters.*

37
After appearing numerous times on the silver screen, **SPIDER-MAN** is also swinging through a Broadway musical, with music by **U2.**

38
The **MOST EXPENSIVE** movie that has been made to date was *Pirates of the Caribbean: At World's End,* with a production budget of about **$300 MILLION.**

39
E.T. the Extra-Terrestrial was originally intended to be a **HORROR MOVIE.**

40
Companies make big money when their products are placed in movies. **RAY-BAN** sales went up after the lead characters wore the sunglasses in *Men in Black.*

41
The mechanical shark used in *Jaws* was nicknamed **"BRUCE."**

42
Steven Spielberg hired a **PALEONTOLOGIST** to make sure the dinosaurs in *Jurassic Park* looked realistic.

43
The Wallace & Gromit claymation film *A Grand Day Out* took the creator **SEVEN YEARS TO MAKE.** Twenty-four frames are needed for each second of film.

44
Artists on the *Finding Nemo* crew visited the **GREAT BARRIER REEF** to get inspiration before starting production.

45
Which superhero is on top? Batman. **THE DARK KNIGHT** is the top grossing superhero movie. It earned more than $530 million.

46
The same actor who played **GOLLUM** in *Lord of the Rings* played **CAESAR** in *Rise of the Planet of the Apes* and the title role in *King Kong.*

47
At the end of the Disney version of *The Little Mermaid,* Ariel marries the prince. In the original Hans Christian Andersen book, she turns into **SEA FOAM!**

48
Actor **TOM CRUISE** does most of his own stunts in the *Mission Impossible* movies.

49
The house that Kevin was left to defend in *Home Alone* was a real home near Chicago, U.S.A. It sold recently for **$2 MILLION.**

50
"WALL-E" stands for Waste Allocation Load Lifter Earth-Class.

50 FACTS ABOUT FLICKS

1
SINCE 1998, ABOUT **430 DAMS** IN THE UNITED STATES HAVE BEEN **REMOVED**, ALLOWING RIVERS TO **RETURN TO THEIR NATURAL FLOW.**

2
THE **SNAKE-NECKED TURTLE,** FOUND IN THE MARSHES AND SHALLOW WATERS OF AUSTRALIA, INDONESIA, AND NEW GUINEA, **SMELLS LIKE A SKUNK.**

3
FEMALE RED-EYED TREE FROGS lay their eggs on the underside of leaves, so they eventually **FALL INTO THE WATER,** where the eggs hatch.

4
THE **ARMORED CATFISH** MAY LOOK AS IF IT SHIMMERS, BUT ITS SHEEN IS ACTUALLY THE REFLECTION OF A THIN LAYER OF CRYSTALS UNDERNEATH ITS SKIN.

25 WONDERFUL

5
MORE AMERICANS FISH THAN PLAY TENNIS OR GOLF.

6
THE RAIN THAT FALLS TODAY IS THE SAME FRESH WATER THAT DINOSAURS DRANK.

7
THE NILE, considered by most to be the world's longest river, stretches about 4,000 miles (6,400 km)—the length of more than 42 million dollar bills lined up end to end.

8
FRESH WATER MAKES UP **LESS THAN THREE PERCENT** OF THE EARTH'S WATER.

9
A BATH USES **75 PERCENT** MORE WATER THAN A **FIVE-MINUTE SHOWER.**

10
WHEN A RIVER OTTER DIVES, ITS EARS AND NOSE CLOSE TIGHTLY TO KEEP OUT WATER.

11
MORE THAN 3.5 MILLION MILES (5.6 MILLION KM) OF RIVERS AND STREAMS FLOW THROUGH THE UNITED STATES.

12
Every person in the United States uses about 100 gallons — or **1,600 CUPS — OF WATER** every day.

13

COLD WATER
WEIGHS MORE THAN HOT WATER.

14

FROZEN WATER (ICE) IS LIGHTER THAN WATER, WHICH IS WHY IT FLOATS.

16

A MINNOW—
A SMALL, SILVERY FISH FOUND IN PONDS, LAKES, AND RIVERS—HAS ITS TEETH IN ITS THROAT.

15

Florida's
EVERGLADES NATIONAL PARK—a wetlands home to panthers, alligators, and leatherback turtles—covers an area about the size of Delaware, U.S.A.

17

DRAGONFLY LARVAE
LIVE UNDERWATER BEFORE THEY BECOME ADULTS THAT FLY.

18

A type of
SALAMANDER called a **MUDPUPPY** spends its entire life underwater like a fish.

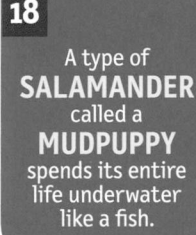

FACTS ABOUT
WATER

19

IT TAKES **2,900 GALLONS (10,977 L) OF WATER** TO PRODUCE ONE PAIR OF JEANS.

20

THERE IS THE **SAME AMOUNT OF WATER** ON EARTH NOW AS THERE WAS **WHEN THE EARTH FORMED.**

21

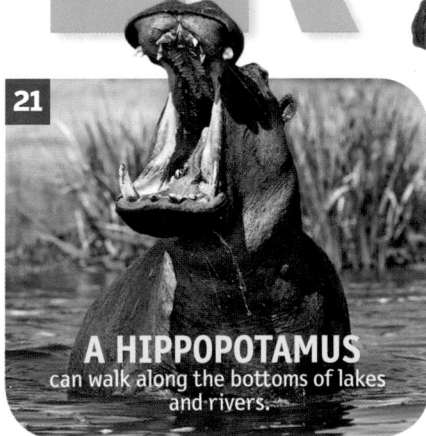

A HIPPOPOTAMUS can walk along the bottoms of lakes and rivers.

22

97 PERCENT OF WATER ON EARTH IS UNDRINKABLE. ANOTHER **2 PERCENT IS FROZEN IN POLAR ICE CAPS.**

23

LESS THAN **ONE PERCENT** OF THE EARTH'S WATER IS AVAILABLE FOR US TO USE.

24

WATER REGULATES THE TEMPERATURE OF THE BODY.

25

A PERSON CAN ONLY LIVE A WEEK WITHOUT WATER.

15 POWERFUL FACTS ABOUT

1 **BARACK OBAMA,** the 44th president of the United States, collects *SPIDER-MAN* AND *CONAN THE BARBARIAN* COMICS.

2 **STEVE JOBS**—co-founder of Apple and largely responsible for the creation of the iPod, iPhone, and iPad—**HAD BEEN TAKING HOME A SALARY OF** $1 A YEAR FROM 1997 UNTIL HIS DEATH IN 2011.

3 **KING TUTANKHAMUN'S NAME WAS LEFT OUT** of all ancient Egyptian records so little was known about him before his tomb was discovered in ALMOST PERFECT CONDITION THREE THOUSAND YEARS LATER.

4 **MOHANDAS GANDHI,** who used nonviolent resistance to help **INDIA GAIN ITS INDEPENDENCE,** refused to use his name to help his son get a college scholarship because he believed **ALL PEOPLE SHOULD BE TREATED EQUALLY.**

5 **CLEOPATRA** was able to sneak past an army to see **ROMAN GENERAL JULIUS CAESAR** by having a **SERVANT WRAP HER IN A CARPET** and deliver her to the royal palace in Alexandria.

6 Between 1957 and 1968 pastor and activist **MARTIN LUTHER KING, JR.** (right) traveled more than **6 MILLION MILES (9.6 MILLION KM)** and spoke more than **2,500 TIMES** on behalf of the American civil rights movement.

WORLD LEADERS

7 In **2010, DILMA ROUSSEFF** became the **FIRST FEMALE PRESIDENT OF BRAZIL.**

8 The U.S. has had **12 DIFFERENT PRESIDENTS** since **KING BHUMIBOL ADULYADEJ (RAMA IX)** became the monarch of Thailand.

9 **PUYI**, the twelfth ruler of the Qing dynasty and **LAST EMPEROR OF CHINA**, became emperor JUST BEFORE HIS THIRD BIRTHDAY.

10 **QUEEN VICTORIA POPULARIZED WHITE WEDDING DRESSES** when she wore one to her **OWN WEDDING IN 1840.**

11 The Roman emperor **CALIGULA LOVED HIS HORSE INCITATUS SO MUCH** that it's been said he **INVITED THE ANIMAL TO BANQUETS** and had intentions of **MAKING IT A PRIEST.**

12 **WINSTON CHURCHILL,** the British Prime Minister during World War II, worked for many years to OVERCOME A SPEECH IMPEDIMENT.

13 Russian Prime Minister **VLADIMIR PUTIN HAS A BLACK BELT IN JUDO.**

14 In 2006, TV host and comedian **CONAN O'BRIEN** ran advertisements supporting **FINNISH PRESIDENT TARJA HALONEN'S BID FOR RE-ELECTION** because she looks like him; **SHE WON.**

15 **POPE BENEDICT XVI** has about **20,000 BOOKS** in his personal library.

1 The minute hand on London's Big Ben clock travels about 118 miles (190 km) a year.

2 It took 20,000 workers 22 years to build India's Taj Mahal.

3 Frank Lloyd Wright's Guggenheim Museum in New York, U.S.A., is as much a work of art as the pieces it holds. A quarter-mile-long (.40 km) spiral ramp leads visitors past hung artwork. Some artists protested its design because they said the curved walls would make it too hard to hang their art.

4 ARCHITECTS HAVE DESIGNED A 65-STORY "EARTH SCRAPER" FOR MEXICO CITY. INSTEAD OF BUILDING UP, THE BUILDING WILL BE 984 FEET (300 M) UNDERGROUND!

5 The Luxor Hotel and Casino in Las Vegas, Nevada, U.S.A., has a spotlight on top of its pyramid that beams the equivalent of 40 billion candles into the sky.

6 The TransAmerica Pyramid, the tallest building in San Francisco, U.S.A., has wings coming out the sides starting at the 29th floor so elevators can go to the pointed top.

7 The 36 columns on the Lincoln Memorial in Washington, D.C., represent the U.S. states in the Union at the time President Lincoln died.

8 After East and West Germany were reunified, two artists wrapped Berlin's historic capitol building, the Reichstag, in 1,076,000 square feet (99,964 sq m) of silvery fabric.

9 THE SQUARE MOAT AROUND CAMBODIA'S ANGKOR WAT IS AS WIDE AS TWO OLYMPIC SWIMMING POOLS AND CAN BE SEEN FROM SPACE.

10 Potala Palace in Tibet sits on a ridge 10,000 feet (3,048 m) high, contains some 1,000 rooms, and has been the home of kings and monks for 1,300 years. The Dalai Lama, however, has not lived there since he went into exile in 1959.

11 Soviet leader Joseph Stalin ordered Moscow's St. Basil's Cathedral, built in the 16th century, to be destroyed and replaced with a subway station. The architect for the job refused and was sent to prison, but the church remained.

12 In addition to being a U.S. President, Thomas Jefferson was an architect. He spent 40 years designing and building Monticello, his home in Virginia. It has 43 rooms, 8 fireplaces, and 13 skylights.

13 In the 1930s, architect Frank Lloyd Wright designed a house in Pennsylvania, U.S.A., called Fallingwater using what he called "organic" architecture. Built over a waterfall, there is a boulder in the living room that is also a fireplace.

14 The Louvre Pyramid in Paris, France, acts as the main entrance to the Louvre Museum. There's a smaller, inverted pyramid in an underground mall in front of the Louvre.

15 The Pompidou, an art, music, and education center in Paris, has a tubed escalator that runs around the outside, which some people call a "hamster walkway"!

16 Rome, Italy's Colosseum once seated 50,000 people, who came to watch gladiators fight to the death. It had trap doors that let fighters make surprise appearances and allowed the dead to be hauled away.

17 There is a Darth Vader gargoyle on the National Cathedral in Washington, D.C., U.S.A.

18 The Burj al-Arab Tower Hotel in the United Arab Emirates's Dubai has a helicopter pad that connects to a penthouse suite and an underwater restaurant reachable only by submarine.

19 Standing 1,483 feet (452 m), the Petronas Towers in Kuala Lumpur, Malaysia, were completed in 1998 and became the first skyscrapers to be taller than any U.S. skyscraper.

20 The elevator ride from the basement parking lot to the top of each of the 88-floor Petronas Towers is 90 seconds.

21 The Petronas Towers are made of 36,910 tons (33,500 MT) of steel—that's heavier than 5,000 elephants.

22 At 1,046 feet (319 m), the Chrysler Building in New York, U.S.A., was the world's tallest building for only 11 months until the Empire State Building was completed in 1931. It is 204 feet (62 m) taller.

23 A highway goes through the fifth through seventh stories of the 16-story Gate Tower Building in Osaka.

24 A PRO SKATEBOARDER DESIGNED A HOME IN WHICH EVERY SPACE IS ROUNDED AND SKATEABLE—EVEN THE CABINETS AND FURNITURE!

25 The Chrysler Building was completed in 1930. Made of shiny alloy with steel eagle gargoyles near the top that stare out over the city, the hope was to create a building so distinctive that it would make the automobile company a household name.

26 The Empire State Building was the world's tallest building for 41 years until the World Trade Center was completed in 1972.

27 THE EMPIRE STATE BUILDING IS STRUCK BY LIGHTNING ABOUT 100 TIMES A YEAR.

28 At Chicago, U.S.A.'s Willis Tower, visitors can see four U.S. states from the sky deck—Illinois, Indiana, Michigan, and Wisconsin.

29 The 16,100 windows of Willis Tower are washed by an automatic window-washing machine.

30 The 986-foot (300.5 m) Eiffel Tower was unveiled in 1889 at the Paris World Fair. It's twice as tall as the Washington Monument, but weighs less.

31 The Eiffel Tower is covered in dark brown paint.

32 Michelangelo, who created St. Peter's Basilica in Vatican City, refused to be paid for his work.

33 "The Crooked House" in Poland isn't a home, but rather holds shops and restaurants. Its wavy architecture looks like the reflection from a fun house mirror.

34 The Pantheon in Rome, Italy, completed in A.D. 123, was built as a temple to the Roman gods. Made of bricks and concrete, it remains almost in its original form today. The 27-foot (8.2 m) oculus, a round opening in the center of the dome, is the only source of natural light in the building.

35 Architects have designed a building for Dubai, U.A.E., called the Da Vinci Tower, which will change shape continuously. Each floor will make one full rotation every 90 minutes.

36 George Washington laid the cornerstone of the U.S. Capitol Building in 1793.

37 Houston, U.S.A.'s air-conditioned Astrodome, built in 1966, was a solution for playing baseball in Texas's hot summer weather. It was the first ball field to have a roof over it.

75 BRAIN-BUILDING ARCHITECTURE

FACTS ABOUT

38 The John Hancock Center, a 1,127-foot (343.5 m) Chicago, U.S.A., skyscraper, is known as "Big John."

39 The world's biggest McDonald's opened in London, U.K., for the 2012 Olympics. It seats 1,500 people and is half the size of a football field.

40 The seven rays on the crown of the Statue of Liberty represent the seven continents.

41 The Statue of Liberty, from the base of the pedestal foundation to the top of the torch, is 305 feet, 6 inches (93 m) tall.

42 Burj Khalifa in Dubai, U.A.E., is the world's tallest building. It's more than half a mile high at 2,716.5 feet (828 meters).

43 Burj Khalifa isn't just the tallest building in the world. It has the most number of stories, the highest outdoor observation deck, and the highest occupied floor.

44 The outside of Kansas City's Public Library garage was designed to look like the spines of books. Some of the titles: *Green Eggs and Ham* and *Goodnight Moon.*

45 A company in Ohio, U.S.A., that makes baskets has an office building in a shape of a picnic basket.

46 Built in 1976, the CN Tower in Toronto is 1,815 feet, 5 inches (553.3 m). The restaurant near the top of the tower rotates once every 72 minutes, giving diners a panoramic view of the city.

47 TAIPEI 101, WHICH OPENED IN TAIWAN IN 2004, IS THE WORLD'S SECOND TALLEST BUILDING. IT HAS 101 FLOORS AND STANDS 1,667 FEET (508 M).

48 Taipei 101 has the world's fastest elevator. It travels at 3,314 feet (1,010 m) per minute, taking just 39 seconds to travel from the ground level up to the 89th floor.

49 When the Shanghai Tower is complete in 2014, it will have an elevator that travels at 3,543 feet (1,080 m) per minute. It will become the tallest building in China and the second tallest in the world.

50 An architect built a four-story house in Malawi shaped like a football.

Taipei 101

51 China has more skyscrapers than any other country.

52 Skyscrapers are designed to sway in the wind.

53 The man who invented the Rubik's Cube was an architect.

54 The tower cranes that work on the very top of skyscraper buildings to add more floors assemble themselves by lifting heavy pieces to lengthen the arm.

55 BECAUSE SKYSCRAPERS ARE SO EXPENSIVE TO BUILD, THEY ONLY EXIST IN DENSE CITIES WHERE IT TAKES UP LESS SPACE TO BUILD UP THAN TO SPREAD OUT.

56 The Gateway Arch in St. Louis, Missouri, U.S.A., is 630 feet (192 m) high. That is also the distance between the two legs.

57 A five-story house in London, U.K., is only six feet (1.8 m) wide.

58 The outside of the Empire State Building is illuminated in different colors at different times—for example, red and green at Christmas and red, orange, and yellow at Thanksgiving.

59 The Washington Monument was built between 1848 and 1884 as a tribute to George Washington's leadership during the American Revolution. There was a 20-year break during construction, and the second batch of stone came from a different quarry, resulting in a visible change in the monument partway up!

60 A house in New Jersey, U.S.A., is shaped like a cookie jar. It doesn't have any corners and has a spiral staircase inside.

61 A congressional mandate states that the Washington Monument has to remain the tallest structure in Washington, D.C., U.S.A.

62 The sphere-shaped Spaceship Earth at the Epcot theme park in Orlando, Florida, U.S.A., is 18 stories high. Inside, riders go on a "time machine" that takes them about two-thirds up the dome.

63 The Pentagon has five sides and five stories, and sits on five acres of land in Virginia, U.S.A.

64 Gargoyles are often found on the outside of Gothic churches. They represent leaving the grotesque outside before entering the serenity inside.

65 In Syria, ancient mud houses were shaped like beehives.

66 U.S. President George Washington oversaw construction of the White House, but never lived in it.

67 A two-story building in South Korea was designed to look like a toilet. A meeting of the World Toilet Association was held in it.

68 Built in the 15th century, the Forbidden City was the home of Chinese royalty, located in the heart of what is now Beijing. It was home to 24 emperors and had 90 palaces and courtyards, 980 buildings, and 8,704 rooms.

69 Shakespeare's Globe in London sits on the site of the original Globe Theatre and is a "best guess" reconstruction of the one built in 1599.

70 Mecca, Saudi Arabia's al Haram Mosque, can hold 820,000 people.

71 There are 10,000 panes of glass in southern California's Crystal Cathedral.

72 SOME PEOPLE IN CENTRAL ASIA LIVE IN YURTS—COLLAPSIBLE DOME-SHAPED STRUCTURES COVERED IN SKINS OR FABRIC.

73 Paris's Notre Dame Cathedral, completed in 1250, contains some of its original stained glass windows. The bell in its South Tower weighs more than five tons (4,536 kg)—that's as much as 20 gorillas!

74 The Krzywy Domek (Crooked House) in Poland was inspired by children's book illustrations. The building peaks in the center and is compressed on both sides, appearing as though it is being sucked up in a vacuum.

75 The Statue of Liberty functioned as an actual lighthouse from 1886 to 1902.

35 FOOD FACTS

1 The most popular fruit in the world is the GRAPE.

2 Some cultures believe eating chickens and turkeys for dinner on New Year's Day will bring setbacks for the rest of the year because the birds scratch backward in the dirt.

3 At the first Thanksgiving, pilgrims and Wampanoag Indians ate birds—likely goose, duck, turkey, swan, or pigeon—venison, corn, shellfish, eels, chestnuts, and squash.

4 MOPANE WORMS are a popular food in some parts of Africa, and in some years more than 1,764 tons (1,600 MT) of the insects are sold in South Africa alone.

5 As American as apple pie, hot dogs are celebrated every July 4 in New York at the INTERNATIONAL HOT DOG EATING CONTEST. The 2011 winner ate 62 HOT DOGS AND BUNS IN 10 MINUTES.

6 People have been FARMING POTATOES for more than 9,000 YEARS.

7 Until about 500 YEARS AGO, farmed carrots were every color but orange; MOST WERE PURPLE.

8 LUCKY CHARMS, first sold in 1964, was the first cereal to include MARSHMALLOWS.

9 The "m" on M&MS wasn't printed on the candies until 1950, nine years after they were first sold.

10 In UKRAINE, SALT is a traditional symbol of FRIENDSHIP.

11 POTATOES in Peru and Bolivia come in different sizes, shapes, and colors. Some have names like Feet of the Lequecho Bird and Makes the Daughter-In-Law Cry.

12 There is a variety of LEMON called a BABOON.

13 People in Asia have been FARMING RICE for thousands of years, and today it is the STAPLE FOOD for about HALF THE WORLD'S POPULATION.

14 In 19th-century America, 7,000 DIFFERENT KINDS OF APPLES were grown; now, FEWER THAN 100 are grown.

15 ANT EGGS are a high-end food in Mexico, where they're known as ESCAMOLES, OR "MEXICAN CAVIAR."

16 Half of all salt is MINED; the other half is harvested from the SEA.

17 NOODLES originated in China more than 2,200 YEARS AGO.

18 You can buy LIQUID SMOKE—SMOKE-FLAVORED WATER—at the grocery store.

19 A fully ripe lime is PALE YELLOW, NOT GREEN.

20 As much as 30 PERCENT of an AVOCADO IS OIL.

21 MUSHROOMS are 80–90 PERCENT WATER.

22 Evidence of humans MILKING ANIMALS in northern Europe dates to 5,000 B.C.; rock drawings of the act appeared later in the Sahara; and cheese has been found in ancient Egyptian tombs.

23 The longest PIZZA ever made stretched 3,745 FEET AND 0.85 INCHES (1,141.5 M) and was created in Spain on May 31, 2011.

FOR THOUGHT

24 COTTON CANDY, introduced at the 1904 WORLD'S FAIR in St. Louis, Missouri, U.S.A., is SUGAR SPUN INTO FINE STRANDS.

25 Ancient Greeks left PILES OF GARLIC along travel routes, believing the practice caused demons following them to lose their way.

26 Fried TARANTULAS are considered a delicacy in CAMBODIA.

27 Ancient Greeks traded their wine and olive oil for FOREIGN FIGS believed to BRING SWEET DREAMS.

28 In Thailand, CRICKETS are farmed for food.

29 On a BANANA PLANT, bunches of the fruit are called "HANDS," and each banana is called a "FINGER."

30 TOOTSIE ROLLS are named after the candy maker's daughter, Clara, whose nickname was "Tootsie."

31 The ancient EGYPTIANS were eating WATERMELON 5,000 years ago.

32 The BLUE in blue cheese is MOLD.

33 HEADCHEESE is a mixture of gelatin and HEAD PARTS, often from a PIG. SWEETBREAD is the PANCREAS of a young animal, such as a calf.

34 TRUFFLES, a prized part of certain fungi, are foraged from the woods by farmers using DOGS AND PIGS THAT SNIFF THEM OUT.

35 EATING CHEESE at the end of a meal slows TOOTH DECAY.

1. Abraham Lincoln was an avid sports fan. In the months leading up to his 1860 election to the presidency, he and his friends gathered in an alley in Springfield, Illinois, U.S.A., to play handball. 2. Because so many football players were in the military during WWII, the Philadelphia Eagles and Pittsburgh Steelers formed a combined team for the 1943 season. They were dubbed the "Steagles." 3. The first Olympic victor was Koroibos, a cook who won a foot race of 600 feet (183 m) in 776 B.C. 4. The coldest game in NFL history occurred on December 31, 1967, when the Dallas Cowboys played the Green Pay Packers in -13°F (-25°C) in Green Bay, Wisconsin, U.S.A. It became known as "The Ice Bowl." 5. Baseball player Ken Griffey, Jr., was allergic to the candy bar that was named after him and featured his image. 6. On October 23, 2011, television cameras spotted what some believed to be a UFO during a New Orleans Saints and Indianapolis Colts game. 7. Babe Ruth hit 54 home runs during the 1920 season. Only one team hit more home runs that year than Babe did by himself. 8. On July 13, 1934, after smacking his 700th career home run, Babe Ruth exclaimed, "I want that ball," before circling the bases. The kid who retrieved it swapped it with him for $20 and an autograph. 9. Football players smear black grease under their eyes to help reduce the sun's glare so they can see the ball better. 10. Michael Jordan always wore his University of North Carolina shorts under his professional uniform for good luck. 11. No other continent besides Europe and South America has produced a soccer team that has won the World Cup. 12. Roger Bannister, a British medical student, was the first person to run a mile (1.6 km) in less than four minutes. He ran one in 3 minutes 59.4 seconds in 1954. 13. Heavyweight boxer Rocky Marciano won 49 straight fights in his career and retired undefeated. 14. Beginning in 1875, the Kentucky Derby is one of the oldest sporting events in the United States. 15. Muhammed Ali, perhaps the world's most famous boxer, picked up the sport when he was 12 years old because he was angry that his bike had been stolen. 16. The term "checkmate," which is the ultimate goal of chess, comes from the Persian phrase "Shah Mat," which means "the King is left helpless." 17. Japan's Nagoya Grand Bowl is the largest bowling alley in the world, with 156 lanes divided between three floors. 18. On May 21, 2011, after scaling Mount Everest, Lakpa Tsheri Sherpa and Sano Babu Sunuwar launched a paraglider from its summit. Once they landed, they proceeded to kayak all the way to the Indian Ocean, completing the first summit-to-sea journey. 19. At a West Michigan White Caps game, you can get a "fifth third burger." That is, five one-third pound (.15 kg) hamburger patties on one giant bun. 20. Formula One race car drivers can sweat off up to six pounds (3 kg) during a race. 21. Twenty-one out of the 22 players on Bulgaria's 1994 World Cup Soccer team had last names ending in the letters "ev" or "ov." Petar Mikhtarski was the only one who did not. 22. NHL player Dave "Tiger" Williams spent the equivalent of 66 full games in the penalty box—the most of any player to date. 23. In 1970, 55 people crossed the finish line of the New York City Marathon. In 2011, 47,323 people crossed it. 24. Bossaball, played in Europe and South America, is a hybrid of volleyball, soccer, gymnastics, and a Brazilian martial art called capoeira—and it involves trampolines. 25. Cheese rolling is a sport in which an eight-pound (3.6 kg), wheel-shaped hunk of cheese is rolled from the top of a steep hill and competitors chase it to the bottom. 26. Ice hockey pucks are frozen before games because they slide better and bounce less than warm pucks. 27. The weight limit for jockeys in the Kentucky Derby is 126 pounds (57.2 kg), including the jockey's equipment. 28. On Christmas Day 1965, a man named Sherman Poppen built a toy for his daughter by combining a pair of snow skis into one wide board and attaching a rope to steer with while standing. The toy, which his wife called a "snurfer," was one of the first snowboards. 29. "Heliskiing" is a form of skiing in which, instead of a chairlift, a helicopter takes skiers to the top of a mountain to ski down it. 30. Adventure athlete Andrew Skurka has hiked more than 25,000 miles (40,000 km)—that's the equivalent of walking around the Earth one time. 31. American cyclist Lance Armstrong survived cancer and went on to win cycling's most important race, the Tour de France, a record seven times. 32. Pugil is Latin for "boxer." The sport of boxing is sometimes referred to as pugilism. 33. Former baseball pitcher Turk Wendell would chew four pieces of licorice while he pitched and then brush his teeth between every inning. 34. Evel Knievel, a daredevil motorcycle rider who performed death-defying stunts throughout the 1970s, holds the world record for "most bones broken in a lifetime." 35. The first African-American man to become world heavyweight boxing champion also received a patent for improving the household wrench. 36. The 1972 Miami Dolphins are the only NFL team in history to finish an entire season undefeated. 37. Mark McGwire's record-setting 70 home runs in the 1998 season traveled a total of more than 29,000 feet (8,839 m)—the same as the height of Mount Everest. 38. The fastest runners reach incredible speeds by using as much as 1,000 pounds (453.6 kg) of force with a single leg during each step. 39. Unlike in boxing, there are no weight classes in sumo. 40. Jordan Romero finished the challenge of climbing the tallest mountain on every continent when he was 15 years and 165 days old—a world record. 41. It took almost two and a half years for British Army captain Ed Stafford to walk the entire 4,000 miles (6,437 km) of the Amazon River. 42. At 120 miles per hour (193 kph), a Formula One race car generates so much down force that it can drive upside down on the roof of a tunnel. 43. In September 1971, the Pittsburgh Pirates were the first Major League Baseball team to send an all-minority lineup onto the field. They went on to win the World Series that year. 44. In 1962, the San Francisco Giants' manager, Alvin Dark, said of his rookie pitcher, Gaylord Perry, "There'll be a man on the moon before Gaylord Perry hits a home run." Seven years later, one hour after Neil Armstrong stepped foot onto the moon, Gaylord Perry hit his first major-league home run. 45. Professional players can make soccer balls curve in midair because of the Bernoulli principle: If a ball is kicked with spin, it will experience less air pressure on one side than on the other, causing it to curve. 46. The longest tennis match in history took place at Wimbledon in 2010. It was played over 3 days, lasted 183 games, and took 11 hours and 5 minutes to complete. 47. In 2002, "Mr. Met," the mascot for the New York Mets had a birthday party attended by many other Major League Baseball mascots. 48. In 1984, West Virginia's Georgeann Wells became the first woman to slam-dunk in an official college basketball game. 49. A hot, dry baseball will travel farther than a cold, moist one. 50. The world's fastest human, Usain Bolt, can reach a top speed of just under 28 miles per hour (45 kph). 51. It took Daniel Buettner almost a year to pedal his bike from Alaska to Argentina. It was a 15,266-mile (24,568-km) journey. 52. Ski Dubai in the United Arab Emirates is the Middle East's first indoor ski resort. 53. Several members of the Chicago White Sox were banned from the game after it was discovered they planned to intentionally lose the 1919 World Series against the Cincinnati Reds, earning them the nickname "Black Sox." 54. Baseball teams in the early 19th century didn't play nine innings. They played until the first team scored 21 aces—runs. 55. In a match in 1871, boxers James Mace and Joe Coburn fought for more than an hour without either man landing a solid punch on the other. 56. In 2006, shaman priest Tzamarenda Naychapi traveled to Germany on behalf of the Ecuador national soccer team to drive away evil spirits and bring the team good luck in the World Cup games. 57. Since 1949, the winner of the Masters Tournament—one of the four major competitions in golf—has been awarded a green jacket as a prize. 58. Miller Park, home of the Milwaukee Brewers, holds the Klement's

Sausage Race at the bottom of the sixth inning—a race between people dressed up as different types of sausage. **59.** Eastern Washington University's football field is bright red—matching the school's colors. **60. There are typically 330 to 500 dimples in a golf ball. The dimples help the ball travel higher and farther. 61.** In Major League Baseball, the distance between bases is 90 feet (27.4 m)—a little more than the length of two yellow school buses. **62. The Wife Carrying World Championships are held each year in Finland; men race over hilly terrain carrying their wives on their backs or over their shoulders. 63.** The highest-paid athlete in 2011 was golfer Tiger Woods, who made around $75 million. **64. In 1962, Maryland was the first U.S. state to adopt an official sport—jousting. 65.** Joe Alexander of Germany set a world record in 2010 by breaking 24 concrete blocks while holding an unbroken raw egg in the hand of the arm used for breaking the blocks. **66. Lauren Woolstencroft, who was born without legs below the knees and without a left arm below the elbow, is one of the best alpine skiers in the world and won five gold medals at the 2010 Paralympics in Vancouver. 67.** Boston's Fenway Park is the oldest baseball stadium in the U.S. still in use. The left field wall is known as the "Green Monster." **68. Unlike most professional sports, a clock isn't used in baseball and the time of the game is unlimited. 69.** Each regulation baseball has 108 red double stitches (or 216 single stitches). **70. Kareem Abdul-Jabbar, the NBA's all-time leading scorer, collects rugs. 71.** Early basketball games in the United States used peach baskets as the hoops, so people had to climb a ladder to retrieve the ball after they made a shot. **72. Footballs are nicknamed "pigskins" because they were originally made from inflated pigs' bladders. Now, they are made from rubber and cowhide. 73.** Formula One race car drivers must do special exercises for their neck muscles, which are put to the test when handling the force of turning corners at extremely high speeds. **74. Three consecutive strikes in bowling is called a "turkey." 75.** In a deck of playing cards, all four kings have beards but only three of them have mustaches. The one without a mustache is the King of Hearts. **76. Patrick Roy—one of the best ice hockey goaltenders in history—talked to his goalposts, and he claimed they talked back to him. 77.** In underwater hockey, teams use short sticks to push a heavy puck across pool floors and into their opponents' goal. **78.** Figure skater Kristi **Yamaguchi was born with a foot condition and began skating to strengthen her feet and ankles. 79.** In 1935, runner Jesse Owens set four world records in less than an hour. **80. Before a sumo tournament, wrestlers perform an "entering the ring" ceremony. It ends with the highest-ranked wrestler clapping his hands and stomping his feet to attract the attention of the gods and drive evil from the sumo ring. 81.** In 1951, Althea Gibson became the first black tennis

100 WINNING FACTS ABOUT SPORTS

player at the Wimbledon tournament. Later in life she also became a professional golfer. **82. Freya Hoffmeister is the first woman ever to paddle around the entire continent of Australia. The 8,569-mile (13,760-km) trip took 332 days. 83.** Downhill skiers control their momentum by traveling in an S-shaped path down the slope because it slows them down. **84. Luge athletes can reach speeds of more than 95 mph (153 kph) while sliding down the track on their sleds. 85.** The temperature of an Olympic swimming pool must be between 77 and 82°F (25 and 28°C). The surrounding air must be kept within three degrees of the pool water. **86. At 60 years old, Jack LaLanne swam the mile (1.6 km) from Alcatraz Island to Fisherman's Wharf in San Francisco, U.S.A., while handcuffed, shackled, and towing a 1,000-pound (453.6-kg) boat. 87.** The "Legend of the Octopus" is a tradition in which Detroit Red Wings hockey fans throw real octopi onto the ice for good luck. **88. On Halloween night 2009, the San Antonio Spurs and Sacramento Kings basketball game was delayed because someone released a live bat into the arena. 89.** Third baseman Wade Boggs was very superstitious: He ate chicken on every game day and drew a Hebrew symbol in the dirt each time he stepped up to the plate. **90. Egyptians played a sport similar to baseball called "tipcat." 91.** Extreme Ironing competitors have ironed clothes on the top of Mount Rushmore, while parachuting, in the wilderness, and even underwater. **92. Quidditch, the sport played on broomsticks in the popular *Harry Potter* series, is played today in real life by people around the world. The United States has the most registered teams: 572. 93.** Toe wrestling championships are held annually in the town of Wetton in Derbyshire, England. **94. A presidential race takes place at every Washington Nationals baseball game, as Abraham Lincoln, Teddy Roosevelt, George Washington, and Thomas Jefferson race around the bases during the fourth inning. 95.** There's an ongoing debate between the University of Washington and a man named "Krazy George Henderson" over who invented the wave. University students claim they invented it at a homecoming game in 1981. Krazy George, a professional cheerleader, claims he invented it at an Oakland A's vs. Yankees baseball game two weeks before. **96. The first team mascot was an actual bulldog named "Handsome Dan," who supported Yale University athletes in 1889. 97.** The Italian mountain climber Reinhold Messner was the first person to climb all 14 of the world's "eight-thousanders"—peaks which are at least 8,000 meters (26,247 ft). **98. Studies show that athletes who wear red are more likely to win their contest. 99.** The Faroe Islands' national football team plays on a field that sits on the edge of the sea. A boat stands by in the water to collect any balls that are accidentally kicked off the field. **100. The Olympics were established in 776 B.C. to honor Zeus and to bring peace to Greece.**

7
Asian elephants are more easily trained for **TRANSPORTATION AND LABOR** than African elephants.

20
"ELEPHANTS EARS" are a sugary, fried pastry dough sold at some fairs and carnivals.

1
African elephants are the **LARGEST LAND MAMMALS** on Earth. They are slightly larger than their Asian elephant cousins.

14
Trunks are also used as **SNORKELS** when elephants wade in **DEEP WATER.**

27
Elephants have **FOUR MOLARS,** one on the **TOP** and one on the **BOTTOM** of both sides of their mouth.

8
Elephants can travel up to **90 MILES** (145 km) per day.

21
An elephant smells the air by raising its trunk like a **SUBMARINE PERISCOPE.**

2
African elephants have **LARGE EARS** that resemble the continent of Africa. Asian elephants have **SMALLER, ROUNDED EARS.**

15
An elephant's trunk is controlled by over **100,000 MUSCLES.**

28
ONE ELEPHANT MOLAR can weigh as much as 11 pounds (5 kg) and be the **SIZE OF A BRICK!**

9
An adult African elephant's trunk is about **SEVEN FEET (2 M) LONG.** That's longer than your bed!

22
A MOTHER ELEPHANT can use her trunk to lift or nudge a calf through difficult terrain, to pull another elephant out of the mud, or to lift a newborn elephant to its feet.

3
Elephants are pregnant more than **TWICE** as long as human moms are.

16
At birth, a calf's trunk has no **MUSCLE TONE.** It takes several months for a calf to gain full control of its trunk.

29
Many elephants have been **KILLED FOR THEIR VALUABLE TUSKS,** which are made into jewelry and piano keys. When turned into art or other material, tusks are called ivory.

10
The trunk is actually an **ELONGATED NOSE** and upper lip.

23
Male elephants use their tusks to **BATTLE** one another.

4
African elephants live up to **70 YEARS.**

11
An elephant can suck up as much as **TWO GALLONS** (7.5 L) of water into its trunk at a time. It then sticks its trunk into its mouth and blows. The water goes right down its throat.

17
TWO FINGERLIKE PARTS on the tip of an African elephant's trunk are used for things like **PICKING A BERRY** from the ground or plucking a single leaf off a tree.

24
African male and female elephants have tusks, but **ONLY MALE ASIAN ELEPHANTS DO.**

30
An elephant's long nose **CAN SMELL WATER SEVERAL MILES AWAY.**

5
At their shoulder, African elephants are **8.2 TO 13 FEET** (2.5 to 4 m) **TALL.**

18
An Asian elephant has just **ONE FINGERLIKE PART** on its trunk.

31
An elephant's skin is so sensitive it can **FEEL A FLY** land on it.

12
"Lucy the Elephant" is an **ELEPHANT-SHAPED SIX-STORY BUILDING** in Atlantic City, New Jersey, U.S.A. Visitors climb spiral staircases in her legs to get to the seat on her back.

25
TUSK SIZE AND SHAPE run in the family—much like some of the features you inherited from your parents.

6
African elephants weigh 5,000 to 14,000 pounds (2,268 to 6,350 kg). That's bigger than **TWO LARGE SUVS!**

19
Elephants are close living relatives to the extinct **WOOLLY MAMMOTH.**

32
TUSKS ARE AN ELEPHANT'S TOOLS: They use them to dig for water and roots to eat and as crowbars to pry bark from trees.

13
Elephants use their trunk to spray water over their body to **STAY COOL.** Then they sprinkle dust on themselves for **SUNSCREEN.**

26
Elephants' tusks are actually **TEETH.**

✱ YOU HAVE LEARNED **3,020** FACTS

50 ENORMOUS FACTS ABOUT ELEPHANTS

33 The "Dumbo the Flying Elephant" ride at Disneyland was originally designed to have all pink elephants, like the ones in **DUMBO'S NIGHTMARE.**

34 Elephants **FAVOR THEIR RIGHT OR LEFT TUSK,** just as humans favor their right or left hand.

35 An elephant's feet are hooved with **SPONGY PADS** that absorb its weight.

36 Elephants **FEEL SOUND VIBRATIONS** through the ground. Scientists think they can feel the movement of other herds up to 20 miles (32 km) away.

37 **FEMALES STAY WITH THEIR HERD THEIR WHOLE LIFE.** Males only stick around until they are 12 to 15 years old, then they live alone or form **"BACHELOR" HERDS** with other males.

38 It is **ILLEGAL** to trade ivory today, but poachers continue to kill elephants.

39 When baby elephants are born, they weigh about **200 POUNDS** (91 kg). That's as much as a **LARGE ADULT HUMAN.**

40 Newborn elephants are **THREE FEET (1 M) TALL**—about the height of a sofa.

41 A baby elephant is called a **CALF.** It drinks its mom's milk until it is four or five years old.

42 Calves sometimes suck their trunks for comfort just like **BABIES SUCK THEIR THUMBS.**

43 Elephants sometimes make **PURR-LIKE** sounds when content.

44 African elephants eat up to **300 POUNDS** (136 kg) of food per day. That's like eating **1,200 HAMBURGERS!**

45 Elephants use their mouths and trunks to **GRUMBLE, GROWL, AND TRUMPET.** This is how they talk to each other.

46 **PACHYDERM** is a term used to described elephants, rhinos, and hippos. Pachyderm means **"THICK SKIN."**

47 **ELEPHANT SEALS** got their name because of their large size—and because the males have elephant **TRUNK-LIKE NOSES.**

48 At only 64 minutes long, *DUMBO* is one of Disney's shortest **ANIMATED FEATURE FILMS.**

49 Sometimes elephants hook their trunks together in a kind of **ELEPHANT HUG.**

50 Elephants' ears give off heat to **KEEP THEM COOL** in hot temperatures.

1

THE LARGEST U.S. BILL PRODUCED TODAY IS THE $100 BILL. BUT LESS THAN 45 YEARS AGO, YOU COULD PAY FOR STUFF WITH A **$10,000 bill!**

2 The word "money" comes from Juno Moneta, the **ROMAN GODDESS** who protected all currency.

4  **A SPECIAL INK** in the 50-euro note (used in the European Union) changes yellow stars to orange and a blue signature to green when held under black, or ultraviolet, light.

3 Coins in ancient China were minted with **HOLES IN THE CENTER** so they could be strung and carried more easily. Some countries still use coins with holes, including Denmark, Japan, Papua New Guinea, and the Philippines.

5 Some experts claim the smallest coin in history is the quarter silver tara of Vijayanahar, an Asian empire from 1336 to 1646. It has a diameter of .16 inches (4 mm), roughly **THE SIZE OF A FLEA.**

25 MONEY
THAT WILL MAKE YOU

6 ### Is Canadian money crazy? Nope, just loonie.
That's the nickname for the Canadian one-dollar coin, which features the image of a loon, a bird commonly found in Canada.

7 In 2007, Mongolia issued a commemorative coin with a portrait of U.S. President John F. Kennedy. If you push a tiny button, the coin plays a sound bite from a speech.

9 Not all coins are round. The Cook Islands minted a triangular two-dollar coin. A square 15-cent coin is still in circulation in the Bahamas.

8  There's a zoo's worth of animals on money around the world, including **LIONS** in South Africa, **DOLPHINS** in Iceland, **HUMMINGBIRDS** in Brazil, and **KANGAROOS** in Australia.

10 Whale teeth were once highly treasured currency in Fiji. In the 19th century, a single **WHALE TOOTH** was worth one canoe.

11  In 2008, Chile's 50-peso coins were issued with the **name of the country misspelled as "CHIIE."** The coins were used for more than a year before anyone noticed the typo.

12 The U.S. Mint's first gold and silver coins had no numbers on them. The only way to tell them apart was by their size.

13

In 2009, the Bank of England recycled old and damaged banknotes into **COMPOST THAT WAS SOLD TO FARMS.**

14 Nearly two dozen countries—from Australia to Nigeria to Mexico—print money on **SHEETS OF PLASTIC** instead of paper. These brightly colored bills are so tough they can be washed with soap and water.

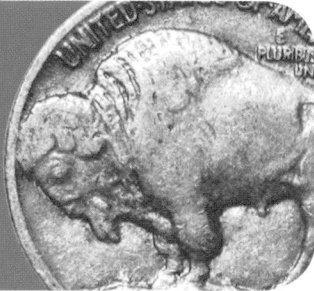

15 IT'S BELIEVED THAT THE BISON ON THE U.S. BUFFALO NICKEL WAS MODELED AFTER A REAL ANIMAL NAMED BLACK DIAMOND THAT LIVED IN NEW YORK CITY'S CENTRAL PARK ZOO FROM 1893 TO 1915.

16 The picture of Miss Liberty on the front of an 1839 U.S. cent looked so ridiculous to many people that the coin was nicknamed "SILLY HEAD."

FACTS
SAY KA-CHING!

17 **A red Canadian coin** LOOKED SO UNUSUAL THAT U.S. MILITARY AGENTS FIRST THOUGHT IT WAS A SPY COIN EMBEDDED WITH A RECORDING DEVICE.

18 In 1685, soldiers in Quebec, Canada, were paid in **PLAYING CARDS** after the French colonial government ran out of money.

19 In Venezuela, you can pay for things with a coin worth **12 ½ céntimos.** (A CÉNTIMO IS VENEZUELA'S SMALLEST CURRENCY, LIKE A U.S. CENT.)

20 A 1933 U.S. gold **double eagle coin** sold for more than $7.5 million at auction in 2002, the most expensive ever.

21 Some nomadic African tribes cast their metal money as jewelry such as **BRACELETS AND ANKLETS.** That made it easy for them to carry money as they moved from place to place.

22 When it was printed in 1946, the **HUNGARIAN 100 MILLION BILLION PENGŐ** was the largest bill ever issued. It was worth about 20 U.S. cents.

23 THE WORD "NICKEL" COMES FROM A GERMAN WORD THAT MEANS "RASCAL." MINERS COINED THE TERM BECAUSE NICKEL ORE LOOKS LIKE VALUABLE COPPER, AND THE "RASCALLY" NICKEL WOULD SOMETIMES FOOL THEM.

24 IN NORWAY, butter WAS ONCE ACCEPTED AS CURRENCY FOR TRADING.

25 Until the early 1900s, a whole coconut was the accepted form of currency in the Nicobar Islands, west of Thailand in the Indian Ocean.

15 SATISFYING FACTS

❶ LEAVES CHANGE COLOR IN AUTUMN because shorter days and longer nights cause trees to **STOP PRODUCING CHLOROPHYLL,** the substance that helps leaves make food and gives leaves a green color.

❷ In the **WINTER OF 1998–99, MOUNT BAKER, WASHINGTON,** set the **RECORD FOR MOST SNOWFALL EVER MEASURED** in the United States in a single season with **1,140 INCHES** (2,895.6 cm). That's nearly enough to cover a **TEN-STORY BUILDING.**

❸ BEAVER, OKLAHOMA, U.S.A., hosts the **WORLD COW CHIP THROWING CHAMPIONSHIP CONTEST** every spring.

❹ According to **GREEK MYTHOLOGY,** the seasons were caused when Hades, god of the underworld, took Persephone, goddess of spring growth, to be his bride. She was **OBLIGATED TO VISIT HIM UNDERGROUND FOUR MONTHS OF THE YEAR,** at which time the **EARTH BECAME COLD AND LIFELESS.**

❺ When it's **SUMMER IN THE NORTHERN HEMISPHERE,** it's **WINTER IN THE SOUTHERN HEMISPHERE** and vice versa.

❻ Seasons are the result of the **EARTH REVOLVING AROUND THE SUN ON A TILTED AXIS.** The tilt causes different parts of the world to receive **DIFFERENT AMOUNTS OF SUNLIGHT AT DIFFERENT TIMES OF THE YEAR.**

❼ Because the **AMOUNT OF SUNLIGHT AT THE EQUATOR** stays pretty much the same year-round, countries in that region **DON'T HAVE FOUR SEASONS.** Months of the year are instead divided into a **WET SEASON AND A DRY SEASON.**

ABOUT SEASONS

8 The **SWEDISH TOWN** of **GÄVLE** constructs a **43-FOOT (13-M) GOAT MADE OF STRAW** every year during the holiday season.

9 SPRING SHOWERS OCCUR IN OUTER SPACE, TOO. Images show that METHANE RAIN has fallen on the deserts of **TITAN, SATURN'S LARGEST MOON.**

10 The MOST POWERFUL VOLCANIC ERUPTION in recorded history was so strong that its ash in the air **CHANGED THE WORLD'S CLIMATE,** causing 1816 to become known in parts of Europe and North America as **"THE YEAR WITHOUT A SUMMER."**

11 Every spring, **CHANDLER, ARIZONA, U.S.A.,** hosts the **OSTRICH FESTIVAL,** a weekend event with music, a parade, and **OSTRICH RACING.**

12 ON SATURN, a season lasts about SEVEN EARTH YEARS.

13 SOME CHINESE BELIEVE THAT SPIRITS GET A MONTH-LONG SUMMER VACATION, when they return to enjoy food and entertainment during what is known in Asia as the HUNGRY GHOST FESTIVAL.

14 SEASONAL ALLERGIES affect more than **35 MILLION AMERICANS. THAT'S A LOT OF TISSUES!**

15 Every winter, the town of **KEMI, FINLAND,** builds the **SNOW-CASTLE,** a structure that features **12-FOOT (3.7-M) WALLS, A HOTEL, AND A RESTAURANT—** all made entirely of snow. Natural snow is too soft, so the snow for the castle is made from seawater.

1 Europe is the second smallest continent—but its coastline of some 24,000 miles (38,000 km) would nearly stretch around the Earth.

2 BULGARIAN FIRE DANCERS DANCE OVER BURNING EMBERS BAREFOOT, JUST AS THEIR ANCESTORS DID THOUSANDS OF YEARS AGO.

3 The Caspian Sea is the world's largest body of water completely surrounded by land. It's larger than Japan.

4 Cheese plays a big role in Switzerland's history. Fondue, bread dipped in warm cheese, started out in Switzerland. The holes in Swiss cheese are called "eyes."

5 Seven European countries start with the letter "S": San Marino, Serbia, Slovakia, Slovenia, Spain, Sweden, and Switzerland.

6 During a bullfight, a popular activity in Spain, a bullfighter called a matador waves a red cape to get the bull to charge. Bulls are color-blind, but the movement attracts them.

7 Russia, the largest country in the world, covers 11 time zones and two continents (Europe and Asia).

8 Eurasian otters, found all over Europe, are very playful. Sometimes they play "tag," and slide down mud banks, or slip and slide in the snow.

9 Austria is sometimes called "The Land of Music" because many classical artists lived in Vienna. Today, almost every town in Austria has a band or orchestra.

10 Latvian cuisine includes a cold sour-cream soup and *spekapīrādzini* (bacon pies).

11 The Palace of Parliament in Romania's capital can be seen from space. Some 20,000 people worked to build it, starting in July 1984.

12 Nightingales are a type of bird found in forests and dry woodland areas of Europe and Southwest Asia. They migrate south and spend winters in Africa.

13 In Rome you'll find the Bocca Della Verità (which means "the mouth of truth"), an ancient stone mask carved out of marble. Legend says that if you put your hand in its mouth, if you are a liar the mask will gobble it up.

14 THE SMALL COUNTRY OF MONACO OFFERS LUXURY RESORTS ON THE MEDITERRANEAN. ONE HOTEL OFFERS AN EIGHTH-FLOOR SUITE FOR ABOUT $14,000 A NIGHT.

15 Porto Santo in the Madeira Islands holds a weeklong festival devoted to Christopher Columbus every September. His first child was born in the city.

16 Finland's capital, Helsinki, is the northernmost capital in Europe, and stretches across more than 300 islands.

17 Mount Etna, a volcano on the island of Sicily in the Mediterranean Sea, is almost always erupting. There are three observatories on the volcano.

18 About one-third of all the world's raspberries come from Serbia.

19 LEGOs were first created in Denmark. When a giant, eight-foot-tall (2.4 m) LEGO man washed ashore in Florida, U.S.A., it was traced back to a Dutch artist.

20 A MAN ONCE RODE HIS BIKE DOWN THE 1,665 STEPS OF THE EIFFEL TOWER IN PARIS, FRANCE.

21 The first circus was held in Rome, Italy.

22 Some 10,000 avalanches happen every year in the Swiss Alps.

23 The Sami people of Scandinavia are excellent reindeer herders. Reindeer can walk 3,000 miles (5,000 km) a year.

24 An Irish poet wrote a play that only lasts for 35 seconds.

25 The International Court of Justice is headquartered in The Hague, Netherlands. It's located in the Peace Palace.

26 The Alps have more than 30,000 animal species and 13,000 plant species, making them a biodiversity hot spot.

27 Many parts of the autobahn, or German highway system, have no speed limit. The first part was completed in 1932, and the system now stretches for 6,800 miles (11,000 km).

28 In Russia, it's bad luck to shake hands through a doorway.

29 The largest known super-colony of ants stretches nearly 4,000 miles (6,440 km) through Portugal, France, Spain, and Italy.

30 The first chocolate shop in Switzerland opened in Bern in 1792.

31 More than 400 species of European butterflies take to the skies. The yellow-and-black swallowtail can be found flitting across alpine meadows.

32 The London, England, subway system is called the "Tube" or the "Underground." It's estimated that half a million mice live in the system.

33 Iceland has two main zones of volcanism because it is located on the boundary of tectonic plates.

34 European bison almost went extinct, but now they are trying to make a comeback. These bison are the largest herbivores in Europe.

35 Finland has some 188,000 lakes.

36 Portugal's only national park, Peneda Gerês, is home to ancient Roman roads and early human rock structures called dolmens.

37 THE WORLD'S LEAST POPULOUS COUNTRY— VATICAN CITY—RECORDED 798 CITIZENS IN 2011. IT IS LOCATED WITHIN ROME, ITALY.

38 The language of Luxembourg—Luxembourgish—is close to German. Newspapers publish in German, but officials use French for administrative tasks.

39 More people with red hair are born in Scotland than anywhere else in the world.

75 FASCINATING FACTS ABOUT EUROPE

40 The flag of the European Union has a circle of 12 yellow stars on a blue background. The stars symbolize harmony and unity.

41 The English Channel stretches 21 miles (32 km) between England and France. The quickest swim across it took a little more than seven hours, but the longest took more than a day!

42 Disneyland Paris opened in 1992. Some 15 million tourists visit the park each year, and it is Europe's most popular destination.

43 The deepest lake in Europe is found in Norway. Lake Hornindalsvatnet is 1,686 feet (514 m) deep.

44 IRELAND HAS NO NATIVE SNAKES. THE LEGEND IS THAT ST. PATRICK FORCED THEM TO LEAVE.

45 The Berlin Wall, which divided Germany for 28 years, came down in 1989. It contained 302 watchtowers and 259 paths for guard dogs. Today, pieces of the wall are in museums around the world. You can also buy pieces of it on eBay.

46 Hungary's capital, Budapest, has more than 100 thermal springs. Be careful when soaking in the spas and baths since some of the waters can reach a scalding 168°F (76°C).

47 Venice, Italy, has no roads but has canals instead. The city is actually more than 100 islands connected by a canal system.

48 Every person in Iceland is required to learn to swim. It's the law!

49 Duffel bags are named for a Belgian town where the cloth used to make them comes from.

50 An annual trumpet festival in Serbia attracts people from all over the world to play and dance. It also includes a contest for best trumpeter.

51 The Statue of Liberty in New York City was constructed in France.

52 THE FIRST WORLD TOE WRESTLING COMPETITION WAS HELD IN DERBYSHIRE IN THE UNITED KINGDOM IN 1976.

53 The Leaning Tower of Pisa began to lean with the addition of the third floor. The 14,000-ton (12,700 MT) medieval tower took over 800 years to fully complete and leans 16 feet (5 m) off-center.

54 A man holds the record for holding the most straws in his mouth—400—while performing in Germany.

55 The "Running of the Bulls" in Pamplona, Spain, can be traced back to the 14th century.

56 Muchanaghederdauhaulia is the longest place name in Ireland, and it is located in Galway County.

57 In France and Spain, instead of a tooth fairy, a legendary tooth mouse comes to collect children's teeth.

58 The most chocolate in the world is sold at Brussels National Airport in Belgium.

59 Showing your palm to someone is offensive in Greece.

60 Putting your hands below the table during a meal in France, Germany, and Austria is considered rude.

61 The biggest Ferris wheel in Europe, the London Eye, takes 30 minutes to rotate and travels so slowly that passengers can get on and off without the wheel stopping.

62 Russia's capital, Moscow, is the largest city in Europe, and in 2011 boasted 79 billionaires—more than New York, London, and Los Angeles.

63 Istanbul, Turkey, is the only large city that stretches across two continents, Europe and Asia. About 70 percent of Istanbul's residents live in the European sector.

64 It's estimated that there are more bicycles than people in Amsterdam.

Eiffel Tower, Paris, France

65 In the summer, parts of Sweden have 24 hours of daylight, but in midwinter the sun doesn't rise above the horizon for two months.

66 Germany hosts the Mud Olympics each year.

67 Germany also hosts a plastic duck race, during which about 6,000 plastic ducks are released into the Neckar River.

68 THE EIFFEL TOWER IN PARIS, FRANCE, IS REPAINTED ABOUT EVERY SEVEN YEARS. IT TAKES A TEAM OF 25 PAINTERS USING MORE THAN 1,500 BRUSHES A YEAR TO PAINT THE MONUMENT.

69 William the Conqueror hunted boar and deer in England's New Forest. Now a national park, the woods are home to 500-year-old oak trees and Britain's only poisonous snake—the adder.

70 A totally upside-down house in Trassenheide, Germany is a very wacky tourist attraction. Everything is upside-down on the inside, too, even the toilet.

71 The United Kingdom's current monarch, Queen Elizabeth II, has her own YouTube channel.

72 Wales's Snowdonia National Park boasts King Arthur among its most famous inhabitants. It's said that he battled king-killing giant Rhita Gawr on the top of Snowdon, the park's namesake and highest peak.

73 Fire Rock is a sun-shaped sphere of rock in the Czech Republic's Bohemian Switzerland National Park and is believed by some to have been created by a lightning strike.

74 Belarus, located in eastern Europe, means "White Russia."

75 Mount Sibilla in Italy is named for the legendary prophetess named Sibyl. It is said that knights traveled from across Europe to her remote cave in hopes of gaining advice and her wisdom.

HEADS UP!
35 FACTS ABOUT

1 SPACE JUNK is any human-made object orbiting Earth that no longer serves a useful purpose.

2 In 2009, an old Russian satellite and a working U.S. satellite CRASHED INTO EACH OTHER over Siberia, creating more than 2,000 new pieces of space junk orbiting Earth.

3 In 2011, the Earth-orbiting International Space Station CHANGED COURSE to avoid hitting a four-inch (10-cm) piece of space junk left over from the 2009 satellite collision.

4 Between April 2011 and April 2012, the 861,804-POUND (391 mt) International Space Station changed course four times to avoid colliding with space junk.

5 In January 2001, a 154-pound (70-kg) CHUNK OF ROCKET landed about 150 miles (240 km) from Saudi Arabia's capital, Riyadh.

6 Space junk includes fragments from rockets and satellites as well as everyday items like WRENCHES dropped during construction of the International Space Station.

7 During astronaut ED WHITE'S historic 1965 spacewalk, he ACCIDENTALLY DROPPED A GLOVE, which has since fallen out of orbit.

8 Most space junk floats within 1,243 miles (2,000 km) of Earth's surface, but the GREATEST AMOUNT OF DEBRIS is found between 466 and 590 miles (750–950 km) above Earth.

9 The largest space junk is about the SIZE OF A REFRIGERATOR; the smallest includes TINY FLECKS OF PAINT.

10 Scientists estimate there are about 500,000 PIECES OF SPACE JUNK between 0.39 and 3.9 inches (1-10 cm) in diameter orbiting Earth.

11 There are tens of millions of space junk particles SMALLER THAN 0.39 INCHES (1 cm) floating around Earth.

12 Space junk orbiting WITHIN 373 MILES (600 km) of Earth takes approximately 25 YEARS TO FALL BACK to the planet.

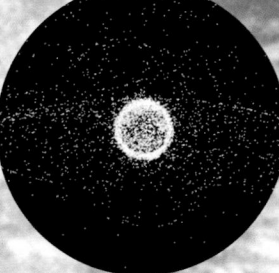

13 Space junk about 500 MILES (805 km) above Earth will REMAIN IN ORBIT FOR DECADES.

14 In 2007, CHINA FIRED A MISSILE at an unused weather satellite, adding more than 3,000 NEW PIECES of space junk to Earth's orbit.

15 Space junk in the "PIZZA BOX," an imaginary box about 1 mile x 30 miles x 30 miles (1.5 x 50 x 50 km) surrounding the International Space Station, is closely monitored.

16 When space junk falls on LAND, it's often in SPARSELY POPULATED REGIONS, such as Siberia, Western Australia, and northern Canada.

17 All space junk is property of the government that built it and possibly HAZARDOUS TO TOUCH, so if you find a piece, CALL THE POLICE.

18 A piece of space junk ONLY 0.39 INCHES (1 cm) in diameter can CATASTROPHICALLY DAMAGE A SATELLITE.

19 In January 1997, LOTTIE WILLIAMS was walking through a Tulsa, Oklahoma, park when a small, lightweight piece of space junk —part of an OLD ROCKET— BRUSHED HER SHOULDER.

20 ANYTHING DROPPED from the International Space Station, which floats about 248 miles (400 km) above Earth, falls to the planet WITHIN ABOUT A YEAR.

SPACE JUNK

21 Though people have been **BRUSHED BY SMALL, LIGHTWEIGHT PIECES OF SPACE JUNK** falling to Earth, the debris has never caused any serious injury or property damage.

22 Because oceans cover the majority of Earth, **MOST SPACE JUNK** that reaches the planet's surface **LANDS IN THE SEA.**

23 **TWENTY-SIX PIECES** of an old satellite weighing about **1,200 POUNDS** (544 kg) fell to Earth in September 2011.

24 A **551-POUND** (250-kg) stainless steel tank from an old rocket landed near **GEORGETOWN, TEXAS, U.S.A.,** in January 1997.

25 Space junk within **1,243 MILES** (2,000 km) of Earth circles the planet at a **SPEED OF ABOUT** 4.35–4.97 **MILES PER SECOND** (7–8 KM PER SECOND).

26 Scientists are tracking approximately **22,000 EARTH-ORBITING** pieces of space junk larger than 3.9 inches (10 cm) across.

27 A person's **ANNUAL RISK** of being injured by space junk falling to Earth is **ONE IN TRILLIONS.**

28 The **INTERNATIONAL SPACE STATION** needs about **30 HOURS NOTICE** to get out of the way of space junk.

29 Space junk **ABOVE 621 MILES** (1,000 km) will circle Earth for at **LEAST A CENTURY.**

30 In the past **40 YEARS,** an average of one cataloged piece of space junk has fallen to Earth **EACH DAY.**

31 The **VANGUARD 1, A 3.2-POUND** (1.47-KG) **SATELLITE** launched into space in 1958, is the **OLDEST PIECE** of space junk and will remain in orbit well into the **NEXT CENTURY.**

32 The **134-TON** (121-MT) **RUSSIAN SPACE STATION MIR** broke up over the Pacific Ocean on its return to Earth, and people in **FIJI** reported seeing gold and white lights.

33 **SKYLAB,** the **UNITED STATES'S FIRST SPACE STATION,** fell to Earth in July 1979 and scattered debris across the Indian Ocean and Western Australia.

34 On February 22, 2012, a piece of space junk 3.3 feet (1 m) in diameter **LANDED IN A SMALL BRAZILIAN VILLAGE** after orbiting Earth for 15 years. The junk damaged a few trees but caused no injuries.

35 When the probability of colliding with space junk is **GREATER THAN ONE IN 10,000,** the International Space Station is moved unless doing so would create an additional risk for astronauts.

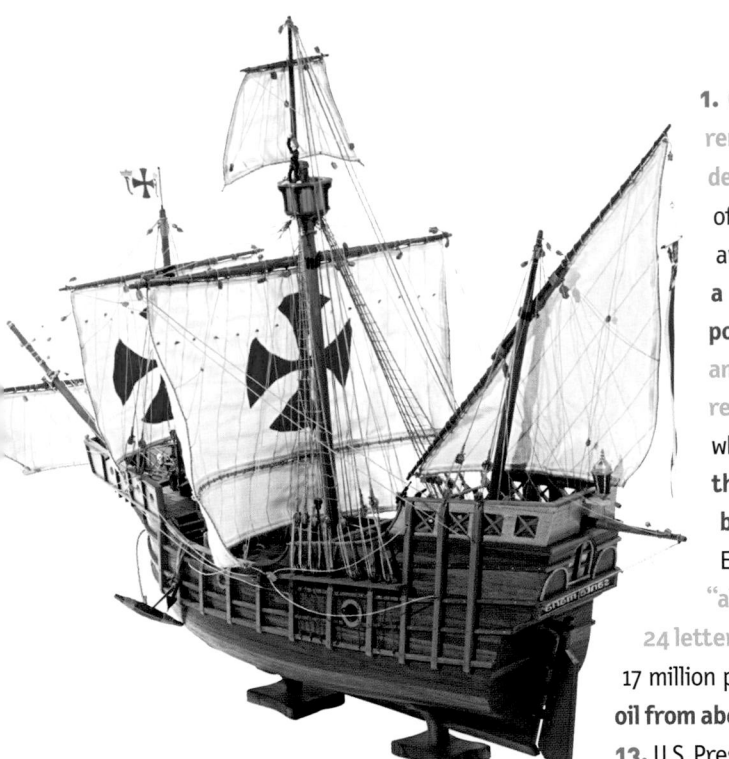

1. George Washington had a false set of teeth made from hippo tusks. **2.** Lifeboats were removed from the *Titanic* so first-class passengers had more room to stroll the deck. That decision left more than 1,000 people stranded aboard the sinking ship. **3.** To help win one of the most important battles of World War II, the British and U.S. militaries created fake army camps to confuse the Germans. **4. When Christopher Columbus reached the Americas, a great exchange occurred. The Europeans brought horses and pigs and returned with potatoes and turkeys. 5.** In the United States, color TV was introduced in 1951. **6.** Men in ancient Rome didn't like to have hair on their arms. They went to special shops to have it removed. **7.** The first "e-book" in the United States was the Declaration of Independence, which was made available on a computer network back in the 1970s. **8. A man who lived during the third or fourth century B.C. used pine resin and plant oil to gel his hair. His preserved body was found in a peat bog. 9.** In 1415, the Chinese reached Africa by boat before the Europeans. Admiral Zheng traveled with 28,000 men and more than 250 boats. **10.** The word "alphabet" comes from two Greek words: *alpha* and *beta*. The ancient Greek alphabet has 24 letters. **11.** Many immigrants arriving to the United States entered at Ellis Island, New York. Some 17 million people came through Ellis Island from 1892 to 1924. **12. The Trans-Alaska Pipeline carries oil from above the Arctic Circle to the Alaska coast. Completed in 1977, it's 800 miles (1,287 km) long. 13.** U.S. President Theodore Roosevelt had more than 40 pets. **14.** People during ancient China's Shang

100 HISTORY FACTS WORTH REPEATING

Dynasty read the bones of sheep and oxen for guidance. **15.** The city of St. Petersburg, Russia, suffered through a 900-day siege during World War II. **16. There are nine justices on the U.S. Supreme Court. In 1790, when the first court met, the justices wore white wigs, which was the fashion at the time. 17.** In 1848, the United States signed a treaty with Mexico and gained land that now makes up all or part of eight states. The treaty also ended the Mexican-American War. **18.** Meriwether Lewis and William Clark traveled for more than two years to chart America's wilderness in the early 1800s. **19.** The first reported bank robbery in U.S. history occurred in 1831 when the City Bank of New York was robbed. **20. Washington, D.C., became the capital of the United States in 1792. A French artist and engineer, Pierre L'Enfant, carefully planned the city. 21.** Portugal was known as a powerful empire built on trade from oceangoing ships. When Portuguese explorer Vasco da Gama first arrived in India, however, the Indian princess didn't want to trade anything for the goods he had brought. **22.** Florence Nightingale, who lived in the 19th century, helped establish nursing as a respectable career. Her parents didn't want her to become a nurse; they wanted her to get married instead. **23.** Camels that carried goods on the Silk Road linking China to the West could smell water underneath the Taklamakan Desert. **24. In the 1800s, a reporter went to Africa to try to locate a European named David Livingstone, who had spent years mapping Africa's rivers and lands. When he found him, accounts say he said the famous phrase, "Dr. Livingstone, I presume." 25.** The Chinese created toothbrushes in the 1400s by plucking bristles from Siberian hogs and fastening them onto handles. **26.** The 132 rooms in the White House have changed throughout the years. The first president to live there was John Adams in 1800. **27.** The late Princess Diana of England had two wedding dresses in case the first one was revealed before her wedding to Prince Charles. **28. The Pony Express was used to carry mail across the United States. At its peak, it had 80 riders and more than 400 horses. 29.** Pakistan used to be divided in two: East and West Pakistan. In 1971 East Pakistan broke off and became Bangladesh. **30.** The Romans called the passageways to a theater or colosseum, *vomitoria*. These passages were so efficiently designed that Rome's packed 50,000-seat Colosseum could empty in 15 minutes. **31.** The Chinese built a 2,500-mile (4,000-km)-long pipeline to carry natural gas. It crosses 37 rivers and 3 mountain ranges. **32. In 1931, archaeologists uncovered the remains of a seventh-century Anglo-Saxon ship in a grassy hill. It contained a nobleman's helmet made of iron, bronze, and tin—one of only three ever found in England. 33.** England's Queen Elizabeth I refused King Philip of Spain's offer of marriage—and would later defeat Philip's armada in one of the most important naval battles in world history. **34.** Before Charles Darwin and his theory of evolution made the Galápagos Islands famous, they were pirate hideouts. **35.** In 1998, Canada's first diamond mine started production. Today, some 15 percent of all diamonds come from Canada. **36. The first European known to visit Madagascar arrived there because his ship had blown off course. 37.** A fire during the War of 1812 burned many of the Library of Congress's books.

To help make up for the loss, Congress purchased books from Thomas Jefferson's collection. **38.** Within the span of one year—1960—17 former European colonies became independent nations in Africa. **39.** In 1848, gold was discovered in California, U.S.A., causing the Gold Rush. Huge numbers of people traveled to the area to try their luck at finding gold. **40. During the Civil War, the Union army was nearly twice the size of the Confederate army. 41.** Jamestown, Virginia, became the first permanent British settlement in North America in 1607. The harsh winter of 1609 killed many of the colonists, and only 60 out of 214 survived. **42.** Civil rights leader Martin Luther King, Jr.'s mother was a schoolteacher. His father was a Baptist minister. **43.** The Suez Canal, linking the Mediterranean and Red Seas, was built in the 19th century. It shortened the trip between India and the United Kingdom by 6,000 miles (9,660 km). **44. South Africa named an armored combat vehicle used in the military after the honey badger, which is a tough weasel that will open bees' nests to get to the larvae. 45.** Nazi Germany controlled France for most of WWII. French resistance fighters worked to interrupt German communication and supply lines. **46.** In ancient Egypt, landowners' boundaries were marked with stones, and owners had to swear they didn't move them to increase their plot. **47.** The Norse explorer Leif Ericsson heard a story that ship-owner Bjarni Herjólfsson had sailed off course and spotted land and forests. Leif bought Bjarni's boat and landed in North America around A.D. 1000. **48. Ancient Greeks had dinner parties featuring roasted birds, snails, and grasshoppers. 49.** The great Frankish ruler Charlemagne was a noted patron of learning, and mastered several languages, but could never learn to write properly. **50.** Canada's Nunavut territory has a caribou, a narwhal, and an igloo on its coat of arms. **51.** American explorer Henry Hudson's crew turned against him and put Hudson, his son, and anyone loyal to them in a boat without oars or food. No one knows what happened to them. **52. Aztec boys had their hair cut at age ten, but a section of hair was left long. This piece was cut off once the boy had taken his first prisoner during a battle. 53.** King Kamehameha of Hawaii was hidden in a cave as a boy so that he wouldn't be killed. **54.** Since the 19th century, Switzerland has been neutral in all wars. **55.** At the age of three, children in ancient Greece were given miniature jugs to mark the end of their babyhood. **56. Camp cooks for cowboys in the American West were known as "cookies." They were also called bean masters and biscuit shooters. 57.** British leader Winston Churchill originally used the term "iron curtain" to describe the nondemocratic nations of Eastern Europe after World War II. At the time, barbed-wire fencing even separated some gardens into two sides. **58.** The Opet Festival in ancient Egypt lasted for as long as 27 days. It celebrated the flooding of the Nile. **59.** The highest battlefield in the world is located on a glacier between India and Pakistan. Troops have battled from time to time since 1984 through blizzards and bitter cold, but a cease-fire was called in 2003. **60. Kenya's motto, "Harambee!" means "let's pull together." The country's first president, Jomo Kenyatta, who was elected in 1964, introduced the term. 61.** In 1870, an inventor unveiled a short subway tunnel with one car in New York City. It wasn't until 1904, however, that the New York subway first opened. **62.** Dice playing was so frowned upon by German authorities in the medieval period, that in 1452, authorities in Nuremberg burned 42,000 dice. **63.** In the late 1400s, European explorers came to the ancient kingdom of Benin in today's Nigeria looking for gold. Since the kingdom lacked gold, its people wore necklaces made from coral. **64. Ethiopia is the only African country never colonized. 65.** The country of Chile made slavery illegal in 1823—42 years before the end of the American Civil War. **66.** Ulysses S. Grant was fined for speeding down a Washington, D.C., U.S.A., street in a horse-drawn carriage. **67.** The capital city of Ireland, Dublin, wasn't founded by the Irish—it was founded by Vikings. **68. Roman emperors wore wreaths made from leaves and branches of the laurel tree on their heads instead of crowns. 69.** In the United States, people used to think tomatoes were poisonous, so in 1820 a man proved they weren't by eating one in public. **70.** In ancient China, different dynasties created rules about clothing colors. During and after the Sui Dynasty, for instance, only the emperors could wear yellow. **71.** When the Beatles went to India in 1967, the first to return to England was Ringo Starr, the drummer, who complained that the food was too spicy. **72. The "S" in President Harry S. Truman doesn't stand for a name. 73.** Sweden built a great warship in 1628, but it sank before it ever made it to sea. Today, you can see it in a museum. **74.** English explorer Sir Francis Drake looted Spanish ships he encountered on his voyages. He shared the treasure he took with the Queen of England, Elizabeth I. **75.** The first toilet recorded in history is more than 2,800 years old. King Minos of the Mediterranean island of Crete used it. **76. The Soviet Union's (now Russia) first McDonald's opened in 1991 in Moscow. It was the largest McDonald's in the world at that time. 77.** The Native American princess Pocahontas saved the life of John Smith, who was a leader of the Jamestown Colony in Virginia. **78.** Frederick Douglass disguised himself as a sailor to escape slavery. **79.** Nigeria launched its first satellite into space in 2003. It was carried on a Russian rocket. **80. People in ancient China paid taxes, but they were in the form of grain or working for the government. 81.** French explorers settled in Canada, and today Montreal is the second largest French-speaking city in the world. **82.** SpongeBob SquarePants began as a TV show on Nickelodeon in 1999. **83.** The ancient Greeks used the stars to navigate their boats. **84. The Black Death began in China and the interior of Asia in the 1300s, arriving in Europe when infected corpses were catapulted into a town in Crimea. 85.** Cesar Chavez, a Mexican-American, campaigned for better conditions for people who worked on farms. In 1968 he went without eating for 25 days in support for the United Farm Workers. **86.** Of all the countries in Europe, Denmark has the oldest royal line. The royal family began with King Gorm more than 1,000 years ago. **87.** People watch male camels wrestle as a spectator sport in Turkey. **88. U.S. President Abraham Lincoln kept important papers inside his top hat. 89.** The Dutch first settled New York City in 1612. They called it "New Amsterdam." **90.** Nearly 400 years ago, the most important export in Venezuela was cocoa. **91.** Mount Rushmore, a mountain with four American Presidents' heads carved onto its face, took about 14 years to complete. **92. Cinco de Mayo is a holiday celebrating the Mexican defeat of the French in an 1862 battle. 93.** Before he was President, Andrew Jackson was shot in the chest in an 1806 duel. He remained standing, firing and killing his opponent. **94.** Spanish mission buildings in modern-day California, U.S.A., were made out of straw and horse droppings. **95.** The ancient Greeks called outsiders "barbarians," because they couldn't understand what they were saying. To them foreign words sounded like "bar-bar." **96. Catherine the Great led Russia for 30 years, but she was actually German and her birth name was Sophie. 97.** President Barack Obama appeared in a 2009 Spider-Man comic book. **98.** In 221 B.C. an Emperor Shi Huangdi united all of China. His name, pronounced "chin," led to the name "China." **99.** Sandwiches take their name from the fourth Earl of Sandwich, John Montagu. He realized he could put a filling between two slices of bread, similar to snacks he had seen in the Middle East, and he could eat and still play cards. **100. In ancient Rome, you could buy hot food right from people selling it from stalls on the street. Most apartments didn't have a kitchen.**

1
The part of the brain associated with math was **15 PERCENT LARGER** than average in Albert Einstein.

2
The human brain weighs about **THREE POUNDS** (1.4 kg).

3
On average, **MEN'S BRAINS ARE LARGER** than women's (because their bodies are bigger).

4
The human brain has about **100 BILLION NEURONS**, nerve cells that transmit information. An octopus brain has about **300 MILLION NEURONS.**

5
Your brain wiring determines whether you are a "MORNING PERSON" or an "EVENING PERSON."

6
RELAX: Stress weakens the brain's ability to process memories.

7
Food passes through a **GIANT SQUID'S BRAIN** on the way to its stomach.

8
When preparing a body for **MUMMIFICATION**, the Egyptians removed the brain through the nose and discarded it; they thought the brain was worthless.

9
Try new things: Research shows that **BEING CURIOUS** increases the number of connections between brain cells.

10
The human skull, which protects the brain, is made up of **22 BONES.**

11
If you could touch your brain, it would feel like a **MUSHROOM.**

12
In 1929, the invention of the **EEG**, or electro-encephalogram, allowed scientists to watch brain wave activity as it happens.

13
MRI, or magnetic resonance imaging, creates a detailed, **3-D MAP** of the brain.

14
HEADACHES occur outside, not inside, the brain.

15
An octopus brain is the size of a **DIME**, but it can solve simple problems like moving barriers to get to food.

16
The brain determines whether you are **RIGHT-HANDED** or **LEFT-HANDED**; men are more likely to be left-handed.

17
No two brains are alike, even among **IDENTICAL TWINS.**

18
By age six, the human brain is already **90 PERCENT** of its adult size.

19
Girls have the greatest number of **NEURONS** in their brains at age 11, boys at age 12.

20
KIDS' BRAINS pick up another language more easily than adults' do.

21
Human brains shrink with age; **CHIMP** brains do not.

22
It's a myth that humans use only **10 PERCENT OF THEIR BRAIN**; though nobody knows the exact fraction, scientists believe we use most or all of our brain.

23
In rural western Kentucky, **SQUIRREL BRAINS** are considered a delicacy.

24
The brain works best when it focuses on **ONE TASK AT A TIME.**

25
A large part of the brain's circuitry is devoted to the **HANDS, LIPS, AND TONGUE.**

26
During sleep, your brain makes **MEMORIES.**

27
A **DREAMING** brain is just as active as an awake brain.

28
Brain cells called mirror neurons are responsible for **LAUGHTER AND YAWNING BEING CONTAGIOUS.**

29
A **SPERM WHALE'S** brain weighs more than five times a human's.

30
A **DOG** brain weighs as much as 13 quarters; a **CAT** brain weighs 5 quarters; and a **HAMSTER** brain weighs about as much as one-quarter the weight of a quarter.

31
A 150-pound (68 kg) person's brain is about **2% OF THEIR TOTAL BODY WEIGHT.**

32
The human brain is **78% WATER.**

33
BRAIN CORAL, a group of reef-dwelling animals living together in a colony that resembles a giant brain, can weigh more than a ton (0.9 MT).

34
Scientists aren't sure what causes "BRAIN FREEZE."

35
BRAIN ISLAND is located between the tip of South America and the tip of Antarctica.

36
All the neurons, or nerve cells, in the brain lined up side by side would be 621 MILES (1,000 KM) LONG, about the distance from Atlanta, Georgia, to Washington, D.C., U.S.A.

37
Information in the nervous system, which includes the brain, can travel as fast as 268 MILES PER HOUR (431 KPH)!

38
Movement on the LEFT SIDE of the body is controlled by the right side of the brain, and movement on the RIGHT SIDE of the body is controlled by the left side of the brain.

39
Studies show that GROUND-UP COCKROACH BRAINS fight harmful bacteria. Scientists are investigating whether they could one day be used in medicine.

40
For the most part, humans are born with ALL THE NEURONS they will ever have.

41
Animals can lose the ABILITY TO SNEEZE if a certain part of their brain is damaged.

42
Brain cells use ELECTRICITY AND CHEMICALS to communicate with each other.

43
The connections between neurons in the brain create a network that resembles a SPIDERWEB.

44
As the brain ages, it loses neurons but is able to form NEW CONNECTIONS between remaining neurons.

45
AWAKE BRAIN SURGERY is exactly what it sounds like: An operation is performed on your brain while you're awake.

46
More than 30,000 NEURONS would fit on the head of a pin.

47
In 2008, archaeologists in England unearthed a 2,500-YEAR-OLD HUMAN BRAIN that was surprisingly well-preserved, thanks to a quick burial and cool soil temperatures.

48
Your brain is WRINKLED.

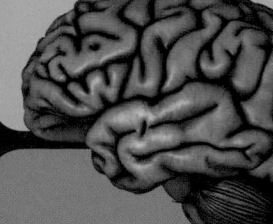

49
It would take more than 3,000 YEARS to count all the neurons in your brain.

50
The adult human brain is about 3.7 INCHES (93 mm) tall, 6.6 INCHES (167 mm) long and 5.5 INCHES (140 mm) wide.

50 MiND-BENDiNG FACTS ABOUT THE BRAIN

1 In northern Australia, people dine al fresco on the first Monday in August in celebration of **PICNIC DAY.**

2 Since 1994, people in Turkmenistan have set aside a day in August to celebrate the country's melons—the aptly named **MELON DAY.**

3 During Iceland's **THORRABLOT WINTER FESTIVAL,** locals celebrate by eating a Viking dish of rotten shark meat.

4 Indians place bowls full of milk next to snake holes and worship at temples dedicated to serpents during **NAG PANCHAMI,** the Hindu festival honoring snakes.

5 For **LOI KRATHONG,** people in Thailand light candles and incense and set them adrift on rivers or release paper lanterns into the sky.

6 For more than 40 years, Chicago, U.S.A., has dyed its namesake river green in celebration of **ST. PATRICK'S DAY.**

7 The first **THANKSGIVING** in Plymouth, Massachusetts, lasted for three days, and more Indians than Pilgrims attended.

8 During **BELTANE,** the 2,000-year-old Celtic celebration of the return of summer, paraders in Edinburgh, Scotland, paint themselves red or blue, juggle fire, and carry flaming torches.

9 President Abraham Lincoln proclaimed **THANKSGIVING** a national holiday in 1863 after being persuaded by Sarah Josepha Hale, author of the poem "Mary Had a Little Lamb."

35 FACTS ABOUT

10 On December 26, people in Great Britain, Canada, Australia, and New Zealand celebrate **BOXING DAY** by watching sports, shopping, and eating Christmas leftovers.

11 In some countries, children are told stories of the evil **KRAMPUS,** a beast-like creature who joins St. Nick, supposedly to **PUNISH MISBEHAVING CHILDREN.**

12 The ancient Celtic festival of **SAMHAIN,** a precursor to Halloween, included playing tricks on people and displaying lanterns made out of hollowed-out turnips.

13 Mexicans honor deceased loved ones on the **DAY OF THE DEAD** by celebrating at street festivals and bringing dead relatives' favorite foods to their gravesites.

14 **INTERNATIONAL WOMEN'S DAY** has been celebrated on March 8 around the world for nearly 100 years.

15 German immigrants in Pennsylvania originally used badgers to predict the weather on what is now known as **GROUNDHOG DAY.**

16 People in Thailand ring in the **LUNAR NEW YEAR** with the world's largest water fight. Water balloons, buckets, and hoses are used to soak others during the Songkran Festival.

17 On **NEW YEAR'S EVE** in Japan, temple bells ring 108 times: 8 times to ring out the old year, 100 to ring in the new. People wake up hours later to watch the first sunrise.

18 **BERMUDA DAY,** May 24, is traditionally the first day of the year that Bermudans take a dip in the ocean.

19 During the Jewish holiday of **PASSOVER,** people eat while reclined on pillows to symbolize freedom.

20 All Jewish holidays begin at **SUNDOWN.**

21 In Sweden, girls dress up as witches, knock on doors, and ask for candy and coins on **EASTER EVE.**

22 During the festival of **DIWALI,** Hindus light candles and set off fireworks to symbolize the victory of good over evil.

23 May 25th is celebrated as **AFRICAN UNION DAY** throughout the continent.

24 In Australia, **SANTA** arrives on **WATER SKIS;** in Ghana, he emerges from the **JUNGLE.**

25 Because it's based on a lunar calendar, the holy Muslim month of **RAMADAN** can occur in spring, summer, fall, or winter.

26 During the month of **RAMADAN,** adults and teenagers don't eat, drink, or even **CHEW GUM** from sunrise to sunset.

27 Every year, more than one billion people in 192 countries celebrate **EARTH DAY,** the world's largest nonreligious celebration.

28 **MIDSUMMER'S EVE,** a national holiday in Sweden and Finland, celebrates the Northern Hemisphere's longest day of the year—the summer solstice.

HOLIDAYS TO MAKE YOU CHEER

29 During **CHINESE NEW YEAR,** people decorate with gold to bring wealth and red to bring luck.

30 In China, people believe that the **MORE FOOD YOU MAKE** on New Year's Eve, the more you will have next year.

31 The letters on a dreidel, a toy played with during **HANUKKAH,** stand for "A Great Miracle Happened There." In Israel, they stand for "A Great Miracle Happened Here."

32 On December 10, 2010, **194,672 LIGHTS** were lit on a Christmas tree in Belgium, setting a new **WORLD RECORD.**

33 Sweethearts candies celebrating **VALENTINE'S DAY** first appeared in 1902, with messages like "Be Mine" and "Be True." Today's messages include "Tweet Me" and "Text Me."

34 Every year on October 9, South Koreans celebrate their **ALPHABET.**

35 Many children in Spain don't get their Christmas presents until January 6, **THREE KINGS DAY.**

15 FACTS ABOUT MEDICINE

1 No medicine exists to cure PROGERIA, a rare disease that causes young people to AGE PREMATURELY so that by **AGE 12 THEY LOOK ELDERLY.**

2 A **LAB IN INDIA** has developed medicines from COW POOP AND URINE.

3 In ancient Egypt, priests applied an **OINTMENT OF HONEY MIXED WITH HUMAN BRAINS**—and maybe some **ANIMAL DROPPINGS**—to treat eye irritations.

4 Some men and women who are **UNHAPPY WITH THEIR WRINKLES** seek injections of BOTULINUM, OR BOTOX—an extremely potent neurotoxin, or POISON, that acts on the nerves.

5 If you caught a **FEVER IN ANCIENT CHINA,** your doctor would have prescribed **HOT EARTHWORM SOUP.**

6 The **CADUCEUS,** a symbol for doctors, shows **TWO SNAKES CRISSCROSSED ON A WINGED STAFF.** It represents the GREEK GOD HERMES, who delivered information.

7 HIPPOCRATES, considered the father of medicine, thought that **DIET AND EXERCISE WERE IMPORTANT** for good health. The Greek physician also **RECOMMENDED QUIET AND BED REST.**

8 In Europe in the 1500s, a common cure for an infected cut was to put **MAGGOTS IN THE WOUND.** Maggots—the larval (or baby) form of flies—munched all the rotten meat, LEAVING BEHIND HEALTHY TISSUE. The treatment is still used today.

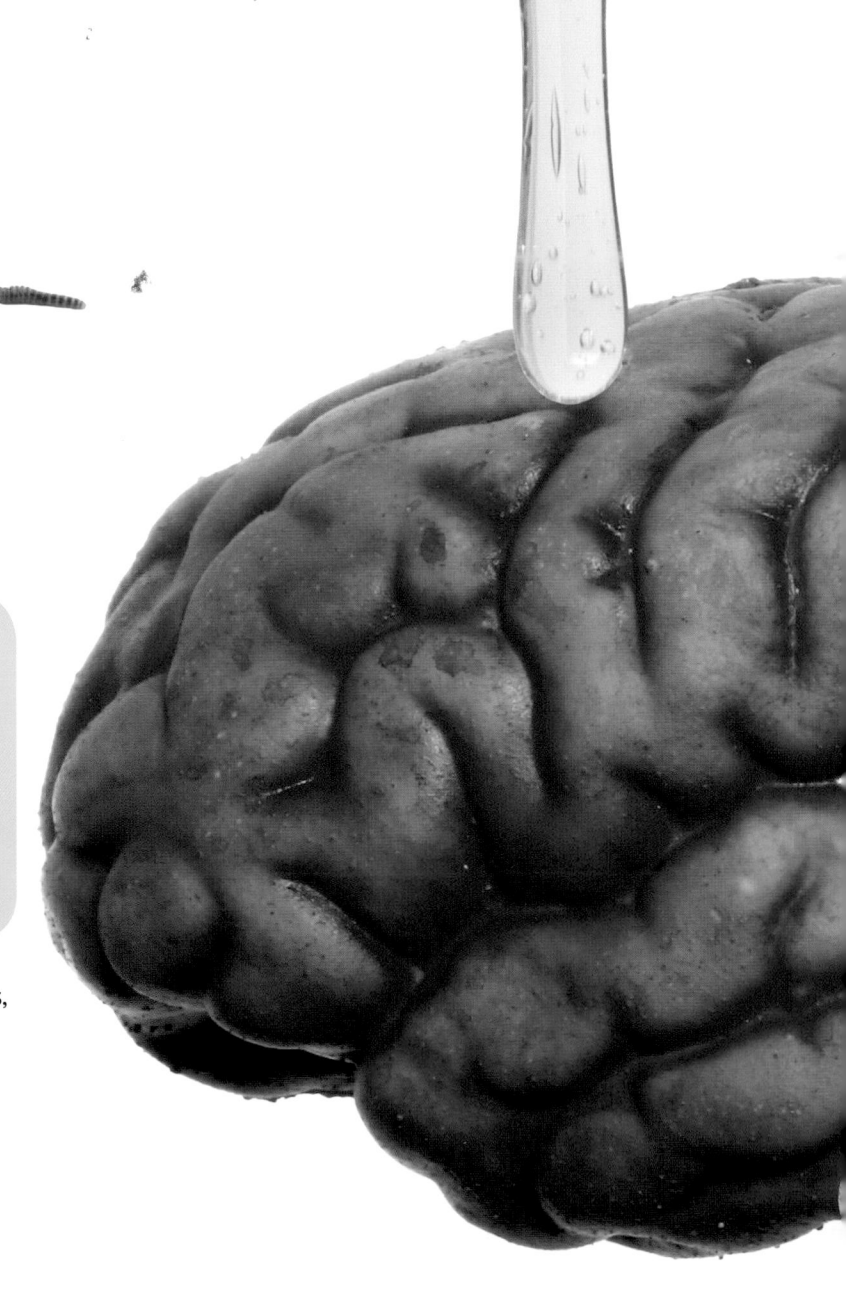

TO CURE YOUR CURIOSITY

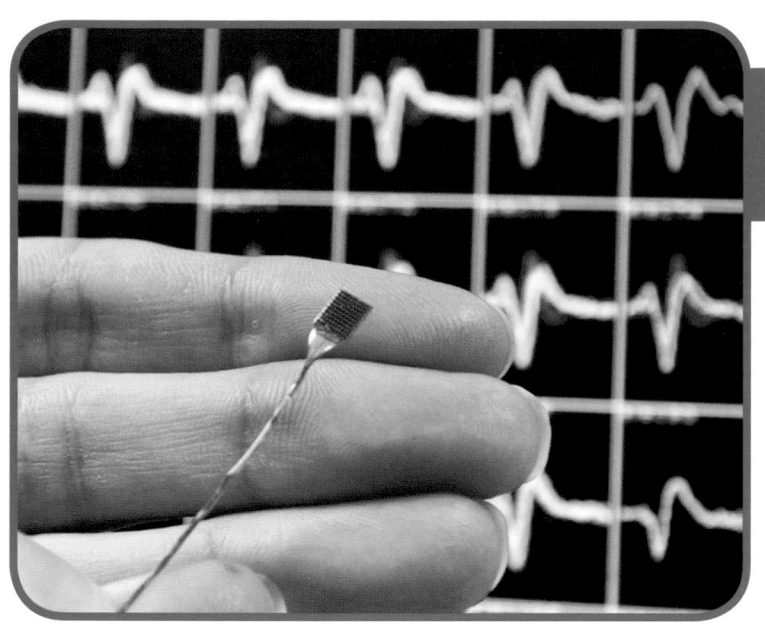

9 Scientists have developed a **COMPUTER CHIP THEY CAN IMPLANT IN THE BRAIN OF A PARALYZED PERSON.** The patient can then send signals to a computer **JUST BY THINKING.**

10 Some drugs prescribed by doctors have **WEIRD SIDE EFFECTS.** One drug to treat bladder infections can **TURN YOUR URINE BLUE** and another to treat bed-wetting can TURN YOUR URINE GREEN.

11 Some doctors use A TOOL THAT VIBRATES on the area where a shot will be given to **CONFUSE THE PATIENT'S SENSES** and make the shot less painful.

12 An English doctor made the discovery of **HOW BLOOD CIRCULATES** throughout the body nearly 400 YEARS AGO. During this time doctors thought that the liver made blood from food.

13 In Europe in the 1800s doctors attached **BLOODSUCKING LEECHES TO A SICK PERSON** to heal them. As many as **100 LEECHES** might feed off a patient in one session!

14 Some American Indian tribes thought SNAKES CAUSED STOMACH ACHES. To help heal from them, medicine men would make **PRAYER STICKS SHAPED LIKE SNAKES.**

15 The **MOST CONTAGIOUS DISEASE IS THE COMMON COLD,** which can be caused from around **100 DIFFERENT VIRUSES** but medicine won't cure it.

1 A SWORDFISH CAN SWIM ABOUT AS FAST AS A CHEETAH CAN RUN.

2 AN OSTRICH EGG WEIGHS LESS THAN 2 PERCENT OF THE ADULT'S WEIGHT.

A WREN EGG WEIGHS ABOUT 13 PERCENT OF THE ADULT'S WEIGHT.

3 HUMMINGBIRDS CAN FLY 385 BODY LENGTHS PER SECOND; A FIGHTER JET CAN FLY 150 BODY LENGTHS PER SECOND.

4 SOME FROGS CAN LEAP MORE THAN 20 TIMES THEIR BODY LENGTH.

5 A MONARCH BUTTERFLY'S 2,800-MILE (4,506-KM) MIGRATION IS EQUIVALENT TO A PERSON WALKING AROUND EARTH 11 TIMES.

25 FACTS OF EPIC

6 A BUTTERFLY WEIGHS LESS THAN A PAPER CLIP.

7  A SEA TURTLE CAN WEIGH AS MUCH AS A WATER BUFFALO.

8  DINOSAURS LIVED ON EARTH 800 TIMES LONGER THAN HUMANS HAVE EXISTED.

9 It would take a stack of more than NINE EMPIRE STATE BUILDINGS to equal the average depth of the ocean.

10 FLAMINGOES HAVE THE LONGEST LEGS RELATIVE TO BODY SIZE OF ALL BIRDS.

11 ONE YEAR ON NEPTUNE LASTS ABOUT 165 EARTH YEARS.

12  SOME GIANT JELLYFISH HAVE TENTACLES THAT EXTEND ONE-THIRD THE LENGTH OF A FOOTBALL FIELD.

13 KIWIS
—CHICKEN-SIZED BIRDS—
lay eggs almost as large as those of an emu—birds that are about **3 TIMES TALLER AND 20 TIMES HEAVIER.**

14 SNOW LEOPARDS CAN LEAP AS FAR AS 45 FEET (13.72 M)—THE LENGTH OF A HUMPBACK WHALE.

15 A BIG CAT'S **SENSE OF SMELL** IS 20 TIMES STRONGER THAN A HUMAN'S.

16 WHAT HUMANS CAN SEE FROM 5 FEET (1.52 M), HAWKS CAN SEE FROM 20 FEET (6.1 M).

17 RABBITS HAVE ALMOST TWICE AS MANY TASTE BUDS ON THEIR TONGUES AS HUMANS.

PROPORTION

18 THE HUMAN BODY IS ROUGHLY 60 PERCENT WATER.

19 ABOUT 70 PERCENT OF EARTH'S SURFACE IS COVERED WITH WATER.

20 MORE THAN 95 PERCENT OF THE UNIVERSE IS INVISIBLE.

21 THE SUN IS 99.8 PERCENT OF ALL THE MASS IN OUR SOLAR SYSTEM.

22 THE TALLEST LIVING MAN IS **8 FOOT, 3 INCHES** (2.5 M)—MORE THAN FOUR TIMES THE HEIGHT OF THE SHORTEST LIVING MAN.

23 Humans and slugs share more than **50 PERCENT** of their genes.

24 EIGHTY PERCENT OF ALL LIVING THINGS ON EARTH ARE **INSECTS.**

25 FROM FINGERTIP TO FINGERTIP, ORANGUTANS' OUTSTRETCHED ARMS ARE LONGER THAN THEIR BODIES.

1 More than 800 people created more than 4,000 pieces of coral out of yarn, plastic bags, and cassette tape to make a huge artistic reef at the Smithsonian's National Museum of Natural History.

2 The building blocks of reefs, coral polyps, are smaller than a baby's fingernail.

3 CORAL REEFS ARE ALIVE, AND THEY USE STINGING CELLS TO CAPTURE THEIR FOOD.

4 Lobe coral takes the shape of a huge flying saucer.

5 A reef fish called a fang blenny feeds on the mucus of other fish.

6 An underwater restaurant in Israel lets you dine while watching marine life on a Red Sea coral reef.

7 Thousands of miles (kilometers) of reefs located in the Caribbean provide local residents and tourists with food and sightseeing spots.

8 Reefs cover about 100,000 square miles (256,000 sq km) of ocean—that's about twice the size of Greece.

9 Because of the reflection of sunlight off the coral and how shallow the water is, from the air reefs appear to be a lighter blue than the surrounding ocean water.

10 Coral reefs are called the rain forests of the sea because they are home to a diverse number of species.

11 Australia's Great Barrier Reef is so big it can be seen from space.

12 Coral reefs have been valued at giving $30 billion in economical benefits to the world every year.

13 Some deep-sea coral will grow 1,650 feet (500 m) below the ocean's surface.

14 Animals hide everywhere on a reef, and no nook or cranny is left unused.

15 Poisonous sea snakes eat coral reef animals but must come to the surface to breathe air.

16 A hotel in Las Vegas features a 20,000-gallon (75,700 L) aquarium with colorful corals.

17 The giant brain coral can grow six and one-half feet (2 m) across. It can live for 100 years.

18 Reef fish called humphead wrasses can grow to be seven feet (2 m) long.

19 One Australian scientist discovered more than 100 new species of coral.

20 The English explorer Capt. James Cook discovered the Great Barrier Reef when his ship crashed into it.

21 QUEENSLAND GROUPER FISH CAN BE AS BIG AS A REFRIGERATOR.

22 One type of coral is called candy coral because it looks like candy, but don't eat it!

23 The Bermuda islands and the Bahamas are really ancient coral reefs.

24 There is a U.S. Navy base on a reef in the middle of the Indian Ocean.

25 Australia's Great Barrier Reef isn't one long, unbroken reef, but a system of more than 3,000 reefs.

26 Two-thirds of warm-water reefs are in danger of disappearing.

27 A quarter of all species of fish live around coral reefs.

28 THE DEAD-MAN'S FINGERS CORAL LOOKS LIKE A HAND WITH STUBBY FINGERS.

29 The barrel sponge is so large you could easily fit inside one.

30 Coral reefs make up less than one percent of the Earth's surface.

31 Chemicals from coral reefs are used as medicine.

32 For coral reefs to thrive, the water has to be clear so the sun can shine through it.

33 Coral reefs like warm water, but not too warm—that puts the coral animals under stress, sort of like how you feel when you are overheated.

34 Necklaces and rings can be made from coral, but some jewelers no longer sell them as a way to help protect the oceans.

35 Film designers built 12,996 corals for the computer-generated characters to swim through in one scene in the movie *Finding Nemo*.

36 Coral polyps have one opening, so they eat and get rid of their waste in the same place.

37 Coral colors come from the algae that live within the coral.

38 A super luxurious resort hotel in Fiji lets you stay in underwater rooms that overlook a coral reef.

39 Most moray eels hide in coral reef crevices with only their heads sticking out. At dusk they come out to hunt.

40 The invention of the rubber facemask in the 1930s allowed divers to explore reefs.

41 Mangrove forests located on the shore near reefs provide an important nursery for young reef fish.

42 In Australia, coral towers that rise near the surface of the water are called "bommies."

43 Reef parrotfish eat coral, and their droppings become the white sand on nearby beaches.

44 The ocean's most venomous animal, the box jellyfish, lives along the Great Barrier Reef. It can kill a person with a swipe of its tentacles.

45 AUSTRALIAN LIFE-GUARDS HAVE BEEN KNOWN TO WEAR PANTY HOSE TO PROTECT THEM-SELVES FROM DEADLY BOX JELLYFISH STINGS.

46 A colorful sea snail called the flamingo tongue lives on Caribbean reefs. It has a leopard-spotted fleshy covering, called a mantle, that the snail sometimes uses to completely cover its shell.

47 Hawksbill turtles eat corals.

48 Small lionfish with poisonous spines will sometimes threaten human divers.

49 The Pacific Ocean is home to the most coral reefs.

50 Snorkeling is a great way to see coral reefs, but don't touch the coral because that could kill an entire colony.

75 COOL FACTS ABOUT CORAL REEFS

51 Nudibranchs are colorful marine snails that lack a shell, but their vibrant color announces that they are poisonous.

52 CORAL TROUT START OUT AS FEMALES AND TURN INTO MALES.

53 Coral reefs can be found on the shores of 109 countries.

54 Visitors must scuba dive into the ocean to reach an undersea lodge in Key Largo, Florida, U.S.A.

55 Sea turtles live around reefs and lay their eggs on the surrounding sandy beaches. The sand's temperature determines whether the babies are male or female.

56 Malé, the capital city of the island nation of the Maldives in the Indian Ocean, is on a coral island.

57 The Great Barrier Reef is home to both huge whale sharks, which can reach 40 feet (12 m) in length, and tiny three-quarter-inch (8-mm) -long infantfish.

58 The U.S. tested nuclear weapons on coral atolls in the Pacific Ocean.

59 Whip corals can be straight or grow to look like coiled whips.

60 The "lips" of giant clams contain algae gardens that provide the clams' food.

61 A seahorse takes two and one-half days to travel 0.6 miles (1 km).

62 Clown anemone fish make their home in an anemone's tentacles but don't get stung by them.

63 Coral Pink Sand Dunes State Park in Utah, U.S.A., features wavy-looking dunes of pink coral sand.

64 CORAL REEFS HELP PROTECT BUILDINGS FROM WAVE AND STORM DAMAGE.

65 Dubai is home to the world's largest aquarium panel. The aquarium showcases a coral reef and holds 2.6 million gallons (10 million L) of salt water.

66 Coral polyps and sea anemones are relatives.

67 Poison from the geographic cone snail can kill a human, but collectors love its black-and-white shell.

68 No two giant clams have the same coloring.

69 Some sea cucumbers expel sticky thread to capture their enemies.

70 Reef cuttlefish can turn vibrant colors like black, gold, and red and even zebra stripes when startled.

71 When fire coral touches skin, it causes a painful burning sensation and a red rash.

72 Reef fish all have different jobs to do, and this allows the reef to function like a city.

73 Stinging tentacles surround a sea anemone's mouth.

74 Goby fish live in fan corals similar to the way birds live in trees.

75 Endangered sea turtles breed and feed on reefs in the Andaman Sea off of the coasts of Myanmar and Thailand.

35 AMAZING FACTS

1 Africans speak more than 2,000 DIFFERENT LANGUAGES.

2 The board game MANCALA (also called kalah) originated in Africa.

3 The oldest dunes in the NAMIB DESERT are at least 34,000 YEARS OLD.

4 NINE out of TEN PEOPLE in Rwanda are farmers.

5 Nairobi, the capital of Kenya, means "COOL WATER" in the Maasai language.

6 Most GOLD AND DIAMONDS in the world come from African mines.

7 The hottest air temperature recorded on Earth—a broiling 136.4°F (58°C)—was recorded in 1922 at Al'Aziziyah, Libya.

8 Africa produces 68 PERCENT of the world's total cocoa beans, the bean used to make chocolate.

9 NGORONGORO CRATER is the largest caldera (land that collapses after a volcanic eruption) on Earth that is not filled with water.

10 In Djibouti's Gulf of Tadjourah, WHALE SHARKS feed on plankton from November to January during their annual migration.

11 Libya is one of the only countries that has NO NATURAL RIVERS.

12 Churches in Lalibela, Ethiopia, were CARVED DIRECTLY FROM STONE.

13 Grasslands cover more than 40 PERCENT of Africa.

14 More than HALF THE GOLD ever mined on Earth came from mines near Johannesburg, South Africa.

15 Ten African leaders have won the NOBEL PEACE PRIZE.

16 PLAINS ZEBRAS will migrate more than 300 miles (480 km) in a clockwise movement through Tanzania and Kenya.

17 ZANZIBAR, an island off Africa's east coast, is made up entirely of coral.

18 FOUR of the FIVE FASTEST LAND ANIMALS live in Africa.

19 Madagascar is home to some 100 species of LEMURS.

20 South Africans enjoy eating spiced sausage called BOEREWORS.

21 In 1990 Namibia became the most recent African country to gain its INDEPENDENCE.

22 The GOLIATH FROG, the world's largest, lives in Cameroon and Equatorial Guinea.

23 Africa is the second largest continent: ONLY ASIA IS LARGER.

24 Two countries have AFRICA in their names: the Central African Republic and South Africa.

25 MOUNT KILIMANJARO, Africa's tallest mountain, stands 19,340 feet (5,895 m) tall. That's roughly 1,018 ADULT GIRAFFES stacked on top of each other.

26 The OKAVANGO DELTA in Botswana can be seen from space.

27 The SAHARA DESERT covers 11 COUNTRIES.

28 In Nigeria it's considered RUDE TO EAT WHILE WALKING.

29 Due to the large number of shipwrecks that have occurred there, part of Africa's western coast is often referred to as "SKELETON COAST."

ABOUT AFRICA

30 Millions of years ago, Africa was part of a huge continent called GONDWANALAND, along with India, South America, Australia, and Antarctica.

31 A South African invented the VACUUM CLEANER that cleans swimming pools.

32 LESOTHO is a small African country about the size of the U.S. state of Maryland.

33 While Egypt is famous for its PYRAMIDS, Sudan has more, but they are smaller.

34 Africa accounts for 20 PERCENT of Earth's land surface.

35 Madagascar, the world's FOURTH LARGEST ISLAND, is a nation off the east coast of Africa.

African Elephants

100 MARVELOUS MAMMAL FACTS

Sugar Glider

Lion

1. Mammals have fur or hair and are warm-blooded. They feed their young with milk. **2. The okapi, the only living relative of giraffes, can clean its eyes with its tongue.** **3.** Blindfolded harbor seals can use their whiskers to determine the shape of an object. **4. Humans are just 1 of about 4,000 mammal species on Earth. 5.** The first mammal may never be known. **6. An adult pink fairy armadillo is the size of a soda can. 7.** Most mammals only see in black and white. **8. Some bats live up to 30 years. 9.** Bats make up almost a quarter of all mammal species. **10. Some mammals glide through the air—like flying squirrels and flying lemurs—using parachute-like wings. 11.** Sugar gliders, a type of possum, can glide 200 feet (60 m) between trees. They steer with their tails, which are as long as their bodies. **12. Much like cats, bats groom themselves constantly. 13.** Hippos show they claim a territory by yawning. **14. If a porcupine is in danger, it may back into an attacker and poke it with its quills. 15.** Platypuses, found only in Australia, are one of the few mammals that lay eggs. **16. A giraffe can use its long tongue to reach up an extra foot (30 cm) to grab food. 17.** Not all mammals live on land. Whales and manatees spend their entire lives in water. **18. Tasmanian devils are the size of a grain of rice when they're born. 19.** Some mammals are born blind. **20. A beaver's eyelids are transparent so it can see as it swims underwater. 21.** A beaver's warning signal to predators is whacking its tail on the water's surface. **22. A newborn manatee is about the same weight as a large dog. 23.** Moose are strong and quick: 90 percent escape when being attacked by a pack of wolves. **24. The pygmy shrew of**

North America is only two inches (5 cm) long and weighs less than a dime! **25.** Whales evolved from mammals that once lived on land about 60 million years ago. The front legs evolved into flippers and the back legs disappeared, although small leg bones remain. **26. An elephant brain weighs eight pounds (3.6 kg). A human brain weighs about 3 pounds (1.4 kg). 27.** A squirrel has such a keen sense of smell that it can find a nut buried under a foot (0.3 m) of snow. **28. One ear of the African elephant can weigh more than 100 pounds (45 kg). 29.** A skunk can spray an object nine feet (2.7 m) away. **30. Coyotes have scent glands between their toes that are used to mark their territory. 31.** When prairie dogs meet, they "kiss" to identify what group the other is a member of. **32. Porcupines can float. 33.** Warthogs don't have warts. **34. Mammals have small bones in their ears that help them hear better than non-mammals. 35.** A giant anteater can lap up 35,000 ants and termites in one day. **36. Capybaras, the world's largest living rodents, weigh as much as 140 pounds (64 kg) and are close relatives of the much smaller guinea pig. 37.** Male cats are called toms. Females are called queens. **38. The two-toed sloth sleeps 15 to 18 hours a day. Even when it's awake it doesn't get around much. Its climbing speed: six to eight feet (1.8 to 2.4 meters) per minute. 39.** The jaguar, the biggest cat in South America, is nocturnal. **40. Wombats can take up to 14 days to digest a meal. It takes humans between one and three. 41.** A group of wombats is called a wisdom. **42. Like the giant panda, the red panda grazes on bamboo and lives in trees. While their faces resemble a raccoon's and their name suggests they are related to the panda, they are in fact believed to be in their own family. 43.** The Chinese name for red panda is *hun-ho*, which means "fire fox." **44. Crabeater seals don't eat crabs! They strain krill out of the water using their special teeth. 45.** Wildebeest migrate over 900 miles (1,450 km) across Africa's Serengeti plains each year in search of food. Herds can number as many as 500,000. **46. Most cats have 18 toes, but one cat in Canada has 28! 47.** Hyenas are considered scavengers—they eat the leftovers from other animals' kills. The spotted hyena is capable of eating every part of an animal, including the bones. **48. Fennec foxes have ears that are about a third of their body length, and that give them excellent hearing and help keep them cool. 49.** Caribou migrate in herds of up to 500,000. Domesticated caribou are called reindeer in Europe and Asia. **50. Caribou are the only deer species in which both males and females grow antlers. Male antlers can measure 51 inches (130 cm). 51.** Tigers are lions' closest relatives. If you were to remove a lion's and tiger's coat, their bodies are so similar that only an expert could tell which was which. **52. A lion's roar can be heard up to five miles (8 km) away. 53.** A puma, also known as a mountain lion or cougar, can kill prey seven times its own weight. **54. Lynx have tufts of hair on the ends of their ears that may be used like whiskers to feel things. 55.** A golden retriever won a world record by holding five tennis balls in its mouth at once. **56. There are more dogs in the U.S. than babies. 57.** If a camel doesn't have enough fat stored up, its hump droops. **58. A giraffe's heart is two feet (0.6 m) long! 59.** A group of hippos is called a bloat. **60. Hippos can go three weeks without eating. 61.** A mare in Kansas holds the world record for the longest horse mane. It measured 12 and a half feet (381 cm). **62. Arctic foxes' fur changes color with the seasons. It's white in winter and brown in summer. 63.** Rams sometimes battle by butting heads for 24 hours straight! **64. Most wolves live in a pack of between four and seven. 65.** Members of the "big cat" families—like lions, tigers, and jaguars—can roar. Smaller cats cannot. **66. Female mountain goats are called nannies. 67.** Aye-ayes and lemurs are only found on Madagascar, an island off of Africa. **68. Wolverines are members of the weasel family and have short legs and wide feet for running quickly through the snow. They travel as much as 15 miles (24 km) a day looking for food. 69.** The clouded leopard's tail is as long as its body, which helps it climb a branch upside down. **70. A hedgehog has 3,000–5,000 quills on its back. 71.** When a hedgehog feels threatened, it rolls into a tight ball, protecting its soft belly. **72. While pigs do roll in the mud (to protect themselves from sunburn), they are considered one of the cleanest farm animals. 73.** Female lions are faster and more successful hunters than the males. **74. Cows eat and chew for four to six hours a day. 75.** Moose antlers can span more than six feet (1.8 m) across. **76. There are about 1.4 billion cattle and about 1.1 billion sheep in the world. 77.** If you were to put all of Earth's 7 billion humans on a giant scale, we would weigh 350 million tons (317 MT). **78. Chinchillas, native to Chile, are known for their soft fur and are often kept as pets. Only a few thousand survive in the wild, however. 79.** Naked mole rats, which are almost completely hairless and have wrinkly gray or pink skin, have large front teeth they use for digging tunnels underground. **80. About 30 percent of all U.S. households have a cat; about 40 percent have a dog. 81.** Trained cheetahs were used by 16th century royalty to hunt gazelles. **82. Newborn giraffes are six feet (1.8 m) tall. 83.** Koalas have unique fingerprints just like humans. **84. Kangaroos can't walk backward. 85.** Koalas sleep as many as 20 hours a day. **86. Unlike most domestic cats, tigers like the water. 87.** Honey badgers don't get their name from eating honey; they eat larva in a honeybee hive. Their thick skin can withstand the bees' stings. **88. A newborn pronghorn calf can walk an hour after it's born. 89.** Spotted hyenas make a noise that sounds like a human laugh when they are nervous or excited. **90. Pot-bellied pigs are used by law enforcement because they're good sniffers! 91.** Matschie's tree-kangaroos spend most of their time up in trees eating leaves. **92. When musk oxen are threatened by predators, they form a circle around their young. 93.** Musk oxen, which weigh as much as 900 pounds (408 kg), live in the Arctic and eat grasses and lichen. **94. Polar bears have an outer coat of fur that sticks together to keep their undercoat dry. 95.** A rabbit's teeth grow its entire life. **96. A polar bear can smell a seal on the ice 20 miles (32 km) away. 97.** "Groundhog" and "woodchuck" are common terms for the same animal. **98. Opossums sometimes "play dead" for hours. 99.** Some kangaroos can jump five times their body length in one jump. **100. Numbats, a type of anteater, have a long, sticky tongue they use for catching termites. They can eat tens of thousands a day!**

Rabbit

1 EUROPEAN SETTLERS brought honeybees to the Americas in the 1600s.

3 Female honeybees carry pollen in BASKETLIKE STRUCTURES on their HIND LEGS.

9 Honeybees have to make about ten million trips to and from the hive to COLLECT ENOUGH NECTAR to make one pound (0.45 kg) of honey.

10 When honeybees return to the hive with nectar, they THROW IT UP into the mouths of worker bees that either eat it or store it in cells.

16 A KILLER BEE STING is not deadlier than that of a regular honeybee. A killer bee—a hybrid of two kinds of honeybee—is just more aggressive.

21 In the United States, North Dakota produces the most honey—46.4 million pounds (21,000 MT) in 2010, about the weight of 128 BLUE WHALES.

27 Each honeybee colony has only one queen, who lays as many as 1,500 PINHEAD-SIZED EGGS a day.

4 Honeybees use a LONG TUBE on their head called a PROBOSCIS to suck flower nectar.

17 Queen bees PRODUCE CHEMICALS that GUIDE THE BEHAVIOR of other bees in the hive.

28 For a nest, honeybees require a space that could hold about FOUR ONE-GALLON (15 L) MILK JUGS.

11 Worker bees called NURSE BEES check on each baby honeybee more than 1,000 times a day.

22 Honeybees OOZE BEESWAX FROM THEIR ABDOMENS to build the six-sided cells of a hive.

5 Honeybees are NEAT FREAKS. It takes 15 to 30 worker bees 40 minutes to CLEAN EACH EGG CELL.

18 When a hive gets too hot, worker bees will crowd around the queen and FLAP THEIR WINGS to create a cool breeze for her.

29 Worker bees CLEAN AND FEED THE QUEEN HONEYBEE, and even carry away her waste.

2 Americans consumed 410 MILLION POUNDS (186,000 MT) of honey in 2010.

12 Honeybees also try to STEAL HONEY from other hives.

23 A honeybee colony's residents ALL SMELL ALIKE.

6 When the water in stored nectar evaporates, or turns into gas, what's left behind is HONEY.

30 When a worker bee is done collecting nectar, she flies in a straight line—A BEELINE—back to the hive.

13 Honeybees "TALK" to each other by DANCING; how fast a bee dances and the shape it makes communicate the distance and direction of flowers.

24 Male honeybees, called DRONES, DON'T HAVE STINGERS.

7 Honeybees can protect plants from hungry caterpillars. The BEES' BUZZING SCARES THEM OFF.

19 Only THREE PERCENT of people stung by a bee develop anaphylaxis, a SEVERE ALLERGIC REACTION.

31 A honeybee SWARM can contain as many as 30,000 BEES.

14 Worker honeybees GROW to be about A HALF AN INCH (15 mm) long.

25 When a worker bee hatches, the first thing she does is turn around and CLEAN HER CELL so it's ready for the next egg.

8 Honeybees are usually attracted to YELLOW, BLUE, and PURPLE flowers.

20 Humans have been EATING HONEY for more than 3,000 years.

32 BEESWAX is used for candles and also to coat jellybeans.

15 Honeybees are FOUND on every continent but ANTARCTICA.

26 Honey's TASTE AND COLOR depend on the kinds of flowers honeybees collect nectar from.

50 SWEET FACTS ABOUT BEES

33 Drones, male honeybees, are **KICKED OUT OF THE HIVE** when food supplies run low as **WINTER APPROACHES.**

39 Bee colonies will split up when it becomes **TOO CROWDED** in a hive. The queen and more than half of the worker bees leave the hive and form a swarm, and elder bees scout out **LOCATIONS FOR A NEW NEST.**

40 Baby honeybees—called larvae—**DINE ON ROYAL JELLY,** which worker bees squeeze from their heads, and beebread, a mix of honey and pollen.

45 All the bees in a hive have the **SAME MOTHER—THE QUEEN.**

48 In spring and summer, **HONEYBEES WORK** about **EIGHT HOURS A DAY.**

34 Worker bees—**ALWAYS FEMALE**—are the majority of a honeybee colony.

43 A honeybee colony needs about **40 POUNDS** (18 kg) **OF HONEY,** collected during warmer months, to survive the winter.

46 Many U.S. crops depend on honeybee pollination, which makes the bees worth **BILLIONS OF DOLLARS.**

50 **GUARD BEES** defend honeybee hives from intruders like bears and honey badgers, which are named after their favorite food.

41 Honeybees have a **SEPARATE STOMACH** just for honey.

35 Because beehives are dark, honeybees **COMMUNICATE THROUGH TOUCH** when inside.

44 Honeybee colonies can hold as many as 80,000 **BEES.**

49 The unexplained disappearance of a hive's honeybees is called **COLONY COLLAPSE DISORDER.**

47 A honeybee dies after it **USES ITS STINGER** on another animal.

36 Only older **(THREE WEEKS OLD!)** worker bees **FORAGE FOR NECTAR** and bring it back to the hive.

37 A honeybee has **950,000 NEURONS,** or nerve cells, in its brain; a human has 100,000,000,000.

38 A honeybee **QUEEN** can live as long as **FIVE YEARS;** by comparison, drones live for only a **FEW WEEKS.**

42 To **AVOID BEING STUNG** by a honeybee buzzing around you, it's best to **STAND STILL.**

1 A DESIGNER HAS CREATED "LIVING" SHOES —ONCE YOU HAVE WORN THEM OUT YOU CAN PLANT THEM AND THEY WILL SPROUT FLOWERS.

2 Countries have different "CARBON FOOTPRINTS" (the amount of greenhouse gases emitted by the country). THE UNITED STATES HAS A FOOTPRINT ABOUT 18 TIMES THAT OF PERU. Qatar has the largest footprint per person, and the Democratic Republic of Congo has the smallest.

3 YOU CAN LIVE IN A STRAW HOUSE. Houses that use straw bales as insulation are more ENERGY EFFICIENT than standard housing, and they use stalks that would be burnt otherwise.

4 Electric cars cost TEN CENTS LESS PER MILE (1.6 km) to drive than a car that runs on gas. A trip between San Francisco and Los Angeles, California, U.S.A., costs $34 less in an ELECTRIC CAR.

5 DOG POOP WAS USED TO POWER A LIGHT IN A PARK IN MASSACHUSETTS, U.S.A.

25 GREEN FACTS

6 A year's worth of the AVERAGE AMERICAN KID'S LAUNDRY would weigh 500 pounds (227 kg). That's heavier than a gorilla!

7 "Vampire" appliances SUCK UP ENERGY even when they are not being used. A TV and its remote use more energy while they are off during the day than they do when you watch TV for four hours.

8 Earth-friendly apartments, shops, cinemas, and schools in a Beijing, China, neighborhood are kept cool in the summer and warm in the winter by 655 GEOTHERMAL (UNDERGROUND) WELLS.

9 SOME LARGE WIND TURBINE BLADES (THAT PRODUCE GREEN ENERGY) CAN STRETCH 112 FEET (34 M). THAT'S TALLER THAN A TEN-STORY BUILDING.

10 Riding on a train for 1,000 miles (1,609 km) PRODUCES LESS THAN HALF THE CARBON EMISSIONS THAN TAKING THE SAME JOURNEY BY PLANE.

11 WRITING A HOMEWORK REPORT CAN BE "GREEN." A DESIGNER HAS CREATED A DESK FROM WHICH YOU CAN POWER YOUR COMPUTER USING THE DESK'S SOLAR PANELS.

12 Throughout the world, about 1 MILLION PLASTIC BAGS ARE USED EVERY MINUTE.

13 Carbon dioxide, the gas that makes your soda fizzy, is **ALSO LINKED TO CLIMATE CHANGE.**

15  INSTEAD OF GAS-GUZZLING LAWN MOWERS, THE INTERNET COMPANY GOOGLE USES GOATS TO **TRIM ITS LAWN.**

16  **EARTH-FRIENDLY BAMBOO** —it grows quickly and can be used instead of slower-growing trees—has been used to make everything from **FLOORS AND CLOTHES TO RADIOS AND EVEN AN IPAD STYLUS (PEN).**

14 **GO PORTABLE** to reduce your carbon footprint. Laptop computers use **50 TO 90 PERCENT LESS ENERGY** than desktop computers.

17 In the U.S. and Great Britain, a **FRUIT OR VEGETABLE TRAVELS** an average of 1,200 miles (1,931 km) from farm to table!

THAT CAN SAVE THE WORLD

18 Putting on a **WARM SWEATER** instead of **TURNING UP THE HEAT** can keep 1,000 pounds (454 kg) of carbon dioxide out of the atmosphere every year.

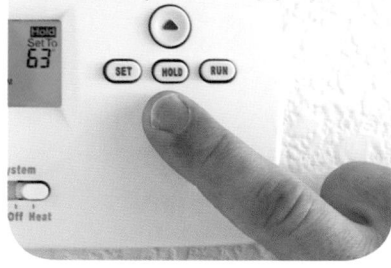

19 WORLDWIDE, PEOPLE RECYCLE ABOUT ONE-THIRD OF ALL ALUMINUM PRODUCTS. THAT'S **19.8 MILLION TONS** (18 MILLION MT).

20 BIOFUEL IS FUEL MADE FROM PLANTS LIKE SOYBEANS OR CORN. A jet using biofuel flew from New Jersey, United States, to Paris, France, in 2011.

21 Turning off your computer when it is not in use and using **"SLEEP" MODE** CUTS ITS ENERGY USE BY 85%.

22 **"GREEN" GUITARS** CAN BE MADE OUT OF RECYCLED MATERIALS SUCH AS PLASTIC BOTTLES AND INDUSTRIAL PIPES.

23 **EARTH HOUR** occurs every March, when people turn off their lights for an hour to raise awareness about climate change. In 2011, people in 135 countries and 5,200 cities took part.

24 A designer has created a cell phone with a casing **MADE OUT OF GRASS.** After the life of the phone is over, it decomposes and the screen and the **KEYS CAN BE RECYCLED.**

25 As much as **90%** of the energy used by standard lightbulbs escapes as heat and is not converted into **USABLE LIGHT.**

15 FACTS ABOUT PARANORMAL

1 PARANORMAL ACTIVITY is anything that is not SCIENTIFICALLY EXPLAINABLE.

2 A POLTERGEIST is a NOISY, MISCHIEVOUS GHOST.

3 ESP STANDS FOR "EXTRASENSORY PERCEPTION," or the ability to obtain information WITHOUT USING THE FIVE SENSES: sight, smell, touch, hearing, or taste.

4 PHASMAPHOBIA is a fear of GHOSTS.

5 There are multiple reports of a BRITISH SOLDIER HAUNTING THE WHITE HOUSE.

6 The busy QUEEN VICTORIA MARKET IN MELBOURNE, AUSTRALIA, is BUILT ATOP A CEMETERY and reportedly haunted by the ghosts of those STILL BURIED BENEATH the building.

7 Rumor has it that ENGLAND'S HAMPTON COURT PALACE IS HAUNTED by the ghost of an EXECUTED QUEEN. Neighbors claim to HEAR HER SCREAMS, and during two separate tours of the palace on the same night, TWO VISITORS FAINTED AT EXACTLY THE SAME SPOT.

ACTIVITY TO MAKE YOUR SKIN PRICKLE

8 Some people believe a **OUIJA BOARD** can be used to **COMMUNICATE WITH SPIRITS** by allowing the dead to move a playing piece over the board's letters and symbols to spell out a message.

9 TELEKINESIS is the ability to **MOVE OBJECTS WITHOUT TOUCHING THEM.**

10 A set of **TAROT CARDS** includes 22 picture cards—such as Death, the Hanged Man, and the Magician—**USED FOR FORTUNE-TELLING.**

THE MAGICIAN

11 NECROMANCY is **CONJURING THE SPIRITS OF THE DEAD** to reveal the future or influence it.

12 In the SEVENTH MONTH OF THE LUNAR CALENDAR, people across Asia celebrate the **HUNGRY GHOST FESTIVAL,** a day when the doors to the spirit world are believed to open and **THE LIVING LEAVE FOOD OFFERINGS FOR GHOSTS** in search of food.

13 A SHAPE-SHIFTER is a mythical creature able to **CHANGE FORM—FROM A HUMAN TO A WOLF,** for example.

14 PALMISTRY is the practice of "READING" THE LINES on a person's palms to **PREDICT THEIR FUTURE AND DESCRIBE THE PERSON'S PERSONALITY.**

15 TELEPATHY IS DIRECT MIND-TO-MIND COMMUNICATION without words or gestures.

The Line of Heart
The Line of Head
The Line of Life

75 EARTH-SHAKING FACTS

1. Tiny pieces of space debris colliding with Earth add about 100 tons (90.7 MT) to our planet every day.

2. Today, 175 countries observe Earth Day.

3. THE AMAZON RAIN FOREST PRODUCES ABOUT 20 PERCENT OF EARTH'S OXYGEN.

4. Earth is 7,926 miles (12,756 km) wide.

5. It takes Earth 365.26 days to orbit the sun. The extra one-quarter of a day each year is usually observed every four years on February 29, during a Leap Year.

6. The Outback makes up about 70 percent of Australia's land, but only about 3 percent of the country's population lives there.

7. The average surface temperature on Earth is 46°F (7.7°C).

8. Mount Everest was once simply known as "Peak 15."

9. Earth's atmosphere is 78 percent nitrogen, 21 percent oxygen, and one percent argon.

10. Humans drilling for oil once caused an earthquake that measured 5.5 on the Richter scale.

11. If you were to stand at the ocean's deepest point, the water pressure would make it feel like 50 jumbo jets were piled on top of you.

12. When Washington's Mount St. Helens erupted on May 18, 1980, within three minutes the blast blew down and scorched 230 square miles (595 sq km) of forest.

13. Earth is not a perfect sphere: It's flattened at the poles and bulges at the Equator.

14. All water on Earth is recycled, so in a sense, you are drinking water that dinosaurs drank millions of years ago.

15. Only 2.5 percent of Earth's water is fresh water, and lakes and rivers hold less than one percent of it.

16. The Mid-Atlantic Ridge, an underwater mountain range, runs nearly the entire length of the Atlantic Ocean.

17. Yellowstone National Park is home to about 60 percent of the world's geysers—hot water and steam ejected from the Earth.

18. Six hundred million years ago, Earth was home to one giant supercontinent named Pannotia, and one giant ocean called Panthalassic.

19. Earth's core is solid metal surrounded by liquid metal.

20. EARTH IS ABOUT 4–5 BILLION YEARS OLD.

21. Earth is covered in about 16 tectonic plates that are on average 60 miles (96.5 km) thick.

22. North America and Africa are moving apart about as fast as human fingernails grow.

23. Earth is home to at least 5,000 different cultures.

24. You'd have to swim about 6.7 miles (10.9 km) down to reach the deepest point in the sea, the Pacific's Challenger Deep.

25. Earth is the only planet in our solar system with plate tectonics.

26. At about 840,000 square miles (2,175,600 sq km), Greenland is the world's largest island.

27. The Nile River has long been considered the longest river in the world, but a group of scientists who recently mapped the Amazon River claim it is 65 miles (105 km) longer than the Nile.

28. The Caspian Sea, the world's largest lake, was reportedly named "sea" because when the ancient Romans arrived there, they found the water to be salty.

29. Sixty million years ago, 42-foot-long (13 m), 2,500-pound (1,135-kg) snakes slithered across Earth's tropical rain forests.

30. At 1,500 feet (457 m), the highest dunes in the Sahara Desert are taller than the Empire State Building in New York, U.S.A.

31. Water flows down the drain both clockwise and counterclockwise in both the Northern and Southern hemispheres.

32. Four oceans are officially recognized—the Pacific, Atlantic, Indian, and Arctic—but there is support for naming a fifth ocean near Antarctica the Southern Ocean.

33. More than 80 percent of Earth's surface, both above and below sea, is shaped by volcanoes.

34. Light from Earth's major urban areas is visible from space.

35. Earth spins on its axis at a speed of more than 1,000 miles per hour (1,600 kph).

36. Earth travels at about 66,700 miles per hour (107,300 kph) while orbiting the sun.

37. An object the size of Mars slammed into Earth more than four billion years ago, breaking off a chunk of the planet that later became the moon.

38. Most major animal groups appeared on Earth more than 550 million years ago.

39. Earth's crust is about 3 to 6 miles (4.8 to 9.6 km) thick under the oceans and as much as 25 miles thick (40.2 km) under the continents.

40. In the 1970s, Russian scientists tried to drill a hole through Earth's crust, but they only made it 7.6 miles (12.2 km) in 19 years.

41. Earth's solid metal core is about as hot as the surface of the sun— about 9,000°F (about 5,000°C).

42. Earth's atmosphere has no real boundary; it just grows thinner and thinner until it fades into space.

43. All weather occurs within eight miles (12.8 km) of Earth's surface.

44. We couldn't live on Earth without ozone—a form of oxygen that protects the planet from the sun's powerful ultraviolet rays.

45. IT TAKES THREE DAYS TO FLY TO THE MOON FROM EARTH.

46. Scientists predict that North America and Africa will collide in about 250 million years.

47. Most objects on a collision course with Earth burn up in the planet's atmosphere and never make impact.

48. Tortoises have lived on Earth for about 230 million years, since the beginning of the age of the dinosaurs.

49. Alaska experiences an average of 60 earthquakes a day.

50. Large cities, major roads, bridges, airports, and dams are all visible from space.

51. The deepest lake on Earth is Asia's Lake Baikal, a little more than a mile (1.6 km) deep.

52. If a full gallon jug represented the world's water, freshwater would equal only about one tablespoon.

53. There may be more than 25,000 islands in the Pacific Ocean.

54. Fiji alone consists of 332 islands.

55. The Pacific Ocean is about 15 times larger than the United States.

56. There are two types of monarch butterfly. One is found in North America, the other in South America. Scientists believe that the two species separated about two million years ago when world sea levels were much higher than today.

57. On Antarctica, there are mountains more than 16,000 feet (4,877 m) tall covered in massive ice sheets.

58. More than half of Earth's seven billion people live in Asia.

59. More than 300 species of tree frog live in Earth's tropical rain forests. They all have a special sticky pad on each toe that helps them move on the undersides of leaves.

60. Asia has more farmers and more cities with a population of a million or more than any other continent.

61. The Ganges Delta in Asia is shaped like a triangle. The middle of the delta is made up of swamps, forests, small islands, and creeks.

62. The geographic North Pole lies roughly in the middle of the Arctic Ocean beneath 13,000 feet (3,962 m) of water.

63. North America's Great Lakes hold about 20 percent of Earth's fresh water.

64. If everyone on Earth jumped at the same time, it would have no effect on the planet's motion.

65. Straddling the Peru-Bolivia border, Lake Titicaca is the highest in the world, perched at about 12,500 feet (3,810 m) above sea level.

66. Earth's temperature rises slightly during a full moon.

67. There are about 3,000 lightning flashes on Earth every minute.

68. When flowers are in bloom in North America's Sonoran Desert, bees and birds pollinate them during the day. At night, bats take over the job.

69. Scientists predict that with the movement of Earth's plates, San Francisco and Los Angeles—which now are separated by about 380 miles (611 km)—will lie next to each other in about 15 million years.

70. There are about half a million detectable earthquakes in the world each year.

71. The interior of Antarctica experiences icequakes, tremors within the ice sheet that covers the continent.

72. Earthquakes don't cause volcanic eruptions.

73. POWERFUL EARTHQUAKES CAN SHORTEN A DAY ON EARTH, BUT ONLY BY A FEW MILLIONTHS OF A SECOND.

74. Forests cover about 30 percent of the planet's land.

75. The International Date Line is an imaginary line that zigzags between Russia and Alaska and down the Pacific Ocean. It separates two consecutive calendar days, so that the date in the Eastern Hemisphere—to the left of the line—is always one day ahead of the date in the Western Hemisphere—to the right of the line.

35 THiNGS

1 What is TREASURE? It is money, sparkling jewels, and precious metals stored up or HIDDEN away, sometimes lost and then rediscovered.

2 Robert Louis Stevenson's 1883 *TREASURE ISLAND* popularized the idea of pirates flying the Jolly Roger and carrying treasure MAPS.

3 An estimated THREE MILLION vessels—from Phoenician merchant ships to Japanese submarines—have been LOST at sea.

4 For 300 years Spanish ships called GALLEONS spilled the treasure they were transporting into the Caribbean waters while EXPLORING the Americas.

5 A galleon is also the name of coin CURRENCY in the *HARRY POTTER* books.

6 In the 1980s, an explorer in the FLORIDA KEYS, U.S.A., found $450 million worth of treasure from a 1622 Spanish SHIPWRECK.

7 Marine archaeologists and treasure hunters are at ODDS: Archaeologists believe shipwrecks should be PRESERVED. Treasure hunters feel they are a public resource.

8 No wreck is too deep: Today, REMOTELY OPERATED vehicles run by people on the ocean's surface can be used to EXPLORE deepwater wrecks.

9 Modern-day treasure hunting called GEO-CACHING involves people using a GPS to locate items HIDDEN by other players.

10 Egyptians believed GOLD covered the SKIN of the gods.

11 When King Tutankhamun's TOMB was discovered in 1922, so was a massive volume of GOLD, JEWELS, and ART. His gold funeral mask is on display in Cairo, Egypt.

12 Egypt's finest GOLDSMITHS crafted King Tut's innermost COFFIN from nearly 250 pounds (113 kg) of PURE gold.

13 The only TREASURE chest known to be owned by a pirate is on display at a museum in Florida, U.S.A. The 400-YEAR-OLD chest weighs 150 pounds (68 kg)—without any LOOT in it.

14 The world's largest jade BUDDHA is 8 feet (2.4 m) tall, weighs 4.5 TONS (4.1 MT), and is valued at more than $1 million.

15 PEARLS are formed inside mollusks after an irritating object gets TRAPPED inside. The mollusk creates a PROTECTIVE layer to seal it off. That becomes the PEARL.

16 Only ONE out of every 10,000 wild mollusks contains a PEARL.

17 The LARGEST treasure hunt game involved 250 PARTICIPANTS in Romania in 2010.

18 Treasure Island is a small MAN-MADE island in the San Francisco Bay, U.S.A. It was built in 1937 and named for the FAMOUS book.

19 A man using a METAL DETECTOR found a hoard of gold valued at SEVERAL million dollars in a FARMER'S field in England.

20 In 1927, future U.S. PRESIDENT FRANKLIN D. ROOSEVELT joined a group to SEARCH for the LOST TREASURE of Oak Island off the coast of CANADA. The search came up empty.

21 While his ship, *Queen Anne's Revenge*, is thought to have been found off the coast of North Carolina, U.S.A., in 1996, Blackbeard's pirate TREASURE IS STILL MISSING.

22 Gold was very rare until discoveries in the MID-1800S. NINETY percent of existing gold has been MINED since then.

23 Tougher than STEEL, the finest Chinese JADE is far more valuable than GOLD.

24 The 45.52-carat HOPE DIAMOND is on permanent display at the SMITHSONIAN INSTITUTION in Washington, D.C., U.S.A. Some say it is CURSED.

25 Astronomers discovered a STAR that is made of a 10-billion-trillion-trillion CARAT diamond.

26 In the 19th century, STEAMSHIPS carrying gold from the California GOLD RUSH of 1849 sank in Atlantic storms.

27 Black, white, gold, and even purple pearls have been PRIZED around the world since ANCIENT times. Those made naturally are the most VALUABLE.

28 The word "diamond" comes from the Greek word *ADAMAS*, or "unbreakable." DIAMOND is the hardest of all MINERALS.

29 Silver is CHEAPER than gold because it is more common and prone to TARNISH.

30 The Spanish thought PLATINUM was silver when they found it in the 1500s. But it's more RARE than silver and has a higher MELTING point.

TREASURED

31 India was the world's only significant SOURCE OF DIAMONDS until the 18th century.

32 Black diamonds—or "CARBONADOS"—found in South America and Africa may NOT have been made here on planet EARTH. Some scientists believe they were formed in space.

33 William Kidd, a 17th-century pirate, supposedly BURIED his loot in New England and maybe the Caribbean. Some think it was seized by the government. Others think it's still HIDDEN.

34 A gold nugget found in CALIFORNIA weighed a whopping 160 POUNDS (72.6 KG)—as much as 12 BOWLING balls.

35 SCROOGE McDUCK was named the richest FICTIONAL character in the world by *Forbes* magazine in 2011. He is worth (a fictional) 44.1 billion dollars.

Clownfish

100 FACTS ABOUT OCEANS

1. Ninety percent of all volcanic activity on Earth occurs in the ocean. **2.** An area the size of New York State, U.S.A., on the South Pacific ocean floor is home to 1,133 active volcanic cones and sea mounts. **3.** In 2012, James Cameron, director of *Avatar*, became the first solo explorer to reach the deepest depth of the ocean. **4.** Earth's longest mountain range is under the sea. The Mid-Ocean Ridge is four times longer than the Andes, Rockies, and Himalayas combined. **5.** Canada has 15 percent of the world's coastline—more than any other country. **6.** At the deepest point in the ocean, the pressure is more than eight tons per square inch (1.1 MT per cm). **7.** The temperature of almost all deep-ocean water is just barely above freezing. **8.** If all of the gold in the world's seawater were sifted out, there would be enough for each person on Earth to claim nine pounds (4 kg). **9.** The world's tallest known iceberg—found off the coast of Greenland—was just a few feet shorter than the Washington Monument in Washington, D.C., U.S.A. **10.** If all of the oceans' salt content could be collected and dried out, it would cover all of Earth's continents in five feet (1.5 m) of sodium. **11.** Scientists measure the age of fish by counting lines in their bones, just like the rings in a tree. **12.** The most primitive fishlike animals on Earth have sucking mouths, like lampreys, which are mostly bottom-dwellers. **13.** Sturgeons live 50 years or more and can weigh more than 1,000 pounds (454 kg). **14.** Sharks have eyelids, but most other fish don't. **15.** Tuna can swim in quick bursts at 50 mph (80 kph). **16.** Most fish can't swim backward. **17.** Most fish are unable to appreciate the colorful lures used to attract them because they are color-blind. **18.** Two of the four flatfish families have their eyes on the left side of their body. The other two families have their eyes on the right. **19.** Puffer fish puff up by pumping water into special sacs. Out of water they will still inflate by using air. **20.** An electric eel discharges some 350 volts—more than an electrical outlet in your house! **21.** A giant squid is as long as a six-story building is high. **22.** Scientists once tracked a lobster as it traveled 225 miles (362 km). **23.** A lobster's teeth are in its stomach. **24.** There's a type of land hermit crab in the Pacific islands that eats coconuts. **25.** A sea turtle can stay underwater for up to two hours without coming up for air. **26.** It would take a stack of more than nine Empire State Buildings to equal the average depth of the ocean. **27.** A dolphin's flipper has five digits, similar to a human's hand. **28.** Humans have only explored 5 percent of the ocean. **29.** The Monterey Bay Submarine Canyon off California, U.S.A., is deeper than the Grand Canyon. **30.** The Gulf Stream off the U.S. Atlantic seaboard flows 300 times faster than the typical flow of the Amazon River. **31.** If you take a gulp of seawater, you may have just swallowed hundreds of thousands of phytoplankton and tens of thousands of zooplankton. **32.** Sand is made of tiny pieces of worn-down rock. Wind, water, and glaciers pick up the pieces and leave them in the ocean where they become sediment or on land, where they form our sand dunes. **33.** Kelp is harvested to make cosmetics and toothpaste. **34.** Lionfish are sometimes called turkeyfish because their fins look like turkey feathers. **35.** Green sea turtles weigh about 300 pounds (135 kg)—that's as much as a male lion. But while lions live about 15 years in the wild, green turtles live about 100. **36.** Starfish aren't fish. Sea stars—as they're properly called—are echinoderms, related to sand dollars, sea urchins, and sea cucumbers. **37.** Some sea stars have more than 40 arms! If an arm is lost, they can grow a replacement. **38.** Jellyfish are about 95 percent water. **39.** Jellyfish don't have a brain, blood, or a heart! **40.** Sea stars take out their stomach to eat! They put it over prey, cover the prey with digestive juices, and then slurp it up. **41.** The sunflower sea star has 24 arms and is considered fast moving, as far as sea stars go. When looking for food it can travel 40 inches (1 m) in a minute. **42.** Scientists can determine how old a sand dollar is by counting the growth rings on its exoskeleton. Most live between six and ten years. **43.** An abalone has bluish-green blood. **44.** When a sea cucumber feels threatened, it can shoot out some of its internal organs! It grows replacements. **45.** Oval-shaped comb jellies have eight rows of tiny comblike plates that they beat to move through the water. Their main prey: other jellies. **46.** Giant clams, the largest clams in the world, can grow to be more than four feet (1.2 m) long. They spend their adult life attached to the same spot. **47.** All clownfish start out as male. As they grow, some males change into females. **48.** The anglerfish has a "rod" on the end of its snout with a glow of light at the end. The light is really millions of light-producing bacteria. **49.** At 5,000 pounds (2,268 kg), ocean sunfish are the world's heaviest bony fish. Still, their size doesn't keep orcas and sea lions from preying on them. **50.** Sea lions are often seen bodysurfing. **51.** Sea lions sometimes keep their flippers out of the water to regulate their body temperature. **52.** Once each year, elephant seals come ashore and shed a layer of skin and their fur. **53.** Sea otters sometimes wrap themselves in kelp when resting to keep from drifting away. **54.** Sea otters' coats have pockets. They have flaps of skin under their front legs, which they use to store food, while their paws are free to continue diving. **55.** A nautilus swims by making jets. By shooting water out of its funnel, it can swim forward, backward, or sideways. **56.** Cuttlefish ink was once used for writing and drawing. **57.** Cuttlefish can instantly change their skin color and pattern. **58.** The giant Pacific octopus has about 2,200 suction cups total on its eight arms. **59.** Seals have small front flippers, whereas sea lions have long ones, helping them "walk" better on land. Sea lions also have small flaps for ears, and seals don't have external ears. **60.** Dolphins have longer noses, bigger mouths, and a more curved dorsal fin than their porpoise cousins. Dolphins also make more noise. **61.** The threadfin butterfly fish has a spot near its tail that looks like an eye, perhaps to confuse predators. Its real eye is disguised under a black strip. **62.** Sawfish have a six-foot (2-m) -long nose that looks like a saw. It uses it to dig for prey in the ocean floor. **63.** Swordfish can travel as fast as 60 miles per hour (96 kph). That's as fast as a car travels on a highway! **64.** A flying fish can glide as much as 600 feet (180 m) over the water. **65.** The tripod fish has thin, long fins that it "stands" on while waiting for prey on the ocean floor. **66.** The eelpout, which lives near hydrothermal vents, is a long, white fish that doesn't have scales.

THAT WILL MAKE YOUR HEAD SWIM

67. Orcas have been known to attack polar bears. **68.** The frilled shark was thought to be extinct until 2007, when a Japanese fisherman found a live one washed up on the shore. **69.** Sea horses have no teeth or stomach. **70.** Plesiosaurs, giant long-necked marine reptiles, swam in the oceans 80–215 million years ago—the same time dinosaurs roamed the Earth. **71.** The largest crocodiles on Earth are strong swimmers and have been spotted far out at sea near Australia and Southeast Asia. Called "salties" by Australians, they can be 17 feet (5 m) long. **72.** Narwhals are called the "unicorns of the sea." Their spiral tusk can be 8.8 feet (2.7 m) long. **73.** Manatees can hold their breath for 15 minutes underwater. **74.** Manatees were once mistaken for mermaids by sailors. **75.** A giant squid's eye is as big as a watermelon. **76.** Scallops have about 60 eyes around the edge of their shell to detect motion, light, and darkness. **77.** Blue whale calves grow at a rate of 11 pounds (5 kg) per hour. **78.** The dwarf goby fish is just 0.3 inches (6 mm) long. **79.** Both male and female walruses have tusks. They use their tusks—which can be about three feet (1 m) long—to haul themselves out of the water and to dig holes in the ice. **80.** Sponges don't have eyes or a mouth and they can't move on their own. **81.** Bottlenose dolphins live 40–45 years in the wild. **82.** Beluga whales stick to swimming in cold waters. They can be found in the Arctic Ocean and near Russia, Canada, Greenland, and Alaska, U.S.A. **83.** Giant tube worms can grow to be more than six feet (1.8 m) tall and are found near hydrothermal vents in the Pacific Ocean about one mile (1.6 km) below the water's surface. A plume from a worm's opening collects nutrients from the surrounding water. **84.** The oarfish, the longest bony fish in the world, can reach lengths of 50 feet (15 m). Some people report seeing a sea serpent when they spot one. **85.** Green sea turtles sometimes migrate more than 1,400 miles (2,253 km) to lay their eggs. **86.** A group of jellyfish is called a smack. **87.** Oil from some fish is used in shampoo. **88.** Bluefish tuna is prized seafood used in sushi. A 444-pound (201 kg) bluefin tuna once sold in a Japanese fish market for $173,600. **89.** Diatoms—algae with hard shells—are used in pet litter, cosmetics, and tooth polish. **90.** Life began in the oceans 3.1-3.4 billion years ago. **91.** When a blue whale exhales, the air comes out its blowhole at 300 miles per hour (483 kph). **92.** A sailfish hits its prey with its nose, which either stuns or kills it. Then it eats it. **93.** Giant kelp can grow up to two feet (0.61 m) a day. **94.** Scottish law once required that fishermen wear a gold earring. If they died at sea, the earring was used to pay funeral expenses. **95.** The Arctic Ocean is the smallest of Earth's five ocean basins. Still, it's one and a half times as big as the United States. **96.** Stingrays are in the same family as sharks. **97.** Salt in the ocean comes from eroding rocks on land! **98.** Orcas are sometimes called the "wolves of the sea" because they live and hunt together. A group of orcas is called a pod. **99.** Orcas have about 45 three-inch-long (7.6 cm) teeth. They only use them for ripping prey. They don't chew their food. **100.** There are some 1,250 known species of sea cucumber.

Longsnout Seahorse

50 POWERFUL FACTS ABOUT POPULATION

1
IN 1800, the world's population was ONE BILLION.

2
IN 1930, the world's population was TWO BILLION. By 1999, it had grown to SIX BILLION.

3
IN OCTOBER 2011, experts think the world population hit SEVEN BILLION.

4
We'll probably hit NINE BILLION by 2045.

5
About every second, FIVE PEOPLE ARE BORN, AND TWO PEOPLE DIE.

6
IN 1960, the average person lived to be 53 YEARS OLD.

7
In 2010, the average person LIVED TO BE 69 YEARS OLD.

8
We don't all share: 5 PERCENT of us use 23 PERCENT of the world's energy.

9
THIRTEEN PERCENT of the world's population doesn't have access to CLEAN DRINKING WATER.

TO UNDERSTAND HOW BIG OF A NUMBER SEVEN BILLION IS:

10
It would TAKE 200 YEARS TO COUNT TO SEVEN BILLION OUT LOUD.

11
SEVEN BILLION TEXT MESSAGES are sent in the U.S. every 30 hours.

12
If all SEVEN BILLION EARTHLINGS stood shoulder-to-shoulder, we would only fill up the city of LOS ANGELES.

13
If you walked SEVEN BILLION STEPS, you would have walked around the globe 133 TIMES.

14
Combined, the SEVEN BILLION ON EARTH speak 7,000 LANGUAGES.

15
A QUAHOG CLAM CAN LIVE SEVEN BILLION SECONDS, or 220 YEARS.

16
If seven billion people had one BIG DANCE PARTY and everyone had six square feet (.55 sq m) of dance floor, we could fit in RHODE ISLAND OR FRENCH POLYNESIA.

IF YOU LOOKED AT ALL SEVEN BILLION PEOPLE TO FIND OUT WHAT WAS MOST TYPICAL ABOUT EARTHLINGS:

17
Most of us are RIGHT-HANDED.

18
There are MORE MALES THAN FEMALES, but just barely.

19
The MEDIAN AGE of our world's population is 28.

20
In HOLLAND, the typical man is five feet 11 inches (180 cm). In PERU, he is five feet four and one-half inches (164 cm).

21
In JAPAN, a woman typically lives to be nearly 86 YEARS OLD. In AFGHANISTAN, she lives to be 45.

22
More than 100 BILLION PEOPLE have lived on Earth since the dawn of humans.

23
Of all the people ever born, only SEVEN PERCENT ARE ALIVE TODAY.

24
The human population has divided itself up to live in 194 COUNTRIES.

25
When AGRICULTURE BEGAN, about 8,000 B.C., the population of the world was around FIVE MILLION.

26
By A.D. 1, people only numbered 300 MILLION. That's about the population of the U.S. today (312 million).

27
By 1650, the world population had risen to about 500 MILLION.

28
In 1900, the world's LARGEST CITY WAS LONDON, ENGLAND. It was home to 6.5 million people.

29
At the turn of the 19th century, the TOP 10 BIGGEST CITIES were in Europe and North America, except for Tokyo, Japan (which came in at number seven).

30
Today, none of Europe's cities are on the top-10 most populous list. NEW YORK, U.S.A., and MEXICO CITY, MEXICO, are the only two from North America.

31
More than a third of the world's people lives within 62 MILES (100 KM) OF A SHORELINE.

32
In 1800, 3 PERCENT of the world's population lived in cities. That number grew to 14 PERCENT in 1900, and 30 PERCENT in 1950. Today, 50 PERCENT of the population lives in cities.

33
In 1950, there were 83 CITIES with a population over ONE MILLION. Today, there are more than 400. Twenty-one cities have a population of more than TEN MILLION.

34
CHINA is the world's most populated country, with 1.34 BILLION PEOPLE. India is a close second with more than 1.24 billion.

35
The U.S. CENSUS BUREAU gathers data from countries around the globe to keep track of the world's population for what it calls WORLD POPCLOCK.

36
WORLD POPCLOCK keeps track of births and deaths and uses mathematical models to predict world population growth.

37
A THIRD of the world's population LIVES IN CHINA AND INDIA.

38
Today, MOST POPULATION GROWTH occurs in the world's POOREST COUNTRIES—and within the poorest parts of those countries.

39
Why is the PLANET'S POPULATION GROWING SO FAST? Improved sanitation and medicine in developing countries have reduced deaths, while the number of births has stayed high.

40
In developed countries, WOMEN HAVE AN AVERAGE OF 1.7 CHILDREN, except in the United States, where women have an average of 2 CHILDREN.

41
LIFE EXPECTANCY, a reflection of a nation's health and economy, is HIGH THROUGHOUT THE DEVELOPED WORLD.

42
The country with the HIGHEST AVERAGE LIFE EXPECTANCY is MONACO—with a total of 89.68 years.

43
Over the past 50 years, the world's population growth rate has SLOWED FROM 2.1 TO 1.2 PERCENT PER YEAR.

44
The WORLD POPULATION grows by about 83 MILLION ANNUALLY.

45
In 2012, *FORBES* magazine listed QATAR as the RICHEST COUNTRY IN THE WORLD.

46
Population experts are called DEMOGRAPHERS. They also study housing, food, schools, natural resources, and roads.

47
In developed countries, MORE WOMEN BEGAN WORKING OUTSIDE THE HOME and more kids enrolled in school. This led to SMALLER FAMILIES.

48
In the U.S., grandma doesn't always live with family. Only about 20 PERCENT OF OLDER AMERICANS live with their extended families.

49
A century ago, about 70 PERCENT OF OLDER AMERICANS lived with their grown children and extended family.

50
The MOST DENSELY POPULATED COUNTRY IN ASIA IS SINGAPORE. Its density is 19,389 people living in a square mile (7,486 people per sq km).

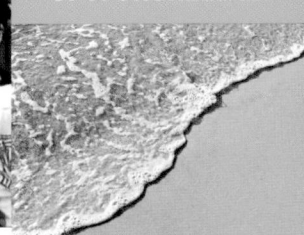

1

Red is the most common color of food packaging. It's believed to make you **HUNGRY.**

2

In the book *The Wonderful Wizard of Oz*, Dorothy's slippers were described as silver. **RUBY RED SLIPPERS** were chosen for the 1939 movie so they would stand out against the **YELLOW BRICK ROAD.**

3

BLOOD ORANGES ARE ORANGE ON THE OUTSIDE AND **CRIMSON RED ON THE INSIDE.**

4

BLACK & WHITE AREN'T TRULY COLORS. Black absorbs all visible colors and none are reflected. White is when all visible colors are blended.

5

The Golden Gate Bridge is painted **INTERNATIONAL ORANGE.**

25 COLORFUL

6

The color of a firework depends on the kind of chemical it is made from. **DIFFERENT CHEMICALS** produce different colors when they are heated.

7

All school buses in the United States and Canada are painted **NATIONAL SCHOOL BUS GLOSSY YELLOW.**

8

OSCAR THE GROUCH WAS ORIGINALLY ORANGE.

9

MOOD RINGS are made from **LIQUID CRYSTALS** that change color with **TEMPERATURE.**

10

ALEXANDRITE is a stone that actually **CHANGES COLOR** when the lighting changes.

11

The most popular color car in North America is **WHITE**. **BLACK** is most popular in Europe, and **SILVER** is most popular in Asia.

12

DARKER-COLORED POPSICLES MELT FASTER THAN LIGHTER-COLORED ONES.

13  Carrots aren't just orange. They come in **PURPLE, YELLOW, RED, WHITE, AND BLACK.**

14 The original M&M colors were **RED, YELLOW, GREEN, BROWN, ORANGE, AND VIOLET.**

15  Mickey's Sorcerer's Hat at Disney's Hollywood Studios in Florida, U.S.A., is painted with a custom technique called **"CHAMELEON PAINT,"** which shifts colors as you move around it.

16 **THE WHITE HOUSE HAD SPECIAL CRAYON BOXES MADE FOR IT,** which included the colors "Lincoln Penny," "U.S. Mint" and "Rockets Red Glare."

17 **ZEBRAS** are drawn to black-and-white. If stripes are painted on a wall, they'll go stand by it.

FACTS

18 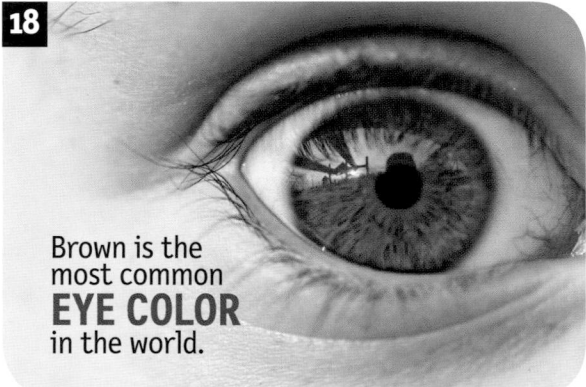 Brown is the most common **EYE COLOR** in the world.

19 Lobster blood is colorless. It turns **BLUE** when exposed to **OXYGEN.**

20 Studies show that **PAINTING YOUR ROOM BLUE** could make you more **CREATIVE.** It may remind us of sunshine, but yellow is not calming. Green is considered restful.

21  Sailfish can instantly change their color—say from blue to yellow—confusing their prey long enough to **MAKE A KILL.**

22 A giraffe's tongue is bluish black. Some scientists think the color might keep it from **GETTING SUNBURNED.**

23  The **FAVORITE COLOR** of William, the Duke of Cambridge, is blue. Duchess Catherine's is **WHITE.**

24 **"ONCE IN A BLUE MOON"** is really when two full moons appear in a single month— which happens about every **2.5–3 YEARS.**

25 **SOME RIVER DOLPHINS ARE BRIGHT PINK!**

15 MOVING FACTS

① Some **SPERM WHALES** swim enough miles in their lifetime while migrating to **CIRCLE EARTH SEVERAL TIMES**.

② In a gray whale's lifetime, it will swim a great enough distance while migrating **TO TRAVEL TO THE MOON AND BACK**.

③ Each year, **TENS OF MILLIONS OF MONARCH BUTTERFLIES** head south for the winter, traveling up to 2,500 miles (4,000 km) from Canada and the eastern United States to Mexico and California.

④ Tuna cover great distances while migrating; one fish tagged in **MEXICO TURNED UP NEAR JAPAN**.

⑤ Shortly after hatching in fresh water, **SALMON MIGRATE TO SALT WATER,** where they spend their adult lives until returning years later to the place where they were born—sometimes more than 1,500 MILES (2,500 km) away—to lay eggs and die.

⑥ In **BOTSWANA, AFRICA,** as many as **30,000 ZEBRAS** migrate each year.

⑦ Migrating birds determine their routes by detecting changes in day length; the position of the sun, moon, and stars; and variations in Earth's magnetic field. **BIRDS ON A REPEAT JOURNEY EVEN REMEMBER LANDMARKS AND FAMILIAR SMELLS.**

⑧ On **AUSTRALIA'S CHRISTMAS ISLAND,** up to **120 MILLION RED CRABS MIGRATE ANNUALLY FROM FOREST TO SEA** along nearly the exact same 5-mile (8-km) route, which includes 40-foot (12-m) cliffs and **AGGRESSIVE YELLOW CRAZY ANTS.**

ABOUT MIGRATIONS

9 **RUBY-THROATED HUMMINGBIRDS,** which weigh only one-eighth of an ounce (3 g), migrate as far as **1,900 MILES** (3,000 km) between Canada and Central America, sometimes flying nonstop over the Gulf of Mexico.

10 **FRESHWATER EELS ARE BORN IN THE SEA.** After hatching, they migrate to rivers and lakes and live there for decades before returning to the ocean—a journey of **PERHAPS THOUSANDS OF MILES**—on dark nights to lay their eggs.

11 A MIGRATING MONARCH BUTTERFLY can flap its wings up to **2,000 TIMES A MINUTE**.

12 **AFRICAN ELEPHANTS,** the largest land animals on Earth, walk **280 TO 435 MILES** (451 to 700 km) during their migration in Mali.

13 Walruses in the Pacific Ocean **MIGRATE WITH MOVING ICE,** swimming around it and **CLIMBING ATOP IT TO REST AND HAVE BABIES.**

14 Every spring, MEXICAN FREE-TAILED BATS MIGRATE UP TO 1,000 MILES (1,609 km) from **MEXICO TO TEXAS'S BRACKEN CAVE,** home to about 20 MILLION of the bats from March to October.

15 LEATHERBACK TURTLES which weigh up to **1,770 POUNDS** (800 kg), make epic oceanic migrations, sometimes swimming across the Atlantic Ocean, and females may spend as little as two hours out of each year on land.

75 DOGGONE

Doberman Pinscher

1 Dogs have been trained to get money out of ATMs (they just need a little help with the PIN).

2 The Basenji, a dog from Africa, doesn't bark, it yodels.

3 Sony's $2,000 robot dog, Aibo, could speak 1,000 words, react to commands and hand motions, and take pictures with cameras behind its eyes.

4 WHEN A SCHNAUZER AND A POODLE HAVE A PUPPY IT'S CALLED A SCHNOODLE.

5 Some 78 million dogs are pets in the United States. That's about one dog for every four people.

6 Pampered pooches can get spa treatments or go to doggie gyms. They even get their teeth brushed and a finish of breath spray.

7 Dogs have a sense of smell that is at least 1,000 times better than that of humans.

8 DOGS CAN FIND HIDDEN TREATS WHEN HUMANS POINT TO THEM. CHIMPANZEES HAVEN'T BEEN ABLE TO DO THE SAME THING.

9 Some 12,000 years ago, an early human and a dog were buried in the same grave. Scientists are not sure if the dog was a pet or not.

10 A Japanese toy dog is made so that it looks like it's actually peeing.

11 The earliest animal in the dog family tree was a small tree climber that arose in North America more than 40 million years ago.

12 Yorkshire terriers were originally bred to catch rats.

13 SOME OWNERS PAY TO BREED CLONES (COPIES) OF THEIR BELOVED PETS.

14 Greyhound racing involves greyhounds chasing a lure around the track. In many cases the lure is a fake rabbit, but some tracks use lures shaped like bones.

15 You can buy matching sunglasses for you and your dog.

16 Dogs are used to track black bears, cougars, and grizzlies in the mountains of Montana, U.S.A., to help scientists track the health of these wild animals. They also track native plants.

17 TILLMAN, A SKATEBOARDING BULLDOG, CAN SKATE 328 FEET (100 M) IN LESS THAN 20 SECONDS. HE ALSO LIKES TO SKIMBOARD.

18 Australian cattle dogs are part dingo, Dalmatian, Australian kelpie, and an extinct dog called the black bobtail—plus a few others.

19 Ancient Egyptians believed that the dog's cousin, the jackal, guided souls to the afterlife. A network of sacred tunnels in Egypt contains some eight million mummified dogs.

20 The wet surface of a dog's nose helps it sort out the odors it smells.

21 SOME DOGS ENJOY JUMPING ON TRAMPOLINES.

22 Sled dog teams leave from Anchorage, Alaska, to race in the Iditarod. Teams take 9 to 12 days to complete the 1,150-mile (1,850-km) race, which was first held in 1973.

23 There are between 350 and 400 different dog breeds.

24 Some specially trained dogs work in hospitals to give kids recovering from surgery a chance to pet and brush them, or just toss a ball.

25 The smallest dog breed in the world, the Chihuahua, is also the name of a state in Mexico.

26 Presidents Barack Obama, George W. Bush, and Bill Clinton all had dogs whose names started with the letter B: Bo is President Obama's Portuguese water dog; Barney and Miss Beazley were President Bush's Scottish terriers, and a Labrador retriever named Buddy belonged to President Clinton. Even the Prime Minister of Russia's dog is named Buffy.

English Bulldog

FACTS

27 Augie, a golden retriever from Texas, U.S.A., holds the world record for gathering and holding the most tennis balls in his mouth—five!

28 In Switzerland, dogs were used to deliver milk to remote homes on their own. They could fit small milk carts through mountainous paths.

29 Dogs of the United States Department of Agriculture's Beagle Brigade work in 21 airports in the U.S. to make sure travelers don't smuggle illegal vegetables, fruits, and meats into the country.

30 Dogs will respond to a high-pitch whistle that humans can't hear.

31 Australian cattle dog Bluey was the oldest dog on record, at 29 years and 5 months.

32 THE COAT OF ARMS FOR CANADA'S YUKON TERRITORY INCLUDES A HUSKY. THESE DOGS ARE USED FOR PULLING SLEDS AND HUNTING.

33 Border collies have been able to learn human words—one Border collie named Chaser knows more than 1,000 words.

34 Prairie dogs aren't dogs, they're rodents. Their underground burrows can stretch for miles (kilometers).

35 Labrador retrievers are the most popular dog breed.

36 Artist William Wegman poses his Weimaraners in human settings.

37 Most dog owners in the United States own just one dog, but 28 percent own two, and 12 percent have three or more dogs.

38 Black and tan coonhounds, bred specifically to hunt, chase prey up trees and then start barking. They even chase mountain lions and bears.

39 Now your dog actually can eat your homework! That is, you can buy dog biscuits with the word "homework" written on them.

40 A researcher compiled a list of the 50 most popular dog and cat names. Dogs in movies, like Marley and Beethoven or even seemingly common Fido and Lassie didn't make the list. But Snoopy made the top-50 list of cat names!

41 Wolves and dogs have the same number of teeth—42.

42 Sirius, or the dog star, is the brightest star in the sky. It's nearly 25 times as luminous as the sun.

43 The Newfoundland, a breed developed in Canada, has webbed feet and can swim in very cold water. One rescued 20 sailors in 1919 by pulling their lifeboat to safety.

44 Dogfish are a small kind of shark. The most widely known species is also called the "spurdog" or "skittle" dog.

45 If something is said to be "going to the dogs," people mean it is ruined.

46 Scientists think that wolves howl to greet each other, tell others where they are, and define their territory.

47 It costs around $60,000 to train a U.S. Navy SEAL dog.

48 A Jack Russell terrier once popped 100 balloons in less than 45 seconds.

49 The Lewis and Clark expedition, which helped map the American West, brought along a Newfoundland dog named Seaman.

50 DOGS ARE CONSIDERED PUPPIES FOR THEIR FIRST TWO YEARS OF LIFE.

51 A Neapolitan mastiff once had a litter of 24 puppies.

52 German shepherd Rin Tin Tin, a heroic military dog of old movies that was rescued from a WWI battlefield, was nominated best actor for the first Academy Awards in 1929, but didn't win. The award went to human runner-up Emil Jannings.

53 A terra-cotta figure of a pet dog found in Greece looks like it has a wagging tail. It was crafted 2,500 years ago.

54 A puppy with pug and beagle parents is called a puggle.

55 THE ALASKAN MALAMUTE CAN WITHSTAND TEMPERATURES TO -70°F (-56°C).

56 The first hot dog stand opened in 1916 on Coney Island, New York. Today, the U.S. city that eats the most hot dogs is not New York but rather Los Angeles.

57 If humans varied in size as much as dogs, the smallest would be 2 feet (0.6 m) tall; the tallest, some 31 feet (9.4 m).

58 Some dogs will howl when they hear music. Most of the time, it's from hearing a wind instrument, like a clarinet or saxophone, and sometimes from humans singing!

59 Dogs carry around their puppies by grasping the loose skin on their necks called scruff. Don't worry, it doesn't hurt.

60 Every day 70,000 puppies and kittens are born in the U.S.

61 A puppy with miniature pinscher and poodle parents is called a pinny-poo.

62 Some pet owners have a microchip implanted in their dog to make tracking a lost dog easier. One chip helped find a dog who wandered 750 miles (1,207 km) from his home in Sacramento, California, U.S.A.

63 A mix between a dog and a coyote is known as a coydog.

64 Some scientists think that as gray wolves started hanging around human campfires thousands of years ago they became tamer on their own, instead of being tamed by humans.

65 People will pay lots of money for guard dogs, often specially trained German shepherds. One businessman bought his guard dog for $230,000.

66 A sled dog named Balto led a team of dogs that brought medicine to Nome, Alaska, U.S.A., in 1925 and prevented an epidemic. The team traveled 700 miles (1,130 km) in about six days, even through a blizzard. A famous statue of Balto is in New York's (U.S.A.) Central Park.

67 Dingoes, wild dogs of Australia, are considered by some scientists to be their own species. The term dingo is also used in Malaysia, New Guinea, and the Philippines for wild dogs.

68 YOU CAN BUY A DIAMOND COLLAR FOR A DOG THAT COSTS ABOUT $3 MILLION.

69 Dogs were used to rescue people trapped in the snow at the St. Bernard Pass between Switzerland and Italy. Now known as St. Bernards, these dogs rescued some 2,000 people over a 200-year period.

70 By 1980, the red wolf was extinct in the wild. A small population was reintroduced into eastern North Carolina, U.S.A., but the species is still considered critically endangered.

71 According to mythology, baby brothers Romulus and Remus were left in the woods to die but were found and nursed by a wolf. Legend says the two brothers went on to found the Italian city of Rome in 753 B.C.

72 Some people think that the Chesapeake Bay retriever started out as a breed when two puppies were rescued from an English shipwreck in 1807. These dogs can retrieve hundreds of waterfowl a day.

73 Dogs are seen in a 2,650-year-old mural in Assyria, an ancient kingdom in the Middle East.

74 While all of the collies that played Lassie in the classic movies were male, some of the stunt doubles were female.

75 The American Eskimo dog is nicknamed the "Eskie." These dogs were the first trained to walk across tightropes in circus acts.

Bulldog Puppy

35 FASCINATING
THE FUTURE

1 Skin-mounted **DERMAL DISPLAYS** will turn your forearm into a TV screen so you can check your email or display cool animated tattoos.

2 Reading your friend's mind takes on new meaning with the invention of **SYNTHETIC TELEPATHY,** which allows you to transmit certain thought patterns.

3 Remote-controlled **COCKROACHES** will be able to **CRAWL INSIDE RUBBLE** to search for earthquake victims.

4 Kitchens will have **TINY FOOD FACTORIES** that "print" your favorite meals right on the plate.

5 Oceangoing pioneers plan to build a **FLOATING CITY,** complete with swimming pools and tree-filled parks.

6 **MULTIMEDIA WALLPAPER** will turn walls and ceilings into larger-than-life video displays.

7 **SENSORS** sewn into your jacket will warn of oncoming traffic if you forget to look both ways.

8 You'll pump your car full of **BIOFUEL ALGAE** grown in artificial saltwater lakes in the world's deserts.

9 The prospect of auto accidents in the sky is so scary that we likely won't see **FLYING CARS** for a long time.

10 Tomorrow's mug-size **QUANTUM COMPUTER** will pack thousands of times more processing power than today's laptop.

11 Films shown in 3-D **HOLO-THEATERS** will be worth watching twice— so you can catch the action from different angles.

12 Imagine **A HOUSE LIKE A TREE,** with a roof that captures sunlight for energy and walls that heal like bark when scratched.

13 Splurge on candy bars, then swallow a **NUTRIBOT PILL** filled with microscopic robots that zap the junk from your junk food.

FACTS ABOUT

14 Computers and phones will be woven into your clothes by 2020, when such **WEARABLE ELECTRONICS** will be the height of fashion.

15 In 30 years some robots will have **REAL BRAINS** grown from human brain cells.

16 Tomorrow's **SMART HOUSES** will check the weather for more efficient heating and cooling.

17 **WEARABLE SENSORS AND DISPLAYS** will turn the world into one big website, letting you click on people and products just by looking at them.

18 Ask for a reading lamp in the near future and poof!—a **HOLOGRAPHIC LIGHTBULB** will appear above your head.

19 **SOCIAL NETWORKING SITES** like Facebook will soon track every little thing about you—even your heart rate!

20 Your closet will contain just one **ALL-PURPOSE NANOFIBER OUTFIT** that changes shape and color.

21 Harry Potter's invisibility cloak will become a reality thanks to lightbending nanofibers sewn into **STEALTH CLOTHING.**

22 Special desktop **OBJECT PRINTERS** will print complete products— from a comb to a cell phone to another printer.

23 **MICROSCOPIC MEDICAL NANOROBOTS** will repair your body's old cells and cure diseases, increasing your life span by hundreds of years.

24 Roads will be safer once **ROBOTIC AUTOCARS** do the driving for us.

25 Some scientists believe that in about 20 years a computer's **ARTIFICIAL INTELLIGENCE** may exceed a human's.

26 **WIRELESS ELECTRICITY** will be beamed through the air to power homes, cars, and airplanes.

27 Humanoid **SPACE ROBOTS,** controlled from Earth, will replace astronauts.

28 Soldiers of the future will feel like superheroes when they strap on strength-boosting robotic outfits called **EXOSUITS.**

29 **EYE IMPLANTS** will let you see farther in the dark.

30 Someday, high-tech **FLOATING HOTELS** will drift through the skies like airborne cruise ships.

31 **CYBERNETIC IMPLANTS** will let us surf the Internet with our brains!

32 Cloning technology could bring extinct animals like the woolly mammoth **BACK TO LIFE.**

33 **FLYING DRONES** will deliver packages and pizzas by the year 2020.

34 Cities will create lanes for speedy personal transportation vehicles such as motorized chairs and **ELECTRIC HOVERBOARDS.**

35 **ROBOTS** will work alongside humans to help with dirty or dangerous work.

1. A megacity is an urban area of more than ten million people. **2.** In 1975, the world had only three megacities: New York/Newark, U.S.A.; Mexico City, Mexico; and Tokyo, Japan. **3.** Today, there are 21 megacities. **4.** By 2025, there will likely be 30 megacities. **5.** By 2050, seven out of ten people will probably live in a megacity. **HERE ARE TEN OF THE WORLD'S LARGEST MEGACITIES TOKYO, JAPAN: 6.** Tokyo is the largest city in the world, with a population of about 37 million **7.** The Sumo Museum in Tokyo is dedicated to sumo wrestling, the 2,000-year-old national sport in which most matches last less than a minute. **8.** About 10 percent of Japan's entire population lives in Tokyo. **9.** Tokyo's Shinjuku Station is the busiest train station in the world. More than three million commuters use it every day. **10.** To save room on bike parking, Tokyo has "cycle trees," automatic, multilevel parking lots that hold up to 6,000 bikes. **11.** In a Tokyo McDonald's, you can order a shrimp burger. **12.** Tokyo Tower looks like the Eiffel Tower, but it's red and 26 feet (7.9 m) taller. **13.** Vending machines around the city offer more than just salty snacks—you can find ones that sell umbrellas, sneakers, and neckties! **14.** Tokyo has a museum all about parasites! Visitors can see a pickled tapeworm specimen that is nearly 29 feet (9 m) long—that's about as long as a killer whale! **15.** Tokyo's massive domed ballpark is nicknamed "The Big Egg" because of its white roof. It is the home of the Yomiuri Giants. **16.** Tsukiji, one of the largest fish markets in the world, sells more than 400 different types of seafood. **DELHI, INDIA: 17.** Its population is more than 22 million. **18.** Delhi is the capital of India. **19.** It is home to an international museum of toilets, which contains toilet artifacts that date back to 2500 B.C. **20.** Auto rickshaws—three-wheeled motorized carts—are a popular way to get around the city. **21.** Delhi is famous for mithai—fancy, often colorful Indian sweets. **22.** The Red Fort, built in 1648 as a royal palace, earned its name from the red sandstone walls that stand 75 feet (23 m) high. **23.** Trained langur monkeys have been brought to the city to scare off the thousands of pesky rhesus monkeys that roam the streets. **24.** When in Delhi, the word for "hello" and "good-bye" is *Namaste*. **25.** Delhi's Jama Masjid, the largest mosque in India, can hold 25,000 people. **26.** Delhi is situated on the Yamuna River, considered by Hindus to be one of the two most sacred rivers in India. **SÃO PAULO, BRAZIL: 27.** Its population is more than 20 million. **28.** Locals call the city "Sampy." **29.** In 2014, São Paulo will host the World Cup, the first time since 1950. **30.** Pelé, considered by many to be the greatest soccer player to have ever played the game, started his career in São Paulo. Between 1956 and 1974, he scored a total of 1,220 goals. **31.** In the same space as São Paulo, you can fit the entire population of Greece. **32.** Buttered sweet corn on the cob and creamy sweet corn juice are popular foods you can buy on the streets of São Paulo. **33.** São Paulo is nicknamed *terra da garoa*, "land of drizzling rain." **34.** The people of São Paulo are known as paulistas. **35.** Even though most people speak Portuguese in São Paulo, people of Italian descent outnumber people of Portuguese descent. **36.** More Japanese live in São Paulo than in any other community outside Japan **37.** All those people create a lot of trash. The city has figured out a way to convert methane gas from the trash into fuel that helps power the city. **MUMBAI, INDIA: 38.** Its population is more than 20 million. **39.** For centuries, Mumbai was called "Bombay." **40.** Bollywood, India's film industry, is based in Mumbai. **41.** Bollywood produces more movies than Hollywood. **42.** Although nicknamed the "City of Dreams," Mumbai's slums are among the largest in the world. **43.** In Dharavi, a Mumbai slum, as many as 18,000 people crowd into a single acre (0.4 ha). **44.** Mumbai is also one of the richest cities in India. **45.** There are 17 public restrooms for every one million people in Mumbai. **46.** Mumbai's most popular sport is cricket. One of the oldest cricket clubs in India is located in Mumbai. **47.** India's official national sport is field hockey. **MEXICO CITY, MEXICO: 48.** Its population is about 20 million. **49.** Mexico City sits at an altitude of 7,340 feet (2,240 m). **50.** The city sprawls over the site of Tenochtitlan, capital of the Aztec Empire until it was conquered by the Spanish in 1521. **51.** Artist Frida Kahlo was born in Mexico City. Her house is called "La Casa Azul" (The Blue House). **52.** Lucha libre, which means "free wrestling," began in Mexico City in the 1930s and is characterized by colorful masks and entertaining moves. **53.** Popocatépetl is an active volcano that can be seen from the city. It's

100 FACTS ABOUT

the second highest volcano in North America. **54.** In Aztec, *El Popo* means "smoking mountain." **55.** Mexico City is known for earthquakes, or tremors. An 8.1-magnitude earthquake struck in 1985. **56.** Mexico City is nowhere near the ocean, but truckloads of sand, some palm trees, and beach chairs were recently brought in to make ten fake beaches around public swimming pools. **57.** You can take a ride on a brightly painted gondola called a "trajiner" along the canals that the Aztec once dug for farming. **NEW YORK CITY/NEWARK: 58.** Its population is just under 20 million. **59.** There are almost 12,000 licensed yellow taxis in New York City. **60.** Two million people crowd New York City's streets to watch the Macy's Annual Thanksgiving Day Parade. **61.** Most of the parade's giant balloons are five to six stories tall. **62.** The Statue of Liberty, located in Upper New York Bay, has an 8-foot (2.4-m)-long index finger and a 35-foot (10.7-m) waistline. **63.** People of all ages can take a flying trapeze class at Trapeze School New York. **64.** More than 4,000 flights leave New York and Newark's three major airports every day. **65.** New York has the most extensive subway system in the world. Laid end to end, the train tracks would stretch from New York City to Chicago (more than 700 miles, or 1,127 km). **66.** New Yorkers fold their floppy pizza in half and eat it like a sandwich. **67.** In New York's Central Park, kids can climb into the lap of an oversized bronze statue of famous children's author Hans Christian Andersen. At his feet: a bronze duck in honor of his famous story "The Ugly Duckling". **SHANGHAI, CHINA: 68.** Its population is about 17 million. **69.** *Shanghai* means "above the sea" in Chinese. **70.** Shanghai's famous snack is *xiao long bao,* soupy pork dumplings. **71.** It is considered China's richest city. **72.** The city, which was once just a small fishing village, is located at the mouth of the Yangtze River. **73.** The city's magnetic-levitation, or "maglev," train reaches speeds of 267 miles per hour (430 kph). Magnets are used to create lift and thrust. **74.** People in Shanghai speak Shanghaiese. **75.** When in Shanghai: "Thank you" is *Xie Xie.* **76.** The city's tallest building is the Shanghai World Financial Center. It stands 1,614 feet (492 m). **77.** Century eggs—duck eggs preserved in ash and salt for about 100 days—are a traditional food. The egg whites turn gray, making them look old. **KOLKATA, INDIA: 78.** Its population is about 16 million. **79.** Kolkata used to be known as "Calcutta." **80.** The city is one of the last places where human-powered rickshaws are still used. **81.** Cricket and soccer are played at the city's 90,000-seat Eden Gardens stadium. **82.** Nobel Peace Prize winner Mother Teresa left her teaching job at a convent to devote herself to helping and living among the poorest people in the slums of the city. **DHAKA, BANGLADESH: 83.** Its population is about 15 million. **84.** Dhaka is the capital of Bangladesh. **85.** Dhaka is among the fastest growing cities in the world. From 1990 to 2005, the city doubled in size — from 6 to 12 million. **86.** Bangladesh is about the size of the U.S. state of Iowa. **87.** It has more people than Russia. **88.** Some children whose homes have been flooded attend school on a boat instead of in a traditional classroom. **89.** By 2025, it is predicted that Dhaka will be larger than Mexico City and Shanghai. **90.** Many people are moving to the city to escape flooding in the countryside from the rising sea waters due to climate change. By 2050, a large part of Bangladesh could be permanently underwater. **91.** The people of Dhaka speak English and Bengali. **KARACHI, PAKISTAN: 92.** Its population is more than 13 million. **93.** Karachi is locally known as the "City of Lights." **94.** Karachi is located on the coast of the Arabian Sea—where locals and tourists come for the golden beaches and resorts. The tomb of Mohammed Ali Jinnah, the founder of Pakistan, is located in the heart of Karachi, and to many, is the city's symbol. **95.** The city is hit by monsoon rains—long periods of downpour and strong wind— every year in late summer. **96.** The rupee is the currency of Pakistan. **97.** Every year, giant olive ridley and green sea turtles return to parts of the Karachi shoreline to lay their eggs. **98.** Karachi is the financial center of Pakistan. **99.** But half of the people live in slums. **100.** The city is 60 times more crowded than it was when modern-day Pakistan formed in 1947. It grows by 6 percent—about 780,000 people— each year.

MEGACITIES

1
HORSES, WILD ASSES, DONKEYS, AND ZEBRAS are all related—they belong to the same scientific genus, *Equus*.

2
Early humans DREW PICTURES OF HORSES on cave walls.

3
Baby horses (FOALS) can STAND UP almost immediately after birth.

4
In Greek mythology, the centaur is HALF HORSE, HALF MAN.

5
The Duke of Wellington's horse, Copenhagen, was BURIED WITH MILITARY HONORS IN 1836.

6
The HAIRS in a horse's tail are of varying lengths.

7
Horses and ponies are measured in "HANDS," and each hand is about four inches (10 cm) in height.

8
PONIES, as a rule of thumb, measure LESS THAN 14.2 HANDS in height (about 58 inches, or 147 cm) to their withers (which are sort of like their shoulders).

9
There are THREE ZEBRA SPECIES: plains zebra, mountain zebra, and Grevy's zebra.

10
The AFRICAN WILD ASS lives in some tough places, including Ethiopia's Danakil Desert, where temperatures can soar ABOVE 120°F (49°C).

11
A foal born with a horse mother and zebra father is called a ZORSE.

12
The V-SHAPED PART on the underside of a horse's hoof is called the FROG.

13
PONIES ARE SMALLER, but wider and stockier than most horses.

14
When born, ZEBRA STRIPES ARE BROWN, not black.

15
"Feral" horses have been running wild on ASSATEAGUE ISLAND (located in Maryland and Virginia, U.S.A.) for some 300 YEARS.

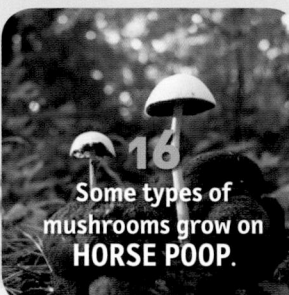

16
Some types of mushrooms grow on HORSE POOP.

17
Horses only have ONE STOMACH. Cows have four.

18
It is not uncommon for a RACEHORSE to have a COMPANION—usually a dog, cat, goat, chicken, or even a monkey—TO KEEP IT COMPANY.

19
For horses and ponies, to "SHY" means to move away sideways from an object out of fear.

20
Zebras will form a MIXED HERD with giraffes and wildebeests.

21
You can get a good idea of HOW OLD a horse is by looking at its TEETH.

22
Though horses today have a SINGLE-TOED HOOF, they didn't always. It evolved from a MULTI-TOED HOOF over time.

23
HORSE-DRAWN CHARIOTS were raced in the ancient Greek Olympics, from 700 to 40 B.C.

24
The PONY EXPRESS mail service began in 1860 and eventually used 400 to 500 horses to deliver letters.

25
The domesticated horse that we know today originated in western MONGOLIA some 4,000 YEARS AGO.

26
You can tell the different species of zebras apart by their STRIPE PATTERNS— the plains zebra has the most widely spaced stripes.

27
Since the 1800s, "PONY" has been used as a slang word for MONEY.

28
Horses lived in North America millions of years ago but died off during a MASS EXTINCTION. They returned only when they were brought by European explorers.

29
APPALOOSAS have patterned coats and striped hooves.

30
Horses will enter into a DEEP SLEEP for less than an hour a day, but they will SLEEP LIGHTLY for another two hours and be drowsy for about two more hours.

31
A horse or pony that hasn't been ridden much is called "GREEN."

32
The THOROUGHBRED RACEHORSE SECRETARIAT ran the Kentucky Derby (1.25 miles, 2 km) in less than two minutes.

33
Horse racing is one of the OLDEST SPORTS in the world.

34 The **PONY EXPRESS** operated in the United States for less than two years before it was replaced by the **TELEGRAPH.**

35 When a **MALE DONKEY** and a **FEMALE HORSE** have a foal, it's called a **MULE.**

36 LEONARDO DA VINCI, the famous Italian artist, included many horses in his works.

37 The tallest **WILD ASSES** are only **FIVE FEET (1.5 M) TALL** at their shoulder.

38 A mare (a female horse) can have **ONE FOAL EVERY TWO YEARS.**

39 The **PRZEWALSKI'S HORSE** is the only truly wild horse whose ancestors were never domesticated—but today it exists only in captivity.

40 There are about **400 BREEDS** of domesticated horses.

41 A **MALE DONKEY** is called a **JACK.**

42 Montana, Wyoming, and Colorado, U.S.A., all have places called **HORSE CREEK,** but only Montana has a town called **PONY.**

43 A horse's **BRAIN** is about the size of a **BAKED POTATO.**

44 The **EARLIEST DATED FOSSIL** of a horse is the **55-MILLION-YEAR-OLD "DAWN HORSE,"** *Eohippus.*

Appaloosa

45 Donkeys are distinguishable from horses by their **VERY LARGE EARS.**

46 A racehorse named the **GREEN MONKEY** once sold for **$16 MILLION.**

47 GREVY'S ZEBRAS, which live in eastern Africa, are **ENDANGERED.** There are less than 1,000 left in the wild.

48 Nearly 200 Thoroughbreds have been inducted in the **NATIONAL MUSEUM OF RACING AND HALL OF FAME.**

49 MINIATURE HORSES can be used as **THERAPY ANIMALS** to help disabled children.

50 A **MARE** is a female horse, but mare is also the name for **BASALT PLAINS** on the moon.

SADDLE UP for 50 FACTS ABOUT HORSES & PONIES

1

The Abominable Snowman, ALSO CALLED THE YETI, IS SAID TO LIVE IN THE HIMALAYAN MOUNTAINS IN NEPAL.

2

The animatronic abominable snowman that appears in the Matterhorn Bobsleds ride at Disneyland is affectionately referred to as **HAROLD.**

4

Yetis have been described as **HALF MAN, HALF BEAST.** Skeptics say yeti tracks are actually created by humans, bears, or falling lumps of snow.

3

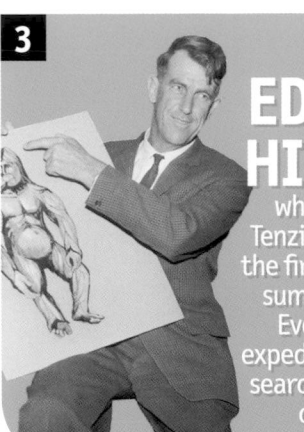

EDMUND HILLARY, who along with Tenzing Norgay was the first to reach the summit of Mount Everest, led an expedition in 1960 to search for evidence of the yeti.

5

India has its own version of the yeti—an ape-like creature called *mande barung*— or forest man.

25 CREEPY FACTS ABOUT

6

3,000 sightings of Bigfoot HAVE BEEN REPORTED SINCE THE 1800s.

7

BIGFOOT IS ALSO CALLED **Sasquatch,** WHICH MEANS **"wild man."**

8

Bigfoot investigators say prints of those big feet are on average **16 INCHES (40.6 CM) LONG** and **7 INCHES (17.8 CM) WIDE.**

9

AT A **BIGFOOT MUSEUM** IN CALIFORNIA, U.S.A., YOU CAN CHECK OUT "BIGFOOT EVIDENCE"— PLASTERED FEET AND HANDPRINTS.

10

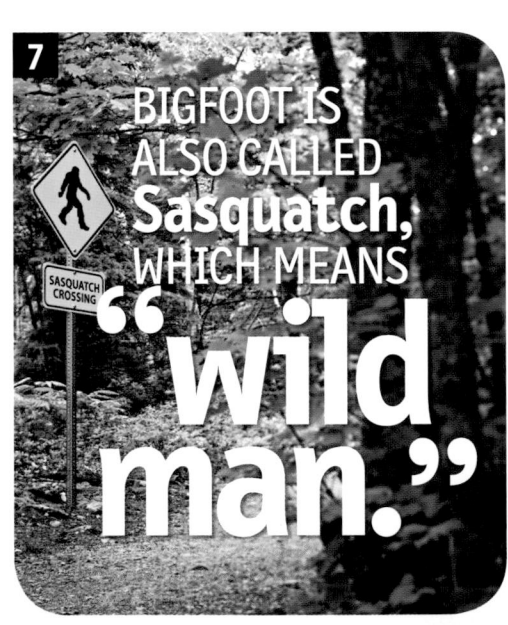

A Russian scientist once suggested Bigfoot was a remnant of **NEANDERTHAL MAN,** but most scientists don't agree.

11 A RESEARCH TEAM ONCE USED **600** SEPARATE SONAR BEAMS AND SATELLITES TO TRY TO FIND SCOTLAND'S LOCH NESS MONSTER, "NESSIE." THEY CAME BACK EMPTY-HANDED.

12 One man recently gave away **50,000** disposable cameras and offered **$2 MILLION** for evidence of Nessie.

13 Some people think Nessie is the sole survivor of the **LONG-EXTINCT PLESIOSAURS.**

14 **SEEING IS BELIEVING?** A survey team once hid a fence post below the water on Loch Ness and briefly raised it in front of tourists. When asked to draw what they'd seen, some drew a monster.

CRYPTIDS*

15 Hundreds of people have reported seeing a similar creature in Lake Champlain in the U.S. and have named it "CHAMP."

* A creature whose existence is disputed or unproven by scientific evidence.

16 Australian folklore describes a **SWAMP-DWELLING MONSTER** called a bunyip that likes to gobble up humans. Some accounts say it looks like a hippo or a manatee.

17 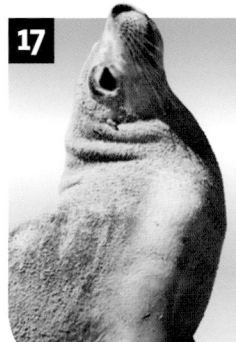 Where the stories might have started: Seals very occasionally found themselves up a stream and would have been an unusual site in the Australian interior.

18 In Australia, the QUEENSLAND TIGER is said to be the size of a large dog with tiger stripes along its back and sharp claws that it's not afraid to use. Sightings have been reported for centuries.

19 Believers think the QUEENSLAND TIGER is a descendant of an extinct marsupial cat.

20 In Mongolia's Gobi Desert, a bright red "death worm" as long as five feet (1.5 m) is said to live under the sands. It reportedly shoots poison and can deliver a powerful electric shock.

21 Some people believe the worm could really be an unidentified burrowing reptile, or a species of cobra.

22 A seven-foot-tall (2.1 m) creature with red eyes and massive wings named "MOTHMAN" was reportedly seen on several occasions in West Virginia, U.S.A., in the 1960s.

23 Point Pleasant, West Virginia, hosts a MOTHMAN festival every year. Pizza has been sold depicting Mothman: His eyes are made of red peppers, wings from mushrooms, and pepperoni for the body.

24 **The chupacabra** has been described as kangaroo-like, but also part gargoyle, with sharp claws and red eyes. In the 1990s in Puerto Rico, some believed it sucked out farm animals' blood.

25 Recently in Maryland, U.S.A., a creature with the "tail of a rat, the ears of a coyote and the head of a deer" was caught. Many thought this was proof that the chupacabra existed, but it was really a fox with hair-loss disease.

15 FACTS TO TOY

1 FAO SCHWARZ toy store in New York, U.S.A., has a **GIANT PIANO KEYBOARD** you play with your feet.

2 A woman created **CANDY LAND** more than 60 years ago to cheer up kids who were **SICK WITH POLIO.**

3 The world's best-selling board game, **MONOPOLY,** has been produced in 37 LANGUAGES and played by more than **500 MILLION PEOPLE.**

4 A jeweler made an **18-KARAT-GOLD MONOPOLY BOARD,** valued at **$2 MILLION,** which included a set of dice with 42 specially cut diamonds for each dot.

5 BARBIE is named after the **INVENTOR'S DAUGHTER, BARBARA.** Since her creation in 1950, she has had more than **100 JOBS.**

6 *SUPER MARIO BROTHERS* is the second-best-selling video game of all time (it was pushed out of the number 1 spot by *Wii Sports*).

7 SCRABBLE was first named **CRISS-CROSS WORDS.**

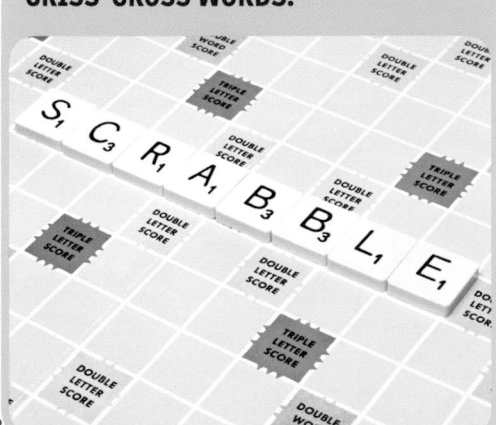

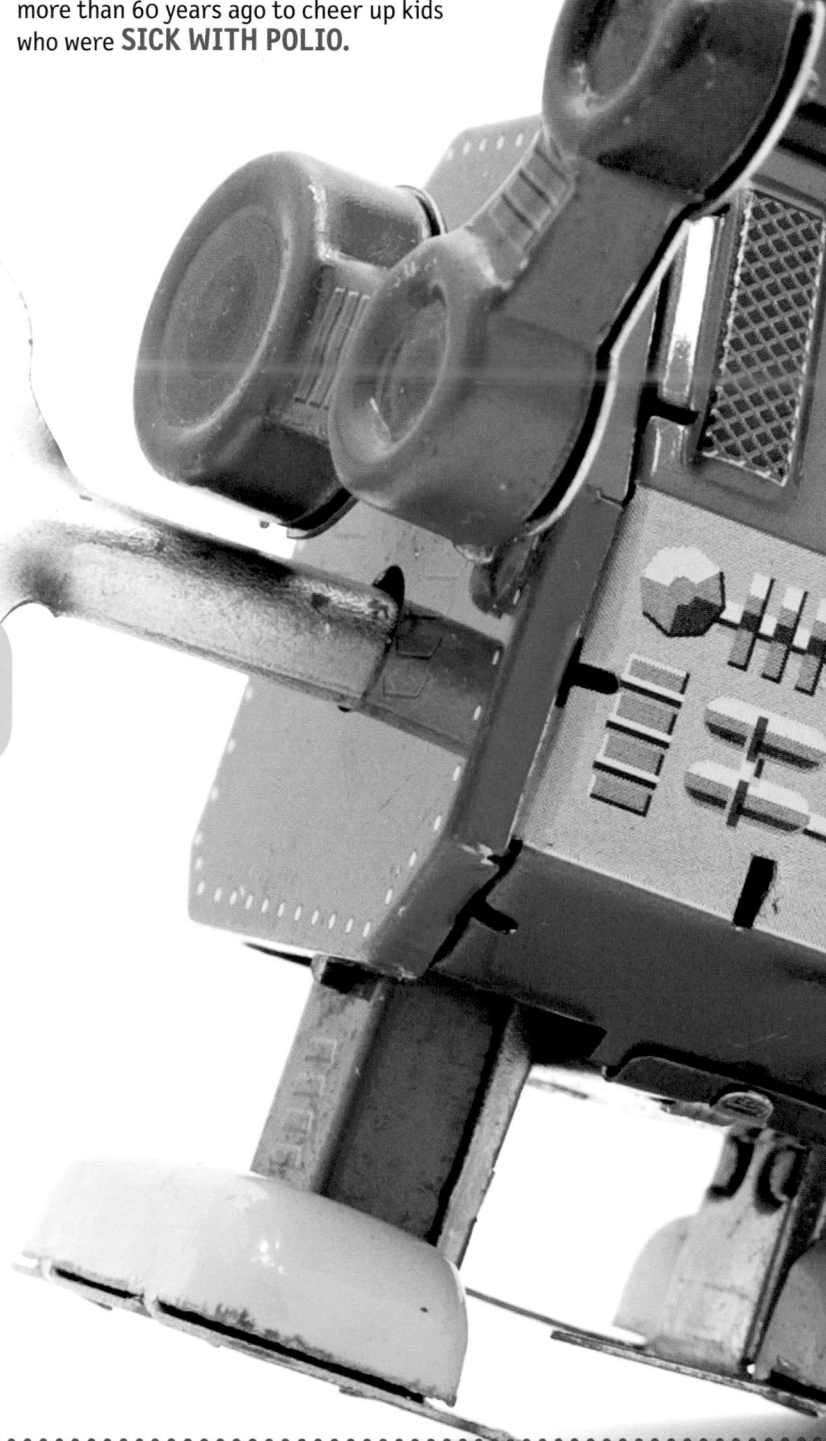

AROUND WITH

8 In many parts of the world, **CHECKERS** is known as **DRAUGHTS.**

9 Originally, **MR. POTATO HEAD PARTS** went on a **REAL POTATO,** not a plastic one.

10 The **EASY-BAKE OVEN** was inspired by **NEW YORK CITY, U.S.A., PRETZEL VENDORS.**

11 The name of the man on the Operation game is **"CAVITY SAM."**

12 **SILLY PUTTY,** the **VIEW-MASTER** viewer, the **JIGSAW PUZZLE,** the **HULA HOOP,** and **G.I. JOE** are in the U.S.A.'s **NATIONAL TOY HALL OF FAME.**

13 **PLAY-DOH** was originally used as **WALLPAPER CLEANER.**

14 In the past 60 years, **LEGO** has made more than **320 BILLION LEGO BRICKS.** That's **46 LEGOS FOR EVERY PERSON ON THE PLANET.**

The game that ties you up in knots!
Twister

Kids · AGE 6+ · ADULT ASSEMBLY REQUIRED

15 MORE THAN A THOUSAND TWISTER MATS ONE **GAME PLAYED ON A FOOTBALL FIELD.**

75 FACTS ABOUT ANCIENT CULTURES THAT STAND THE TEST OF TIME

1 A "thumbs up" from spectators at a gladiator battle in ancient Rome was not a good gesture: It was a vote in favor of killing a gladiator.

2 Of the Seven Wonders of the World, only one still stands—the oldest, the 4,500-year-old Great Pyramid of Egypt.

3 Chairs in ancient Egypt had legs shaped like animal limbs.

4 Tea originated in China millennia ago, possibly around 2,700 B.C. when, according to a Chinese legend, dried tea leaves fell into a cup of water served to an emperor.

5 IN ANCIENT GREECE, COINS WERE DECORATED WITH IMAGES OF BEES.

6 About 4,000 years ago, people in China began cultivating fish and seaweed for food.

7 The Romans believed cinnamon was sacred, and wreaths made from the plant's leaves often decorated Roman temples.

8 Two thousand years ago, people in India used flax and hemp—two kinds of plants—and hair to stitch up wounds.

9 Ancient Egyptians lined linen bandages with honey to get them to stick to the skin.

10 The ancient Greek physician Galen wrapped skin sores with figs, later shown to contain a substance that can speed healing.

11 Near Mexico's Gulf Coast lie giant stone heads and cities carved by the ancient Olmec around 1,200 B.C.

12 The ancient Maya of southern Mexico and parts of Central America developed a picture-based written language in 300 B.C., about 2,850 years after the ancient Egyptians developed their hieroglyphs.

13 Bright-red skeletal remains of the ancient Maya reveal they coated their dead in the red mineral cinnabar.

14 The ancient Maya created both a 260-day calendar and a 365-day calendar.

15 Ancient Maya nobles pierced their skin with spines from stingrays as part of a blood sacrifice made to the gods.

16 Chocolate sweetened with honey or mixed with water was a popular beverage among the ancient Maya and is still drunk by their descendants today.

17 The ancient Maya considered the green gemstone jade to be the symbol of kings, and the green feathers of the quetzal bird were a key part of royal costumes.

18 The ancient Egyptians called their picture-based written language *medu netjer*, which means "words of god." The ancient Greeks renamed the writing system hieroglyphs, or "sacred carvings."

19 Ancient Egyptian kids played hockey with sticks made from palm branches and pucks made from leather pouches stuffed with papyrus, a plant material more famously used as paper.

20 One of ancient Egypt's most famous rulers, King Tutankhamun (Tut), was probably only nine years old when he became king.

21 Going against the tradition of the time, the ancient Egyptian pharaoh Akhenaten ordered artists to portray him realistically, so depictions show him with a potbelly.

22 The tomb of an ancient Egyptian teacher is inscribed with the message "Listen all of you! ... Anyone who does anything bad to my tomb, then the crocodile, the hippopotamus, and the lion will eat him."

23 A slender region called Mesopotamia in between the Tigris and Euphrates Rivers in what is now Iraq has been home to many great civilizations—including Sumeria, Babylonia, and Assyria—since about 3,500 B.C.

24 ANCIENT SUMERIAN KINGS AND QUEENS LIKED TO PLAY BOARD GAMES.

25 There were no stones available around many of the oldest Mesopotamian cities, so people created structures out of mud and bricks.

26 People have lived in the Citadel—the world's oldest neighborhood, in northern Iraq—for at least 7,000 years.

27 The earliest writing, cuneiform, was inscribed on clay tablets and dates to around 3,200 B.C. Over 3,000 years, it was used to record about 15 different languages, including Sumerian, Akkadian, Babylonian, and Assyrian.

28 The saying "an eye for an eye" is from one of nearly 300 laws written by the ancient Mesopotamian ruler Hammurabi, who believed that blindness should be the punishment for blinding someone.

29 Ancient Mesopotamians built ziggurats—terraced pyramids—to honor the gods and get people as close to them as possible.

30 According to legend, an ancient Babylonian king built the Hanging Gardens of Babylon—one of the Seven Wonders of the World—to cheer up one of his wives.

31 The ancient Olmec gave the cocoa tree, used to make chocolate, its earliest known name: *kakawa*.

32 Newgrange, an ancient Celtic site in Ireland, is 600 years older than Egypt's Giza Pyramids and 1,000 years older than England's Stonehenge.

33 Ancient Celts, who regarded wild pigs as sacred, gave each other pig-shaped bronze tablets as a token of friendship.

34 The ancient Celts believed the head was the seat of the soul.

35 At the height of its power, the Inca empire was ten million people strong and covered an area nearly as wide as the continental United States.

36 The ancient Celts used an early form of hair gel made from vegetable oil and resin, a sticky substance from trees.

37 The walls of ancient Celtic homes were made of woven willow branches smeared with mud and animal dung.

38 The ancient Celts in Europe were trading goods with people in China more than 2,500 years ago.

39 The ancient Egyptians and their powerful neighbors to the south, the Nubians, flip-flopped back and forth over who controlled whom for thousands of years.

40 Archaeologists have found the remains of eagles, wolves, pumas, rattlesnakes, and beheaded humans in the Pyramid of the Moon, an abandoned temple in the ancient city of Teotihuacan, in present-day Mexico.

41 Ancient Africans created thousands of rock art images using animal tails, quills, feathers, and bones as paintbrushes and paint made from ocher (a natural pigment), fat, egg yolk, and blood.

42 Ancient Romans wore soccus, leather indoor shoes that were the predecessors of socks.

43 The ancient Romans paid taxes.

44 The diverse peoples of the vast Roman Empire used Latin to communicate with each other.

45 ROADS BUILT BY THE ANCIENT ROMANS ARE STILL INTACT AND IN USE TODAY, FROM EUROPE TO THE MIDDLE EAST.

46 The ancient Romans loved to bathe in large public baths, but before dipping into a cool pool of water, Romans were blasted with hot air to sweat out impurities.

47 THE INCA BUILT 14,000 MILES (22,500 KM) OF ROADS.

48 The 4,500-year-old city of Mohenjo Daro in present-day Pakistan was one of the largest metropolises of its time, with a population of 35,000.

49 Between 750 and 550 B.C., the ancient Greeks established 200 colonies throughout the Mediterranean.

50 Wherever the Greeks started colonies, they built theaters, some of which are still used today and are so cleverly built that even people in the back seats can clearly hear the actors speaking on stage.

51 The Parthenon—an ancient Greek temple built to honor the goddess of art and wisdom, Athena—was badly damaged in 1687 when it was hit with a cannonball during a war.

52 A Greek city-state, which the Greeks themselves called a *polis*, was a city and the rural lands outside its walls.

53 Citizens in the ancient Greek city-state of Sparta—Spartans—voted by pounding on their shields.

54 Alexander the Great expanded the ancient Greek empire surrounding the Mediterranean all the way east to India.

55 The Inca of Peru had no official alphabet or writing system but did make knots in colored strings called *quipus* to keep track of the calendar and livestock.

56 An Inca burial site was found 20,702 feet (6,310 m) high in the Andes.

57 The Chavín, the earliest ancestors of the Inca, arrived in present-day Peru around 1200 B.C., possibly from another part of the continent, since their temples had carvings of monkeys and alligators, which don't live in the area but are found in forests to the east.

58 From about 150 B.C. to A.D. 750, Teotihuacan—in present-day central Mexico—was the largest city in the Americas, with about 100,000 to 200,000 inhabitants.

59 Almost 500 years ago, the Spanish seized the Aztec capital of Tenochtitlan, founded in 1325, and built Mexico City right on top of it.

60 The Hohokam, who lived in present-day Arizona, U.S.A., as long as 1,800 years ago, played a game that involved using elbows and knees to pass a small ball through high, courtside iron rings.

61 In 290 B.C., the Egyptian pharaoh Ptolemy Soter began building the world's first lighthouse in the harbor of the city of Alexandria.

62 The Achaemenid Persian empire, formed in 550 B.C., extended from modern-day Turkey and Egypt to northern India and Central Asia, but much of what we know about these people comes from ancient Greek writers.

63 In China, the earliest writing dates to around 1200 B.C. and was inscribed on the bones of animals.

64 The earliest coins were used in the seventh century B.C. in the ancient kingdom of Lydia, in modern-day Turkey. Made from a mixture of gold and silver, the coins followed a strict weight standard and had designs only on one side.

65 HORSE RIDING BEGAN ABOUT 6,000 YEARS AGO IN CENTRAL ASIA, BUT SADDLES WEREN'T USED UNTIL 5,700 YEARS LATER.

66 In Greek mythology, a sphinx had a woman's head and a lion's body; ancient Egyptians believed a sphinx had the body of a lion and the head of either a human, hawk, or ram.

67 About 2,600 years ago, people in the ancient Egyptian city of Bubastis began burying cat mummies—eventually thousands of them—in a special cemetery.

68 Ancient kingdoms on the Arabian Peninsula were based on the control and trade of frankincense and myrrh, used as fragrances.

69 Ancient stone sculptures found on the Pacific island of New Guinea date to around 1500 B.C. and depict humans, birds, and long-nosed creatures that resemble echidnas, egg-laying mammals that live on the island today.

70 Flutes carved from the leg bone of a crane more than 8,000 years ago in ancient China are the earliest complete, playable, multinote instruments discovered.

71 The ancient Phoenicians of the eastern Mediterranean region used marine mollusks to make a highly prized purple dye.

72 ACCORDING TO ANCIENT WRITINGS, THE ROMAN EMPEROR CALIGULA WANTED TO MAKE HIS HORSE A SENATOR.

73 Australian Aborigines, the world's oldest living culture, have existed for at least 50,000 years.

74 Ancient Romans living in cooler climates had homes with central heating—hot furnace air was pumped into a chamber beneath the floor of a house.

75 In A.D. 79, the Roman towns of Pompeii and Herculaneum—each with a population of about 10,000—were destroyed by the eruption of Mount Vesuvius, which buried the cities in ash and lava.

35 FACTS THAT WILL ROCK

1 ROCKS are made up of a mix of minerals.

2 GRAPHITE is a soft mineral used in PENCILS.

3 VOLCANIC ERUPTIONS can CARRY DIAMONDS to the Earth's surface from MORE THAN 60 MILES (96 km) UNDERGROUND.

4 The brightly colored OPAL IS AUSTRALIA'S NATIONAL GEMSTONE.

5 An Australian man found a 60-POUND (27 kg) GOLD NUGGET near a school using a metal detector.

6 Humans moved the GIANT BLUESTONES used to build STONEHENGE AS FAR AS 140 MILES (225 km) approximately 4,500 YEARS AGO.

7 There are more than 4,000 known minerals.

8 FLUORITE can glow under ULTRAVIOLET LIGHT.

9 A LIGHTNING STRIKE can MELT TOGETHER SAND OR ROCK forming tube-shaped fulgurites.

10 EGYPT'S PYRAMIDS at Giza and the SPHINX ARE MADE OF LIMESTONE, a rock that consists mostly of calcite. That's a mineral formed by the REMAINS OF TINY SEA CREATURES.

11 Ancient humans CHIPPED AWAY AT FLINT to make ARROWHEADS AND OTHER SHARP WEAPONS and tools.

12 The name "PETER" comes from the GREEK WORD FOR STONE OR ROCK.

13 The HOBA METEORITE weighs about 66 TONS (60 MT). The outer-space rock contains MINERALS RARELY FOUND ON EARTH'S SURFACE.

14 The CHOL INDIANS of Mexico BELIEVE CRYSTALS HAVE MAGICAL POWERS.

15 The characters on the ROSETTA STONE, which helped decipher Egyptian hieroglyphs, are carved into granodiorite.

16 Natural ice formations, such as ICEBERGS AND ICICLES, ARE CONSIDERED MINERALS.

17 Standing 1,142 feet (348 m) above the surrounding desert, AUSTRALIA'S LARGEST ROCK, ULURU, was actually FORMED UNDERWATER.

YOUR WORLD

18 The LINCOLN MEMORIAL STATUE in Washington, D.C., U.S.A., was carved from GEORGIA MARBLE.

19 MAGNETITE is NATURALLY MAGNETIC.

20 The U.S. FIVE-CENT COIN is made of 25 PERCENT NICKEL and 75 PERCENT COPPER. Both are minerals.

21 A professional ROCK EXPERT is called a PETROLOGIST.

22 The BEAUTIFUL STRUCTURES OF PETRA in Jordan were cut into SOFT SANDSTONE ROCK CLIFFS more than 2,000 years ago.

23 Legend says that the MINERAL AQUAMARINE was found in the TREASURE CHESTS OF MERMAIDS. Sailors wore it for good luck.

24 Royalty in ancient China wore BURIAL SUITS MADE OUT OF JADE because they believed the mineral would help PRESERVE THEIR BODIES.

25 The OLDEST ROCKS ON EARTH are about FOUR BILLION YEARS OLD.

26 The GOLD BURIAL MASK OF KING TUT is decorated with blue rocks called LAPIS LAZULI and the minerals TURQUOISE, CARNELIAN, AND QUARTZ.

27 The ancient AZTECS USED GLASSY VOLCANIC ROCKS called obsidian AS MIRRORS.

28 The HUGE ROCK STATUES ON EASTER ISLAND off Chile were carved from compacted VOLCANIC ASH CALLED "TUFF."

29 The SHINY CHROME ON CARS comes from the MINERAL CHROMITE.

30 The four granite presidential heads at MOUNT RUSHMORE are ERODING ABOUT 1 INCH (2.5 CM) EVERY 10,000 YEARS.

31 SAPPHIRES AND RUBIES are both the same mineral: CORUNDUM.

32 SALT was once considered SO VALUABLE that ancient Roman soldiers were paid partly in the mineral INSTEAD OF MONEY.

33 PUMICE, a type of volcanic rock, CAN FLOAT ON WATER.

34 The HOPE DIAMOND is valued at more than $200 MILLION. The 45.5 CARAT GEMSTONE was donated to the Smithsonian Institution in 1958 —and sent by regular mail.

35 Invented in 1839, the first successful CAMERAS USED SILVER to help process photographs.

100 GEOGRAPHY FACTS THAT WILL POINT YOU IN THE

1. Mongolia, the most sparsely inhabited country on Earth, averages only about four people in every square mile (2.6 sq km)! **2.** The largest collection of maps—more than four million—belongs to the U.S. Library of Congress. **3.** Maps have helped people find their way for about 3,500 years. The earliest were drawn on clay tablets. **4.** The world's longest hot dog—668 feet, 7.62 inches (203.80 m)—was created in Paraguay in 2011 to commemorate the country's 200th anniversary. **5.** The Mississippi River drains 40 percent of the continental United States. **6.** On November 8, 2005, the city of Hillsdale, Michigan, U.S.A., elected 18-year-old high schooler Michael Sessions as mayor. He fulfilled his mayoral duties after school. **7.** Prince William, Duke of Cambridge, has a degree in geography. **8.** Cairo, Egypt, is the largest city in both Africa and the Middle East. **9.** Iceland's capital, Reykjavík, is the world's northernmost capital city. **10.** In 1513, a Turkish admiral created the oldest-surviving map showing a detailed look at the Americas. He used one of Christopher Columbus's maps for reference. **11.** The first new country of the 21st century, Timor-Leste, gained its independence from Indonesia in 2002. **12.** The highest point in Australia—the 7,310-foot-(2,228-m)-tall Mount Kosciuszko—is only about one-quarter the size of Mount Everest. **13.** The lowest point on Antarctica's surface is 8,383 feet (2,555 m) below sea level—but it's covered with ice. **14.** The Andes Mountains make up the entire west coast of South America. **15.** Though Europe and Asia are a giant landmass, the Ural Mountains divide the two continents. **16.** Almost half of the Netherlands is below sea level. **17.** Russia is the largest country in the world, spanning 6,592,850 square miles (17,075,400 sq km) across Asia and Europe. **18.** Ninety-five percent of Saudi Arabia is desert. **19.** Dutch is the official language of the South American country of Suriname. **20.** Dutch men are on average taller—6 feet (1.83 m)—than any other country's male population. **21.** Africa has more countries than any other continent. **22.** La Paz, Bolivia, sits at 11,897 feet (3,626 m), making it the world's highest capital city. **23.** The Strait of Gibraltar, a body of water just 36 miles (58 km) long, separates Europe from Africa. **24.** The Isthmus of Panama, which connects North America with South America and separates the Pacific Ocean from the Atlantic Ocean, is only about 30 miles (50 km) wide at its narrowest point. **25.** Yellowstone National Park's Old Faithful geyser blasts water and steam out of the earth and 184 feet (55 m) into the air about every 92 minutes. **26.** A volcano in Canada, Mount Garibaldi, erupted through a glacier. **27.** Beneath the surface of North America's deepest lake, which sits inside a volcano, is another volcano. **28.** Asia likely got its name from the Assyrian word *asu*, which means "sunrise, east." **29.** The ancient Greek city of Byzantium was renamed Constantinople in A.D. 330 and renamed again in 1930 to Istanbul, the capital of Turkey. **30.** On January 22, 2010, 5,387 citizens of South Korea's Taebaek City participated in a snowball fight, the world's largest. **31.** Great Britain is an island that includes England, Scotland, and Wales. **32.** Birmingham, Alabama, U.S.A., is known as the "Pittsburgh, Pennsylvania of the South," because of its large iron and steel industries. **33.** A state, city, waterfall, island, lake, mountain, river, and province are all named after Britain's Queen Victoria. **34.** The country of Lesotho is completely surrounded by the country of South Africa. **35.** People in Belgium don't speak Belgian, they speak Flemish and French. **36.** A forest more than 11 times the size of Texas, U.S.A., stretches across Russia and as far west as Norway. **37.** Russia produces more natural gas than the next top six producing countries combined. **38.** Only about one-sixth of Russia's population—fewer than 25 million—lives in Siberia, a frigid expanse of land covering northern Asia. **39.** The world's longest railroad tunnel links Japan's two largest islands, Honshu and Hokkaido, and is 33.46 miles (53.85 km) long. **40. About 900,000 square miles (2.3 million sq km) of farmland in northern China are blown away by the wind each year. 41.** Tokyo's busiest train station serves more than two million passengers a day. **42.** Asia's Dead Sea is 1,380 feet (421 m) below sea level, nearly the length of the Empire State Building with its antenna. **43.** Thailand is the only country in Southeast Asia that's never been under colonial rule. **44. Oregon, U.S.A.'s D River is only 120 feet (37 m) long—shorter than an Olympic-size**

RiGHT DiRECTION ▶

swimming pool. **45.** On March 14, 2010, 22-year-old Katie Spotz completed her solo, 70-day paddle across the Atlantic Ocean, between Africa's Dakar, Senegal, and South America's Georgetown, Guyana. **46.** Drought and irrigation have reduced Central Africa's Lake Chad to one-twentieth its original size. **47.** South Africa's Kruger National Park, which covers more area than Israel, is the largest park in Africa. **48. Namibia's "Big Daddy" sand dune rises 1,200 feet (366 m). 49.** Australia's largest lake, Lake Eyre, isn't even 20 feet (6 m) deep. **50.** The National Geographic Society organized the first international geography contest in 1993; three teams competed in London. The competition—now called the National Geographic World Championship—is held every other year, and has included teams from as many as 18 different regions. **51.** Argentinians eat 150 pounds (68 kg) of beef per person each year. **52. More people live in California, U.S.A., than in Canada. 53.** In Christmas, Florida, U.S.A., the average temperature on December 25 is 71°F (22°C). **54.** The capital of the African country of Burkina Faso, Ouagadougou, is pronounced wah-ga-DOO-goo. **55.** In 1873, the two cities of Buda and Pest, divided by the Danube River, united to become Budapest. **56. Dalmatian dogs come from the Dalmatia region along Europe's Balkan Peninsula. 57.** Finland has more than 185,000 lakes. **58.** There's a statue of the Little Mermaid in Copenhagen, Denmark's harbor. **59.** Mount Etna, on the island of Sicily, is known as the home of the Greek god Zeus. **60. The country of South Sudan declared its independence from Sudan on July 9, 2011. 61.** Asia's Lake Baikal is home to about 1,500 plants and animals found nowhere else on Earth, including the world's only freshwater seal. **62.** About 35,000 people live in the country of Monaco's 0.8 square miles (2 sq km). **63.** Almost half of South America's land lies in Brazil. **64. The final question of the 2011 National Geographic Bee was: "Thousands of mountain climbers and trekkers rely on Sherpas to aid their ascent of Mount Everest. The southern part of Mount Everest is located in which Nepalese national park?" Answer: Sagarmatha National Park. 65.** Thirty-five islands in the Persian Gulf make up the country of Bahrain. **66.** Saudi Arabia has more oil reserves than any other country in the world. **67.** One-quarter of New Zealand's population lives in the city of Auckland. **68. People live on only 36 of Tonga's 170 islands. 69.** The island country of Tuvalu's highest point is only about 16 feet (5 m) above sea level. **70.** Papua New Guinea's mountainous interior is so rugged that it wasn't explored by outsiders until the 1930s. **71.** India has more than three times the population of the United States, but only about one-fifteenth the number of cars. **72. The vast majority of Egypt's 78,629,000 people live along the banks of the Nile River. 73.** In March 2011, Reza Pakravan bicycled across the Sahara in 13 days, 5 hours, 50 minutes, and 14 seconds—the fastest trip across the desert by bike to date. **74.** About 12,000 years ago, the Sahara had a wetter climate and was covered with forests. **75.** It would take about two days to drive the roughly 3,000 miles (4,828 km) between the U.S. towns of Boring, Oregon, and Ordinary, Virginia. **76. North America's most densely populated country, Barbados, holds 1,693 people per square mile (2.6 sq km). 77.** In the 12th century, a Muslim scholar made an atlas showing most of Europe, Asia, and North Africa for the first time. The map took 15 years to make and was created centuries before Marco Polo or Columbus explored the world. **78.** Part of the nation of Armenia lies entirely within Azerbaijan. **79.** There are no tornadoes on Antarctica. **80. Nepal's flag, which resembles two stacked triangles, mimics the country's famous Himalayan peaks and is the only national flag that isn't a rectangle or a square. 81.** Indonesia is home to more Muslims—202,900,000—than any other country. **82.** Botswana has more government-protected land—18.2 percent—than any other African nation. **83.** More than six million Kenyans work in the coffee trade. That's 15 percent of the population! **84. More than half of the world's diamonds are mined from Africa. 85.** Only 61 percent of India's population can read. By comparison, the United States, the United Kingdom, Russia, and Japan have populations that are 99 percent literate. **86.** Russia's seaport of Murmansk lies above the Arctic Circle, but thanks to warm currents, it is ice-free year-round. **87.** The vast majority of Russia's 142 million people live west of the Ural Mountains, in the European part of the country. **88. In the early years of cartography, or mapmaking, Muslims usually drew their maps with South facing upward and north downward while Europeans did the opposite. 89.** The interior of Antarctica averages less than two inches (5 cm) of snow a year. **90.** More than half of Bolivia's population is Amerindian, the native people of the continent. **91.** Europe's six smallest countries could fit inside the smallest U.S. state, Rhode Island, with room to spare. **92. Portugal is the world's leading producer of cork. 93.** People in Fiji practiced cannibalism until the late 1800s. **94.** Japan builds more cars, almost ten million in 2008, than any other country. **95.** Due to the construction of the Three Gorges Dam on China's Yangtze River, more than one million people living in the area were forced to move. **96. Indonesia has more square miles of coral reefs—51,020 (132,132 sq km)—than any other country. 97.** Mexico takes its name from the word *Mexica*, another name for the native Aztec people who ruled the country until Spanish conquerors took over in 1521. **98.** When traditional drums were banned in Trinidad in 1884, plantation workers used 55-gallon (208 L) oil drums instead as instruments, the origin of the Caribbean's characteristic steel drums. **99.** Some of Colombia's emerald mines were once worked by the Inca, who considered the stones sacred. **100. The world's oldest space-launch facility is in Kazakhstan.**

1
Olympic **GOLD MEDALS** are actually more than **90 PERCENT SILVER.**

2
A Chinese man built a **BICYCLE THAT LOOKS LIKE THE OLYMPIC RINGS.**

3
The Olympics were first written about in **776 B.C.**, when the games were held at the sacred site of **OLYMPIA, IN GREECE.**

4
In ancient Greece, Olympic athletes **COVERED THEIR BODIES IN OLIVE OIL AND FINE SAND**, in part to protect their skin from the sun.

5
WOMEN, SLAVES, AND FOREIGNERS COULDN'T PARTICIPATE in the ancient Olympics, only free, Greek men.

6
CHEATERS in early Olympic Games had to **PAY A FINE** that was used to erect a statue of Zeus, called a *Zane*, with the cheater's name inscribed on the base.

7
There were **NO TEAM SPORTS IN THE ANCIENT OLYMPICS**; early events included horse races, the pentathlon, foot races, boxing, and wrestling.

8
The symbol of the Olympics, **FIVE INTERLOCKED RINGS**, represents the **FIVE CONTINENTS** in competition. North America and South America are considered one continent.

9
Early Olympic **STADIUMS WERE RECTANGULAR** and participants **RAN IN A STRAIGHT LINE** instead of on a circular path around an oval stadium.

10
On the third day of the ancient Olympics, **100 COWS WERE SACRIFICED** to honor Zeus and other gods.

11
In A.D. 393, emperor Theodosius I **BANNED THE OLYMPICS.** Farms grew over Olympia and its ruins weren't discovered until 1776.

12
An early Olympic wrestling event called **PANKRATION** allowed any move except biting, gouging out eyes, and putting fingers in an opponent's nose.

13
The **FIRST MODERN-DAY** Olympics were held in **1896**, in Athens, Greece, and **245 ATHLETES** from 14 different countries competed.

14
The **FIRST OLYMPIC WINTER GAMES** weren't held until **1924.**

15
The Winter and Summer Olympic Games were held the **SAME YEAR EVERY FOUR YEARS FROM 1924–1992.** Since 1994, the games are held alternately every two years.

16
WOMEN first took part in the **1900 OLYMPICS**, held in Paris, France, competing in tennis, sailing, croquet, horseback riding, and golf.

17
OLYMPIC TORCHES LIT in Olympia have made their way to host stadiums on five continents through snow, over water, by airplane, and **ATOP A HORSE AND A CAMEL.**

18
In the 2010 Winter Olympics, **WOMEN PARTICIPATED** in nearly **50 PERCENT** of the events.

19
The Summer Olympics scheduled for **2016** in **RIO DE JANEIRO, BRAZIL**, will be the first time the games—winter or summer—have ever been held in South America.

20
There were **NO OLYMPIC GAMES** from 1940 to 1944 because of **WORLD WAR II.**

21
For the **1932** Olympics, held in Los Angeles, U.S.A., European athletes had to cross the Atlantic by boat, then take a train across the U.S., a journey that took **THREE WEEKS.**

22
On an Olympic podium, the **SILVER MEDALIST** stands to the right of the **GOLD MEDALIST**, the **BRONZE MEDALIST** to the gold medalist's left.

23
The first **EIGHT FINISHERS** in an Olympic event have their names read aloud and **RECEIVE A DIPLOMA.**

24
When the ancient Greeks were at war with each other, they **CALLED A TRUCE** to hold the Olympics.

25
The Olympics began as a way to honor **ZEUS, KING OF THE GREEK GODS.**

26
In 1958, an old Olympic running track was **UNEARTHED** that measured 232 yards (212 m). Ancient Greek legend says that **HERCULES** paced it out, exactly 600 steps.

27
In **SYNCHRONIZED SWIMMING**, teams of two or eight athletes perform in unison routines set to music played on loudspeakers both above and below water.

28
In ancient Greece, first-place Olympic winners were **CROWNED WITH OLIVE WREATHS** and presented with a **RED WOOL RIBBON AND A PALM LEAF.**

29
The first competition for **WHEELCHAIR ATHLETES** was held on the day of the opening ceremony of the 1948 Olympics, in London, England.

30
Four hundred athletes from **23 COUNTRIES** participated in the first **PARALYMPIC GAMES**, held in 1960 directly following the Olympics in Rome, Italy.

31
The youngest individual gold-medal winner is **MARJORIE GESTRING**, who won the springboard diving title at the 1936 Olympics when she was **13 YEARS** and 268 days old.

32
The 2008 Beijing Summer Olympics had the **MOST OFFICIAL MASCOTS** of any Games: Characters represented an Olympic flame, panda, fish, Tibetan antelope, and swallow.

33
Between 1956 and 1964, Soviet gymnast **LARISA LATYNINA** collected 18 Olympic medals—the most of any athlete to this day.

34
Swimmer **MICHAEL PHELPS** has **WON MORE MEDALS, 16,** than any other man, and **MORE GOLD MEDALS, 14,** than any other man or woman.

35
The **OLYMPIC SHOT,** a metal ball thrown in the shot put event, weighs **16 POUNDS** (7.26 kg) for male competitors, **8.8 POUNDS** (4 kg) for female competitors.

36
Only men compete in the ten events that make up **THE DECATHLON;** women compete in the seven events that make up **THE HEPTATHLON.**

37
The official name of the Summer Olympics is **THE GAMES OF THE OLYMPIAD.**

38
JACKIE JOYNER-KERSEE set the Olympic women's record for **FARTHEST LONG JUMP—24.28 FEET** (7.4 m) in a single leap—in 1988.

39
FIVE OLYMPIC athletes have won medals in **BOTH WINTER AND SUMMER** events.

40
The **YOUTH OLYMPIC GAMES,** for athletes ages 14–18, were held for the first time in 2010, in Singapore.

41
Competitors in **OLYMPIC WALKING RACES** must have **ONE FOOT TOUCHING THE GROUND** at all times.

42
The **STONE USED IN OLYMPIC CURLING,** a winter sport that appears similar to a game of shuffleboard played on ice, is **42.1 POUNDS (19.1 KG) OF POLISHED GRANITE.**

43
Balls in **TABLE TENNIS** matches can reach speeds of up to **93 MILES PER HOUR** (150 kph)—about the same as athletes in luge competitions.

44
At the 2016 Summer Olympics, athletes will compete **IN GOLF FOR THE FIRST TIME SINCE 1904.**

45
ARCHITECTURE, PAINTING, SCULPTURE, LITERATURE, AND MUSIC competitions were part of the Olympics from 1912 to 1948.

46
All sports in the Summer Olympics must be popular with men in at least **75 COUNTRIES** on four continents and with women in at least **40 COUNTRIES** on three continents.

47
At **64 YEARS AND 257 DAYS OLD, OSCAR SWAHN** became the oldest Olympic gold medalist when he won a 1908 shooting event.

48
At the 1936 Berlin Games, African-American track and fielder **JESSE OWENS** won four gold medals, broke or equaled nine Olympic records, and set three new world records.

49
Although **WEIGHTLIFTING** has been part of the Olympics since ancient times, **WOMEN DIDN'T COMPETE** in the sport until 2000.

50
There are **NO MOTORIZED SPORTS** allowed in the Olympics.

50 WINNING facts ABOUT THE OLYMPICS

1 The **MONARCH BUTTERFLY** eats only **POISONOUS MILKWEED PLANTS,** making both the caterpillar and the adult butterfly a dangerous snack for birds, lizards, and mammals.

2 MANY BUTTERFLIES, LIKE THE **ORANGE-AND-BLACK VICEROY,** MIMIC THE APPEARANCE OF THE **POISONOUS MONARCH** SO PREDATORS WILL BE AFRAID TO EAT THEM.

3 Just as a skunk's stench warns predators to leave it alone, the caterpillar of the **ZEBRA SWALLOWTAIL** has a **NASTY ODOR** to help keep it safe from hungry animals.

4 THE GRASS BLUE BUTTERFLY IS ABOUT THE SIZE OF A **PENNY.**

24 BEAUTiFUL FACTS ABOUT

5 THE GREEN-VEINED CHARAXES BUTTERFLY FROM AFRICA **DIVE-BOMBS ANY INTRUDER,** FROM INSECT TO HUMAN.

6 **OWL BUTTERFLIES** have patterns on their wings that resemble the large eyes of an owl, which **SCARE AWAY PREDATORS!**

7 A butterfly begins life as a caterpillar that emerges from a tiny **EGG.** Once grown, the caterpillar becomes a **PUPA.** Inside the pupa, the caterpillar transforms into a butterfly. This process of completely changing its physical appearance is called **METAMORPHOSIS.**

8 BIRDWING BUTTERFLIES HAVE A WINGSPAN NEARLY AS **WIDE AS A BASKETBALL.**

9 SOME BUTTERFLIES LIVE ONLY A **FEW DAYS.**

10 Many butterflies, like the **INDIAN LEAFWING,** are so well camouflaged that they look just like a leaf!

11 ALONG THEIR MIGRATION ROUTE, MONARCH BUTTERFLIES STOP TO REST IN THE **OYAMEL FOREST** OF MEXICO. DURING THE HEIGHT OF THE SEASON, THERE ARE ENOUGH BUTTERFLIES IN THE FOREST TO **COVER 11 FOOTBALL FIELDS.**

12 BUTTERFLIES **TASTE WITH THEIR FEET.**

13

THE RED ADMIRAL BUTTERFLY
makes a remarkable round-trip journey between Africa and Europe.
MONARCH BUTTERFLIES migrate from Canada to Mexico.

14

SOME CATERPILLARS GROW TO **MORE THAN 100 TIMES** THEIR ORIGINAL SIZE.

15

Some butterflies **SLEEP THROUGH THE WINTER,** seeking shelter in caves, trees, **OR EVEN HUMAN HOMES.**

16

THERE ARE ABOUT **20,000** SPECIES OF BUTTERFLIES **WORLDWIDE.**

BUTTERFLiES

17

The **BLUE MORPHO BUTTERFLY** appears in different colors when observed from different angles.

18

All butterflies have **MICROSCOPIC SCALES** on their wings.

19

SOME BUTTERFLIES, LIKE THE GLASSWING SPECIES, HAVE SEE-THROUGH WINGS.

20

A butterfly's body temperature must be between about **60 AND 110°F (15.6 AND 37.8°C)** to fly, but it can't generate its own body heat so it **SUNBATHES TO KEEP WARM.**

21

BUTTERFLIES LIVE ON ALL CONTINENTS EXCEPT **ANTARCTICA.**

22

When a butterfly breaks open the shell of its pupa, IT MUST STRETCH OUT ITS WINGS AND LET THEM DRY BEFORE TAKING FLIGHT.
If it doesn't extend its wings quickly, they will dry wrinkled and it won't be able to fly.

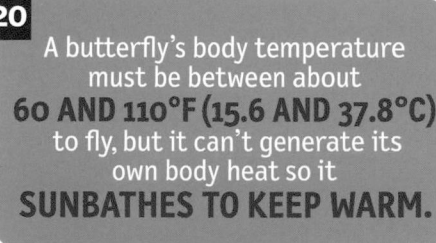

23

BUTTERFLIES' **ANTENNAE** ARE SMOOTH, WHEREAS MOTHS' ANTENNAE ARE FURRY OR FEATHERY IN APPEARANCE.

24

BUTTERFLIES COMMUNICATE mostly through chemical signals, but some, such as **MALE CRACKER BUTTERFLIES,** can make a crackling sound by rubbing their wings together.

75 WiLD FACTS ABOUT

1 "Pea soup" fog is any thick and heavy fog. It gets its name from London during the Industrial Revolution, when coal smoke coated the city with yellow smog, which the people nicknamed pea soup.

2 A mirage gives the appearance of a giant lake in the middle of a desert. What it really is: a reflection of the sky on a layer of hot air.

3 Satellites up to 1,000 miles (1,609 km) above Earth keep track of the weather below.

4 ANCIENT GREEKS BELIEVED THAT WIND WAS THE EARTH BREATHING.

5 When it is winter in the United States, it is summer in Australia.

6 In cold weather when you can "see" your breath, you're actually seeing water vapor released from your mouth that has turned into tiny visible droplets.

7 Hawaii, U.S.A., is one of the wettest places in the world. It averages 450 inches (1,143 cm) of rainfall a year.

8 San Francisco, U.S.A., is known as "Fog City." Summer fog is caused by warm air mixing with the cool water coming into the San Francisco Bay.

9 Nighttime rainbows are called moonbows! They rarely occur because the moon must be very bright and be positioned in just the right way in relation to the rain.

10 Hoarfrost is when spiky ice freezes on plants.

11 An avalanche can reach speeds of 80 miles per hour (130 kph) within about five seconds.

12 IN THE U.S. ALONE, LIGHTNING STRIKES THE GROUND 25 MILLION TIMES A YEAR.

13 The highest weather station on Earth is located at 26,000 feet (7,925 m) on Mount Everest.

14 The "eye" of a storm is the calm center of a tropical storm surrounded by thunderstorms.

15 A raindrop's top speed is 18 mph (29 kph).

16 The typical lifetime of a fluffy cotton ball–looking cumulus cloud is 5–40 minutes.

17 An inch of snow falling evenly on 1 acre (.4 ha) of ground is equivalent to about 2,715 gallons (10,277 L) of water.

18 We get sniffles in the winter because common-cold viruses survive better when there's low humidity, like during the winter.

19 Snowflakes formed in clouds usually take about an hour to reach the ground.

20 The largest hailstone ever recorded in the United States was about the size of a soccer ball.

21 During the especially cold winter of 1898–99, ice floated down the Mississippi River into the Gulf of Mexico, U.S.A.

22 The average width of a tornado is the length of four soccer fields.

WEATHER!

23 The United States has about 1,000 tornadoes a year—more than any other country in the world. Tornado Alley is the name of the mid-U.S. section where most violent tornadoes occur.

24 Dorothy may have left Kansas in a tornado for the Land of Oz, but more violent tornadoes are "born" in Oklahoma than in any other U.S. state.

25 Most hurricanes are about 300 miles (483 km) across!

26 There is no difference between a hurricane, a cyclone, and a typhoon. Different parts of the world use different names to describe these tropical storms.

27 Tornadic waterspouts are weak tornadoes that form over the water and sometimes come on land.

28 Tornadoes can happen any time of year and any time of day, but most occur in spring and summer between 3 p.m. and 9 p.m.

29 A supercell thunderstorm is a long-lasting, severe storm that can produce violent tornadoes.

30 ALL SNOWFLAKES HAVE SIX SIDES.

31 An avalanche, which is a moving mass of snow, can travel as fast as 245 miles per hour (394 kph)—that's three times faster than an Olympic downhill skier!

32 Clouds sometimes look dark when they get thick because they let through less light.

33 Raindrops are shaped more like hamburger buns than teardrops!

34 Two feet (61 cm) of water from a flash flood can float a large car.

35 A lightning flash is no more than one inch (2.5 cm) wide.

36 The "doldrums" is an area of the ocean near the equator that is calm with light, shifting winds.

37 You can tell the outside temperature by listening to a cricket's chirps! For a rough estimate in Fahrenheit, count the number of chirps in 15 seconds and add 37.

38 Most tornadoes spin counterclockwise in the Northern Hemisphere and clockwise in the Southern Hemisphere.

39 The longest recorded distance a tornado has traveled is 218 miles (352 km) through three U.S. states in 1925.

40 In 1947, the U.S. military sprayed dry ice on an Atlantic hurricane to try to weaken it. It didn't work.

41 Fossilized imprints of raindrops were found in India, proving that rain fell on Earth at least 1.6 billion years ago.

42 The world's tallest snowman was a girl! She measured 122 feet, 1 inch (37.21 m).

43 The world record for the most people making snow angels at the same time is 8,962.

44 The world's largest snowball fight had 5,387 participants.

45 Derechos are long-lived windstorms accompanied by fast-moving thunderstorms. Derechos is a Spanish word meaning "straight ahead."

46 U.S. states Hawaii and Alaska have the same record high temperature—100°F (38° C).

47 For a tropical weather system to be classified as a hurricane, the winds must be 74 miles per hour (64 knots) or higher.

48 IN 1948, NIAGARA FALLS STOPPED RUNNING. ICE JAMMED A RIVER THAT FLOWED TO THE FALLS FOR ALMOST TWO DAYS.

49 If a hurricane has had a devastating impact, its name is "retired" for at least ten years.

50 Eighty percent of lightning strike victims survive.

51 The most powerful tornadoes can derail a train and rip pavement off a street.

52 There are about 2,000 thunderstorms happening somewhere on Earth at any one time.

53 There is fog on Mars.

54 A cloud droplet is 100 times smaller than a raindrop. It takes 100,000 cloud droplets to make a snowflake.

55 No two snowflakes are alike.

56 Capped column snowflakes look like a spool of thread under a microscope. They often fall during warmer snowfalls.

57 DIRTY SNOW MELTS FASTER THAN CLEAN.

58 Pinecones can predict the weather! In dry weather, the scales open, and when rain is on the way, they close.

59 Some people think it will be a severe winter if squirrels have bushy tails in the fall, but scientists have not found evidence to support the theory.

60 Commercial jets have de-icing equipment on their wings because the temperature high in the atmosphere is below freezing.

61 A cloud can only form when there is enough moisture in the air and the moisture can be lifted into the cooler atmosphere to condense.

62 Scientists point laser beams at clouds to see how high they are.

63 To a meteorologist—a person who studies the weather—a "light rain" is less than 1/48 inch (0.5 mm). A "heavy rain" is more than 1/6 of an inch (4 mm).

64 According to Norse mythology, Thor, the god of thunder, made thunder by banging his heavy hammer in the clouds.

65 The snowiest places on Earth aren't necessarily the coldest! Very cold air can't always hold enough moisture for precipitation.

66 About 1,000 years ago, hailstones the size of baseballs dropped from the sky at 100 miles per hour (160 kph), hitting people living in the Himalaya.

67 BEFORE THEY WERE TOYS, KITES WERE FLOWN IN CHINA THOUSANDS OF YEARS AGO TO INDICATE THE STRENGTH OF THE WIND.

68 People say it is "raining cats and dogs" when it is pouring outside. In Serbia, it once rained frogs! Scientists think they were picked up from a pond by a waterspout or tornado and dropped on a nearby town.

69 An electrical discharge during thunderstorms can produce a blue-green glowing light called St. Elmo's Fire, usually seen at the tip of an object, like a ship at sea.

70 Rogue waves are walls of water ten stories high that occur in the middle of the ocean. They aren't caused by earthquakes, like tsunamis. Scientists aren't sure how they form.

71 The world's largest meteorology lesson was attended by 16,110 people.

72 Some airplane pilots have reported seeing a full-circle rainbow. We can't see them on land because the horizon blocks the view.

73 A halo sometimes appears around the sun when sunlight passes through a cloud with ice crystals. These crystals split the sunlight into seven colors that make a ring around the sun.

74 In a double rainbow, the inner rainbow has the red on the top. The outer one has the red on the bottom!

75 In the 18th century, a weather-related fashion accessory was all the rage: The Franklin wire was attached to hats and dragged along the ground to divert lightning from the wearer.

1 MALE PLATYPUSES are one of only a FEW VENOMOUS MAMMALS: They have sharp spurs on their hind feet that PIERCE THEIR VICTIMS AND DELIVER A POWERFUL TOXIN.

2 An EASTERN BROWN SNAKE can kill a person with JUST ONE BITE.

3 ONE STING from an Arizona bark scorpion is POWERFUL ENOUGH TO SERIOUSLY INJURE OR KILL A PERSON.

4 The world's largest lizard, a KOMODO DRAGON, has a VENOMOUS BITE.

5 RATTLESNAKE VENOM is deadly, but the roughly 8,000 PEOPLE IN THE UNITED STATES who are bit each year usually SURVIVE, THANKS TO QUICK TREATMENT.

6 POLAR BEARS lie in wait at holes in the ice and ATTACK SEALS THAT POP TO THE SURFACE for a breath of air.

7 CROCODILES KILL and eat many kinds of animals, including ZEBRAS, WATER BUFFALO, AND EVEN SHARKS.

8 The BLUE-RINGED OCTOPUS, which weighs 0.9 ounce (26 g), has a VENOMOUS BITE THAT CAN KILL A HUMAN IN 15 MINUTES.

9 The VENOMOUS SPINES on a STINGRAY'S TAIL can deliver a FATAL BLOW.

10 Just ONE DROP OF VENOM from the HOOK-NOSED SEA SNAKE can KILL A PERSON.

11 A GREAT WHITE SHARK, which uses 3,000 jagged teeth to kill prey, can SMELL A TINY AMOUNT OF BLOOD IN THE WATER UP TO 3 MILES (4.8 KM) AWAY.

12 STONEFISH STING would-be predators with 13 spines that contain VENOM STRONG ENOUGH TO CAUSE PARALYSIS AND DEATH.

13 A BOX JELLYFISH'S TENTACLES, which can grow up to 9 feet (2.7 m) long, are packed with ENOUGH TOXINS TO KILL 60 PEOPLE, and death can occur in as few as four minutes.

14 ANACONDAS SUFFOCATE THEIR PREY, which includes animals as large as MONKEYS, PIGS, AND DEER, and then SWALLOW IT WHOLE, HEADFIRST.

15 SCORPIONS CAN CONTROL THE AMOUNT OF VENOM they inject into a victim; BIGGER ANIMALS GET BIGGER DOSES.

16 In 2010, A MOUNTAIN GOAT in Washington, U.S.A.'s Olympic National Park FATALLY INJURED A HIKER.

17 One PUFFER FISH has enough TOXIN TO KILL 30 PEOPLE. Despite this, specially trained chefs PREPARE THE FISH FOR DARING DINERS.

18 A BROWN BEAR'S LONG, NONRETRACTABLE CLAWS CAN KILL another animal in ONE SWIPE.

19 AFRICAN BUFFALOES, considered by some the DEADLIEST ANIMAL IN AFRICA, have large, thick horns and move in herds of thousands.

20 KING COBRAS grow up to 18.5 feet (5.7 m) long and are the LARGEST VENOMOUS SNAKES IN THE WORLD.

21 Venom from a CONE SHELL, a kind of sea snail, can PARALYZE IN SECONDS AND EVENTUALLY KILL.

22 When ELEPHANTS FEEL THREATENED, they stab with their tusks, trample with their feet, and USE THEIR TRUNKS TO PICK UP AND THROW ATTACKERS THROUGH THE AIR.

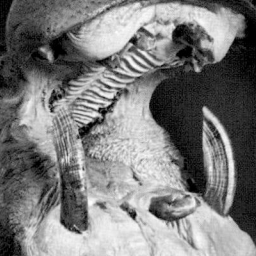

23 HIPPOS USE THEIR POWERFUL JAWS and 20-INCH (51-CM)-LONG CANINE TEETH TO ATTACK ANIMALS (including humans) that get too close to calves.

24 An angry HIPPO CAN OUTRUN and OUTSWIM A HUMAN.

25 About 1 IN 4,000 PEOPLE are severely ALLERGIC TO BEE VENOM AND CAN DIE from just one untreated sting.

26 A tiny frog named TERRIBILIS IS THE MOST DEADLY FROG of all— just one has ENOUGH POISON TO KILL 20,000 MICE.

35 LETHAL FACTS ABOUT

27 The BROWN RECLUSE SPIDER'S BITE can go unnoticed for days, but its powerful poison can cause injuries that TAKE MONTHS TO HEAL AND, IN RARE CASES, LEAD TO DEATH.

28 The venomous bite of a BLACK WIDOW SPIDER makes it difficult to breathe and swallow, but only rarely kills humans.

29 According to the INTERNATIONAL SHARK ATTACK FILE, in 2010, there were 79 SHARK ATTACKS around the world, but of those ONLY SIX WERE FATAL.

30 A recent study in Tanzania found that LIONS are more likely to ATTACK HUMANS IN THE TEN DAYS FOLLOWING A FULL MOON.

31 HAIRY BRISTLES on two-inch (5-cm)-long oak PROCESSIONARY CATERPILLARS CAUSE RASHES, ASTHMA ATTACKS, AND DEADLY ALLERGIC REACTIONS.

32 A PERSON CAN DIE minutes after touching the TOXIC SKIN OF A POISON DART FROG.

33 Of the roughly 3,000 SNAKE SPECIES in the world, ONLY ABOUT 300—or 10 percent—CAN KILL HUMANS with their venom.

34 Each year, 2 TO 3 MILLION PEOPLE DIE FROM DISEASES TRANSMITTED BY MOSQUITOES, considered the deadliest animals in the world.

35 The GIANT PACIFIC OCTOPUS, which can grow to 16 feet (5 m) and weigh as much as 110 pounds (50 kg), uses POWERFUL SUCKERS TO CATCH AND PRY OPEN PREY.

Terribilis Frog

DEADLY ANiMALS

1 CLIMATE CHANGE IS CAUSED BY GREENHOUSE GASES THAT TRAP SOME OF THE EARTH'S HEAT. ABOUT 80 PERCENT OF GREENHOUSE GAS EMISSIONS ARE FROM CARBON DIOXIDE.

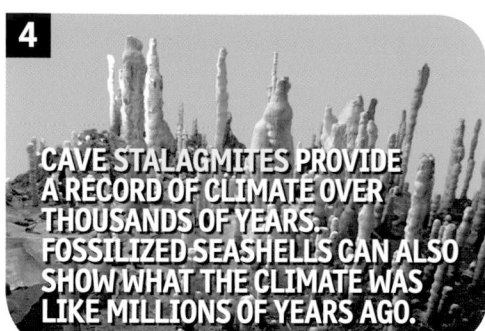

2 A VOLCANO ERUPTION IN 1883 LOWERED TEMPERATURES AND CHANGED THE EARTH'S CLIMATE FOR FIVE YEARS.

3 WITHOUT EARTH'S ATMOSPHERE, THE AVERAGE TEMPERATURE WOULD BE A FRIGID 0°F (-18°C).

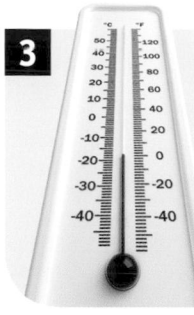

4 CAVE STALAGMITES PROVIDE A RECORD OF CLIMATE OVER THOUSANDS OF YEARS. FOSSILIZED SEASHELLS CAN ALSO SHOW WHAT THE CLIMATE WAS LIKE MILLIONS OF YEARS AGO.

5 Harnessing energy from **OCEAN WAVES** can produce "clean" energy and help fight global warming.

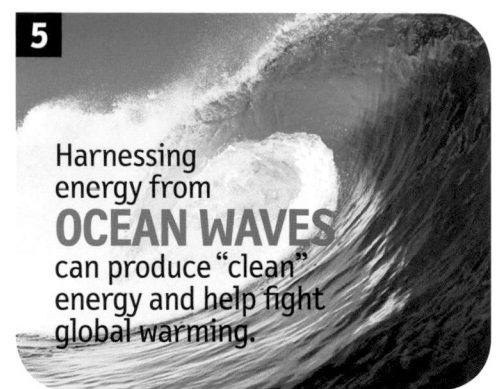

25 FLUCTUATING FACTS

6 Climate change also causes **WILD WEATHER.** In 2004, for the first time on record a hurricane hit Brazil.

7 **CLEAN ENERGY** can be produced naturally from the warm temperature of the ground. Just six feet (1.8 m) underground, the temperature can be a **STEADY 75°F (24°C).**

8 **BEETLES** IN ALASKA, U.S.A., THAT THRIVE DURING WARMER SUMMERS HAVE EATEN FOUR MILLION ACRES (16,187 SQ KM) OF SPRUCE TREES.

9 Since 1880, the Earth has **WARMED** 1.4°F (0.8°C) on average— which can be the difference between an ice cube or a puddle of water.

10 **DESERTS** COVERED THE **AMAZON** RAIN FOREST DURING THE JURASSIC PERIOD, SOME 200 MILLION YEARS AGO.

11 **MOUNT KILIMANJARO** in Africa may lose its snow-covered top within 20 years.

12 **NINETEEN** of the Earth's **TWENTY** **HOTTEST YEARS** (since records have been kept) have occurred since **1980.**

※ YOU HAVE LEARNED **4,714** FACTS

13 Climate change might increase the cost of **CHOCOLATE** by making it hard or impossible to grow in West Africa.

14 WARMING TEMPERATURES MEAN THAT SOON SHIPS CAN PASS RIGHT ACROSS THE NORTH POLE DURING THE SUMMER (SINCE IT WILL BE ICE-FREE).

15 WITH AN ELEVATION OF ONLY EIGHT FEET (2.4 M) ABOVE SEA LEVEL, RISING SEA LEVELS COULD MAKE THE ISLAND NATION OF THE MALDIVES DISAPPEAR.

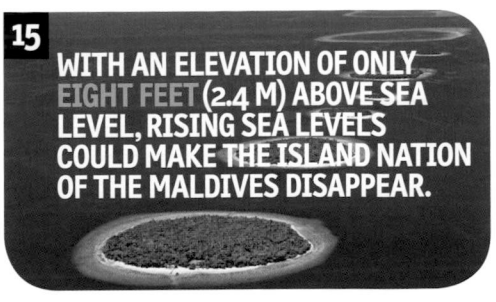

16 GLACIER NATIONAL PARK IN MONTANA, U.S.A., IS LOSING ITS GLACIERS BECAUSE OF GLOBAL WARMING—SOME SCIENTISTS BELIEVE ALL OF THEM COULD BE GONE BY 2030.

17 SCIENTISTS STUDY GLACIAL ICE TO HELP THEM UNDERSTAND WHAT THE CLIMATE WAS LIKE IN THE PAST.

ABOUT
CLIMATE CHANGE

18 Scientists think that **MELTING ICE** will cause sea levels to rise between 7 and 23 inches (18 and 59 cm) by 2100, possibly more if the poles continue to melt.

19 IN 2005, MUMBAI, INDIA, RECEIVED **37 inches** (94 CM) OF RAIN IN 24 HOURS— THE MOST EVER RECORDED.

20 IN THE ALPS, SOME OWNERS OF SKI RESORTS USE WHITE BLANKETS TO COVER SKI SLOPES TO SLOW DOWN MELTING.

21 AS THE **PERMAFROST** —FROZEN SOIL—THAWS, IT CHANGES THE SHAPE OF THE GROUND, TURNING A FLAT BIKE PATH NEAR FAIRBANKS, ALASKA, U.S.A., INTO A BUMPY RIDE.

22 A changing climate means **BUTTERFLIES** live in new areas as the temperatures warm. Two-thirds of the 35 butterfly species in Europe have moved northward as far as 150 miles (240 km) in recent decades.

23 ENGINEERS HAVE CREATED FLOATING HOMES IN AMSTERDAM THAT RISE WITH THE SEA LEVEL.

24 The more the ice in **THE ARCTIC** melts, the FASTER it melts.

25 A WIND FARM in Texas, U.S.A., has more than 600 turbines and can provide power to 265,000 homes.

1
HAWKEYE, a cat in California, U.S.A., loves water. Her owner had a **SCUBA SUIT SPECIALLY MADE** that allows her to explore the bottom of her backyard pool.

2
LEATHERBACK SEA TURTLES, the largest of all turtles, can dive up to **4,200 FEET** (1,280 m) and stay down for more than 85 minutes in search of jellyfish.

3
Scuba divers explore under **ICE SHEETS** by cutting a hole in the ice and diving into the water. They use a **STROBE BEACON** to mark the hole so they know where to resurface.

4
WOMEN can dive underwater for longer periods of time than MEN.

5
An American man holds the **RECORD FOR THE DEEPEST SCUBA DIVE.** He dove 1,000 feet (305 m) down into Zacatoa Cave in Mexico.

6
Divers who **SURFACE TOO FAST** can get decompression sickness, also called "THE BENDS"; it can cause confusion, itching, loss of balance, and death.

7
The larvae of the **DRONE FLY** have their own **BUILT-IN SNORKEL**, which can be ten times the length of their bodies.

8
Emperor penguins **SLOW THEIR HEART RATE** to only three beats a minute while diving. While resting, their hearts might beat 72 times a minute.

9
Divers in Japan and Korea use **WEIGHTS ON THEIR BELTS** when diving for oysters and seaweed. This helps them to stay on the seafloor rather than float up.

10
Lifeguards use the **DOLPHIN DIVE** to enter the water quickly. They run into the water until it is about at their knees and then do a shallow dive.

11
American colonists attempted to use a **ONE-PERSON SUBMARINE** during the Revolutionary War to attack the British. It was called the "TURTLE."

12
Diving beetles keep **AIR UNDERNEATH THEIR WINGS** when they dive underwater so they can breathe.

13
It is believed that in ancient Greece, divers were employed **DURING THE TROJAN WAR** to attack enemy ships.

14
Tourists in Hawaii, U.S.A., can dive more than 100 feet (30 m) below the surface in a **48-PERSON SUBMERSIBLE** to sightsee.

15
An early invention for diving was called the **AQUA-LUNG**, which allowed humans to breathe underwater. **JACQUES COUSTEAU** was one of its inventors.

16
JACQUES COUSTEAU, famous ocean explorer, wanted to be a navy pilot. He turned to undersea exploration when he was in a car accident and **BROKE BOTH OF HIS ARMS.**

17
In 1928, an Egyptian man was awarded a gold medal in platform diving—**BY MISTAKE.** The error was soon corrected and an **AMERICAN DIVER WAS AWARDED THE GOLD.**

18
There is a debate as to who holds the record for the **HIGHEST DIVE** into water; one contender needed help getting out of the water, which some claim disqualified him.

19
Scuba divers are also known as "FROGMEN."

20
The Mariana Trench, the **DEEPEST PART OF THE OCEAN**, is deeper than Mount Everest is tall.

21
The deepest part of the ocean is called the **HADAL ZONE**, where it is always **DARK AND COLD.**

22
Platform divers can **SPRAIN THEIR WRISTS** because of the force of hitting the water's surface. They work to keep their hands in the correct position.

23
LEONARDO DA VINCI invented a **BREATHING TUBE**, but it was more than twice as long as our windpipes and would have filled with dangerous carbon dioxide.

24
You can buy **SPONGE-BOB SQUAREPANTS** diving fins. Swim fins can increase the flexibility of your ankles so you can **SWIM FASTER.**

25
Ocean explorer **SYLVIA EARLE** has spent more than **6,000 HOURS** diving—the equivalent of **250 DAYS** in the water.

26
U. S. NAVY SEALS train for combat missions involving diving and underwater swimming. Training takes **30 MONTHS.**

27
PEREGRINE FALCONS are one of the fastest animals in the world and are able to dive for prey at 200 miles an hour (320 kph).

28
The deepest lake in the United States, **CRATER LAKE** in Oregon, is 1,943 **FEET** (592 m) deep and open to divers about four months of the year.

29
Southern **ELEPHANT SEALS** can dive nearly a mile (1,620 m). To cope with the depth's chill, they can shut down the blood pumping to their extremities.

30
In 1992, Richard Presley spent 69 DAYS AND 19 MINUTES in an underwater module off the coast of Florida, U.S.A.

31
Divers explore **DEEP-WATER CAVES OFF BERMUDA** to observe changing sea levels. They look for notches cut in the rock by the waves at lower sea levels.

32
A "DIVE" is slang for a rundown restaurant.

33
JACQUES MAYOL DOVE 282 FEET (86 m) without using any equipment off the coast of an island in the Mediterranean.

37
In the Netherlands **173 PEOPLE IRONED CLOTHES UNDER WATER** for 10 minutes.

34
BASE JUMPERS use a diving board 881 feet (269 m) above the New River in West Virginia, U.S.A.

44
In the 1700s, **HAWAIIAN WARRIORS** had to **DIVE OFF A CLIFF** to prove their loyalty.

Australia 24c
SPERM WHALE

41
IN 1843 the British Royal Navy founded the **FIRST DIVING SCHOOL.**

48
A **SPERM WHALE** can **DIVE DEEPER** than humans in the deepest-diving submarine.

38
WATER SPIDERS spin an underwater web, called a **DIVING BELL,** and spend much of their lives under the bell.

45
The world record for the **MOST PEOPLE SCUBA DIVING** at one time is 2,486.

35
Olympic divers dive off a 3-FOOT, 10-INCH (3-m)-high flexible aluminum board or a solid 33-FOOT, 9.7-INCH (10-m) platform.

42
By just holding their breath, people have been **DIVING FOR PEARLS AND SPONGES** for centuries.

49
Some **SKYDIVERS** turn their heads toward the ground in a maneuver called **HEAD-DOWN FLYING.** They can reach speeds of 180 miles per hour (290 kph).

39
Some dive-bomb pilots **LOSE CONSCIOUSNESS** from the force of pulling the airplane out of a dive.

46
For Olympic diving, the **SMALLER THE SPLASH** when entering the water, the **HIGHER THE SCORE.**

36
One person can fit inside **DEEP FLIGHT I,** a modern submarine that weighs 2,860 pounds (1,297 kg) and has **18 HOURS OF LIFE SUPPORT.**

43
The shipwrecked RMS *Titanic* was discovered using a remotely operated diving vehicle, or **ROV.**

50
To make the biggest splash when doing a **"CANNONBALL"** make yourself as close to **SPHERE-SHAPED** as possible. The rounder you are, the larger the splash.

40
The U.S. NAVY'S **MARINE MAMMAL PROGRAM** trains sea lions and bottlenose dolphins to sniff out underwater bombs.

47
HUMPBACK WHALES flip their tails out of the water before diving in a move called **FLUKING.** Each tail, or fluke, is unique and can help identify individual whales.

50 FACTS YOU CAN REALLY DiVE INTO

35 FACTS ABOUT

1 Parrots don't have **VOCAL CORDS.**

2 If kept in the dark for a long time, a **GOLDFISH WILL TURN GRAY.**

3 A canary can sing **TWO DIFFERENT SONGS** at the same time.

4 President Calvin Coolidge had a pet **PYGMY HIPPOPOTAMUS NAMED BILLY.**

5 Mice can have **150 BABIES A YEAR.**

6 **LAIKA THE DOG** was the first animal to **TRAVEL INTO SPACE.**

7 Ancient Egyptians **MUMMIFIED THEIR PET** cats, dogs, and monkeys.

8 **WESTERN HOGNOSE SNAKES PLAY DEAD** when they feel threatened.

9 **A CHAMELEON'S TONGUE** can stretch to **ONE AND A HALF TIMES ITS BODY LENGTH.**

10 At some pet spas, cats are treated to **CATNIP TEA.**

11 When President **THEODORE ROOSEVELT'S SON** was sick in bed with the measles, his sibling brought the **FAMILY PONY INTO THE WHITE HOUSE** to visit him.

12 **A DOG WILL DRINK OUT OF THE TOILET** because water stays **COOLER** there than in its bowl.

13 **A CAT'S TONGUE HAS HOOKED TASTE BUDS** that work like Velcro to help hold prey in its mouth.

14 **GUINEA PIGS CAN WALK** immediately after being born.

15 **A CAT'S EYE** has **THREE EYELIDS.**

16 You can keep a dog from **SHAKING WATER OFF ITS COAT** by holding its muzzle.

17 Dogs **CAN'T BACK DOWN A TREE LIKE CATS.** They can only come down forward.

18 **CALICO CATS** are almost always **FEMALE.**

19 Hamsters can keep food in **POUCHES IN THEIR CHEEKS FOR DAYS.**

20 **A HAMSTER'S TEETH** never stop growing.

21 The oldest known **KOI FISH** lived to be **226 YEARS OLD.**

22 **DOGS OFTEN YAWN** when they are nervous or excited.

23 Female rabbits are called **DOES,** male rabbits are called **BUCKS,** and baby rabbits are called **KITS.**

24 Dogs pant up to **300 TIMES A MINUTE.**

*YOU HAVE LEARNED **4,799** FACTS

PETS

25 A CAT'S HEART BEATS TWICE AS FAST as a human's.

26 Horses can travel up to 100 MILES (161 KM) IN A DAY.

27 Rats CAN'T BURP.

28 GEORGE WASHINGTON owned more than 30 FOXHOUNDS.

29 When sleeping standing up, A HORSE LOCKS ITS HIND LEGS so it doesn't fall over.

30 In Europe, ferrets have been used to RUN TELEVISION CABLES THROUGH PIPES.

31 More than HALF OF THE HOMES in the United States HAVE A PET.

32 A ST. BERNARD NAMED BARRY was said to have saved more than 40 people during his life.

33 When doing difficult tasks, FEMALE CATS TEND TO BE RIGHT-PAWED, whereas MALES ARE USUALLY LEFT-PAWED.

34 Snakes use their TONGUES TO HELP THEM SMELL.

35 You can sometimes CALM A DOG during a thunderstorm by RUBBING A DRYER SHEET ON ITS FUR.

Ferret

1. Antarctica wasn't known to be a continent until the 1840s. Up until then, people thought it was a group of islands.

2. Antarctica is the windiest continent—some gusts hit the coast at up to 180 miles per hour (300 kph) and can knock people off their feet.

3. **ANTARCTICA IS THE DRIEST CONTINENT. IT IS ACTUALLY A REALLY COLD DESERT.**

4. The geographic South Pole is not located in the same place as the magnetic South Pole, which marks the spot where compass arrows point.

5. In Brazil, you can buy a sweet, fizzy soda called Guaraná Antarctica.

6. Antarctica contains about 90 percent of the Earth's ice.

7. If all of Antarctic's ice melted, the oceans would rise 200 feet (60 m).

8. Dogs are banned from Antarctica because they can infect seals with disease.

9. **ORCAS HUNT IN PACKS IN ICY ANTARCTIC WATERS.**

10. People who work in Antarctica call it "The Ice."

11. A lost emperor penguin that turned up in New Zealand was named "Happy Feet" after the animated movie.

12. Antarctic cod (fish) can survive in icy waters because they produce natural antifreeze in their blood.

13. Aristotle, an ancient Greek philosopher, never saw Antarctica but believed it must exist in order to balance out the lands in the North.

14. There are ATM machines in Antarctica.

15. Three countries—the United Kingdom, Chile, and Argentina—claim the Antarctic Peninsula, which juts toward South America.

16. Antarctica was discovered in the 1820s, but it was more than 75 years before anyone set foot on it.

17. The Earth's crust sags some 3,000 feet (914 m) under the thick, heavy Antarctic ice.

18. Humpback whales live off of tiny Antarctic krill, a shrimplike animal.

19. **ANTARCTICA'S ICE CAP HOLDS 70 PERCENT OF THE WORLD'S FRESH WATER.**

20. Antarctica's tallest mountain is the Vinson Massif, at 16,067 feet (4,897 m).

21. In 1911, Norwegian Roald Amundsen became the first person to set foot on the South Pole.

22. **TENS OF MILLIONS OF YEARS AGO, AUSTRALIA ONCE WAS CONNECTED TO ANTARCTICA.**

23. Antarctica has active volcanoes. Mount Erebus has been active for 1.3 million years and recently started erupting again in 2011.

24. NASA has tested equipment for Mars missions in Antarctica's rocky valleys.

25. Lichens, a type of plant, are adapted to the cold life in Antarctica, but they can grow very slowly. One kind can grow only about 0.4 inches (1 cm) every 1,000 years.

26. The South Pole has six months of darkness and six months of daylight.

27. A meteorite found in Antarctica in 1981 was full of tiny diamonds.

75 ICE COLD

FACTS ABOUT ANTARCTICA

28 Twenty-nine countries operate research stations on Antarctica.

29 Antarctica has plenty of sea mammals, like seals and whales, but no land mammals.

30 The coldest temperature in Antarctica was recorded in 1983 at Vostok Base, a Russian research station: -128.56°F (-89.2°C).

31 More than 99 percent of Antarctica is covered in ice.

32 A cat named Mrs. Chippy went on Ernest Shackleton's famous voyage to Antarctica. She even jumped overboard and had to be rescued.

33 Antarctica's ice has been forming for millions of years.

34 ONLY ABOUT 10 PERCENT OF AN ICEBERG IS VISIBLE ABOVE THE WATER.

35 Scientists and tourists bring some 70,000 seeds to Antarctica each year on their clothing, shoes, and travel gear.

36 Antarctica has no time zone. Each research station keeps the time of its home country.

37 Leopard seals, which live in the waters off the Antarctic coast, can consume a penguin in as little as four to seven minutes.

38 Emperor penguins can dive more than 800 feet (244 m) below the surface.

39 Emperor penguins are the only Antarctic bird that breeds in winter.

40 Weddell seals chew breathing holes in the ice with their sharp teeth.

41 There is no snow in Antarctica's Dry Valleys—and there hasn't been for two million years.

42 Male Adélie penguins will walk 60 icy miles (97 km) to reach their breeding grounds.

43 At least 145 lakes are buried under Antarctica's ice, including one that's about the size of Lake Ontario.

44 Some countries claim parts of the continent, but no country owns Antarctica.

45 When an iceberg's ice melts and refreezes, it can appear striped with different-colored bands.

46 A WANDERING ALBATROSS HAS A WINGSPAN OF UP TO 11 FEET (3.4 M), WHICH IS TALLER THAN ANY HUMAN.

47 Athletes challenge themselves by running a 26.2-mile (42.2-km) marathon or an even longer 62.1-mile (100-km) race in Antarctica. Sometimes penguins race along with them!

48 Antarctica is the only continent that doesn't have ants—but a small insect called a wingless midge does live there.

49 The largest iceberg ever spotted in Antarctic waters measured 208 miles (335 km) long by 60 miles (97 km) wide, making it slightly larger than Belgium.

50 Except for humans, emperor penguins are the only warm-blooded animal to remain on Antarctica for the winter.

51 Blue whales spend their summers feeding in Antarctic waters. They can live to be 90 years old and can weigh up to 200 tons (181,437 kg).

52 During the summer, at least 5,000 people work on Antarctica, but they are still outnumbered by penguins. The number drops during the winter.

53 Icebergs drift at about the pace you walk—3 miles an hour (4.8 kph).

54 Entire mountain ranges are buried under Antarctic ice.

55 The coldest place on Antarctica is the Plateau Station, whose average annual temperature is -70°F (-56.7°C).

56 Workers ride snowmobiles to get around on the Antarctic tundra.

57 Antarctica has the world's lowest elevation not underwater—the Bentley Subglacial Trench at -8,383 feet (-2,555 m).

58 Since the ice above the pole moves, the U.S. research station at the South Pole will be located directly on the South Pole in 2025.

59 When ice starts to form on water it can look like a layer of sludge. This is called "grease ice."

60 A large elephant seal can have 900 pounds (408 kg) of blood.

61 Some king penguins live in colonies of 200,000 birds!

62 Antarctic krill use their front legs to form a "feeder basket" to capture the algae that they eat.

63 An annual rugby match in Antarctica pits Americans against New Zealanders.

64 Leopard seals can puncture rubber boats with their sharp teeth.

65 Male emperor penguins balance a single egg on their feet to keep it warm for about two months.

66 When ice breaks off a glacier to form an iceberg, scientists call it "calving."

67 WEDDELL SEALS CAN HAVE A LAYER OF FAT CALLED BLUBBER THAT IS 4 INCHES (10 CM) THICK.

68 The Adélie penguin was named for the wife of an early French explorer.

69 Southern elephant seals can dive 3,000 feet (914 m) to feed on squid.

70 The 2011 Japanese earthquake sent a tsunami more than 8,000 miles (13,000 km) through the ocean. It crashed into an ice sheet, breaking off an iceberg almost the size of Manhattan, New York, U.S.A.

71 A bird called the brown skua eats penguin eggs and even trash.

72 Millions of years ago, trees grew on Antarctica.

73 People who spend all winter on Antarctica are called "winterovers."

74 Early seafarers believed that the souls of dead sailors were reincarnated as wandering albatrosses, a species of bird.

75 One gigantic iceberg weighed 300 gigatons (661,386,786,554,632.8 pounds or 300,000,000,000,000 kg).

1 Some of our earliest ancestors were about four feet (1.2 m) tall, or the height of a small **chimpanzee** when standing up.

2 In 1859, CHARLES DARWIN published his theory of evolution, in which he said humans evolved from apes. Many people thought he was crazy.

4 Modern humans **LIVED IN AFRICA 100,000 YEARS AGO;** they then migrated to every continent except Antarctica.

3 **EARLY ARTISTS PAINTED CAVE WALLS** with figures of the animals they hunted; they used minerals and either water or their spit to make the paints.

5 In prehistoric times, people ate **DANDELION GREENS** in their salads. We still eat them today!

25 Exciting FACTS

6 A **1.6** MILLION-YEAR-OLD fossil of a preteen-aged boy discovered in Kenya in 1984 and known as "Turkana Boy" has a skeleton shaped much like ours.

7 Our ancestors made tools such as **STONE AXES.** Today, some chimpanzees make spears to hunt other animals for food.

8 Scientists think that we can communicate emotion with **OUR EYES** more effectively than other primates because of the large "whites."

9 We have short hair on our bodies instead of fur to help **KEEP OUR BODIES AND BRAINS COOL.**

10 **HUMANS** AND **NEANDERTHALS** ONCE LIVED SIDE BY SIDE, BUT NEANDERTHALS ARE NOW EXTINCT.

11 SCIENTISTS STUDY CHANGES IN THE SHAPE OF OUR **ANCESTORS' JAWS AND TEETH** TO LEARN ABOUT THE HUMAN FAMILY TREE.

12 An ancient necklace from Burma was made of **MORE THAN 100 HORNET BODIES.**

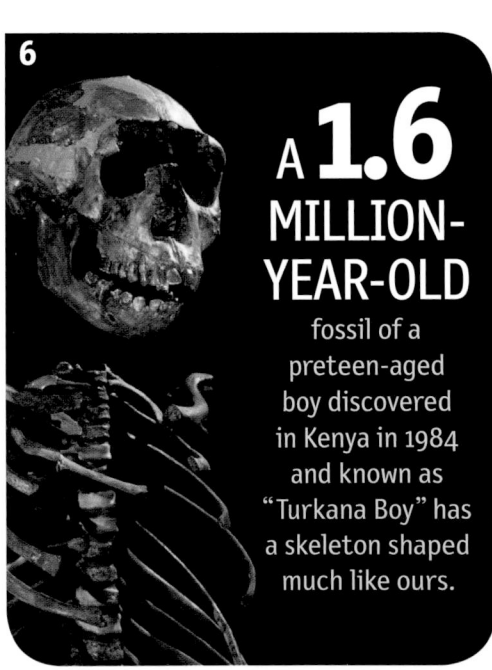

13 When an adult and a child walked across wet volcanic ash some 3.6 million years ago, their path was covered with more ash and then turned into about **70 fossil footprints.**

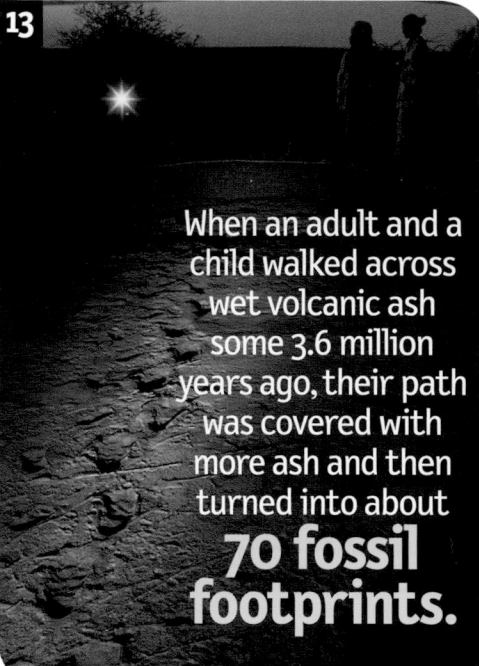

14  Neanderthals **LIVED A TOUGH LIFE;** their fossils show injuries similar to those of rodeo riders of today.

15 SOME RAW FOODS ARE POISONOUS. WHEN EARLY HUMANS STARTED TO COOK THEIR FOOD, THEY DISCOVERED IT UNLOCKED ADDITIONAL NUTRIENTS AND MADE SOME OF THOSE FOODS SAFE TO EAT.

16 Early humans would sometimes carve designs into **ANIMAL ANTLERS.** One piece of carved antler seems to show a lunar calendar, suggesting a way early humans kept track of time.

17 Humans began **MAKING POTTERY** some **18,000 YEARS AGO** in Japan.

ABOUT EARLY Humans

18 Early humans shared some features with today's apes. Both can walk on two feet. But humans went on to **develop larger brains.**

19 Our ancestors began using fire hundreds of thousands of years ago. Once they discovered that rubbing two sticks together created a spark, they could stay warm and cook their food.

20 **Lucy,** a famous fossil of an *Australopithecus afarensis* female, was named after the **Beatles song,** "Lucy in the Sky with Diamonds."

21 When you are cold you might get goose bumps, but our ancestors had longer body hair that would stand up to create a **WARM BLANKET** on their skin.

22 Early humans used needles made of bone to sew **WARM CLOTHES** from animal skins and fur.

23 EARLY HUMANS USED **HARPOON-LIKE** POINTS MADE OF ANTLER TO SPEAR THEIR PREY.

24  **The Bushmen** of Africa's Kalahari Desert still hunt and eat the way their ancestors did.

25 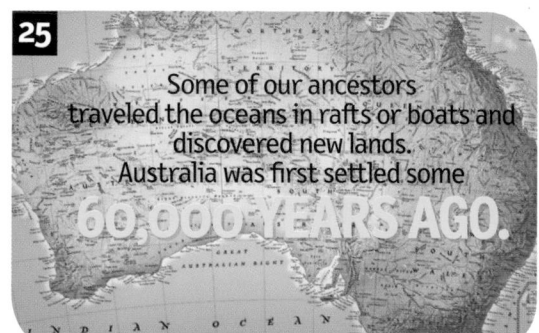 Some of our ancestors traveled the oceans in rafts or boats and discovered new lands. Australia was first settled some **60,000 YEARS AGO.**

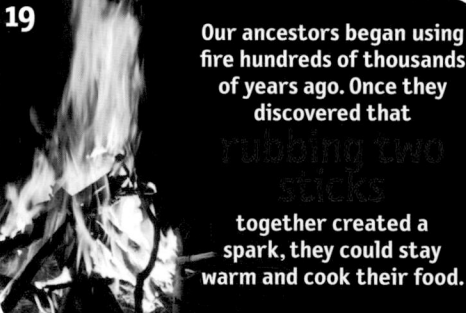

50 FUN FACTS ABOUT NORTH AMERICA

1 RUSSIA is the only country in the world that is LARGER THAN CANADA.

2 Scientists think DINO-SAURS DIED OFF from the effects of a METEOR that left a 112-MILE (180-KILOMETER) HOLE in Mexico's Yucatan Peninsula.

3 To get someone's attention in Guatemala, say "CHHTT-CHHTT."

4 HONDURAS is the only Central American country that DOESN'T HAVE A VOLCANO.

5 More than ten MILLION PEOPLE take cruise ships to the CARIBBEAN EVERY YEAR.

6 A common CANADIAN SNACK IS POUTINE—french fries with gravy and cheese.

7 MCDONALD'S started in 1940 IN SAN BER-NARDINO, CALIFORNIA, U.S.A, as a drive-in restaurant with car hop service. They now have over 33,000 locations.

8 Americans have a total of about $10 BIL-LION IN LOOSE CHANGE just sitting around their homes.

9 Although he is credited with discovering America, CHRISTOPHER COLUMBUS never set foot in what is now the U.S.A. HE FIRST LANDED IN THE BAHAMAS.

10 Most CANADIANS LIVE WITHIN 125 MILES (200 km) of the United States.

11 Only one kind of NATIVE SNAKE IN PUERTO RICO is venomous—the PUERTO RICAN RACER.

12 In Mexico, fami-lies often eat the LARGEST MEAL OF THE DAY BEFORE 4 P.M.; in the UNITED STATES FAMILIES EAT AROUND 6 P.M.

13 The NATIONAL ANIMAL OF HONDURAS is the WHITE-TAILED DEER.

14 Nearly 40,000 PEOPLE WORKED on the PAN-AMA CANAL—linking the Atlantic and Pacific Oceans—at the height of its construction in 1904.

15 CANADIANS eat a type of pudding called "BUGGER-IN-A-BAG."

16 Early Central Americans used to drink HOT CHOCOLATE made from UNSWEETENED CHOCOLATE AND SPICY PEPPERS.

17 The MEXICAN FLAG has an image of an EAGLE PERCHED ON A CACTUS HOLDING A SNAKE.

18 MT. MCKINLEY IN ALASKA, U.S.A., is North America's highest point. It is also called DENALI, which means the "High One" in one Native American language.

19 At a festival in EL SALVADOR, PEOPLE THROW FIREBALLS AT EACH OTHER. It's held in honor of a 1922 volcano eruption.

20 Only 26,000 PEOPLE live in Canada's Nunavut territory, which takes up 20 PERCENT of all of Canada. More than 700 times as many people live in Mexico City.

21
The world's largest canyon, THE GRAND CANYON, IS ABOUT 1 MILE (1.6 KM) DEEP.

22
MEXICO CITY is located close to POPOCATEPETL (Aztec for "smoking mountain"), an active volcano, but the city is not likely to be bothered by any lava.

23
NORTH AMERICA was named after AMERIGO VESPUCCI, an early explorer of the Americas. He even helped Christopher Columbus prepare for some of his voyages.

24
EL SALVADOR is the smallest country in Central America; at its longest it is only 88 MILES (142 km).

25
CANADIAN THANKSGIVING CELEBRATES the HARVEST IN OCTOBER unlike the American Thanksgiving holiday, which is in November.

26
An underground cave in Mexico has the WORLD'S LARGEST CRYSTALS. The longest one is 8 TIMES TALLER than the AVERAGE 10-YEAR-OLD KID.

27
COSTA RICA MEANS "RICH COAST" in Spanish. The Spanish never found much gold, but today the country produces bananas, pineapples, coffee, and sugar.

28
The world's LARGEST SPANISH-SPEAKING POPULATION is found in MEXICO.

29
Visitors sleep in a HOTEL MADE OF ICE IN QUEBEC CITY, CANADA. It's only open a few months of the year.

30
There's a STREET IN TORONTO that's about 1,181 MILES (1,900 km) long; that's longer than the distance from London, England, to Madrid, Spain.

31
The ancient MAYA CHEWED GUM made from TREE SAP.

32
Before the construction of the PANAMA CANAL, ships had to go around South America to get from the Atlantic to the Pacific—an 8,000-MILE (12,800-km) trip.

33
Nearly EIGHT OUT OF EVERY TEN AMERICANS live in a city.

34
GUATEMALA'S NATIONAL BIRD is the QUETZAL, and its money is called the quetzal.

35
Canada's national police officers are called MOUNTIES.

36
SINKHOLES CALLED *CENOTES* on Mexico's Yucatán Peninsula were sacred spaces to the ancient Maya, believed to act as a GATEWAY TO THE UNDERWORLD.

37
The CHA-CHA DANCE originated in CUBA.

38
POLAR BEARS venture as far south as Canada's Hudson Bay to EAT SEALS AND WALRUSES.

39
FRIED BANANAS WITH HONEY is a Central American treat.

40
There have been more than 1,200 INDIGENOUS cultures in North America including NAVAJO, CHEROKEE, AND INUIT CULTURES.

41
Many GREAT BASEBALL PLAYERS come from the DOMINICAN REPUBLIC: Sammy Sosa, David Ortiz, and Albert Pujols to name just three.

42
Scientists have mapped more than 390 miles (628 km) of passages in the world's largest cave system, MAMMOTH CAVE in Kentucky, U.S.A., but there is more to explore.

43
AMERICAN ALLIGATORS live in the southeastern United States. They can bite down with about the SAME FORCE AS IF A MID-SIZE SEDAN FELL ON YOU.

44
A "TICO" is someone who is from COSTA RICA.

45
HURRICANES threaten the eastern coast of North America FROM JUNE TO NOVEMBER. In other places the storms are called typhoons, cyclones, or baguios.

46
HAITI is the only country in the world that WON ITS INDEPENDENCE BECAUSE OF A SLAVE REVOLT.

47
The FIRST NASCAR RACE took place in DAYTONA, FLORIDA, IN 1948.

48
North America's Lake Superior is the WORLD'S SECOND LARGEST LAKE.

49
North America is home to only ONE MARSUPIAL, the OPOSSUM, which is active at night.

50
In CANADA'S BAY OF FUNDY, high tide can come in as high as a 5-STORY BUILDING, or 52 feet (16 m).

35 WILD FACTS ABOUT WACKY HOTELS

1 A hotel in Chile is designed to look like a **VOLCANO.** But instead of lava, a **WATERFALL ERUPTS** at the top.

2 The builders of Burj Al Arab in Dubai, United Arab Emirates, made an island so the **SAIL-SHAPED HOTEL** appears to be cruising 918 feet (280 m) into the Arabian Gulf.

3 Bright orange **METAL PODS** are the rooms of the Capsule Hotel in the Netherlands. The survival pods were once **RESCUE CAPSULES** for workers on offshore oil rigs.

4 You can stand face to face with **POLAR BEARS** in northern Canada's **TUNDRA BUGGY,** an off-road vehicle equipped with an observation deck, a dining room, and sleeping space.

5 **GIRAFFE MANOR** in Kenya is home to nine free-roaming Rothschild's giraffes. And they're **NOT SHY!** Some may stick their heads into your bedroom window or eat food off the breakfast table.

Burj Al Arab, Dubai, United Arab Emirates

6 At a motel chain in Holbrook, Arizona, U.S.A., visitors stay in **WIGWAMS**, domed dwellings used by some Native Americans! Each wigwam is equipped with a hot shower and cable TV.

7 Dog Bark Park Inn in Cottonwood, Idaho, U.S.A., is a **GIANT INN SHAPED LIKE A DOG.**

8 In New Mexico, U.S.A.'s Kokopelli's Cave Bed and Breakfast guests stay in a **ROOM DUG INTO A CLIFF FACE** of 65 million-year-old sandstone.

9 At Out 'n' About Treehouse Treesort in Takilma, Oregon, U.S.A., guests stay in **TREE HOUSES**—some of which are accessible only by **SWINGING BRIDGES** and zip lines.

10 The **AIRPLANE SUITE** in the Netherlands was once an airplane, but it's now a five-star hotel room. The 131-foot (40-m) cabin has a whirlpool bath, a sauna, and flat-screen TVs.

11 Try not to lick the walls! The Palacio de Sal, located on one of Bolivia's salt flats, is **MADE ALMOST ENTIRELY OF SALT.** The hotel also has a salt spa and salt golf course.

12 Have you ever wanted to see a **MERMAID?** This vacation spot comes close! At Weeki Wachee Springs in Florida, U.S.A., performers wear fins and suck on air hoses to pretend to be mermaids.

13 The Everland is a hotel with **ONLY ONE ROOM** that travels around the world! It has parked at places such as the roof deck of the Museum of Contemporary Art in Leipzig, Germany.

14 The Hotel de Glace in Canada is made **ENTIRELY OUT OF ICE AND SNOW.**

15 The deepest hotel room in the world is located **509 FEET (155 M) UNDERGROUND** in an old **SWEDISH SILVER MINE.**

16 The De Vrouwe van Stavoren Hotel in the Netherlands is made out of **RECYCLED WINE BARRELS.**

17 Rooms in Austria's Das Park Hotel are made out of **CONCRETE PIPES.**

18 Germany's Hotel im Wasserturm was Europe's **LARGEST WATER TOWER** during the 19th century.

19 At the Minimalist Hotel in Sweden, guests stay in **TENTS THAT HANG** from trees. The stay includes **ROPE-CLIMBING** training so that you can get to your room.

20 The **LIBERTY HOTEL** in Boston, U.S.A., was once a **PRISON.**

21 The Hotel Kakslauttanen, located above the Arctic Circle in Finland, is a **GLASS IGLOO** perfect for viewing the **NORTHERN LIGHTS** and the shining stars of the Arctic sky.

22 In Christchurch, New Zealand, you can go back in time at **WAGON STAYS,** where visitors can stay in rooms modeled after **COVERED WAGONS** used by pioneers.

23 The Boot Bed 'n' Breakfast in New Zealand is exactly what it sounds like—a cottage **DESIGNED IN THE SHAPE OF A BOOT!**

24 The Crowne Plaza Hotel at Union Station in Indianapolis, Indiana, U.S.A., is built in the city's **FORMER TRAIN STATION.** The hotel offers the option to spend the night in a Pullman train car!

25 The Amazon rain forest's Ariau Amazon Towers is at the **TOP OF THE TREES**—bedrooms, suites, and tree houses are linked by 30-foot (9.1-m)-high **CATWALKS.**

26 The Winvian in Connecticut, U.S.A., features an **AIRPLANE-HANGAR-THEMED COTTAGE** with a 17,000-pound (7,711-kg) helicopter that's been turned into a private lounge.

27 It was an **ELEMENTARY SCHOOL** in 1915, but now the McMenamins Kennedy School's classrooms in Portland, Oregon, U.S.A., are used as guest rooms—complete with chalkboards.

28 Sleeping in a **CLEAR BUBBLE TENT** designed for stargazing and enjoying the outdoors is a popular attraction in the French town of Roubaix.

29 India's Tree House Hideaway has **FIVE TREE HOUSES** that look out into the jungle of a **TIGER RESERVE.** The striped cats can be spotted from the hotel rooms.

30 Guests can stay in a **LIGHTHOUSE** on a deserted Norwegian island only accessible by helicopter. The lighthouse was manned for 100 years and is still a weather observation post.

31 The Propeller Island City Lodge in Berlin, Germany, boasts a room with furnishings hanging from the ceiling, a room completely covered in mirrors, and one with **COFFIN-LIKE BEDS.**

32 **ELEPHANTS** are also guests at Thailand's Anantara Golden Triangle Resort, which has an elephant rescue on site. Guests can even **TAKE A JOURNEY** on an elephant.

33 At Loews Coronado Bay Resort in California, U.S.A., your pooch can ride the waves during a **DOGGY SURFING LESSON.**

34 A New York, U.S.A., luxury hotel has a **"FEED THE PARTY ANIMAL"** menu for four-legged, two-legged, and slithering guests.

35 It may look like a little floating red house on Lake Mälaren in Sweden, but Utter Inn is actually a single hotel room whose **ONLY ROOM IS UNDERWATER.**

15 FINAL FACTS

1 **NOSTRADAMUS,** a 16th-century French astrologer, predicted many things, including **WHEN THE WORLD MIGHT END.** But since his predictions go to the **YEAR 3797,** we will have to wait.

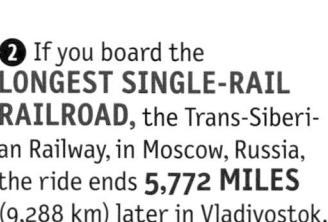

2 If you board the **LONGEST SINGLE-RAIL RAILROAD,** the Trans-Siberian Railway, in Moscow, Russia, the ride ends **5,772 MILES** (9,288 km) later in Vladivostok. **THE ENTIRE TRIP TAKES ABOUT EIGHT DAYS.**

3 On the **50TH ANNIVERSARY** of the U.S. Declaration of Independence, **JOHN ADAMS DIED** in Boston at age 91. Reportedly, he said, **"THOMAS JEFFERSON STILL SURVIVES."** What he didn't know was that Jefferson had died a few hours earlier at his home in Virginia.

4 The most southwesterly part of England is called **LAND'S END.** Basking sharks swim offshore, and dolphins can be spotted from the cliffs.

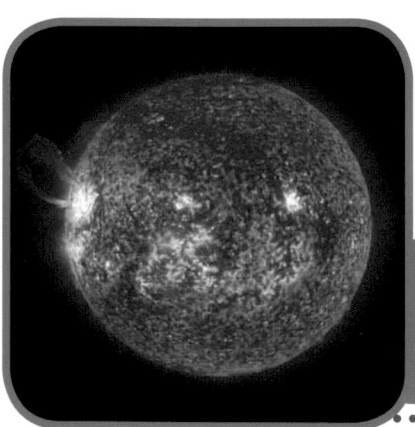

5 A bridge in Sowerby, England, is known as the **"WORLD'S END" BRIDGE.** It was built in the 1600s for packhorses to cross a river to a nearby town.

6 **OUR SUN** will end up as a **WHITE DWARF STAR** when it runs out of fuel in **A FEW BILLION YEARS.**

7 Why can you never reach **THE END OF A RAINBOW?** Because **IT MOVES AS YOU MOVE.** The raindrops reflecting the sunlight that cause the rainbow aren't located in one part of the sky.

ABOUT ENDINGS

8 At the end of the **INDIANAPOLIS 500** the winner **DRINKS A BOTTLE OF MILK.** The tradition began with winner **LOUIS MEYER IN 1936: HE DRANK BUTTERMILK.**

9 USHUAIA, known as the most **SOUTHERN CITY IN THE WORLD,** is located on Tierra del Fuego in Argentina. Puerto Williams, in Chile, is ALSO KNOWN AS THE SOUTHERNMOST CITY, but while it's a little farther south it's also smaller. Most travelers to Antarctica leave from Ushuaia.

10 Dorothy and her friends find EMERALD CITY at the **END OF THE YELLOW BRICK ROAD** in the movie *The Wizard of Oz.* Some people believe that a road of yellow bricks in Peekskill, New York, U.S.A., inspired the author of the book that was later made into the movie.

11 For **30 YEARS NASA'S SPACE SHUTTLE PROGRAM** sent astronauts into space. The program **ENDED ON JULY 21, 2011,** when its 135th mission landed at Cape Canaveral, Florida, U.S.A.

12 The END PHASE OF A FOREST FIRE is the **GLOWING PHASE,** when the charcoal created by the fire burns to leave a small amount of ash.

13 In May of each year **THE NIGHT ENDS FOR 84 DAYS IN BARROW, ALASKA, U.S.A.** The sun won't set for 12 weeks in Barrow, known as **"THE LAND OF THE MIDNIGHT SUN."**

14 J.K. Rowling knew how the **HARRY POTTER BOOK SERIES WOULD END** when she wrote THE FIRST BOOK.

15 Visitors to the **SOUTHERNMOST POINT OF THE UNITED STATES IN KEY WEST, FLORIDA,** find a concrete buoy that says it's only **90 MILES (145 KM) TO CUBA.**

5,000

IF THE **AVERAGE** ADULT READS **250 WORDS** PER MINUTE, IT WOULD TAKE THEM ABOUT **400** UNINTERRUPTED MINUTES TO READ THIS BOOK **COVER TO COVER.**

BEHIND THE FAcTS

Just how did we get **5,000** awesome facts about everything into this book? First, we came up with a list of the coolest stuff there is— stuff we knew kids would really care about. Like peanut butter and space junk. Dolphins and spies. Pets. The brain. Everything. Then we looked at how to get the most possible facts on all this cool stuff onto the pages. Some subjects have 15 facts. Some have 25. Some even have 100! We carefully researched each and every fact to make sure it's absolutely true. And we illustrated and designed the fact pages so well that you'll never get bored looking at them. Then we added up all the facts with the fact ticker to get to 5,000. It didn't take 5,000 people to make this awesome book—but it did take a crew of writers, a gang of editors and photo editors, and a slew of designers— the most awesome book team around!

ILLUSTRATION CREDiTS

AL: Alamy; GI: Getty Images; MP: Minden Pictures; NGC: National Geographic Creative; NGMS: National Geographic My Shot; SS: Shutterstock

COVER (shark), Mike Parry/MP; (dog), Digital Vision; (sea turtle), Rich Carey/SS; (robot), Mondolithic Studios; (saturn), NASA; (chocolate), Elena Schweitzer/SS; (frogs), Gail Shumway/Photographer's Choice/GI; (popsicle), Stephen Coburn/SS; (shield), Johannes Wiebel/SS; BACK COVER: (giraffe), Ilya Akinshin/SS; (brain), mikeledray/SS; (snake), James Steidl/SS; 1 Finnbar Webster/AL; 2-3 stavklem/SS; 5 Leksele/SS; 6-7 Joe Farah/SS; 7 nito/SS; 8 (B), Gary Woodard/SS; 8 (C), Food Features/AL; 8 (E), Uryadnikov Sergey/SS; 8 (A), Aaron Amat/SS; 8 (D), 8 (F) © Carter Archives/ZUMAPRESS.com/AL; 8-9 (CTR), Maren Caruso/Photodisc/GI; 9 (A), Marc Dietrich/SS; 9 (B), Hulton Archive/GI; 9 (C), nito/SS; 9 (D), Joe Potato Photo/iStockphoto.com; 9 (E), NASA; 10 (UP), The Bridgeman Art Library/GI; 10-11 (LO), Marina Kryukova/SS; 12 (UP), Dirk Ercken/SS; 12 (CTR), Big Pants Production/SS; 12-13 (Background), Susan Flashman/SS; 13 (UP), Eric Isselée/SS; 13 (LO), Philip Date/SS; 14-15, Christopher Parypa/SS; 15 (LO), Alexander Cherednichenko/SS; 16-17 (Background), Marlene DeGrood/SS; 16 (LO), Henrik Larsson/SS; 17 (UPLE), MarFot/SS; 17 (UPRT), mrfiza/SS; 17 (CTR), Aptyp_koK/SS; 17 (LOLE), Pan Xunbin/SS; 17 (LORT), Vaclav Volrab/SS; 18 (2), Hiroshi Sato/SS; 18 (4), Brandon Bourdages/SS; 18 (5), mikeledray/SS; 18 (6), Flip Nicklin/MP/NGC; 18 (7), Willyam Bradberry/SS; 18 (8), Goncharuk/SS; 18 (11), Jenny Solomon/SS; 19 (14), guentermanaus/SS; 19 (17), Christian Musat/SS; 19 (15), Larry Foster/NGC; 19 (16), urosr/SS; 19 (18), tubuceo/SS; 19 (20), Nickolay Stanev/SS; 19 (21), Skip ODonnell/iStockphoto; 19 (22), Rich Carey/SS; 20 (UP), Express/Express/GI; 20 (CTR), Stephen Morris/iStockphoto; 20 (LO), Carlos Alvarez/iStockphoto; 20-21 (CTR), Disney XD via Getty Images; 21 (UP), Photo Researchers RM/GI; 21 (CTR), NASA; 21 (LO), Boyer/Roger Viollet/GI; 22, Franco Tempesta; 24 (UP), Venus Angel/SS; 24 (LO), alexxl/SS; 24-25 (Background), Roger Ressmeyer/NGC; 25 (UP), Dja65/SS; 25 (LO), YAKOBCHUK VASYL/SS; 26 (UPLE), SeDmi/SS; 26 (UPRT), emin kuliyev/SS; 26 (CTR), Elena Butinova/SS; 26 (LO), Thomas M Perkins/SS; 27 (UPLE), 3445128471/SS; 27 (CTR), Roman Pyshchyk/SS; 27 (LO), Lisa F. Young/SS; 28, Rich Carey/SS; 29, fivespots/SS; 30 (1), injun/SS; 30 (3), Patrick Poendl/SS; 30 (5), Picsfive/SS; 30 (6), szpeti/SS; 30 (9), NASA; 30 (10), ARNTHOR AEVARSSON/NGMS; 30 (11), Alex Staroseltsev/SS; 30 (8), Eric Isselée/SS; 31 (13), Roger Cotton/iStockphoto; 31 (15), Ben Haggar/NGMS; 31 (14), Andrey Shtanko/SS; 31 (16), Rob Byron/SS; 31 (19), Rob Wilson/SS; 31 (17), Jan Cejka/SS; 31 (22), Craig Dingle/iStockphoto; 31 (25), Ton Lammerts/SS; 32-33 (Background), Hung Chung Chih/SS; 32 (UPRT), Elena Schweitzer/SS; 32 (UPLE), nito/SS; 32 (LOLE), bonchan/SS; 32 (LORT), vichie81/SS; 33 (UP), Lyn Adams/SS; 33 (CTR), Tony Magdaraog/SS; 33 (LO), urfin/SS; 34 (UP), James E. Knopf/SS; 34 (CTR), GI; 34 (LO), Alexander McClearn/AL; 34-35 (CTR), AP Images/Martin Ellard/PA Wire URN; 35 (UP), Hung Chung Chih/SS; 35 (LO), Paul Orr/SS; 36-7, John Carnemolla/SS; 38 (LE), Petoo/SS; 38, Peter Haley/Tacoma News Tribune/MCT/GI; 39 (UPLE), Hadrian/SS; 39 (UP CTR), B Calkins/SS; 39 (UPRT), andersphoto/SS; 39 (LO), Victor Maff/iStockphoto; 40, Mike Parry/MP/GI; 42-43 (Background), Claudio Rossol/SS; 42 (UP), photopixel/SS; 42 (LO), Andrew Cowin/Travel Ink/Corbis; 43 (UPLE), Andrew G./SS; 43 (UPRT), Bartosz Wardzinski/SS; 43 (LO), Wildnerdpix/SS; 44 (1), Igor Karasi/SS; 44 (2), artconcept/SS; 44 (3), Factoria Singular/iStockphoto; 44 (4A), Gerrit_de_Vries/SS; 44 (4B), Gerrit_de_Vries/SS; 44 (6), CLIPAREA l Custom media/SS; 44 (7), Sandra Nicol/iStockphoto; 44 (8), Pete Donofrio/SS; 44 (11), Ashley Whitworth/SS; 44 (12), Mornee Sherry/SS; 45 (13), David Pruter/SS; 45 (14), Brooke Becker/SS; 45 (15), mashe/SS; 45 (16), PD Loyd/SS; 45 (17), Computer Earth/SS; 45 (20), Paul-André Belle-Isle/SS; 45 (22), markrhiggins/SS; 45 (24), Eric Isselée/SS; 46 (UP), Julien Tromeur/SS; 46 (LO), NASA Jet Propulsion Laboratory; 46-47 (CTR), oorka/SS; 47 (UP), Alexey Stiop/SS; 47 (LO), Bettmann/Corbis; 48-49 (Background), Hazysunimages/GI; 48 (RT), Goncharuk/SS; 49 (LE), Dionisvera/SS; 49 (RT), Ivaylo Ivanov/SS; 50 (UPLE), James van den Broek/SS; 50 (UPRT), Kharidehal Abhirama Ashwin/SS; 50 (LO), Andrew Burgess/SS; 50 (Background), Jason Edwards/NGC; 51 (LE), Eric Isselée/SS; 51 (RT), Eric Isselée/SS; 52, renkshot/SS; 54 (UP), Radin Myroslav/SS; 54 (LO), Digital Vision/AL/NGC; 54 (Background), Richard Du Toit/MP/NGC; 55 (UPLE), ylq/SS; 55 (UP CTR), Thomas Koellner/iStockphoto; 55 (UPRT), Dave and Sigrun Tollerton/AL; 55 (LOLE), Katherine Feng/Globio/MP/NGC; 55 (LOCTR), Diane Webb/SS; 55 (LORT), David Steele/SS; 56 (1), brunosphoto/iStockphoto; 56 (3), MarcelClemens/SS; 56 (5), Robert Madden/NGC; 56 (CTR), Thank You/SS; 56 (6), Semen Lixodeev/SS; 56 (7), Jennie Book/SS; 56 (10), Steven Coling/SS; 56 (8), Joey Boylan/iStockphoto; 56 (11), Carolina K. Smith, M.D./SS; 57 (13), Marco Regalia/iStockphoto; 57 (14), Ron Bailey/iStockphoto; 57 (15), Joshua Lewis/SS; 57 (16), Zsolt, Biczó/SS; 57 (18), Andrzej Gibasiewicz/SS; 57 (25), Stephen Coburn/SS; 57 (22), fantuz/SS; 57 (23), Artmim/SS; 57 (24), Gen Productions/SS; 58 (1), Alex Staroseltsev/SS; 58 (2), Keith Hanson/iStockphoto; 58 (3), Arkady/SS; 58 (6), DamianPalus/iStockphoto; 58 (7), andersphoto/SS; 58-59 (CTR), Daniel Laflor/iStockphoto; 58 (UP CTR), Hway Kiong Lim/SS; 59 (9), iofoto/SS; 59 (12), anarhist/SS; 59 (13), MaxPhotographer/SS; 59 (14), BW Folsom/SS; 59 (15), Brooks Kraft/Corbis; 60, Mike Hollman/NGMS; 62, SuperStock RM/GI; 62 (INSET), Library of Congress; 63 (UP), Vladimir Wrangel/SS; 63 (LE), Allstar Picture Library/AL; 63 (RT CTR), Anwar Hussein/WireImage/GI; 63 (LORT), RIA Novosti/AL; 64, Susan Schmitz/SS; 65, Sascha Burkard/SS; 66 (2), A. Längauer/SS; 66 (7), Eric Isselée/SS; 66 (11), Christian Musat/SS; 66 (16), Anan Kaewkhammul/SS; 66 (9), Paula Cobleigh/SS; 66 (5), Photographer/SS; 66-67 (Background), James Galletto/NGMS; 67 (25), Time Life Pictures/USDA Forest Service/Time Life Pictures/GI; 67 (20), Nagel Photography/SS; 67 (47), James Galletto/NGMS; 67 (22), Shironina/SS; 67 (35), Joshua Haviv/SS; 67 (42), Pshenichka/SS; 67 (36), Danny Smythe/SS; 67 (31), BW Folsom/SS; 67 (44), AnutkaT/SS; 68 (3), Jessmine/SS; 68 (4), Chuck Rausin/SS; 68 (6), Constance Roberts/NGMS; 68 (LE CTR), Steve Collender/SS; 68 (7), Abel Tumik/SS; 68 (8), Gorshkov25/SS; 68 (9), Paul Fleet/SS; 68 (12), Matthew Cole/SS; 68 (13), Matthew Cole/SS; 69 (14), David Doubilet/NGC; 69 (15), ngarare/SS; 69 (16), fivespots/SS; 69 (17), picturepartners/SS; 69 (19), Roger Meerts/SS; 69 (20), tubuceo/SS; 69 (18), Audrey Snider-Bell/SS; 69 (23), Mark Kostich/iStockphoto; 69 (24), Sally Scott/SS; 69 (22), Dariusz Majgier/SS; 69 (25), April Cat/SS; 70 (UP), Historocal Picture Archive/Corbis; 70 (CTR), Henry Westheim Photography/AL; 70 (LO), Mathew Imaging/WireImage/GI; 70-71 (CTR), AP Images/Magic Mountain, Craig T. Mathew; 71 (UP), Iain Masterton/AL; 71 (LO), Travel Pictures/AL; 72, Peter Waters/SS; 74 (UPLE), Eric Isselée/SS; 74 (UPRT), vihrogone/SS; 74 (LE CTR), Tischenko Irina/SS; 74 (RT CTR), testing/SS; 74 (LORT), William Warner/SS; 74 (LOLE), Alice Day/SS; 74 (LOCTR), Valentyn Volkov/SS; 75 (UPLE), Mark Rucker/Transcendental Graphics/GI; 75 (UPRT), Graça Victoria/SS; 75 (UP CTR), Awe Inspiring Images/SS; 75 (LOCTR), evantravels/SS; 75 (LOLE), Hayati Kayhan/SS; 75 (LORT), Russ Beinder/SS; 76, NASA/ESA/STScI/AURA; 78 (8), helza/SS; 78 (7), Aaron Amat/SS; 78 (CTR), Michael C. Gray/SS; 78 (15), Brenda Carso/SS; 79 (38), KSPhotography/SS; 79 (32), AnutkaT/SS; 79 (21), SAJE/SS; 79 (46), Jay Paul/Bloomberg News/GI; 79 (28), Senol Yaman/SS; 79 (41), Paul Poplis/GI; 79 (30), V. J. Matthew/SS; 80 (1), Booka/SS; 80 (3), photovideostock/iStockphoto; 80 (5), AP Images/Itsuo Inouye; 80 (CTR), TeddyandMia/SS; 80 (4A), Eric Isselée/SS;80 (4B), Daniel Bendjy/iStockphoto; 80 (CTR), TeddyandMia/SS; 80 (CTR), TeddyandMia/SS; 80 (6), SS; 80 (9), KAZUHIRO NOGI/AFP/GI; 80 (10), MUSTAFA OZER/AFP/GI; 80 (8), Robert Markowitz/NASA; 80 (12), Cristian Mihai Vela/iStockphoto; 81 (CTR), TeddyandMia/SS; 81 (14), Everett Collection Inc/AL; 81 (16), AP Images/ATR Intelligent Robotics and Communication Laboratories, HO; 81 (17), Karwai Tang/WireImage/GI; 81 (CTR), TeddyandMia/SS; 81 (CTR), TeddyandMia/SS; 81 (CTR), TeddyandMia/SS; 81 (19), parameter/iStockphoto; 81 (21), Broccoli Photography/AL; 81 (24), scibak/iStockphoto; 81 (25), Andrea Krause/iStockphoto; 81 (22), Mike Cherim/iStockphoto; 81 (25), Kevin Russ/iStockphoto; 82 (UP), Khoroshunova Olga/SS; 82 (LO), Michel Segonzac/NGC; 82-83 (CTR), Dante Fenolio/Photo Researchers RM/GI; 82 (RT), Kjersti Joergensen/SS; 84, Yarygin/SS; 86 (UP), Pictorial Parade/GI; 86 (LO), Kenneth Garrett/NGC; 87-5 (RT), Kenneth Garrett/NGC; 87 (LE), ITAR-TASS Photo Agency/AL; 88, YorkBerlin/SS; 88, Philipp Nicolai/SS; 90 (1), EcoPrint/SS; 90 (8), kurt_G/SS; 90 (15), David Steele/SS; 90 (10), arnaud weisser/SS; 90 (7), Eric Isselée/SS; 91 (25), Johan Swanepoel/SS; 91 (38), neelsky/SS; 91 (20), Audrey Snider-Bell/SS; 92 (1), Creative Crop/GI; 92 (2), Leser/photocuisine/Corbis; 92 (3), Steven Mark Needham/Envision/Corbis; 92 (5), photographer/GI; 92 (CTR), Creative Crop/GI; 92 (6), Niels Poulsen std/AL; 92 (7), FoodCollection/SuperStock; 92 (8), James L. Stanfield/NGC; 92 (10), Nick Gordon/naturepl.com; 92 (21), Adalberto Rios Szalay/Sexto Sol/GI; 92 (22), Mary Evans Picture Library/AL; 93 (11), Photocuisine/SuperStock; 93 (CTR), Radius/SuperStock; 93 (12), Biwa Studio/GI; 93 (13), Paul Fleet/AL; 93 (14), Food and Drink/SuperStock; 93 (CTR), Radius/SuperStock; 93 (15), age fotostock/SuperStock; 93 (16), INTERFOTO/AL; 93 (17), Radius/SuperStock; 93 (18), Exactostock/SuperStock; 93 (19), Edward Bottomley/GI; 93 (23), Mary Evans Picture Library; 93 (24), Arco Images GmbH/AL; 93 (25), Mary Evans Picture Library; 93, Lew Robertson/Corbis; 94 (LE), Library of Congress; 94 (RT), bumihills/SS; 95 (10), Jarno Gonzalez Zarraonandia/SS; 95 (6), Nick Pavlakis/SS; 95 (7), James P. Blair/NGC; 95 (13), Pecold/SS; 95 (9), Mike VON BERGEN/SS; 95 (15), Kokhanchikov/SS; 96-97, Darren J. Bradley/SS; 98-99, Rob Stark/SS; 99 (UP), Fer Gregory/SS; 99 (CTR), Eric Isselée/SS; 99 (LO), Library of Congress; 100 (LE), Eric Isselée/SS; 100 (RT), Mikhail Melnikov/SS; 101 (UP), Le Do/SS; 101 (LO), Mikhail Melnikov/SS; 102 (UP), Ira Block/NGC; 102 (LORT), Gentoo Multimedia Ltd./SS; 102 (LOLE), Susan Flashman/SS; 103 (UP), Ralf Hettler/iStockphoto; 103 (CTR), Jan Martin Will/SS; 103 (LORT), Leksele/SS; 104 (4), gosphotodesign/SS; 104 (5), Brandon Alms/SS; 104 (6), Rob Hainer/SS; 104 (7), Eric Isselée/SS; 104 (10), Andy Lim/SS; 104 (11), Hugh Lansdown/SS; 105 (13), Wild Wonders of Europe/Lundgren/naturepl.com; 105 (14), bernd.neeser/SS; 105 (15), vadim kozlovsky/SS; 105 (16), Milan Lipowski/iStockphoto; 105 (18), Kenneth C. Catania/NGC; 105 (20 UP), Miles Away Photography/SS; 105 (22), Jason Kasumovic/SS; 105 (23), Fesus Robert/SS; 105 (20 lo), IrinaK/SS; 105 (25), Joel Sartore/NGC; 106-107, Justin Black/SS; 106 (1), Ammit/SS; 106 (7), Julian de Dios/SS; 106 (21), Library of Congress; 106 (28), Ralf Hettler/iStockphoto; 107 (6), Kobby Dagan/SS; 107 (10), Muellek Josef/SS; 107 (17), Eduardo Rivero/SS; 107 (26), Ronald Sumners/SS; 107 (34), Traveler/SS; 108 (UP), Johan Swanepoel/SS; 108 (CTR), EastVillage Images/SS; 108 (LO), Tony Rix/SS; 108-109 (CTR), JaBa/SS; 109 (UP), Mark Beckwith/SS; 109 (UP CTR), Kathy Burns-Millyard/SS; 109 (LOCTR), worldswildlifewonders/SS; 109 (LO), Eduard Kyslynskyy/SS; 110-111, Angelo Giampiccolo/SS; 110 (2), Alessandro Vigano/SS; 110 (6), Science & Society Picture Library/SSPL/GI; 110 (10), DanielW/SS; 110 (13), Gregory Gerber/SS; 110 (16), thefinalmiracle/SS; 110 (17), Astronoman/SS; 111 (19), AGCuesta/SS; 111 (33), Regien Paassen/SS; 111 (45), INTERFOTO/AL; 111 (36), Hung Chung Chih/SS; 112 (4), Steve Cukrov/SS; 112-113 (Background), DNF-Style Photography/SS; 112 (22), ivvv1975/SS; 112 (30), Tierfotoagentur/AL; 113 (14), Library of Congress; 113 (20), Walter Quirtmair/SS; 113 (23), Nici Kuehl/SS; 113 (34), Kellis/SS; 114, Africa Studio/SS; 115, Mushakesa/SS; 116 (LO), Everett Collection Inc/AL; 116 (UP), WronaART/SS; 117 (UP), UNIVERSAL/THE KOBAL COLLECTION/The Picture Desk; 117 (CTR), Juan Camilo Bernal/SS; 117 (LO), © Columbia Pictures/Courtesy Everett Collection; 118 (1), greenland/SS; 118 (2), fivespots/SS; 118 (3), Martin Shields/AL; 118 (5), iofoto/SS; 118 (6), Catmando/SS; 118 (7), Frontpage/SS; 118 (9), saiko3p/SS; 118 (10), CREATISTA/SS; 118 (11), 7Michael/SS; 118 (12), Andi Berger/SS; 119 (13), ifong/SS; 119 (14), Vladimir Melnik/SS; 119 (16), FormosanFish/SS; 119 (15), SHADOWMAC/SS; 119 (18), Joel Sartore/NGC; 119 (17), Subbotina Anna/SS; 119 (20), nito/SS; 119 (19), Uryadnikov Sergey/SS; 119 (23), buradaki/SS; 119 (24), irabel8/SS; 119 (25), greenland/SS; 119 (22), fivepointsix/SS; 120 (UP), Toby Jorrin/AFP/GI; 120 (CTR), Fox Photos/GI; 120 (LO), DeAgostini/DEA Picture Library/GI; 120-121 (CTR), James P. Blair/NGC; 121 (UP), Evaristo Sa/AFP/GI; 121 (CTR), DeAgostini/DAE Picture Library/GI; 121 (LO), RIA Novosti/AL; 122-123, LIN, CHUN-TSO/SS; 124-125 (Background), allylondon/SS; 124 (1), D7INAMI7S/SS; 124 (5), Nayashkova Olga/SS; 124 (7), Albert Michael Cutri/SS; 124 (15), LIN, CHUN-TSO/SS; 124 (18), Stephan Zabel/iStockphoto; 124 (22), Werner Muenzker/SS; 124 (31), hxdbzxy/SS; 125 (14), Dobrinya/SS; 125 (19), Thomas Bedenk/SS; 125 (21), stockerman/SS; 125 (29), Manfred Steinbach/SS; 125 (34), grafvision/SS; 125 (35), Valentyn Volkov/SS; 127, George Dolgikh/SS; 128 (UP), Sean Bolt/SS; 128 (CTR), Henk Bentlage/SS; 128 (LO), Alberto Tirado/SS; 129 (UP), Joe Mercier/SS; 129 (LO), Johan Swanepoel/SS; 130 (1), ultrapro/SS; 130 (4), Irena Misevic/SS; 130 (3), HomeStudio/SS; 130 (6 UP), Peter Spiro/iStockphoto; 130 (6 LO), Diane Picard/SS; 130 (9), holligan78/SS; 130 (8), Neil Overy/SS; 130 (10), Renewer/SS; 130 (11), AP Images/Aliosha Marquez; 131 (13 LE), Olga Kovalenko/SS; 131 (13 RT), AnatolyM/SS; 131 (14), Jan Hopgood/SS; 131 (15), Gregory James Van Raalte/SS; 131 (17), AP Images/Royal Canadian Mint; 131 (18), Picsfive/SS; 131 (19), David Rochkind/Bloomberg via GI; 131 (20), Sotheby's/GI; 131 (24), jeehyun/SS; 131 (22), Laszlo Podor/AL; 131 (23), Zelenskaya/SS; 131 (25), Goncharuk/SS; 132 (UP), Miao Liao/SS; 132 (LO), UladzimiR/SS; 132-133 (CTR), Dmitriy Shironosov/SS; 133 (UP), Robert Matton AB/AL; 133 (CTR), Vishnevskiy Vasily/SS; 133 (LO), Seppo Hinkula/AL; 134-135, Ariwasabi/SS; 136-173 (Background), Time Life Pictures/GI; 136 (UP), NASA; 136 (LO), NASA/JSC; 137 (UP), NASA; 137 (LO), NASA; 138, Ivonne Wierink/SS; 140 (1), Library of Congress; 140 (21), Eric Isselée/SS; 140 (17), Viachaslau Kraskouski/SS; 140, MANDY GODBEHEAR/SS; 140-141 (Background), Sebastian Kaulitzki/SS; 141 (48), Anatomical Design/SS; 141 (25), Sebastian Sparenga/iStockphoto; 142 (UPLE), Library of Congress; 142 (RT), Viacheslav Zhukovskiy/SS; 142 (LO), BW Folsom/SS; 143 (UP), Galina Dreyzina/SS; 143 (LOLE), Chhanda Bewtra/NGMS; 143 (LORT), EdBockStock/SS; 143 (LOCTR), Albert Moldvay/NGC; 144 (UP), Petrenko Andriy/SS; 144 (CTR), Tsekhmister/SS; 144 (LO), Philip Sigin-Lavdanski/iStockphoto; 144-145 (CTR), mikeledray/SS; 145 (UP), AP Images/Chitose Suzuki; 145 (CTR), Sergey Goruppa/SS; 145 (LO), Serhiy Kobyakov/SS; 146 (2 UP), archives/iStockphoto; 146 (2 LO), Glenn Price/SS; 146 (5), Cathy Keifer/SS; 146 (6), EuToch/SS; 146 (7 LE), Hugh Lansdown/SS; 146 (7 RT), Brian Skerry/NGC; 146 (8), DM7/SS; 146 (11), NASA; 146 (12), Undersea Discoveries/SS; 147 (16), Sokolov Alexey/SS; 147 (14), Philip Dalton/AL; 147 (17), Ferenc Szelepcsenyi/SS; 147 (19), Alexey Repka/SS; 147 (21), xfox01/SS; 147 (23), ajt/SS; 147 (24), Mitya/SS; 147 (25), Neale Cousland/SS; 148-149, stephan kerkhofs/SS; 150 (UP), Robert Gebbie Photography/SS; 150 (CTR), Eric Isselée/SS; 150 (LO), Eric Isselée/SS; 150-151 (Background), Graeme Shannon/SS; 151, Lightspring/SS; 152 (UP), Snowshill/SS; 152 (UP CTR LE), Fine Shine/SS; 152 (UP CTR RT), ILYA AKINSHIN/SS; 152 (LOLE), Eric Isselée/SS; 152 (LORT), Tony Wear/SS; 153, Roman Pyshchyk/SS; 154-155 (Background), chinahbzyg/SS; 154 (9), John Kimbler/NGMS; 154 (5), Computer Earth/SS; 154 (14), Mike Flippo/SS; 154 (19), Katrina Brown/SS; 154 (39), Fedorov Oleksiy/SS; 154 (43), Feng Yu/SS; 156 (3), Steven Poe/AL; 156 (4), Nuno Andre/SS; 156 (6), Eric Isselée/SS; 156 (7), Plati Photography/SS; 156 (8), Feng Li/GI; 156 (9), CreativeNature.nl/SS; 156 (12), Picsfive/SS; 157 (13), Liv friis-larsen/SS; 157 (15), Veniamin Kraskov/SS; 157 (16), Dinga/SS; 157 (14), Chris leachman/SS; 157 (17), Sandra Caldwell/SS; 157 (18), topseller/SS; 157 (19), italianestro/SS; 157 (20), Jim Barber/SS; 157 (23), Zadiraka Evgenii/SS; 157 (24), jannoon028/SS; 157 (25), Ivaschenko Roman/SS; 158 (UP), HomeArt/SS; 158 (LO), St. Nick/SS; 158-159 (CTR), Annette Shaff/SS; 159 (UP), nutech21/SS; 159 (CTR), Andriy Zholudyev/SS; 159 (LO), Lamella/SS; 160, NASA; 162-163, Fer Gregory/SS; 164, stockpix4u/SS; 165, Eric Isselée/SS; 166-167 (Background), Faraways/SS; 166 (UP), YanLev/SS; 166, Louella938/SS; 167 (LO), aslysun/SS; 167, Anatoli Styf/SS; 168 (2), Everett Collection, Inc.; 168 (5), Dr_Flash/SS; 168 (7), Rufous/SS; 168 (6), R. Gino Santa Maria/SS; 168 (8), Everett Collection, Inc.; 168 (9), Shannon West/SS; 168 (12), L Barnwell/SS; 169 (13), phloen/SS; 169 (16), LVV/SS; 169 (15), Bea Cooper/AL; 169 (CTR), aida ricciardiello/SS; 169 (18), sonya etchison/SS; 169 (20), NREY/SS; 169 (21), Paul Nicklen/NGC; 169 (22), Nagel Photography/SS; 169 (23), Samir Hussein/Wire Image/GI; 170 (UP), Beata Slonecka/NGMS; 170 (CTR), Victor Malevankin/SS; 170 (LO), WaterFrame/AL; 170-171 (CTR), Jan-Dirk Hansen/SS; 171 (UP), Sari ONeal/SS; 171 (CTR), Hedrus/SS; 171 (LO), Firmin Carpenter/NGMS; 172 (UP), Nikolai Tsvetkov/SS; 172 (LO), WilleeCole/SS; 173, Africa Studio/SS; 174-175 (Background), Mondolithic Studios; 174 (LE), Mondolithic Studios; 174 (RT), Mondolithic Studios; 175 (UPRT), Mondolithic Studios; 175 (LORT), Mondolithic Studios; 175 (UPLE), Mondolithic Studios; 175 (LOLE), Mondolithic Studios; 176-177, gary yim/SS; 178-179 (Background), Andrew Lever/SS; 178 (2), arindambanerjee/SS; 178 (21), Studio 37/SS; 178 (16), James P. Blair/NGC; 178 (12), Groomee/SS; 179 (45), Montenegro/SS; 179 (43), Brenda Carson/SS; 180 (1), ©Buena Vista Pictures/Courtesy Everett Collection; 180 (4), Popperfoto/GI; 180 (3), Bettmann/Corbis; 180 (6), Bettmann/Corbis; 180 (7), David Muir/GI; 180 (9), Gary Crabbe/Enlightened Images/AL; 180 (10), Mikhail Zahranichny/SS; 181 (11), Keystone/Hulton Archive/GI; 181 (12), Jeff Banke/SS; 181 (13), Paul B. Moore/SS; 181 (17), kwest/SS; 181 (20), Michal Cerny/AL; 181 (24), Memo Angeles/SS; 182 (UP), Stephen Harrison/AL; 182 (LOLE), Beepstock/AL; 182 (LORT), incamerastock/AL; 182-183 (CTR), charles taylor/SS; 183 (UP), Finnbarr Webster/AL; 183 (CTR), Judith Collins/AL; 183 (LO), Ben Molyneux/AL; 184-185 (Background), marcokenya/SS; 186-187 (Background), Dirk Ercken/SS; 186 (UP), Vasilius/SS; 186 (CTR), ribeiroantonio/SS; 186 (LO), Gontar/SS; 187 (UP), Kenneth Garrett/NGC; 187 (LO), Smithsonian Institution/Corbis; 188, Kokhanchikov/SS; 190, Sergei Bachlakov/SS; 191 (UP), Bork/SS; 191 (Background), Morgan Lane Photography/SS; 191 (LO), Suzanne Tucker/SS; 192 (1), Jason Patrick Ross/SS; 192 (3), Norman Bateman/SS; 192 (2), Sari ONeal/SS; 192 (8), rsooll/SS; 192 (7), Martin Spurny/SS; 192 (5), Joanna Zopoth-Lipiejko/SS; 192 (16), Ivan Hor/SS; 192 (4), Mark Bridger/SS; 192 (25), Kirsanov/SS; 193 (11), aragami12345s/SS; 193 (13), Giuseppe Lancia/SS; 193 (12), Kirsanov/SS; 193 (19), Hannamariah/SS; 193 (18), Peter Waters/SS; 193 (17), Daleen Loest/SS; 193 (20), Doug Lemke/SS; 193 (21), Kirsanov/SS; 193 (15), SunnyS/SS; 194-195, Shane Kirk/NGMS; 196 (UPRT), Teguh Tirtaputra/SS; 196 (UPLE), Jim Agronick/SS; 196 (LORT), Takashi Usui/SS; 196 (LOLE), Eric Isselée/SS; 196-197 (Background), Dirk Ercken/SS; 197 (RT), Pasi Koskela/SS; 198 (1), Joe Ferrer/SS; 198 (4), Dumitrescu Ciprian-Florin/SS; 198 (2), Hulton Archive/GI; 198 (3), VladisChern/SS; 198 (5), EpicStockMedia/SS; 198 (6), NASA/GSFC; 198 (9), gresei/SS; 198 (10 LE), Ammit/SS;198 (10 RT), apdesign/SS; 198 (8), Andrew Orlemann/SS; 198 (11), DarkOne/SS; 199 (13), leungchopan/SS; 199 (16), Matt Ragen/SS; 199 (14), Amy Nichole Harris/SS; 199 (15), R McIntyre/SS; 199 (17), George F. Mobely/NGC; 199 (19), Indranil Mukherjee/AFP/GI; 199 (20), Melissa Farlow/NGC; 199 (24), Darren Baker/SS; 199 (22), Jens Stolt/SS; 199 (23), Hilda Elisabeth Aardema/iStockphoto; 199 (25), Tharinee M./SS; 200-201 (Background), Strider/SS; 200 (UP), phdwhite/SS; 200 (LOLE), frantisekhojdysz/SS; 200 (LORT), Tatiana Belova/SS; 201 (UP), tristan tan/SS; 201 (LO), Emory Kristof/NGC; 202 (UP), Eric Isselée/SS; 202 (LE CTR), Lobke Peers/SS; 202 (RT CTR), steve greer/iStockphoto; 202 (LORT), Eric Isselée/SS; 202 (LOLE), Narcis Parfenti/SS; 203 (RT), Vitalij Geraskin/iStockphoto; 203 (LE), Ivan Kuzmin/SS; 204-205, Scenic Shutterbug/SS; 206 (1), Eric Isselée/SS; 206 (3), James L. Stanfield/NGC; 206 (2), Patrick Poendl/SS; 206 (5), SeDmi/SS; 206 (6), Kenneth Garrett/NGC; 206 (7), Vladimir Melnik/SS; 206 (8), Aaron Amat/SS; 206 (9), Hans Joachim Hoos/iStockphoto; 206 (10), David Evans/NGC; 207 (13), Kenneth Garrett/NGC; 207 (14), Margo Harrison/SS; 207 (17), De Agostini Picture Library/GI; 207 (19), Péter Gudella/SS; 207 (20), Dave Einsel/GI; 207 (21), Tyler Olson/SS; 207 (23), The Natural History Museum/AL; 207 (24), Chris Johns/NGC; 207 (25), NG MAPS/NGC; 208-209 (Background), 375Ultramag/SS; 208 (6), LittleMiss/SS; 208 (8), STILLFX/SS; 208 (16), IngridHS/SS; 208 (13), Pictureguy/SS; 209 (34), worldswildlifewonders/SS; 209 (38), Graça Victoria/SS; 209 (35), patrimonio designs limited/SS; 209 (39), Alex Uralsky/SS; 209 (31), GrigoryL/SS; 209 (37), Konstantin Sutyagin/SS; 209 (38), nokhoog buchachon/SS; 210-211, Gabriela Maj/Bloomberg/GI; 212 (UP), © APIC/GI; 212 (CTR), stocker1970/SS; 212 (LO), NASA; 212-213 (CTR), Rena Schild/SS; 213 (UP), Chad Buchanan/GI; 213 (CTR), NASA; 213 (LO), nito/SS; 214, Jason Stitt/SS; 215 (UP), Eric Isselée/SS; 215 (CTR), renkshot/SS; 215 (LOLE), Stephen Morris/IS; 215 (LORT), Vishnevskiy Vasily/SS

INdEX

Savitskaya, Svetlana 63
Sawfish 165
Sax, Adolphe 111
Saxon Switzerland National Park 96
Saxophones 111, **111**
Scallops 105, 165
Scansoriopteryx 22
Schadenfreude 27
Schnoodles 172
School buses 168, **168**
Schulz, Charles 78
Science, experimental **114**, 114–115, **115**
Scorpions 12, 55, 91, **91**, 101, 196
Scotch tape 85
Scotland 134
Scrabble 75, 182, **182**
Scrooge McDuck 163
Scuba diving *see* Diving
Sea anemones 149
Sea creatures 82–83, **82–83**, 91, **164**, 164–165, **165**
Sea cucumbers 149, 165
Sea-level rise 199
Sea lions 55, 165, 201
Sea otters 91, 165
Sea pen 83
Sea snails 148, 196
Sea snakes 148
Sea stars 45, **45**, 105, **105**, 164
Sea turtles 146, **146**, 148, 149, 164, 200
Seahorses 54, 83, 149, 165, **165**
Seals 165, 181, **181**, 196
Seasons 132–133, **132–133**, 194
Seaswarm (robots) 81, **81**
Seat belts 85
Seaweed 8, 164, 165
Secret Service, U.S.A. 20, **20**
Secretariat (horse) 178
Seed vaults 49, 115
Senses 17, 40, 72, **104**, 104–105, **105**, 147
Sequoia National Park, California, U.S.A. 96
Serbia 134, 135, 195
Serengeti National Park, Tanzania 97
Servals 109, **109**
Sessions, Michael 188
SETI Institute 47
Seven Wonders of the World 184
Shackleton, Ernest 39, 53, 205
Shakespeare's Globe, London, England 123
Shanghai, China 177
Shanghai Tower, China 123
Shape-shifters 159
Sharks 38, 39, **40**, 40–41, 73, 164, 197
Sheep 97, 153
Shepard, Alan 76
Sherpa, Lakpa Tsheri 126
Shi Huangdi, Emperor (China) 139
Ships 34, **34**
Shipwrecks 73, 162
Shoes 25, 85, 156
Shofar 110, **110**
Shooting stars *see* Meteors
Shots 145
Showers 118
Shrek 116
Siamangs 61
Sibilla, Mount, Italy 135
Sign language 27, 60, 84
Silkworms 100, 101
Silver 163, 187
Silver mines 107
Singapore 32, 167
Singapore Changi airport 112
Sinornithosaurus 23
Sirens (amphibians) 29
Sirius (dog star) 173
Sitar 110, **110**
Size *see* Proportions
Skaftafell National Park, Iceland 97
Skateboarding 85, 114, 122, 172
Skeletons 73, 88, 100
Ski Dubai, United Arab Emirates 126
Skiing 51, 56, **56**, 106, 126, 127, 199
Skin 88, 89, 174
Skittles candy 79
Skunks 153
Skurka, Andrew 126
Skydiving 15, 35, 115, 201
Skylab (space station) 137
Skyscrapers 122, **122–123**, 123
Slavery 139, 209
Sleep 19, 112–113, **112–113**, 129, 140, 178, 203
Sleepwalking 112
Slingshots 98
Slinky 85
Sloth bears 66, **66**, 67, **67**
Sloths 12, 54, 64, 65, 90, 153

Slow lorises 69, **69**
Slugs 147, **147**
Slurpee drinks 57, **57**
"Smart bombs" 98
Smart houses 175
Smart phones 24, 84
Smell, sense of 104, 147
Smith, David "The Bullet" 15
Smith, John 139
Smokey Bear 39, 67, **67**
S'mores 34, **34**, 79
Smurfs **34–35**, 35
Snackbot 80
Snails 148, 149
Snake-necked turtle 118, **118**
Snakes 28, 29, **45**
    babies 55
    bites 28
    Ireland 135
    poisonous 38, 45, **45**, 50, 68, **68**, 69, **69**, 196, 197, 208
    prehistoric 161
    rain forests 65
    tongues 203, **203**
    venom 38, 45
Sneezing 88, 141
Snickersnee 27
Snipe (bird) 15
Snoopy (comic strip character) 15, 76
Snoring 113
Snorkeling 148
Snow 38, 132, **133**, 194, 195
Snow cones 56, **56**
Snow leopards 108, **108**, 147, **147**
Snow White and the Seven Dwarfs (movie) 117
Snowball fights 188
Snowboards 126
Snowdonia National Park, Wales 135
Snowflakes 194, 195
Soccer 107, **107**, 126
Sociable weavers 37
Social networking 175
Socrates (Greek philosopher) 114
Soda 114
Solar energy 14, 30, 31, **31**, 39, 114, 156
Solar system 76
Solar years 75
Solenodon 12
Songbirds 37
Songs 44
Sonoran Desert, Mexico-U.S. 161
Sony Walkman 111, **111**
S.O.S. 38
Sosa, Sammy 209
Soul Surfer (movie) 41
Sound 115
Sound barrier 15
South Africa 150
South America 106–107, **106–107**
South Korea 32, 143
South Pole 204, 205
South Sudan 189
Southern elephant seals 200, 205
Space Camp, Huntsville, Alabama, U.S.A. 77
Space flights and research 76
    animals 17, 202
    future 175
    oldest facility 189
    space junk 136–137, **136–137**, 161
    tourism 14
    women 63, **63**
Space shuttles **213**
    end of program 76, 213
    food 79
    number of missions 15, 76, 213
    passengers 14, 15
    research 77, 101
    sleeping 113
    weight 76
Spaceship Earth, Epcot theme park, Orlando, Florida, U.S.A. 123
Spain 59, 143
Spanish language 209
Spectacled bears 66, **66**, 67
Sperm whales 140, 170, 201, **201**
Sphinx, Egypt 95, 185, 186
Spices 49
Spider-man 117, 139
Spider monkeys 61
Spiders **16**, 16–17, **17**, 59, **68**, 73, 197
Spiderweb, South Carolina, U.S.A. 16
Spielberg, Steven 117
Spies 20–21, **20–21**, 63
Spinosaurus 23
Spirit (Mars rover) 81
SpongeBob SquarePants (TV show) 139, 200

Sponges 148, 165, 201
Sporange 27
Sports 85, 126–127, **127**
Spotz, Katie 189
Spring festivals 132
Spring peepers (frogs) 12
Springsteen, Bruce 111
Spud guns 99
Spy Kids: All the Time in the World (movie) 21
Squid 82, 83
Squirrels 140, 153, 195
Stafford, Ed 126
Stalin, Joseph 122
Star anise 49, **49**
Star-nosed moles 105, **105**
"The Star Spangled Banner" 111
Star Wars (movies) 81, **81**, 97, 98, 111, 116, 122
Starfire Optical Range, New Mexico, U.S.A. 24, **24–25**
Starr, Ringo 139
Stars 77, 163
Statue of Liberty, Buenos Aires, Argentina 106, **106**
Statue of Liberty, New York, New York 123, 135, 177
Steamboat Willie (movie) 116
Stegosaurus 23
Stevenson, Robert Louis 162
Stingrays 68, 165, 196
Stink bugs 101
Stomach 89
Stomach aches 145
Stonefish 196
Stonehenge, England 95, **95**, 186
Storks 37
Strauss, Levi 85
Straw houses 156, **156**
Straws 135
Stress 140
Sturgeons 164
Submarines 84
Submersibles 200
Subways 53, 134, 139, 177
Sudan 151
Sue (dinosaur) 23
Suez Canal 139
Sugar 79
Sugar gliders 152
Sugarhill Gang 111
Sultan bin Salman bin Abdul-Aziz Al Saud 14
Summer 132, 133
Sumo wrestling 32, 126, 127, 176
Sun 76, 77, 147, **147**, 212, **212**
Sun bears 66, **66**, 67
Sunfish 165
Sunflowers 48
Sunuwar, Sano Babu 126
Super Glue 85
Superb lyrebird 36
"Supergun" 99
Superior, Lake, Canada-U.S.A. 209
Supernovas 77
Supersoaker 85
Supervolcanoes 42
Supreme Court, U.S.A. 138
Surface tension 115
Surfing 25, 41, 85, 115
Suriname 188
Sushi 165
Swahn, Oscar 191
Swans 37
Sweat 88
Sweden 135, 139, 143
Swedish language 27
Swimming 25, 63, 127, 135, 190, 200
Swimming pools 44, 151
Swiss National Park, Switzerland 97
Switzerland 134, 139, 173
Swordfish 146, 165
Swords 98, 99
Sydney Opera House, Australia 110
Synchronized swimming 190
Synesthesia 105
Synthetic telepathy 174
Syria 32
Syzygy 26

T
Tabei, Junko 63
Table tennis 191
Tadpoles 54, 55, 73
Taffy 78
Taipei 101, Taiwan **122–123**, 123
Taj Mahal, Agra, India 122

Tamanduas 91
Tamarins 61
Tanks 99
Tapeworms 72
Tapirs 65
Tarantulas 12, 16, 17, 65, 97, 125, **125**
Tarot cards 159, **159**
Tasmania, Australia 51
Tasmanian devils 12, 54, 152
Taste, sense of 104, 105
Tattoos 86
Taxis 52, 53
Taylor, Anna Edson 63
Tea 184
Technology facts 24–25, **24–25**, 174–175
Teddy bears 67
Teeth 78, 88, 89, 125, 128, **128**, 135
Telekinesis 159
Telepathy 159, 174
Telephones 84
Telescopes 24, **24–25**, 47, 85, 115
Television 84, 138
Television remotes 84, 115, 156, **156**
Temperature
    cool facts 56–57, **56–57**
    hot facts 30
Tennis 126, 127
Tents 211
Tenzing Norgay 180
Teotihuacan 184, 185
Teresa, Mother 177
Tereshkova, Valentina V. 63, **63**
Termites 100, 101
Text messages 25, 32, 113
Thailand 142, 143
Thanksgiving 124, 142, 209
Theodosius I, Emperor (Rome) 190
Theremin (musical instrument) 73
Therizinosaurus 23
Thermos 114
Theropod dinosaurs 15
Thomson's gazelles 90
Thorn bugs 91
Threadfin butterfly fish 165
Three Gorges Dam, China 189
3-D 24
Thundersnow 56
Thunderstorms 195
Ticks 100
Tigers 91, 97, 108, **108–109**, 109, 153
Tikal National Park, Guatemala 97
Tillman (bulldog) 172
Timor-Leste 188
Tipcat (sport) 127
Titan (Saturn's moon) 133
Titanic (movie) 116
Titanic, RMS 38, 72, 138, 201
Titicaca, Lake, Bolivia-Peru 107, 161
Toads 28, 29, 30, **30**
Toe wrestling 127
Toenails 88
Toilet paper 10
Toilets 11, 85, 123, 139, 176, 202
Tokyo, Japan 167, 176
Tomatoes 139
Tonga Islands, South Pacific Ocean 189
Tongues 89, 104
Toothbrushes 138
Tootsie Roll Pops 79
Tootsie Rolls 125
Toraja people 33
Tornado Alley 195
Tornadoes 38, 39, 194, 195
Toronto, Ontario, Canada 209
Torpedoes 99
Tortoises 28, 55, 161
Toucans 91
Tower of London 10
Tower of Pisa, Italy 135
Toy Story (movies) 67, 116
Toys 85, 182–183, **182–183**
Trains 24, 52–53, 156, 211, 212
Trampolines 85
Trans-Alaska Pipeline 138
Trans-Siberian Railway 212
TransAmerica Pyramid, San Francisco, California, U.S.A. 122
Transformers: Dark of the Moon (movie) 53
Trap-jaw ants 90, **90**
Trassenheide, Germany 135
Treasure Island (Stevenson) 162
Treasure Island, San Francisco Bay 162
Treasures 162–163, **162–163**
Trebuchet 10
Tree frogs 118, **118**, 161
Tree kangaroos 65, 153

AWESOME CREDiTS

STAFF FOR THIS BOOK
Becky Baines, *Project Editor*
James Hiscott, Jr., *Art Director/Designer*
EmDash, *Designer*
Lori Epstein, *Senior Illustrations Editor*
Annette Kiesow, *Illustrations Editor*
Julie Beer, Michelle Harris, Emily Krieger, Keith Rutowski, *Contributing Writers*
Kate Olesin, *Associate Editor*
Michaela Berkon, Susie Charlop, Molly Gasparre, Riley Kirkpatrick, Carly Larkin, Libby Marsh, *Editorial Interns*
Mary Jones, *Release Editor*
Kathryn Robbins, *Design Production Assistant*
Hillary Moloney, *Illustrations Assistant*
Grace Hill, *Associate Managing Editor*
Joan Gossett, *Production Editor*
Lewis R. Bassford, *Production Manager*
Susan Borke, *Legal and Business Affairs*

MANUFACTURING AND QUALITY MANAGEMENT
Phillip L. Schlosser, *Senior Vice President*
Chris Brown, *Vice President, Book Manufacturing*
George Bounelis, *Vice President, Production Services*
Nicole Elliott, Rachel Faulise, Robert L. Barr, *Managers*

Since 1888, the National Geographic Society has funded more than 12,000 research, exploration, and preservation projects around the world. The Society receives funds from National Geographic Partners, LLC, funded in part by your purchase. A portion of the proceeds from this book supports this vital work. To learn more, visit www.natgeo.com/info.

NATIONAL GEOGRAPHIC and Yellow Border Design are trademarks of the National Geographic Society, used under license.

For more information, please call 1-877-873-6846, visit nationalgeographic.com, or write to the following address:
    National Geographic Partners
    1145 17th Street N.W.
    Washington, D.C. 20036-4688 U.S.A.

Visit us online at nationalgeographic.com/books

For librarians and teachers: ngchildrensbooks.org

More for kids from National Geographic: natgeokids.com

For information about special discounts for bulk purchases, please contact National Geographic Books Special Sales: specialsales@natgeo.com

For rights or permissions inquiries, please contact National Geographic Books Subsidiary Rights: bookrights@natgeo.com

LIBRARY OF CONGRESS CATALOGING-IN-PUBLICATION DATA
5,000 awesome facts (about everything!) / by National Geographic kids.
    p. cm. -- (National Geographic kids)
Includes bibliographical references and index.
ISBN 978-1-4263-1049-2 (hardcover : alk. paper) -- ISBN 978-1-4263-1050-8 (library binding : alk. paper)
1. Curiosities and wonders--Juvenile literature. 2. Handbooks--Juvenile literature. I. Title: Five thousand awesome facts (about everything!).
AG243.A18 2012
031.02--dc23
2012012940

Printed in Hong Kong
20/PPHK/19